COURAGE AND CONVICTION

An Autobiography

General VK SINGH
with Kunal Verma

ALEPH BOOK COMPANY
An independent publishing firm
promoted by *Rupa Publications India*

First published in India in 2013 by
Aleph Book Company
7/16 Ansari Road, Daryaganj
New Delhi 110 002

ISBN: 978-93-82277-57-6
1 3 5 7 9 10 8 6 4 2

Printed and bound in India by Manipal Technologies Ltd, Manipal

Dedicated to
Bharti,
who embarked on this journey with me.
Our daughters,
Mrinalini and Yogja,
whose love and affection made this possible.
And
to all the brave men and officers of the Indian Army
whose unflinching support and courage
enabled me to soar.

'Few men for the right cause brave the disapproval of their fellows, the censure of their colleagues and the wrath of their society. Moral courage is a rarer commodity than bravery in battle or great intelligence. Yet it is the one essential, vital quality for those who seek to change the world which yields most painfully to change.'

The Day of Affirmation Speech, Robert F. Kennedy

CONTENTS

PROLOGUE: THE MOMENT OF TRUTH

The Indian Army flag fluttered on the gleaming black bonnet of the car as we raced through the manicured roads of New Delhi. I looked at my watch, and realized we would be a few minutes early for the meeting with the Minister for Home Affairs. I told my aide-de-camp Captain Prakash to tell the pilot vehicle to slow down slightly.

A week after I had taken over as the Chief of Army Staff (COAS), Naxalite-Maoists owing allegiance to the outlawed Communist Party of India (Maoist) ambushed and killed seventy-six jawans from the Central Reserve Police Force (CRPF) near Chintalnar village in the Dantewada district of Chhattisgarh. Nearly eighty men had made up the CRPF/police team that had been on an 'area domination' exercise in the Bastar tribal region, an area rich in natural resources.

Like the rest of the country, all of us at Army Headquarters were saddened by the incident and the tragic loss of lives. This was one of the bloodiest attacks ever on our security forces, and by the end of the day we had a fair idea of how the CRPF boys had walked into an ambush. The next day, at an interaction with the press, I was asked how a large party of armed jawans could be completely annihilated. After expressing my outrage and the army's solidarity with our fallen comrades, I said it hardly mattered if it was the Border Security Force (BSF), the Assam Rifles, the Indian Army or the CRPF; for any ambush to succeed so dramatically, the organization concerned had to look within itself and review training and operating procedures. Even though this was not on the agenda of the media interaction, the press latched on to this remark and sensationalized the comment, saying, 'Army chief faults the training of the CRPF'.

In the ensuing days, the Ministry of Home Affairs seemed to feel I had encroached on to its turf and there were indications that they were none too happy about my comments (although subsequent findings of the inquiry commission fully supported what I had said). This discomfort was possibly aided by the fact that there was much talk around this time, at various levels, about the army's possible deployment against the Naxalite-Maoist movement. (Though keeping a close watch on the Naxalite-Maoists, the army was not yet directly involved in any way.)

Three weeks had passed since the Dantewada massacre. Owing to various other commitments, the meeting with the home minister had remained pending. Prior to joining politics, Palaniappan Chidambaram had been a corporate lawyer. He had been a key member of the previous two Congress governments. In the wake of the Mumbai terror attack in 2008, Chidambaram had been made the Minister for Home Affairs. Upon taking office, he had promised to tackle the Naxalite-Maoist insurgency on a war footing. With the latest setback hanging in the air and my perceived 'stepping on their turf', I was pretty certain that the official call on the minister would be coloured by the Dantewada event.

The vehicles stopped outside North Block and the security staff led me to the office of the minister. I was ushered in and greeted the minister who was, as always, attired in his trademark crisp whites. He courteously led me to the sitting area at one end of the room.

'So how are things with you, General?'

'All well with the army, Hon'ble Minister.'

Without beating about the bush, Chidambaram came straight to the point. 'You know the Naxal problem is a major national issue. So why do you oppose the deployment of the army in Naxal areas?'

This confirmed my fear that the government was indeed considering asking the army to deploy in the heartland of India. The minister was looking at me intently, a half smile on his lips. For me, it was the moment of truth. Any half-baked answer would open the door. 'I am fully aware of the situation on the ground, Minister. It is a socio-economic and governance issue and needs to be addressed accordingly. At the same time, this is not a secessionist movement and it would not be correct to use the army against our own people.'

My answer did not imply that the people in Kashmir or the Northeast where the army was deployed in anti-insurgency duties were not our own people. In both those regions, as in the Punjab of the 1980s, the insurgents had safe havens across the border and the movements were fanned and stoked by hostile countries. The Maoist problem, ruthless and dangerous as it was, had to be tackled by security forces other than the army. We could offer all the support that the Home Ministry wanted by way of training and logistics, but to get involved in a guerrilla war would impact the operational efficacy of the army. I was determined not to let that happen. The smile never left the minister's face; he was much too suave to show any emotion, but I could sense he hadn't liked my reply.

PART I

THE FORMATIVE YEARS

1

THE BEGINNING

Roots

Every year, as winter set in after the blistering heat of the summer months, the entire Tomar clan would gather in the village of Bapora for the festive season. Jagas (bards) would pull out their ravanhattas (stringed musical instruments) and sing songs that chronicled family history. It didn't make much sense to me as a child and, more often than not, I would nod off; but as I grew older, it became possible to understand and identify with the verses. As the family's history began to get etched in my mind, so did the moral tenets that governed the existence of my people: nothing mattered more to the family than honour. Regardless of the personal cost, situation or circumstance, the code of conduct was encapsulated in one word—izzat.

To be born into the Tanwer (Tomar) clan meant that you either became a soldier or you tilled the land. My grandfather, Daffadar Mukhram Singh, the youngest of three sons, had served with 3 Cavalry. In his days, anyone who owned a horse and could afford to take care of it, invariably joined the cavalry. All five of my father's brothers had followed the drum—Risaldar Major Bannu Singh, OBI, and Daffadar Ram Kanwar Singh (he laid down his life for the Awwal Risala during World War II) were part of Skinner's Horse—while all three sisters married into the army. 1/7 Rajput was almost a family jagir, with brother following brother into it, to the point where for some time almost all the subedar majors of the unit, before and after Independence, were my uncles. Most of the village was either part of the Rajput Regiment or Skinner's Horse.

By the time the sixth and youngest brother lined up to serve in the army, major changes were taking place in the country. A few years before World War II, the British had opened the doors of the army for Indians to serve as regular officers. Hence, Jagat Singh, my father, was commissioned and earmarked for 1/7 Rajput. And here lay a dilemma for the young officer. For, according to family custom, he would have to touch the feet of his elder brothers every time he met them. He asked for an interview with the authorities and highlighted this delicate matter. It was then decided that he be sent to 14 Rajput instead, joining the battalion during the War years.

The Tanwer Rajputs—one of the thirty-six ruling races of India—were a royal Rajput clan of the Chandravanshi (lunar) lineage. They resided mainly in northern India, with a few spilling into areas that are now a part of Pakistan. According to folklore, Tanwer Rajputs are the descendants of the Pandava prince, Arjuna, through his great-grandson Emperor Janmejaya, son of Emperor Parikshit. Though the family traces its roots back to the time of the Pandavas, recorded history goes back to the Tanwer (Tomara) dynasty that ruled Delhi in the mid-eleventh century. Anangpal Tomar II, whose legacy included the construction of Lal Kot, is believed to have appointed his daughter's son Prithviraj Chauhan as heir apparent. Subsequently, Anangpal II had a son, but unwilling to go back on his word to his daughter, he moved away from Delhi and into exile, taking his son with him. My family is said to be direct descendants of this lineage.

Some ballads refer to the fact that Prithviraj Chauhan was merely a caretaker of the throne as long as his grandfather was alive. Prithviraj was never crowned the king of Delhi, adding weight to the view that the Chauhan ruler usurped power from his maternal grandfather. According to another version, Anangpal made Prithviraj the caretaker of his kingdom when he went on a religious pilgrimage, as his own sons were very young at that time. When Anangpal returned, Prithviraj refused to hand over the kingdom.

Whatever the reason for the loss of Delhi, a branch of the Tomar clan established itself in the area of modern Gwalior in northern Madhya Pradesh. The Tomar king Man Singh built the fortress citadel that still stands there. Subsequently, the Mughal emperor Akbar captured Gwalior in 1559. Some Tomar Rajputs converted to Islam during this period of Mughal rule; as a result, Tomar Muslim Rajputs are found in western Rajasthan, Pakistan and Sind. Another part of the clan had earlier established itself as the rulers of Patan in Rajasthan since the twelfth century CE. Patan was the capital of Tanwarawati state and is one of the oldest states still ruled by the Tanwers.

Over the centuries, the Tanwers moved from Delhi to Haryana (Bhiwani, Mahendergarh and Karnal districts), Madhya Pradesh (Gwalior, Morena and Bhind districts), Punjab, Rajasthan (Patan state and surrounding areas), western Uttar Pradesh (Meerut, Badaun, Bareilly, Baraut, Muzaffarnagar, Ghaziabad, Aligarh, and Bulandshahr), eastern Uttar Pradesh and many parts of Himachal Pradesh.

The family can trace its roots back to 1411 when Bapora was first settled, moving from the vicinity of Patan near Neem Ka Thana. At the time, Baba Jagsi Singh called for all castes—though mainly the Rajputs and the Brahmins—to form the village, so that it would be a complete entity by itself. As a child, it made one feel extremely proud to be a part of a much larger community, and tales of valour and honour were everyday fare once the sun set. The bronze, chiselled faces of the villagers, my uncles, their families—this was my world. I knew even then that I was among the toughest of men, the simplest of men, men who would never bow before what they considered unjust or unfair. Each man lived and died by his own set of rules, rules that were ingrained in the character of each of them. As I sat at the foot of the charpoys listening to them talk, I was secure in the knowledge that not one of them, individually or collectively, would ever bend with the wind.

Of Mothers and Fathers

My maternal grandfather, Shimbu Singh, retired as a subedar from the British Indian Army shortly after World War I. Nanaji's village was Bohra Kalan, a part of the old Gurgaon district. The train did not go further than Pataudi Road railway station, after which one had to cover the distance by road. Nanaji had five children—three sons and two daughters (both of whom married into the army). My oldest uncle was in the field of education, while the second looked after the considerable land that my grandfather had acquired. Known as subedar saab in the village, he commanded a lot of respect. My youngest uncle was an advocate in Gurgaon, then a small town on the outskirts of Delhi.

My parents were married in 1949; my father, at the time, was a captain with 14 Rajput. From the few stories I heard subsequently, they were a contented couple. I was born in 1951 in the Military Hospital in Pune, an event that found mention in the 14 Rajput Digest of Service.

My memories of early childhood are somewhat blurred. I know we moved to Kasauli in the Shimla Hills where my father's unit was located. There is a story of a large cobra having come into the compound of our house where, as a one-year-old infant, I was playing on the floor. The house was next to the battalion training ground and word of the snake's entry into Captain Jagat Singh's house spread rapidly. Soon, a crowd of soldiers was at the door, while, the story goes, I was happily playing with the cobra. I was lucky, for the snake obviously did not perceive me as a threat. The men, unwilling to kill naag devta, called the local snake catcher. The snake story then got even more interesting, for after the man had captured the snake, he released it in the forest, saying he had never seen such a noble snake.

It was during this period, around 1952, that my mother was diagnosed with terminal cancer. Her health deteriorated extremely fast. She passed away shortly after we moved from Kasauli to Delhi, leaving my father with a son who was barely beginning to walk. This entire period is a complete blank for me, particularly as no one ever spoke to me about it. I guess I knew something had happened, but the implications of her passing away would dawn on me only much much later. Unfortunately, the only photograph I have of my mother is a slightly blurred studio shot of my parents and me.

Shielded from the tragedy, I guess I was like any other naughty child growing up in the care of my maternal grandparents, who had accepted the responsibility of raising their daughter's only son. I was obviously physically very active, for one of my earliest memories is of getting hurt by running into a door. Nani was soon applying honey to the gash, telling me soothingly that it was an antiseptic. I asked Nani if I could keep the bottle with me and apply it every time I got injured, which was often.

Somewhere during this period, the family decided that my father should get married again. I was oblivious to all this, until my mama arrived to take me to Dehradun to live with my parents. I had no intentions of leaving my nani and resisted violently, even slapping my mama when he tried to carry me off. It must have been heart-wrenching for my grandparents to see me leave, but they knew my place was with my parents. I would learn later that my nani did not speak to my mama for over a year, holding him responsible for having taken me away.

My father was a serious sort of person and, like everyone else who knew him, I too learnt to be careful about not getting on his wrong side. But that was as much as I learnt about my father in those initial years.

I was much too young to have any clear memories of the Indian Military Academy (IMA) when we lived there in early 1955 but I do remember flashes. I was extremely fond of pets and was allowed to keep a dog and a cat. Then my father got posted back to his battalion, 14 Rajput, towards the end of the year. The unit was initially stationed in Anand Parbat in Delhi but was soon set to move to Santa Cruz in Bombay. The entire battalion was put on to a single 'special train', a maddeningly exciting adventure for me: ice slabs in compartments to bring down the temperature, and the novelty of a field telephone with which one could actually talk to people!

We settled down quickly in Bombay. I was enrolled in a preschool class at Sacred Heart. Even at that stage, my Hindi suffered, for teachers in Bombay were not very good at teaching the language.

Soon, my father was posted to the Rajput Regimental Centre at Fatehgarh. As decent schools were scarce in that entire region, it was decided that I should go to Birla Public School (BPS) in Pilani. My father had studied in Pilani, though at a different institution, so it was natural for him to think of sending me there. BPS had a hostel, which probably settled the issue in favour of the school. There was still the tricky business of passing the entrance examination, and as it was deemed that my Hindi was shaky (the result of our stay in Bombay), I was given tuitions by the paltan panditji to polish my language skills.

I travelled to Pilani with my father, much too young to realize what was in store for me. The entrance test for Class II was fun for me as I was also asked to sketch a man. The drawing I produced did not necessarily showcase my artistry—my 'man' was just two round circles with lots of lines shooting off sideways, indicative, I guess, of arms and legs—but I did get through.

Having passed the all-important entrance test (I don't remember if I was tested in Hindi), we went to the hostel, Shishu Griha, designed according to the instructions of Maria Montessori who had visited the school when it was being built. Everything was child-friendly. The beds were small, windows at a level conducive for a child to look out of, and toilet fittings were of a small size and low enough that we had no difficulty using them. I sort of liked the hostel and also the flags of all nations that were part of the United Nations organization.

That evening, I was left in the hostel and my father went to another hostel where arrangements had been made for parents. New entrants to the dorm always invited attention, and there was the resultant teasing and mild ragging. It was like nothing I had experienced before, and I felt bereft of the shelter and safety I had enjoyed with my parents. I decided then and there that I did not want to stay and went to look for my father.

I wept and asked him to take me home. He placated me by saying I had liked the hostel and the flags. But I insisted, and he seemed to relent, saying that I should give it a try for three days after which he would come and take me home. I eagerly waited for the three days to pass, and then some more, but he never came! After a while, as he had no doubt anticipated, I got used to life in the hostel.

School gradually grew on me. The sense of belonging, the friends—I was in an environment that suited me. Most importantly, the food was good, except the milk which was given to us in the afternoon. The common rumour among students was that it was camel milk.

The highlight of each day was the assembly which started with the school prayer written by the poet Maithili Sharan Gupt, followed by a devotional song sung by the music teacher. Another teacher would then explain a shloka from the Vedas and then a senior student would speak on some topic of general interest. Yet another teacher would then test us on our ability to identify the national flags adorning the assembly hall. The last item on the agenda was an exercise in silence. We always emerged from assembly wiser than before.

There were three Vijay Singhs including me in my class, which confused Miss Fosbury, our teacher. We were renamed, for convenience, according to house number: the one with the most senior house number was Vijay Singh. I came next in this hierarchy and was to answer to Vijay Kumar, while the third was to be known as Vijay Pal. Problem solved!

School was a lot simpler in those days when the use of the cane and the occasional slap for any mistake, real or perceived, was considered par for the course. My first brush with authority came in Class III. I was dared by my classmates to start recess early by ringing the gong. I did, and was promptly caught; the teacher then used the wooden mallet on my back and, boy, did I get a first-hand feel of what it was like to be a gong!

was always an event, for it meant getting a soft drink and a snack to eat. During one of these visits home, I was surprised to find that my kid brother had been joined by a baby sister. That completed the family.

Bapora was relatively close to Pilani, and an older cousin would take me to our ancestral home, where my father would also spend a few days. I enjoyed going to the village, for it was fun to be with my cousins. It was also exciting, as one would often be called to the village school to tell the other children what one had studied in Pilani.

Life in the village was rather busy even for visitors. I got involved in the daily chore of fetching water from the village well. At that time there were no taps or running water. We had to fetch water in metal pots or earthen pots. The wells were deep, especially the ones from which sweet drinking water was hauled out. These wells were generally close to the village ponds. The average depth of these wells was between 150 to 200 feet and one needed at least three people to pull out water (two to pull and one to monitor the progress) and then haul the vessel to fill up the various pitchers brought by all and sundry. It didn't stop at fetching water. Using the fodder-cutting machine, we prepared the feed for the cattle, took the cows and buffaloes to the pond for a wash, went to the post office to check for mail, and so on. Being more or less on my own, I would spend the afternoons sitting in the shade reading a book. The evenings were spent playing kabaddi or some other popular game, which would be topped off by visiting the small shops in the village around sunset.

The harvesting season also coincided with our vacations, and that meant helping with the unloading of the grain. The dusty environment coupled with frequent sandstorms during the summer months added to the uniqueness of village life and made me mentally and physically tough.

Our headmaster, Radha Raman Pathak, had a profound impact on us. He encouraged us to be truthful and upright and to fight for what is right. Equally importantly, his unadulterated patriotism rubbed off on all the students.

One day when I was in Class VII or VIII, we had decided on a cycle sortie from Pilani to Jaipur. Good intentions, but by the time we covered the 116 kilometres to Sikar we were exhausted, and took a collective decision to board the train to Jaipur. We spent the day going around the Pink City, and after spending the night at a friend's home, we took the train back, this time up to Chirawa, from where we then cycled back to school. After depositing the cycles, we discussed the vexing problem that was hounding our collective conscience: what would happen if the headmaster learnt that we had cheated on the cycle sortie by travelling by train?

It was decided that we come clean with the headmaster. A la Oliver Twist, I was chosen to go to the office, not only because I was the class head but also because of the general belief that the headmaster had a good impression of me. I gingerly entered his office and told him the truth. As expected, he was infuriated and caught hold of my ear. I received six stinging lashes of the cane on my backside and was told to tell the rest of my gang to pack up and get out of school. The message was accordingly conveyed and we packed and called for rickshaws to take us to the bus stand. The main concern now was explaining our expulsion to our parents. As we approached the school gate on our rickshaws, we found the headmaster standing there. He asked us where we thought we were going. Perplexed, we said we were only following his orders, at which he shouted at us not to be dimwits and to get back into the school and get on with our studies.

Though he never openly acknowledged that he appreciated our truthfulness, we could sense it. In any case, the sheer relief of not being expelled was so great that we literally fell at his feet in gratitude.

Returning to school after our Class IX vacations, some of my close friends decided to take the National Defence Academy (NDA) entrance examination. They broached the subject with me and I promptly asked for a form for myself. We generally hung out together and it was this bond which probably influenced me to apply. Left to myself, I may not have bought the form without my father's permission. One of our teachers who always encouraged students to join the armed forces helped us not only to fill out the forms but also to put together the various support papers that were required. In lieu of my father's signature, the form was countersigned by my housemaster as my guardian (which he literally was, as I had spent the better part of my growing years with him).

When I next went home to the village during the winter vacations, my father was there on short leave. When I told him about the exam, he merely said I was wasting my time and should be concentrating on my board exam curriculum instead. Nevertheless, he reluctantly allowed me to appear for the NDA entrance examination.

Delhi was my selected examination centre and my father arranged for me to stay for two nights with his friend and regimental colleague Colonel Prahlad Singh—who served at Army Headquarters, and lived in the officer's enclave in Dhaula Kuan.

It was winter in Delhi and the sun was setting by the time I started looking for Colonel Prahlad Singh's house. No one seemed to know of the colonel. I was getting frustrated and began considering spending the night either at the bus stand or the railway station. It was then that I saw three boys walking in my direction. In a last-ditch effort, I asked for their help in locating the elusive colonel's house. But by this time, I had forgotten the name of my prospective host and was asking for Colonel Prabhu, further hampering my cause. While this conversation was going on, the mother of one of the boys came along and asked us what was going on. On being told that I had come for the NDA exam to be held the next day, she told her son to take me to their house. I was ordered to park myself in the guestroom and told I could stay there. Shortly thereafter, her husband returned from office and, without any hesitation, seconded his wife's offer. He said he would take me to the exam centre, Delhi Public School on Mathura Road, the next morning and that I was not to worry.

This incident had a profound impact on me and underlined the fact that the armed forces were really one large family. The couple had literally taken me—a complete stranger—off the street and under their wing and they did their best to ensure that I was mentally at ease for what was an important exam. I was given the same love and affection that they would have probably bestowed on their own son if he was appearing for the NDA exam. Much later in life I narrated this incident to a general officer who had come to call on me while I was posted at Ambala. Coincidentally, it turned out that this officer was one of the boys I had met, and he was the son of Colonel Prahlad Singh I had been looking for. The family with whom I had stayed, I learnt, was now living in Chandigarh.

After the exam, I returned to school and geared up for the annual board exams. The NDA results came out just as the school exams were about to begin; while I had cleared the examination comfortably, that wasn't the case with my friends who had also taken the exam. It was an uncomfortable situation to be in.

Back in school, at the beginning of the next academic year, came the notification for the Services Selection Board (SSB). As I had given the air force as my first choice, I was to report to No. 1 Air Force Selection Board in Dehradun. I wrote to my father to seek his permission to go to Dehradun only to be told that I was to forget about it. I decided to go to Roorkee, where he was then posted, to reason with him. As it turned out, the reason for his objection was the fact that I had opted for the air force rather than the army. (My infatuation with the IAF was mainly on account of a cousin I looked up to. He was a test pilot and would serve with distinction and go on to become the Air Officer Commanding-in-Chief, Western Air Command.)

Since I was already in Roorkee, my father reluctantly told me that I could go to Dehradun, but said that he reserved the right to decide whether I could join the services or pursue higher studies. The final decision, he told me, would be taken in consultation with my headmaster.

On passing the SSB and the Pilot Aptitude Battery Test as well as a medical examination in Delhi, I was found fit to join the air force. Now I had to wait for the merit list. Come June, two sets of results brought me joy. I had topped my school in the boards and had automatically qualified for a scholarship due to a fairly high position in the state merit list. This was followed by the NDA results where I had also made the grade as an air force cadet, and my name was high on the merit list here as well. This gave me a lot of satisfaction, for now both avenues were available to me.

This brought my father to the school for the agreed-upon discussion with my headmaster, and the matter was debated at some length, after which the headmaster spoke to me separately to enquire about what I wanted. Knowing that I really wanted to join the NDA, the headmaster went about convincing my father—successfully. The decision made, my father and I returned to the village.

It was then that a discrepancy was highlighted by the UPSC (Union Public Service Commission). In the original UPSC form, my year of birth had been erroneously filled in as 1950, even though the supporting documents and the certificate sent by the school independently had correctly listed the year as 1951. Even though this made absolutely no difference to my eligibility for the NDA, there was a flurry of activity to get the necessary paperwork done to rectify the error. As the Rajasthan Board of Education certificate was yet to reach me, my father got a certificate signed by the commanding officer (CO) of 14 Rajput to verify that my year of birth was indeed 1951. This was based on his own and the battalion's (I was born while my father was serving in the unit) documents. The various papers were then forwarded to the UPSC that accepted the documents and the explanation, and cleared me to join the NDA. The matter having been finally resolved, I embarked on the journey to join the academy almost a week later than the rest of the batch because of this snafu.

National Defence Academy

The National Defence Academy is situated at Khadakwasla on the outskirts of Pune. It was to be my home for the next three years of my life.

The main body of the course had reported to the academy by 7 July 1966. Apart from me, there were a couple of other cadets who had also been delayed owing to documentation problems. This meant that we were the new murgas on the block without the protective shield of the flock. It was a huge culture shock in spite of the fact that I had spent all my school years in a hostel. The first thing I was told to do was to 'shave off that silly moustache' and someone thrust a razor in my hand. I had no clue how to use a razor. In fact, I was hardly aware of the fact that the fuzz on my upper lip qualified as a moustache.

The next command was even harder to comprehend. 'Wipe that silly smile off your stupid face' just didn't make sense, for we were more like frightened rabbits caught in the glare of a car's headlight. However, that didn't stop our tormentors from thinking that we looked amused, which only triggered off another cycle of verbal abuse. It was a vicious loop and it was tough. The brain was numbed and it would stay like that through most of the first term.

When one wasn't hanging upside down, or front-rolling endlessly, or running from place A to place B with bicycles held over our heads, we could appreciate the beauty of the campus: the architectural blend of arches and pillars topped by a dome; the Sudan Block, a three-storied basalt-and-granite structure constructed with Jodhpur red sandstone dominated the sprawling expanse of the academy; the battalion blocks; the parade ground with the huge mast right behind the saluting base; the Bombay Stadium; the Science Block; Habibullah Hall; the airfield with its complement of gliders; Peacock Bay with its boats and yachts; the stables with a wonderful array of horses. The facilities were top-notch and everything about NDA felt larger than life.

According to existing practice, all first-term cadets were housed in I (India), J (Juliet) or K (Kilo) squadrons which all had a sprinkling of third, fourth, fifth and sixth term cadets. I was in K squadron and we called ourselves 'killers', deliberately pronouncing it in a sing-song fashion.

I was asked to join the technical stream—it had recently been decided to club cadets into technical and non-technical streams from the first term rather than the fourth term. We proudly referred to ourselves as the 'experimental course'. The logic behind the move was that all those who were in Class XI or had studied partly in Class XI would be technical while all those who came into the academy after Class X would be non-technical. The technical stream had a larger syllabus to cover, which made the going quite tough. However, a few days after joining the academy, a senior cadet explained to me that if I was an air force cadet aspiring to be a fighter pilot, I was probably in the wrong stream. He suggested I go meet the principal, TN Vyas, and I did so the next day to explain my situation. Without any further ado, I was shifted to the non-technical stream.

Life at the academy was fast-paced and interesting. In hindsight, the endless punishments and ragging helped to toughen us up. Curiously, the system made us tolerant and patient, apart from preparing us mentally to take on life's adversities and conditioning us physically to a point where we believed we could surmount any difficulty.

The training at NDA was excellent—the only institution of its kind where cadets from the army, navy and the air force all train together. The facilities were excellent, though one could have argued that there was always scope for further improvement. The academic content was good and our batch was told that we would have external examinations in our fourth and sixth terms to get our graduation degree. The examinations were held as scheduled but the final graduation degree eluded us due to some bureaucratic snafu. This issue was finally resolved when the NDA became affiliated to the Jawaharlal Nehru University many years later. Recently, this was further improved upon: under my watch as COAS, the NDA course now offers a B. Tech degree and also offers the cadets an honours programme.

The NDA prepares a young man to become physically fit and mentally robust, while also providing academic knowledge and skills in fields such as engineering drawing, woodcraft, metal craft and welding. In addition, cadets are trained in social graces appropriate to the services, all under the watchful eye of superior divisional officers and squadron commanders.

Cadets have qualification standards in swimming, physical training, equestrian skills, and are taken on a variety of outdoor camps where they are exposed to conditions they will sooner or later encounter in their careers. All this makes a young boy just out of school into a confident man who is prepared to shoulder responsibilities as a part of the services. Over the years, the academy has evolved and there have been many changes: more squadrons, an additional battalion and, in academics, the content is far better, with an emphasis on services-beneficial knowledge. Today, cadets are being offered electives that help them specialize in their chosen fields.

NDA cadets are being constantly evaluated—by their instructors, their seniors and even by their peers. The entire system is based on cadet appointments that start by bringing in graded degrees of responsibility. I became a corporal in my fifth term and was appointed the battalion cadet captain (BCC) in my sixth and final term. As the BCC, I also had to function as the academy cadet captain (ACC) for a couple of months. During the fifth term, specific service-oriented classes were started and it was here that I discovered that Major HS Dalal, my squadron commander had, at my father's request, changed my service from the air force to the army.

On the eve of the passing out parade, hardly any of the cadets had slept a wink, so high was the excitement the night before. We had been drilled this way and that until most of us could march around the drill square in our sleep. Everything was gleaming in the morning light as we gathered behind the fort doors, boots shining, dress looking resplendent, swords clanking and the metallic tips of canes catching the glint of the rising sun. The academy brass band then struck up the age-old arti—*Om Jai Jagadish Hare*—and every cadet, regardless of religion, caste or creed, stood stock-still, drinking in the moment.

Soon the bugles sounded and the markers were out. As the BCC, I was to lead my battalion. Commands were shouted, the brass band struck up a marching tune, the doors swung open and we streamed out in our white patrols (again, this was a first, a fitting tribute to the 'experimental lot'). I dug my heels into the ground, knowing that those coming behind me were matching each of my steps. After that, almost everything is a blur, until we slow marched past the saluting base, under the famous mast that represents the navy. Above us, aircraft of the Indian Air Force were thundering past in a fly-past. I banged my foot down on the step that marked the final step; already, in my mind, I was out of the academy. Being an army cadet, now my path would lead me to Dehradun where we were to report to the Indian Military Academy (IMA). I felt very, very good.

2

THE FORMATIVE YEARS

Dignity and Honour

In the larger context of a military career, the move from the NDA to the IMA might well be a small step. However, for a cadet, it was a gigantic leap. We were now GCs (gentlemen cadets) and, as NDA graduates, we were automatically afforded the status of third termers.

My first visit to the IMA was as a kicking and screaming toddler, relocated from my nani's home to that of my father—he was then a platoon commander—and new mother. At that time, I had been too young to appreciate the beauty of my surroundings. The Doon valley is one of the most spectacular places in the country, ideally situated to house educational institutions. To the south lay the jungle-clad Shivalik Hills, the ravine-like terrain ideal training grounds for the GCs. The academy itself was situated on the left bank of the Tons River that gently sweeps down from the Himalayan foothills to the north. At night, the twinkling lights of Mussoorie added greatly to the charm of the place. Boxing in the valley were the Ganga to the east and the Yamuna to the west.

Chetwode Hall, with the drill square extending in front of it, gave the IMA a regal setting. Adding to the grandeur were the Greco-Roman and colonial styled Kingsley and Collins blocks that housed the GCs, while majestic tree-lined avenues were flanked by elegant bungalows that housed the commandant and other senior officers. Originally, the IMA campus had been the Railway Staff College, but in 1932 it was transferred to the army when the academy was set up to train Indians as officers, one of the main demands of the Indian nationalist movement.

We arrived at the IMA towards the end of June 1969, and even though we wore the third term insignia on our collars, we were given the royal boot along with the first-termers who were direct entrants to the academy. Though the NDA had forwarded our documentation directly to the IMA, we were still required to fill a fresh form under the supervision of a junior commissioned officer (JCO) who demanded that we respectfully address him as 'saab'. His orders were clear: we were to enter our date of birth *as it appeared on the UPSC application form when applying for the NDA entrance exam.* When I tried to point out that my year of birth had been corrected, I got a barrage of abuse and had to front-roll a few times. The saab threatened to take even more drastic action. I did as I was told and entered the (wrong) year as it was on the UPSC application form, but managed to get the point across to the authorities somehow who in turn made the correction and, subsequently, the identity card issued to me and all the other relevant documentation reflected my correct date and year of birth. At that point, I could not have imagined that this innocuous incident would have to be explained when a controversy over my age was deliberately created.

IMA places suitable emphasis on services-oriented subjects along with the rest of its academic syllabus. As GCs in the third term, the emphasis was tilted more towards service orientation. I was assigned to Cassino Company, which was located in temporary barracks at a distance from the main academy block. The senior under officer (SUO) was HPS Mann with whom I had had a misunderstanding at NDA. Not surprisingly, I was singled out for special treatment, constantly engaged in push-ups and front-rolls. A hard taskmaster, HPS was very keen that the company did well under his watch, and we would be taken out after dinner to practice for the cross-country run.

There was never a dull moment at the IMA. Service-oriented subjects ensured that we learnt what a platoon commander must know. In addition, many other activities kept us busy. I joined the shikar club and enjoyed the outings on Sundays when we would go out into the other parts of the Doon valley in search of partridge, jungle fowl or duck. The shoots, entirely on the wing, sharpened our reflexes and helped us develop an eye for the ground—a necessary soldierly skill, especially for infantry officers.

My platoon commander was Captain Abhijit Mamik from 5/11 Gorkhas and the company commander was Major Chandra B Khanduri of the First Gorkhas. The latter had a great sense of military history and, as cadets, we imbibed a lot from him. He was posted out during my fourth term, and was replaced by Major Diwan Chand Saraswat from Rajputana Rifles. But our main interaction was with the platoon commander, with whom we forged a special rapport. Abhijit Mamik had come to the IMA after completing his tenure as the aide-de-camp to General GG Bewoor, the army chief. Mamik was a solid professional and the GCs learnt a lot from him.

A few days through my third term, Captain Mamik summoned me to question me about the SUO's complaint that I was creating problems in the company. Since I had been asked, I frankly told him the reason for the SUO's ire. As far as I was concerned, it was the luck of the draw that I should be in the same company as HPS Mann and all I could do was grin and bear whatever he hurled at me. I can only surmise that Mamik then looked at my dossier and the NDA reports, and realized that I was a victim of 'personal score settling'. Whether that was the case or not, fortunately, Bobby Saiyyad took over as SUO from HPS shortly after, and things improved for me.

I was appointed the SUO in my fourth term. Having learnt lessons from the previous term, the handling of the company was reoriented. We had Amar Aul (company sergeant major), VK Sharma (JUO), Balraj Nagal and Sandeep Gupta (sergeants) and Prakash Singh (CQMH). During this period Cassino Company did extremely well and started accumulating trophies in various competitions.

Sometime after the midterm break I found Captain Abhijit Mamik looking distressed and not his usual self during our morning classes. He called me aside after classes got over and asked, 'What the hell did you do yesterday evening?' I was completely thrown, for nothing untoward had happened. He then told me I was to be marched up for manhandling a cadet. As ordered, I went back to change into the appropriate dress for being marched up.

I was marched into the battalion commander's office by the AQ Captain Kanwer Kuldip Singh. Colonel Goverdhan Singh Jamwal, a very fine human being, asked me if I had manhandled a cadet. I answered, 'Negative, sir!'

The complainant was called in and I was asked to look into his eyes and narrate what had happened. On realizing that I was telling the truth, the battalion commander rang up the commandant, Major General Rajendra Prasad, and told him that I was not at fault and could not be punished till a proper inquiry was held. To cut a long story short, the court of inquiry found me 'not guilty' of the serious charge of 'manhandling' but it was decided that some action had to be taken as the junior cadet had been 'bullied'.

A few days later, I was again marched up, this time in front of the officiating commandant. In the hour before the marching in, Academy Subedar Major Ashirvadam (Madras Regiment) had been drilling me and practising the entire procedure of my anticipated detabbing (where rank badges are removed as punishment): with a flourish, he would take off the SUO rank badges from my shoulders, bellowing the commands into my ear from barely six inches away. I was almost stone deaf from these enthusiastic practice sessions. To my immense relief, as the sentence was read out, I realized I was only being demoted to the rank of JUO. This eventuality had not occurred to the subedar major, who just stood there dumbfounded, unable to figure out what to do. Everyone was looking at each other, when finally the subedar major bellowed, 'JUO, march out!' The half grin on my face further added to his discomfiture, and he glared at me until I walked out.

After about a month, my rank was reinstated, and I passed out of IMA as SUO and as the most senior infantry officer in my course. Cassino Company bagged both the academy and chief's banner, a feat achieved after sixteen years. My take-away from the IMA: if you are truthful and have not done anything wrong, then you do not have anything to fear. Additionally, the handling of the company taught me empathy and also taught me that setting a good example encourages people in one's command to excel.

As our time at the IMA drew to a close, all we could talk about was the choice of regiments. A few days prior to the big day when we were to submit our individual choices, the platoon commander told me it didn't matter which regiment I opted for. 'I've decided you are to go to 5/11 GR (Gorkha Rifles).'

Abhijit Mamik was paying me a great compliment, but the situation made me feel extremely uncomfortable. Apart from the fact that I wanted to join the Rajput Regiment where I had not just a parental but a family claim, I did not want it to look as if I was being given preferential treatment. Mamik glowered at me, saying he would take the matter up with my father.

That night I decided to pre-empt the situation and hurriedly wrote to my father, articulating my reasons for not wanting to be sent to my platoon commander's regiment, wanting instead to follow in the footsteps of my uncles and my father. I must have beaten Captain Mamik to the draw, for my father wrote to Mamik telling him that while he appreciated his sentiments about me, I should go where I felt comfortable.

However, only half the battle was won. I then went to Major NK Kapur of the Rajputs to plead my case. The fact that I was in the top ten of the merit list probably got me the Rajput Regiment. I was very happy that I was earmarked for 2 Rajput; going to my father's unit, 14 Rajput, would have meant living in his shadow. I was determined to chart my own course.

The passing out parade at IMA is a major event, not only for the cadets being commissioned, but for rest of the academy too. Our passing-out parade was held on 14 June 1970 and the reviewing officer was Lieutenant General Jagjit Singh Arora, the Eastern Army Commander. As we went through our paces on the drill square for one last time, little did we know that a year later most of us would be going to war under his command.

We still had to wait for darkness to fall before the single star denoting our rank could adorn our shoulders. In those days, the piping ceremony was held with the imposing Chetwode Hall as a backdrop. My parents were not able to attend my passing out parade, so I requested the parents of a coursemate to pip me. It was a proud moment to be commissioned as an officer after four years of hard work and that too in a regiment and a battalion that had a rich history of valour.

▪

2 Rajput, also known as Kali Chindi, is one of the oldest battalions of the Indian Army. Raised at Badgaon on 30 November 1798 as the 1/16 Bengal Native Infantry, its designation was to change eight times during the course of the next century-and-a-half—33rd Bengal Native Infantry in 1824; 4th Bengal Native Infantry in 1861; 4th Regiment of Bengal Infantry in 1885; 4th (Prince Albert Victor's) Bengal Infantry in 1890; 4th (PAV) Rajput Regiment of Bengal Infantry in 1897; 2nd Battalion/7th Rajputs in 1921; 2nd Battalion The Rajput Regiment (PAV) in 1945; and finally 2nd Battalion The Rajput Regiment in 1950. If it sounds confusing on paper, it was even worse when one stepped into the mess, where each and every piece of silver was associated with the various phases of the battalion's history. (Silver refers to trophies that the battalion has collected—the amount of silver is usually indicative of the age and lineage of the battalion.) As a subaltern in the unit, the upkeep of the silver was an added responsibility and we youngsters were supposed to know the entire history like the backs of our hands.

The battalion had an impressive operational record: within five years of its raising, it fought and earned its first battle honour in 1803, at the pass of Leswaree, ousting the French from north India. Thereafter, the unit participated in numerous campaigns, the battles of Kalenjra, Kalunghar, Nahun, Rampore and Gwalior being the most prominent. The siege and capture of Bharatpur Fort alongside 1 Rajput (in 1825) earned the battalion its second battle honour.

The story of the 'tattered flag' during the battle of Bharatpur needs to be told, for in its telling lies the very soul—that is, the deep sense of honour—of not just the Rajput Regiment, but also of the Indian Army. 1 Rajput had been a part of Lord Lake's force when the British had besieged the Bharatpur fortress in 1805.

> After a breach was effected in the fort's walls on 9 January, the British attacked, but were repulsed. A second attack on 20 January was also thrown back. Following about one month of analysis and new breaches, a third attack was made against a new location, on 20 February. This one was repulsed by the defenders with heavy casualties, and a fourth and final assault the next day also failed. In the fourth assault, 1 Rajput lost 180 men out of 400. The assault was partially successful with the colours of the battalion being planted on the rampart, but one after the other, whoever held the colours was shot down. Soon the battalion colours were riddled with shots and in tatters.
>
> New colours replaced the old ones. No one knew about the disappearance of the fragmented old colours. Twenty years later, in January 1826, when 1 Rajput along with 2 Rajput attacked the fort and took it, the sons brought the pieces of the old colours out and tied them to the new colours to remind themselves of the unfinished task of their fathers and uncles that they had to accomplish.*

2 Rajput earned its third battle honour 'Kabul' in 1842, operating as the vanguard of the British Expeditionary Force during the First Afghan War. In 1845-1846, during the First Sikh War, it earned two more hard-fought battle honours: 'Ferozeshah' and 'Sobraon'. The sixth battle honour 'Afghanistan 1870-80' was conferred on it during the Second Afghan War and, finally, for its impressive performance in the upper Burma campaign, the seventh battle honour 'Burma 1885-87' was awarded. Its performance in Burma also earned the battalion the sobriquet 'Kali Chindi' (on account of backings and flashes worn), a name by which it is known across the army.

In the immediate aftermath of the tribal invasion of Jammu and Kashmir, the battalion opened up the route to Rajouri, following its sister battalion 1 Rajput into the Rajouri-Jhanjhar region that saw some desperate fighting against Pakistani raiders. In the limited actions fought by the battalion, it acquitted itself well, earning four Vir Chakras. However, fifteen years later in 1962, the battalion found itself in the vanguard when it was hurriedly deployed along the Namka Chu River just below the Thagla ridge in NEFA (present-day Arunachal Pradesh) when the Chinese launched an attack on 20 October. With no winter clothing, digging tools, basic defensive materials or adequate ammunition, the battalion was virtually decimated. Four officers, seven JCOs and 286 other ranks were killed while the commanding officer,

*Philip Mason, *A Matter of Honour* (1974)

Lieutenant Colonel Maha Singh Rikh, was wounded and taken prisoner along with all those remaining in the battalion.

On that fateful morning, our men had perished fighting waves of attacking Chinese, some going down with stones in their hands, having expended the limited ammunition at their disposal. The second-in-command (2IC), Major Gurdial Singh (later awarded the Mahavir Chakra), and the other officers had all gone down fighting. The Rajputs at Namka Chu, along with 2/11 Gorkhas and elements of Assam Rifles, had stood their ground despite almost impossible odds, giving new meaning to the term 'last man, last round'. The man who was credited with having saved the CO's life and having waged a desperate battle from the CO's bunker on the fateful morning was Second Lieutenant Bhup Singh.

Lal Qila and Rashtrapati Bhavan

After graduating from the IMA, we got a few days' leave and I went home to Bapora. As a newly commissioned officer in the Indian Army, I accompanied my father, who seemed intent on introducing me to the entire district. We also met the district commissioner of Bhiwani, MG Devasahayam, who, prior to joining the administrative service, had been with the Madras Regiment. I would meet him again forty-two years later, after I retired from service, under completely different circumstances.

I then proceeded by train to Delhi and was received at the station by Lieutenant Manyapada Nanjappa Nanaya who was my immediate senior, having passed out of the Officers Training Academy, Madras in March 1970 as a short service officer. At that time, 2 Rajput was partly garrisoned at the historic Red Fort while the other half was at Rashtrapati Bhavan. In those days, there was only one infantry battalion in Delhi which looked after all ceremonial jobs in the capital.

Nanaya gave me a quick 'what-to-expect-on-your-first-day-in-the-battalion' rundown as we entered the crowded walled city of Old Delhi. No one can be immune to the overwhelming sense of history as the imposing Red Fort comes into view. For a newly commissioned 2nd lieutenant in the Indian Army, it was even more significant, and a little intimidating.

The sheer architectural splendour of Shah Jahan's seventeenth-century Lal Qila takes one's breath away. Constructed under the supervision of the Mughal emperor himself, it was built adjacent to the existing Salimgarh Fort that had been built by Salim Shah Suri in 1546. After Shah Jahan decided to shift his capital from Agra to Delhi, work began in 1638, and it took an army of labourers ten years to complete it. Situated on the west bank of the Yamuna, the fort got its name from the red sandstone which was used to put up the massive walls that were protected by moats fed by the river.

As we entered from the Meena Bazaar side through the Lahore Gate, I could hardly believe that this would be my new home for the next few months. Nanaya showed me to my quarters and told me to freshen up, after which I was to make my way to the officer's mess, adjacent to the bachelor's quarters and flanking the ornate Diwan-i-Aam (the hall of public audiences during Mughal times). Sitting in the mess, we could hear the extremely popular sound and light programme that was, and continues to be, a daily evening affair.

Within these regal surrounds, I met Captain Thomas Mathews, who was from the Malabar region of south India. Also from the NDA, Tom was three courses senior to me; with his debonair good looks and languid approach to life, he was the natural ringleader of the junior officers. Tom immediately took it upon himself to welcome me into the unit with the traditional mug of beer. My feeble protests that I didn't drink were brushed aside with disdain and the traditional regimental welcome went down my throat. After a couple of drinks, it all travelled back the other way and Tom just managed to get out of the line of fire. I was to realize subsequently that I was allergic to alcohol, for every time I had to live up to the 'regiment and country', I would develop painful patches on my skin.

The next morning I reported for the morning parade, expecting to see the battalion in reasonable strength. To my disbelief, there were only five officers, an equal number of JCOs and three other ranks. As the only battalion literally 'holding fort' in Delhi, the men used to be on various ceremonial duties which were by and large extremely stressful. The segment stationed at Rashtrapati Bhavan was stretched, and had at least two guard details practising the ceremonial guard of honour that needed to be mounted at Palam airfield whenever any dignitary visited the country. To break the stifling monotony of this mundane work, some of the men who were from villages near Delhi were encouraged to take an out-pass and go to their homes, reporting back by noon on Monday. As a result, Red Fort always had a semi-deserted look even at the best of times.

After completing my documentation, I reported to the adjutant, Captain NK Gupta, who told me I was being slotted into Charlie Company and gave me a quick rundown of the dos and don'ts. Though welcoming and friendly, Nandu Gupta was a stickler for rules and his list of 'dos' was fairly long. After this, I was marched off to meet the officiating commanding officer, Major (later Brigadier) Bhup Singh.

With an impressive upward sweep of a moustache adding to his persona, Bhup Singh interviewed me. He asked all the usual questions: where I had finished in the order of merit at the IMA; what my interests were; and what sport I was interested in. He then decreed that I should take charge of the battalion's athletics team, adding that I should take them out for a run in the morning and oversee their overall training. With a final word of welcome, the interview was over.

I made my way to C Company and was met by the company JCO, Subedar Udai Pratap Singh. Ramrod straight in his bearing, I had seen him earlier at the NDA when he had won the national pole vault championship. He was also a national record-holding swimmer and had been a national level boxer. Topping off an already impressive résumé was the fact that he had also been an instructor at the IMA. He smartly rattled off my duties; orders had already come that I was to be with the athletics team, so I would take them out even before the rest of the battalion fell in for morning drill. After that, I was to be part of the cadre that would carry on till midday, and so on. He then escorted me around the unit lines, familiarizing me with the barracks, the langar, and showing me what was stored where.

Then was the real moment of truth: when an officer comes face to face with the men whom he is to command. The men are invariably going to test you and the thought of falling short is terrifying for any young officer. When the athletics team assembled the next morning at dawn, I met another legend—CHM Nar Singh Chauhan, a services triple jumper who had been in charge of the team. We started off at a brisk pace, heading towards Shantivan on the banks of the Yamuna.

The entire plot had obviously been thought out carefully, for two long distance runners were positioned up front. Fresh out of IMA, I was determined to keep up with them, and I took off after them like a jackrabbit without so much as a backward glance, assuming that the rest were following. The two long-distance runners first went north, crossed the Yamuna by the old iron railway bridge, then doubled back along the opposite bank until we came to the Nizamuddin bridge, crossed back and kept the pace up until, exhausted, we were back at Shantivan. Here to my utter disbelief, I found the rest of the squad relaxing and languidly studying the clouds while lying around on the grassy mounds. When they saw the three of us approaching, they lazily formed up and I realized I had been taken for a ride.

As we made our way back into the Red Fort, Nar Singh Chauhan said to me in full hearing of the others, 'Saab, dopahar ko razai ya kambal ke andar paon rakh kar letiyega, nahin toh pao bhar jayenge aapke.' (Remember to wrap your feet in a quilt or a blanket in the afternoon, otherwise they'll swell up.)

Having survived the morning run, it was soon time for what was to become my daily routine. Rank badges would come off and one would sit with the men as they were briefed about various topics ranging from weapons to map reading. This over, I would proceed to my office where Subedar Udai Pratap Singh would guide me through the daily paperwork, telling me which documents needed my attention and where and what I was to sign. We would then break for lunch and, without fail, Udai Pratap Singh would tell me to report back at C Company at 1430 hours sharp for some duty or the other. This invariably meant that, apart from the subedar saab and myself, even the men would be on call after lunch.

This additional chore had me perplexed for I seemed to be on perpetual duty, but I was too scared to ask. After a week or so, I finally gathered the courage to ask him, 'Saab, yeh hukum kaun deta hai aapko?' (Who is giving you these orders?)

'Koi nahin deta. Hamaara kaam hai aapko sikhana.' (Nobody tells us. It's our job to teach you.)

This was a conversation I would never forget. That was the calibre of our junior commissioned officers, most of them at the time not even matriculates and, by today's standards, they would have been considered uneducated! Like Subedar Udai Pratap Singh, there were scores of JCOs across the Indian Army simply doing what they considered their duty: putting us young officers through virtually every possible scenario which helped us understand the unique functioning of an infantry battalion. Day in and day out, one officer after the other, we were moulded by these steady hands of the battalion that bridged the gap between the men and the officers who would have to lead them into battle.

In the Indian Army, the role of the JCO has not been adequately built upon, and we have failed to optimize a valuable resource pool. Today, four decades later, the JCO rank in each battalion has multiplied manifold, soon to be expanded to almost sixty JCOs to each infantry battalion. The failure to optimize this valuable resource pool is even more alarming given the shortfall in the officer cadre. Given the 'zero error' syndrome that has gripped our command structure today, commanding officers are loath to decentralize control beyond the officers in the unit. As a result, the JCOs often become a liability as they have little or not enough responsibility. A good NCO (non-commissioned officer) cannot become an indifferent JCO overnight.

I took to my new life without any difficulty. Despite the heat and dust of Delhi, I couldn't have been more content. However, I was acutely aware that I still had to surmount an important hurdle, else I would be the perennial new kid in town for the troops. Unfortunately, there are no set templates and the academy does not tell you what to do—when it happens, it just happens!

The athletic team once again reassembled at the crack of dawn and we trooped out of the Red Fort to Shantivan. This time I took charge and told Nar Singh Chauhan to put the two runners in the front with the rest of the squad behind them. I declared I would bring up the rear and if I overtook any one of them, they would have to re-run the entire stretch. Once again we took off, this time with the *entire* athletic team running the gruelling distance. Each man knew they had been caught out and kept up the pace superbly. Back at Shantivan, the heaving, panting mass came to a halt. Before dismissing the squad I took my parting shot: 'Aap sab aaj dopehar ko apne paon kambal mein rakhna, nahin to bhar jayenge!' (All of you keep your feet wrapped in blankets this afternoon, or they'll swell up.)

As we walked back into the Red Fort, I could sense the ice had been broken. Nothing specific that one could put a finger on, just the body language. The men were laughing and joking and I was a part of them. This moment is played out so many times in the army; sometimes you see it, sometimes you don't. The bonhomie, the mutual respect, the bonding, every minute the bond grows and years later the same man will meet you and embrace you regardless of where your respective destinies took you. That kind of brotherhood is something to die for!

My brush with liquor was not yet over, for I still had to meet the commanding officer, Lieutenant Colonel Sohrab Vakil, who had been on leave when I joined the battalion. The colonel was a legendary wine-maker, making his own concoctions from just about every conceivable thing—from bitter gourd to potato! After my initial introduction, it was a matter of time before I had to formally call on him. The commanding officer's residence was situated at the rear of the Red Fort and from there one could see the Yamuna River. As was his wont, he used to bottle his spirits in colourful decanters of all shapes and sizes that he would purchase from the adjoining Jama Masjid market. I was offered some of the improvised nectar on the appointed day. My first experience with beer notwithstanding, I had better luck with wine.

It's amazing how the battalion just envelops you. Everything plays its part—history, traditions, the officers and, of course, the men. In spite of the nature of the duties and the fact that the battalion was split across two locations, 2 Rajput exuded a happy feeling and the men took tremendous pride in themselves. The class composition of the battalion was such that we had Rajput (Alpha and Charlie), Gujjar (Bravo) and Bengali (Delta) companies, which resulted in tremendous competitive rivalry. Each group wanted to be better than the other. In subsequent years, I was to spend most of my time with Bravo, and most old-timers would identify me with the Gujjar troops. They were in a class by themselves, the lords and masters of the universe! Bravo Company was unique: they would always have more ghee, a hookah and double the amount of halwa and churma in their lines and cookhouse. They had an earthy sense of humour and were hardy; no task assigned to them was ever considered impossible.

Inspections were par for the course, and those too were part of my duties. So, as part of my charter, I made my way to Delta Company which had Bengali troops and decided to inspect their cookhouse. I asked the nearest soldier how he rated the food.

'Mota mati,' he replied. Aha! There was mud in the food. Big, fat lumps! I called for the company JCO and decided to berate him.

'Saab, khane me mitti hai.' (There is mud in the food.)

The JCO looked most perplexed: 'Saab, kisne bola?' (Who said that?)

'Maine jawaan se poocha aur woh bol raha hai ki khane mein mota mati hai.' (I asked a soldier and he said there was a lot of mud in the food.)

The JCO, who until then was looking most concerned, could barely stop himself from bursting out laughing! 'Saab, mota mati Bangla mein matlab "generally okay!"'

As each day passed, one got to know the other officers of the battalion. Nandu Gupta, the adjutant, lived in the married quarters along with Major Kanwer Mohinder Singh and the recently-married Kamal Nain Mishra. The others with the battalion at the time were Majors Melvin Mascarenhas, Satish Vashist, Ashok Kumar and 'Uncle' Dharam Pal Kukrety. The quarter master was Captain Prakash Singh (he would ensure that his store was always immaculate and he would not issue anything that would spoil the geometry of the store). I couldn't have asked for a more impressive setting or a more harmonious bunch of officers to start my army career; it had the feel of a tight compact family and I was extremely proud to belong to this battalion.

▪

My maternal grandfather, Subedar Shimbu Singh, was absolutely thrilled when I was commissioned into 2 Rajput as he too had served in the same battalion before and during World War I. He would tell me stories of 2/7 Rajput and talk of the various British officers who had commanded the battalion. On one occasion, the angrez commanding officer decided to visit the subedar saab in his village, where he was accorded a grand reception. Overwhelmed by the hospitality, the CO asked Subedar Shimbu Singh what he could do for him.

'I want your 12-bore gun.'

'Take it,' said the angrez CO, immediately offering the weapon.

'No. I want to buy it.' A price was arrived at and the gun changed ownership.

Now Nanaji had an important task for me. He had lost his discharge book after retirement and he asked me to get him a replacement. I started going through all the old records in the unit and even tried to track down his record of service, but to no avail. All the while, the old man was getting more and more agitated with his incompetent grandson. 'You're in 2/7 Rajput! Why can't you do this?' he would repeatedly ask.

I then decided to expand my search and began to check the digest of service. Sure enough, sometime during World War I, Subedar Shimbu Singh had taken two companies from the battalion and helped raise 13 Rajput. His name was on the nominal rolls of the new unit that had subsequently become the Regimental Centre for the Rajputana Rifles (Shekhawati).

Armed with this information, I wrote to the Regimental Centre in Fatehgarh which informed me that all records pertaining to this lot of men had been sent to the Rajputana Rifles Centre in Delhi. The replacement was issued, and with a great sense of relief I was able to hand over a duplicate discharge book to my nanaji. My reputation was restored. Having one's roots in the historical DNA of the regiment was one thing, getting buried in the sands of time with it was quite another!

It was only a matter of time before I was sent off to Rashtrapati Bhavan. The entire structure, perched atop Raisina Hill, dominated the heart of New Delhi. Just as the Red Fort showcased every aspect of Mughal India,

Rashtrapati Bhavan was all about the British Raj. The planning of New Delhi began in right earnest after the British government decided to shift the capital from Calcutta after the Delhi Durbar in 1911. King George V had laid the foundation stone of New Delhi at Kingsway Camp during the imperial visit. A major part of New Delhi was planned by Sir Edwin Lutyens and Herbert Baker, both prominent twentieth-century British architects.

The central administrative area of New Delhi was laid out as a testament to Britain's imperial aspirations. The foundation stone was shifted from Kingsway Camp to the more centrally located Raisina Hill which was to be the location of the viceroy's residence, later known as Rashtrapati Bhavan. The North and South Blocks of the secretariat building which housed various ministries flanked King's Way which is now Rajpath and extended south up to the World War I memorial—India Gate—that has the names of all Indian soldiers who were killed in Europe. With the circular Parliament building and other imposing structures, the visual impact of New Delhi as the seat of power could not be lost on anyone. The actual contract for the construction had been given to Sir Sobha Singh and was completed by 1931. Lord Irwin, the then viceroy, formally inaugurated Lutyens' Delhi on 13 February 1931.

When the CO was in town, the 2IC, Major Bhup Singh, lived at Rashtrapati Bhavan where the rest of the troops were billeted. Every Thursday, the changing of the guard would take place and we would march down from Rashtrapati Bhavan past South and North Blocks and down the slope to Vijay Chowk. The two detachments would be lined up waiting for the inspecting officer who would be accompanied by a magnificent ram—who, taking his cue from the officer, would lower his head and butt any soldier who was improperly dressed. When the unit had moved to Delhi from Tangdhar in Jammu and Kashmir, the billy goat with his curving Ovis ammon horns was the battalion mascot. Spoilt silly and fed round the clock, the ram grew to the size of a small pony. He was virtually the battalion mascot. The men were more intent on passing muster with the ram rather than the inspecting officer!

President VV Giri had a large extended family and the place was buzzing with activity. We had the squash court and the swimming pool mainly to ourselves, though we rarely had time to use them as various duties kept us on our toes. Despite the pomp and glitter of the presidential complex, all of us were more interested in getting back to the Red Fort. Our own mess cost us ₹5 per day which, when combined with other subscriptions and expenses, added up to roughly more than half our salary. But while messing with the President's Bodyguard, this rate went up to ₹10 per day. Not only was the food in our own mess more affordable, it also tasted better!

Back at Red Fort, we had the annual inspection for which GOC (general officer commanding) Delhi Area, Major General SK Korla, DSO, MC was to visit the battalion. The highly decorated officer was from the old school and, as the only infantry battalion posted in Delhi, we were determined to have everything in top order. Dulled by routine ceremonies, none of the men were proficient with the Tarzan swing anymore. This entailed swinging across a ditch full of water and landing on a platform; it needed perfect timing, or else one landed in an embarrassing muddy heap. Just out of the academy, I was not only nominated to impress the general on the obstacle course, but was to somehow get to the shooting range in time to put a few rounds in the target. This was all part of the 'senior officer management' methods which all units are extremely adept at.

The inspection went smoothly and, as was the norm, we hosted the GOC to a dinner. The general was a renowned drinker and the battalion officers watched in awe as he lived up to his reputation. Then the area was cleared and General Korla treated us to a demonstration of the Highland Swing dance. We all came to the conclusion that it was the ideal way to work off the booze.

Without Fear, Without Pity, Without Remorse

My three months with the battalion came to an end at the beginning of November 1970 as I was detailed to attend the second Young Officers (YOs) Course at Mhow. Switching to the metre gauge railway at Ratlam for the final leg of the journey, I was delighted to find that all my infantry coursemates were also heading for the same destination.

Compared to Delhi, Mhow was a quarter-horse town that lay some twenty-three kilometres from Indore on the Bombay-Agra highway, but it was fast emerging as an important hub for the Indian Army. According to Hindu mythology, it was the birthplace of Parashuram, an avatar of Vishnu, while, more recently, it had produced BR Ambedkar, the father of the Indian constitution.

Mhow got its name from the mahua tree that grew in abundance in the Malwa region (some others claim that Mhow was an acronym for Military Headquarters of War). The black soil and the expansive countryside teemed with painted partridge and a sprinkling of leopards. Militarily, the Malwa region had always been of great importance, especially as it straddled the route taken by Mughal armies that marched on to the Deccan. The region was dominated by the Mandu Fort, which was situated fifty-six kilometres from Mhow and was an integral part of our training area.

The cantonment had been founded after the British defeated the Holkars of the Maratha Confederacy at the Battle of Mahidpur in 1818. The resultant Treaty of Mandsaur stipulated the shifting of the Holkar capital to Indore from Maheshwar, on the banks of the Narmada River. As a result, Mhow was a collection of colonial bungalows and buildings; a couple of churches and a reasonably well-laid-out cemetery.

Major General Onkar Singh Kalkat was commanding the Infantry School. The formation sign of the institution was a bayonet and we youngsters added an unseen motto to it: 'Without fear, without pity, without remorse'. Kalkat was known to be a fitness fanatic who wanted the entire infantry to be fit enough to meet any challenge. Built like an ox, the burly Sikh general was from 8 Gorkhas that was also General (later Field Marshal) Sam Manekshaw's regiment. He was the driving force behind the YOs and, through rain and sunshine, the general was always there, watching the 'boys turn into men'. Ever since the NDA, the army did just that—constantly forced you to earn your spurs. Just when you crested a particular hill, there was inevitably the next mountain to climb.

We were only the second batch in the newly-established YO course. As at the NDA, here too, we would be guinea pigs as the establishment tried to fine-tune YOs. The first course had not been graded. As a result, the establishment didn't know what hit it as all the youthful energy exploded around its ears. Now we were told in no uncertain terms that we would be graded at each and every step. Apart from impacting our future in the army, the grading system was designed to straitjacket us.

The course senior was AK Dutta who was from 3 Jat. He was actually from the course senior to us and had missed the un-graded fun for some reason or the other. He now took pole position, which gave me some breathing space as I was the senior-most infantry officer from within my own batch.

The four-and-a-half month course was divided into three parts: Weapon Leg was followed by the TAC Leg and finally culminated with the Commando Wing. The four years spent at the NDA and then IMA had honed us into extremely fit individuals, and the physical part of the training was not much of a bother. The high point, quite literally, was the 'confidence jump': we had to climb up a huge tower; from there we would have to make our way along a narrow plank, metres above a water tank that looked like a matchbox from where we were. A command would be given and we had to drop, equipment and all, legs ramrod straight into the water below.

The final exercise was a 'treasure hunt' held at Mandu, about a hundred kilometres away from Mhow. As a group, we had to recover the treasure and bring it back safely to a pre-designated spot. The most unlikely looking officer from the group was selected to hide the treasure on his body, while the rest of us formed a protective circle around a decoy. The ruse worked like a charm, as all the other groups went hell for leather after the decoy, allowing the actual treasure bearer to stroll back casually.

At the end of the course, I was awarded the Commando Dagger and the coveted Sam Manekshaw Trophy for topping the course. The course had made us supremely confident of our professional and physical abilities.

The Elusive Certificate

We were granted a few days' leave after the completion of the course, and I headed home to Bapora, hoping to put my feet up and catch up with family. Going through the collection of mail that had been sent to my permanent address, I was amused to find my matriculation (Class X) certificate that had been issued by the Rajasthan Secondary Board of Education, with the stamp on the certificate saying 13 June 1966 and sent to my school in Pilani. The school had then sent the certificate to my father's 14 Rajput postal address, only to find that he had been posted to the Branch Recruiting Office in Rewa and then on to the NCC battalion at Narnaul. By then, the matriculation certificate could have written its own autobiography, for it was forwarded first to Rewa, then to Narnaul only to find that my father had retired from the army by then. It is perhaps a tribute to the postal system that the much-forwarded envelope finally made its way to our house in Bapora where it lay unattended, as no one was residing there at the time.

Even though all my documentation through NDA, IMA and at the time of commissioning correctly reflected 1951 as my year of birth, I knew the matriculation certificate needed to be filed with Army Headquarters. The logical thing to do was to send it to the required branch through the proper channel.

Having exhausted my leave, I made my way to Tamulpur in Assam to catch up with the battalion. One of the first things I did was to send the original matriculation certificate to the Adjutant General (AG) Branch, which is the official record holder and authority on all such matters. After its due verification, the AG's Branch returned it to the battalion. Until the original certificate had been submitted, my commission on paper was 'provisional'. This status was accordingly changed to 'permanent'.

As far as I was concerned, this was all a part of the red tape that drives most young officers crazy. The amount of time spent on documentation and filling forms took the sheen off our main task, which was soldiering. Every new file that landed on one's table was met with an inward groan.

At the time, I was vaguely aware of the fact that there was something called an Army List published by the Military Secretary (MS) Branch. This list was published around this time and had on record the wrongly entered year from the original UPSC form. Even had I known of the error in the Army List, I probably wouldn't have paid much attention, for the only practical purpose that the list served was as a ready reckoner of seniority. In any case, all seniors told us that good officers did not bother about silly things like the Army List, so it did not mean anything at all. In any case, we were told that these lists were riddled with too many errors and were of no practical use. Or at least that's what we all believed at the time.

3

2 RAJPUT AND THE BANGLADESH WAR

War Clouds in the East

While I was still at Mhow, events unfolding in the Eastern Sector would change the face of the subcontinent yet again. On the evening of 12 November 1970, one of the deadliest tropical cyclones lashed the coastal areas of East Pakistan, leaving an estimated five lakh dead in its wake. Horrific pictures of bloated bodies washed ashore filtered through as newspapers reported the extent of the damage. President Yahya Khan and the central government in West Pakistan, far removed from the scene of the disaster, were perceived to be insensitive to the extent of the disaster. A week after the cyclone had struck, students were demonstrating against the president and West Pakistan's indifference towards the Bengali population in Dhaka. By March, the situation had steadily worsened, and it got further accentuated when the Pakistan Army launched Operation Searchlight, aimed at crushing Bengali nationalist sentiment.

Though initially unaware of the extent of the genocide unleashed by the Pakistan Army, we, in India, tried to make sense of the situation as news of mass killings and rapes began filtering in. Pakistan's actions seemed incomprehensible as the systematic killings went on, resulting in a massive exodus of refugees into India—first in the hundreds, then thousands. As things progressed, or rather regressed, it seemed but a matter of time before we would be drawn into a conflict situation with Pakistan, the third since Independence in barely twenty-four years.

At the same time, there had been many changes in the battalion that had, during this period, moved from Delhi to Tamulpur in the Eastern Theatre. Tamulpur was a small settlement some eighty kilometres from Guwahati, a far cry from the hustle and bustle of Delhi. One had to cross the Brahmaputra and get on to the north bank from Guwahati, turn left to Rangia and then head north into the Bodo region. Though the hills of Bhutan were visible to the north, the entire area was low-lying and flat, with paddy fields interspersed with clumps of bamboo stretching in every direction.

Lieutenant Colonel Sohrab Vakil had handed over command to the tall and youthful Lieutenant Colonel (later Major General) Dev Raj Dutt. 2 Rajput was a part of 83 Mountain Brigade, commanded by Brigadier BS Sandhu, which in turn came under 23 Division commanded by Major General RD 'Rocky' Hira. Our new CO was a first-class professional and a hard taskmaster who was focused on making things better for the men. On my return to the battalion with the coveted Commando Dagger and Sam Manekshaw Trophy, he made a big deal of it in the unit durbar and made me feel extremely good. However, that lasted for exactly one day! Nandu Gupta had also handed over charge as adjutant to Captain Kanwer Mohinder Singh.

Major Bhup Singh was still the 2IC; Major RK Raizada was commanding Alpha Company, while Bravo Company was with Major Jagbir Verma (he handed over to Major Dharam Bhalla of 20 Rajput shortly before the war), Charlie Company was under Dharam Pal Kukrety and Delta had Major Kamal Nain Mishra (he later retired as the Judge Advocate General). Support Company had Tom Mathews whose main job was to make sure that the mortar platoon trained hard, while other officers on the battalion's strength included Bhupi Sahi, Vashist, Suresh, Melwin Mascarenhas, Nanaya, PK Gupta, Ashok Kumar and the regimental medical officer (RMO), Captain BK Roy. I was made the intelligence officer (IO) though I was given other odd jobs as well.

Months of ceremonial and guard duties in Delhi had severely impacted the battalion's combat readiness. Training, which is such an integral part of any unit, had been neglected due to commitments during the Delhi tenure and the CO felt we would have to start from scratch. It started with a squad of officers giving a demonstration of how a section and a platoon needed to operate. They were then followed by the JCOs, and finally the men, who would repeat the same thing under the watchful eyes of the CO. Basic combat drills and tactics were practised again and again, and yet again.

The sense of urgency got further heightened when, by mid-April 1971, a provisional government was formed in Meherpur district (in western Bangladesh bordering India) with Sheikh Mujibur Rahman as its president (although he was in prison in Pakistan at this time). By then, fighting between the regular Pakistan Army and the Mukti Bahini was grabbing the headlines, while an estimated ten million refugees were housed in Assam and West Bengal.

The other two battalions that made up the brigade were 3 Dogra, commanded by Lieutenant Colonel Ajit Chopra, stationed at Daranga on the Indo-Bhutan border, and 8 Bihar, commanded by Lieutenant Colonel OP Bisla, which along with the Brigade HQ and an engineer company made up the military camp at Tamulpur. In spite of the deepening crisis all around us, the battalion was given the task of hosting an NCC camp. Not surprisingly, as was the general practice when it came to sundry duties, I was put in charge of this activity.

Saadda Punjabi! Saala Bangali! The genocide of the Bengali population by the Pakistan Army continued unabated as thousands were butchered. President Yahya Khan, unshakeable in the belief that the only way out of the mess was by mass murder, infamously briefed the top brass in East Pakistan saying: 'Kill three million of them and the rest will eat out of our hands'.* On the night of 25 May 1971, Pakistani troops decided to take things further. An Indian post at Dalu Haat, a small checkpoint on the Meghalaya-Bangladesh border south of Tura and a major crossing point for refugees, was attacked at night. The post was held by a section comprising thirteen constables from the 83rd Battalion of the Border Security Force (BSF) who held firm despite nine of the jawans losing their lives in the encounter.

At the NCC camp I got a call from the adjutant to fall back to the unit and report to him immediately. The entire place was abuzz, as the unit had been ordered to move into Meghalaya. The adjutant, busy coordinating everything, barely looked up when I reported to him.

'These are now your babies,' he said, as he handed me a large folder containing various maps. 'As the intelligence officer, stick close to the CO at all times. You are his eyes and ears, literally his shadow. The battalion is being deployed south of Tura, somewhere near a place called Dalu Haat. It's the western corner of Meghalaya. Good luck!'

I studied the map and tried to get as much information as I could about our proposed route, but information pertaining to the Garo Hills was scanty. Though much needed to be done, it was decided that we would move by the evening in a long convoy, heading east and then south towards Guwahati. We crossed the Brahmaputra river by the bridge at Saraighat and then headed west again, keeping the hills of Meghalaya to the south and the expanse of the river to the north. We had gone a short distance in this direction when it was discovered that the spare barrels of the battalion's light machine guns (LMGs) had been left behind. The adjutant, Kanwer Mohinder Singh, was

---

*Philip Henser, 'The war Bangladesh can never forget', *The Independent*, 19 February 2013.

hopping mad and he laid down the battalion's wartime mantra at the side of the road in the middle of the night. 'Check, recheck, and then check the recheck!' A vehicle with an appropriate escort had to double back to get the spare barrels and catch up with the unit.

I was stuffed in the back of the CO's jonga, and from my position could barely look out of the vehicle, having to twist and turn to get a view of the outside as the darkness of the night dissipated into the grey light of dawn. My navigational abilities were already being tested to the full for, as the IO, I was always expected to know where we were at any given time.

The convoy turned south just before Goalpara and we snaked our way into the West Garo Hills. The region was mostly deserted, with but a few isolated settlements. Before noon, we had reached the BSF camp at Tura, a small town that was also the district headquarters. It was decided that we would take a short break and then proceed along the Tura-Mymensingh road. This was now technically BSF territory, but after the Pakistani assault on this post, and according to wartime norms, the army was moving in. The southward move continued and by late afternoon we had reached our new location—a position that was tucked into the hills approximately three kilometres short of the border post of Dalu Haat. Leaving the unit to settle in for the night, the CO's party drove down to the border post, where everything was quiet, though signs of the earlier attack were visible.

A battery of 76 mm Yugoslav guns from 57 Mountain Regiment had also arrived and the artillery battalion was settling down near our camp. The long road journey behind them, the men had quickly cleared the area and set up camp. There were two wooded hilly spurs with a narrow valley in between, and this was our battalion's new location. As darkness had set in early, the men, in spite of the long drive, were hard at work in the light of hurricane lamps. Already Battalion HQ was up and running, around which all other tented infrastructure was rapidly being set up. I made sure the CO's tent was up and all his things were in place, after which I went looking for a place for myself.

In the clearing of the valley, there were a couple of jhum huts, basic contraptions of bamboo and thatch. I headed for them but found three company commanders already settled there for the night. My lieutenant rank badges were obviously not going to get me entry into the exclusive club, so I quickly backtracked and clambered on to a three-ton vehicle. There I set up my camp cot on the corrugated metal floor and tucked in for the night. Completely exhausted, I was vaguely aware that it had started to rain. In a matter of minutes, I was fast asleep.

Meghalaya literally means the land of the clouds, and when it rains, it rains! The monsoon-laden clouds sweep in from the flat lowlands across East Pakistan and deposit enough precipitation to make the Garo, Khasi and Jaintia Hills look like giant forest-covered sponges.

The three-ton with its canvas flaps down proved to be the perfect outdoor caravan, for soon the water outside was gushing around the tailboard. For the unfortunate company commanders in the jhum hut, the flimsy roofing had offered no protection against nature's drenching, with most of their belongings almost getting swept away. Once the sun was up and I emerged fresh and dry, the three soaked and grumpy majors made caustic remarks about intelligence officers who reserved the best accommodation for themselves.

The new location was teeming with leeches, supplemented by a more than healthy population of snakes. To complicate matters further, the reptiles had a way of showing up wherever the CO went. Fortunately, we didn't have a case of snake bite, though each man invariably plucked off at least three or four swollen balloon-like leeches off his body through the day. Stemming the flow of blood from the leech bites was a constant problem, but after a while one barely bothered with the gross creatures.

There were hardly any Garo people around, and standing on the down slope towards East Pakistan, we could see for miles. About fifteen kilometres to the west, the Brahmaputra, called the Jamuna at this point, flowed in a north-south direction. Directly ahead of us was Mymensingh, which was locally known as Nasirabad. To the east, a bit further away, flanking the Khasi Hills, lay the important garrison town of Sylhet.

The slopes leading up to Dalu Haat were extensively cultivated with pineapples. But the trouble was that there was no one to buy them from. The few locals we did come across—shy, simple Garos—would smile at us, revealing their betel-nut-stained red teeth, and tell us to simply help ourselves, refusing any payment. At Mahendraganj, to the west of our location, there existed a system of barter trade amongst the locals at the border. For ₹25, we could get twenty chickens. Soon we were fed up of drinking fresh pineapple juice and eating chicken. The saving grace, especially for our Gujjar company, was the abundance of desi ghee which came from across the border at very reasonable rates.

My immediate buddy sharing my tented accommodation was the regimental medical officer (RMO), Captain Roy, who is a senior cardiologist today with a large hospital and healthcare group. Being paired with Roy was a huge advantage, for his big fat medical books reinforced the wooden planks that made up our beds.

The Mukti Bahini

The battalion's area of responsibility (AOR) extended along the base of the Meghalaya Hills. We were responsible for the area extending up to Baghmara in the east and to Mahendraganj in the west. The entire frontage was under the operational control of the BSF, who now had our companies deployed in support, and hence the battalion was now responsible for all operational matters.

As the IO, my job took me wherever the CO went. The next day I went with him on the road to Haluaghat, a post between our camp and Baghmara. Once there, we made our way to the BSF post where we were met with the trademark steaming mugs of tea.

In command of the post was a burly Sikh senior inspector, equivalent to a JCO, with two stars on his shoulders. Before joining the BSF, the inspector had been with the Punjab Armed Police. A long way from his village, he and his men were now living under the threat of a Pakistani attack ever since the Dalu Haat incident. Looking around the post, Colonel Dutt asked, 'Agar Pakistani aa gaye to kya karoge, saab?' (If the enemy approaches, what will you do?)

Looking almost disdainful at being asked such a question, the inspector said in chaste Punjabi, 'Saab, ithe inne kande lagye han, jharian han, ki koi je aa gaya te saare kapde phat jane hain, pher vee je koi pahunch gaya tey assi lathi mar mar ke unna nu bagha diyange.' (Sir, there are so many thorns and bushes that anyone coming here will have all his clothes torn. Even if someone makes it through, we'll bash them with lathis until they run away.)

To that, the CO could only utter, 'Shabash,' and we made a quick exit to visit the next post.

The situation in the refugee camps was pathetic. At first, officials had tried to help, but the sheer magnitude of the influx had resulted in complete chaos. There were stories of some border guards and officials exploiting the situation. These stories were extremely upsetting, especially as the Indian

Army was simultaneously gearing up to fight a conventional war on behalf of these very people. Tagging along with the CO, I saw the condition in the camps: inadequate shelter and food provisions coupled with filth and squalor, and the threat of an epidemic looming large.

Delta Company was the first to come in contact with the Mukti Fauj, as they had advanced before the rest of the unit. They were part of the FJ Sector, which was located south of Tura and was commanded by Brigadier 'Baba' Sant Singh, MVC and bar. All men were operating in mufti, which meant that even the sentries posted were in lungis, t-shirts and casual footwear. When Dev Raj Dutt came to check on the men, he was greeted with loud 'Joy Bangla' salutes. Seeing Rajput soldiers dressed like this was already irking the CO, who told the company commander that the boys needed to stick to the standard 'Ram Ram Saab' or 'Jai Hind'. So much for maintaining secrecy!

We all got our fair share of thrills as we routinely went in with the Mukti Bahini to register targets. Usually we would have a sprinkling of our boys mixed with the freedom fighters, and on one occasion I found myself on a reconnaissance of a bridge with the Mukti Bahini. The sentries sensed our presence and started shouting. I froze and, to my absolute horror, realized that my entire group had melted into the darkness. Dressed in a lungi and a t-shirt, I had to find the way back on my own.

Sometime in August, Baba Sant Singh came up with the ambitious plan of the Mukti Bahini launching an attack from Mahendraganj with the intention of capturing Kamalpur, from where the objective was to take control of the road and reach Mymensingh within three days. Major Zia (later President of Bangladesh) was the brigade commander and he had three or four Mukti Bahini units, with a fair sprinkling of soldiers from East Bengal Rifle (EBR) units under his command. 2 Rajput was to provide support, hence Bravo Company under Major Jagbir Verma along with our battalion Tac HQ was moved to Mahendraganj.

H-hour arrived and was greeted with a whole lot of firing. The 76 mm guns that were deployed in our support also joined the party but there was absolutely no movement on the part of the Mukti Bahini to move forward and press on with the attack.

Orders promptly came down from FJ Sector to send in Bravo Company. The din of gunfire was deafening, but nothing was happening. Major Verma promptly sent a message to Battalion HQ asking for the IO who would lead the way with the first platoon. Fortunately for me, the CO told Verma to get on with the job, telling him that it was his company and that his officers should lead the attack. While all this was going on, the gunfire began to fizzle out and with it died Baba Sant Singh's ambitious attack plan. The entire lot of Mukti Bahini and EBR troops had fallen back. All sorts of reasons were offered for this amazing turn of events, the most popular being that the Bangla force was facing Pakistani Punjabi troops (31 Baluch) who were uncouth and abusing the Bengalis. Their sensitivities offended, they had apparently decided to get out of earshot. In reality, the Bangla force was facing battle-hardened Pakistani troops, who were able to bring down accurate machine gun fire to foil any plans of a frontal attack.

Kamalpur was strongly fortified and held by determined troops and this is evident from the fact that the town could not be captured even when the war broke out. The defences had to be bypassed en route to Mymensingh. This garrison surrendered only on 16 December when the ceasefire was declared.

To expect the Mukti Bahini to perform in set piece battle conditions was unrealistic. The cadre was, by and large, a medley of students and non-military personnel who had been cobbled together to take on the Pakistani regular units and the Razakars (paramilitary force of Pakistan Army). 1 EBR had earlier tried to take on the same Pakistani garrison at Kamalpur and had suffered heavy losses. The rank and file of the Mukti Bahini was hardly trained in regular combat, they had limited leadership and a deep-rooted psychological fear of the Pakistan Army. This was perfectly understandable given what they had suffered at the Pakistan Army's hands.

These aspects notwithstanding, their contribution cannot be downplayed, for they provided guides, linguistic support and in-depth knowledge of the terrain. They were also good at hit-and-run type of operations that sapped the morale of the Pakistani forces. Individually, when functioning with our units, they were outstanding—motivated and steady under the most trying conditions. As they got more and more battle hardened, they fought some extremely successful actions.

For the battalion, the raids and isolated skirmishes with Pakistani soldiers were a perfect way to get inoculated for battle. The ceremonial duties of Delhi were soon a distant memory and, day by day, the men were getting sharper for actual combat. Our little interlude in Meghalaya proved to be exactly what the unit needed. We were ordered back to Tamulpur sometime in October. The CO then decided to test the unit in conventional operations and moved us to Daranga—a foot march of over twenty kilometres.

I was sent to do a reconnaissance of the advance landing ground (ALG) at Daranga with the intention of leading a full battalion advance-and-attack on the objective. I came back and reported that the best way to the Daranga ALG was to move along the only road that would take us to the objective, as all other approaches were through paddy fields. I got it in the neck from all and sundry.

'What sort of an intelligence officer are you? How can we walk down a road that is bound to be defended?' was the general refrain.

So after darkness had descended, I found myself moving through paddy fields with the various battalion companies strung out behind me. As the leading element, I had the easiest time of it, for as each man stepped in the wet mud that made up the bunds, bits of it collapsed. The rear elements soon lost their olive green look and were covered in mud from head to toe. Eventually, the only two people who hadn't lost their footing in the mud were Bhup Singh—wearing a long US Army trench coat which made him look stately and dignified—and me. Cursing, slipping and falling, we eventually made it to the end of the paddy fields from where a small track led to the forming up place marked by the intelligence section. It was then that Bhup Singh stepped into what looked like a small puddle, but was in reality a deep pit. He was completely muddied and soaked, to the amusement of all who had admired his poise and the trench coat. It then started to rain and, within minutes, the ALG was submerged under six inches of water. After the attack drill was over, the CO and Bhup spent the night sitting back-to-back on the ALG, while I did the same with Tom Mathews, the mortar platoon commander.

The CO was extremely pleased with the way the exercise had gone off. As a reward for the good work done, I was given seven days casual leave. Taking advantage of my good fortune, I went to Guwahati and somehow managed to get a seat on an An-12 to Bagdogra. On the flight I started to feel unwell, and stayed on board the aircraft when everybody else disembarked at Bagdogra and was 'manifested' afresh. Thus my onward status to Delhi was that of a stowaway. The amusing part was that each time the crew did a pre-flight headcount they got a different figure! The inability of most crews to do an accurate headcount on a loaded aircraft was something I noted; it would come in handy subsequently while on another mission.

I went to Bapora and met all my people. The return trip went off smoothly, but when I reached Guwahati I was told that 2 Rajput had already moved from Tamulpur. Major KN Mishra, the Delta Company commander was also trying to catch up with the battalion, so together we boarded a train that would take us to Dharmanagar on the Assam-Tripura border.

The Lumding-Haflong line skirted the Jaintia Hills and then headed south. The visually spectacular route was also notorious for robberies and, to our utter disbelief, someone stole Major Mishra's shirt by inserting a wire through the tiniest of openings in the window. At Dharmanagar, we disembarked and found that the rest of the battalion had got in just twelve hours ahead of us.

The Belonia Bulge

6 Rajput was stationed in north Tripura under the command of Lieutenant Colonel Hardev Singh, who hosted us, and the unit seemed to be in good spirits, waiting like the rest of the Indian Army for something to happen. In the evening all officers of 2 Rajput arrived for the barra khana being held in our honour wearing 'Rajesh Khanna' kurtas, a rage at that time in Delhi. Sitting in Tripura, far removed from the fashion buzz of the capital, our hosts thought this was the official dress of 2 Rajput!

Next day, we moved further south, moving through the night, going past Agartala where yet another sister battalion, 18 Rajput under Ashok Kalyan Verma was positioned. We crossed Udaipur and set up a tented encampment in the middle of a forested area short of Belonia. The respite lasted only a few days for we were soon tasked to make inroads into the Belonia Bulge. The brigade's plan was simple. The entire region along the Belonia-Feni axis, extending from Basura, Goashipur and Kahua to the area around Parshuram, was to be cleared by the brigade. Operating in civilian clothes, we were to lend support to the Mukti Bahini operating inside East Pakistan as a part of this task. 3 Dogra was to clear Parshuram; 2 Rajput was to lay blocks in the south towards Goashipur and Kahua; and 8 Bihar was to clear areas northwest of Parshuram.

We moved in the night and cut off the approaches to Parshuram. The new unit location was quite bare: a dighi (pond) with half a dozen thatched huts in the area. We quickly prepared a proper bunker for the CO that was also to be his command post. The company locations had already been marked and they got down to preparing their own defences. It was a period of hectic activity and the unit settled in quickly. Facing us at Belonia and Parshuram were troops of Pakistan's 53 Infantry Brigade. The enemy's defences in the area were based on inhabited areas along the Belonia-Feni road. The brigade's tactic was to infiltrate troops, along with the Mukti Bahini, and establish blocks. Cut off from the rear, there was then no chance of any reinforcements influencing the battle. Once the blocks were established, the assaulting units were to reduce the defences. The Bangla force was under the overall command of Major Rafique. Once 3 Dogra neutralized the Parshuram defences, the brigade was to gradually consolidate.

On the third day, one of the company locations came under fire at around 1030 hours from Pakistani artillery guns that fired a couple of smoke shells. Even as these landed, our position came under attack as four F-86 Sabres screamed in and strafed the area. One of our boys, a kitchen helper, stuck his head out to see what the aircraft were doing and was killed in the air attack. He was the battalion's first casualty in the Bangladesh War.

Battalion HQ also came under fairly heavy Pakistani shelling. The first time they opened up, we had the CO and the HQ detachment safely ensconced inside the bunker, but I was caught outside. I immediately dived into one of the thatched huts. When the CO realized I was outside while we were being shelled, he gave me a real rollicking.

While we made sure that the CO was always safe inside the bunker, Melvin, Tom Mathews and I often slept in the huts. We would draw lots to see who would sleep next to the brick wall, for often at night, the trigger-happy Mukti Bahini personnel would start firing. On a couple of occasions, the odd bullet would smack through the hut. Quite naturally, the side towards the thatched wall was not particularly popular.

The Pakistani 105 mm guns were a constant menace, but we got used to being under fire soon enough. The air strikes, however, were something else altogether. The Sabres came in on two more occasions; during one of the air raids I was caught in the open along with some men while we were shifting a dismantled 106 mm recoilless gun (RCL). We hugged the ground as close as we possibly could, with cannon fire exploding all around us. The second time we came under an air attack, Major Vimal Shingal, the brigade major (BM) called up the unit and got Tom Mathews, who was officiating as adjutant, on the line. Though they could see the aircraft from the brigade location, they were not under attack themselves and Shingal told Tom to do something.

'Do what? Throw stones?' retorted Tom.

The end result was that some L/70 anti-aircraft guns were deployed to protect us, but these were kept well back from the border as we were still not officially at war. To complicate matters, the Mukti Bahini was also reporting the presence of Pakistani armour in the area. Though there had been no visual sighting of tanks, they could often be heard at night. This resulted in our moving our 106 mm recoilless guns well forward beyond the company positions. Extremely heavy, weighing upward of four hundred kilograms, this weapon is usually mounted on a jeep or a jonga, but here they had to be dismantled, manually transported and positioned in an anti-tank configuration. It would later transpire that there was no Pakistani armour in the area and the sound was in fact that of a bulldozer that sometimes worked at night.

The Dogra Regiment had captured some Pakistani troops from 15 Baluch who were ferrying supplies on a railway trolley between Parshuram and Belonia. My CO handed me a copy of the situation report (SITREP) that 3 Dogra had sent to Brigade HQ. I finished reading the rather long narration of events and looked at the CO.

'What do you make of it?' he asked me quietly.

We had been monitoring the particular operation (as had 8 Bihar) and we knew the basic details. 'Yeh to, sir, story jiada hai.' (This is more a story, sir.)

'Well, that's the way it goes,' said a bemused Dev Raj Dutt. As the intelligence officer, it was also my job to file our own SITREPs and reports to Brigade HQ after each operation. He smiled wryly and added tongue-in-cheek: 'I hope your writing skills can match this!'

'I can only write what happens,' I replied frankly. The CO nodded, gave me the once over and took the paper back from me. It was not mentioned again, but the incident stayed with me forever. Warlike conditions create situations where people who are extremely keen on getting accolades and awards often distort events, cataloguing them at variance with what actually happened. As the war unfolded, there were instances where some citations were written even before the action had taken place. The worst part of this was that there were instances of men who were actually busy fighting and had no time to 'project themselves', and were as a result, unrecognized, and left out of the final list of awards.

Another sharp lesson was hammered home after an officer from 8 Bihar, the third battalion in our brigade group, was wounded. Unable to evacuate the officer in time, the men watched in horror as he bled to death. This had a huge impact on me and, later, when I was in a position where I could do something about it, I did my best to address this problem.

The golden hour, when a casualty must be treated and evacuated, is critical and we studied the possibility and logistics of providing field medical support rather than transporting battle casualties to medical care elsewhere.

By the middle of November, we, along with the Mukti Bahini, had complete control of the area in the Belonia Bulge. Two platoons of 2 Rajput and a company of the BSF were also launched to clear the area around Belonia railway station. Direct firing of our 106 mm recoilless guns had destroyed most Pakistani bunkers. This enabled one platoon each of 2 Rajput and the BSF to occupy the first row of bunkers and probe forward. The remaining force did an outflanking move and captured Lichi Bagan, and the entire area was cleared by the early hours of 9 November.

Behind Enemy Lines

A few days later, an indicator that war would soon be declared formally came when we were told that we could revert to being in uniform. The unit was also asked to de-induct and we were shifted into another forested area west of Belonia in what is today the Trishna Wildlife Sanctuary, south of Rajnagar. On 30 November, the unit celebrated its Raising Day with more than its usual gusto and fervour and by the evening the celebrations had taken their toll on the men and officers alike. Later that evening, there was a call from Brigade HQ asking the unit to perform certain tasks. The CO looked around for the adjutant, but couldn't find him; he then tried to get the assistant adjutant and couldn't find him either. Ultimately, he got hold of me and I told him quite frankly that everyone in the unit was sleeping off the effects of the celebrations. With a resigned look on his face, the CO reached for the field telephone and informed Brigade HQ that 2 Rajput was not available that evening owing to its Raising Day. 'Give us a task tomorrow, and we'll do it!'

The next day, the battalion received a fresh task from Brigade HQ. According to intelligence sources, the Pakistani force aligned against us was deployed in a strong defensive position at Chauddagram. A few regular Pakistan Army companies along with a fair number of Razakars held these positions. It was believed that their artillery regiment of 105 mm guns was positioned somewhere in the vicinity of Parikot, east of Laksam, a few kilometres behind Chauddagram. The brigade commander wanted a patrol to go into East Pakistan with a Mukti Bahini guide and pinpoint the exact location of the guns. He also wanted the patrol to scout for two locations where the battalion could take up blocking positions to cut off the Chauddagram axis once the fighting began.

The CO assembled the battalion officers and outlined the task given to us. He asked for volunteers but the idea of romping around behind enemy lines in the middle of the night was too daunting. The process of elimination led the CO to eventually look in my direction. 'VK?' If there was a question mark attached to my name, I for one didn't notice it.

'No problem, sir! When can I set out?'

'Good. Then you take ten boys from Delta Company. Rendezvous with the Mukti Bahini guide and set off at dusk from here.' He tapped the map, indicating the launch-off point.

All the other officers were looking at me the way one looks at a sacrificial lamb. 'Sir,' I said, trying to sound deadpan, 'can I take a few boys from Alpha Company?' Delta Company had Bengali boys who were comparatively physically weaker when it came to carrying loads over long distances, and this exercise entailed traversing more than thirty kilometres of enemy territory. I was calculating on taking a few Rajput and Gujjar boys who could carry some serious weaponry in case we ran into a fire fight.

'No,' said the CO, 'you can hand-pick the chaps but only from Delta Company. Good luck!' The briefing was over and so were any doubts that lingered in my mind.

During the next few hours, I carefully studied the map, familiarizing myself with the terrain. I was getting a lot of advice from the other officers, each one suggesting how best to proceed, which men to take with me and what to do in case of various contingencies. I told everybody not to worry, and that the task was now my problem and it would be completed. In my own mind, I was working out my reaction to various possible scenarios. If we stuck to the basics of infiltration and kept things simple, with a bit of luck, we would be back with the required information.

I knew the Delta Company boys fairly well and selected a section strength of ten men, the most senior being an NCO. I briefed them, telling them we had to go a long distance behind enemy lines and that it would be absolutely imperative for them to keep pace with me. Having assigned individual duties, I made sure each man understood what was expected of him. Having ensured that all the required gear was checked, all we could do was wait for the sun to set.

At the appointed hour, once again dressed in civilian clothes, we started to move towards the international border. I was in for a rude shock, for the entire countryside was bathed in a swathe of bright moonlight. How the hell could brigade have overlooked this, I wondered, but it was too late now and we were soon at the crossing point where the Mukti Bahini guide was waiting for us. He quietly told me of the gaps between the Pakistani positions and we set off in a single file, crossing the border a couple of kilometres south of Chandul, somehow trying to make ourselves invisible in the bright moonlight. We had our first stroke of luck, for dense waist-high mist began to envelop the open countryside. I started to breathe easier, for the mist would make it a little easier for us to avoid detection.

We entered a path that led up to a village, but the guide stopped us at the outskirts. He whispered to me that the area was guarded by a village volunteer force that was tasked by the Pakistan Army to ensure that no Mukti Bahini elements passed through. After a quick discussion, he went ahead with one of the boys to make contact with the village sentries. For a few horrible minutes, we just sat there, with all sorts of negative thoughts flashing through our heads. The guide, however, had nerves of steel and he got the village volunteers together at a single spot. Before any of them could react, we quietly surrounded them and disarmed the entire lot. Obviously, I couldn't risk leaving the villagers now, so I ordered them to fall in behind the guide and lead the way.

We passed through three more villages, and each time we followed the same drill. Eventually, I had more than two dozen captive men with me. I was in a quandary, for I wasn't sure what I would do with the prisoners once we got close to Parikot. However, yet again we were lucky, for we came upon a deserted school building. I quickly herded the entire lot into the school and locked them into a room. They were told that we would blow up the building at the slightest noise from them. The poor souls were still unsure about our identity, and were probably too terrified of being discovered by Pakistani Razakars to try anything clever.

Parikot was a small settlement, with houses on either side of a river. The river itself was spanned by a single bridge, which was guarded by Razakars. The guns, as per my appreciation, were positioned on the other side. I now had to take a call. Either swim across the water body or take out the guards on the bridge. I was still weighing my options when a Pakistan Army jeep appeared on the bridge and a JCO loudly went about checking on the sentries. The jeep drove off but now we knew exactly where the four sentries were. I decided that our best option now was to silence them and get across the bridge, finish the task of locating the guns and get back before the jeep came back to check again.

Having decided to eliminate the sentries, we began to inch forward towards the bridge, using hand signals to communicate. Sentry silencing is one of the basic drills taught to us, and for me this was going to be the moment of truth. Yet again, for the third time, lady luck smiled on us. There were a few muffled shouts from across the river and then the 105s fired—first, the flashes lit up the night sky and then the sound of the blast followed, shattering the stillness of the night. One, two, three, four, five, six...one after the other the guns fired into the night at a distant target. Never in my life would I be so delighted to see enemy guns open up, for now all I had to do was take a reading of each muzzle flash and zero in positively on the location of each gun. Having mapped the location of the battery across the river, we headed back.

Had we silenced the sentries on the bridge, it would almost certainly have been a chase down to the border with the angry Pakistanis hot on our tails. At that point, we were more than fifteen kilometres behind enemy lines. Not wanting to look a gift horse in the mouth, we backed away from the bridge. I still had to find suitable locations to deploy the battalion in a blocking position. I had identified possible points on the map and, along with the guide, scouted around (though the guide seemed perplexed at my wasting precious time walking around uncharted area). After that, it was a mad dash to get back into Indian territory before first light. Pakistani vehicle-borne patrols were out, but I told the boys to stick to the track and make a dash for it. We had just about crossed the international border when the sun peeped over the horizon.

Till then, I had maintained complete radio silence. Having covered more than thirty kilometres, the boys were exhausted but elated, and we were welcomed into a BSF post with hot mugs of tea. I then got through to Battalion HQ who sent a vehicle to pick us up. The CO, I was told, had not slept through the night, anxiously waiting for news of the patrol. There was a lot of excitement and I was debriefed in detail. Towards the end of the debrief, the CO asked me, 'Why didn't you bring the village security teams back with you? Had you done that, I would have recommended you for an award straight away.' I told him that such an action would have jeopardized our mission and would have resulted in Pakistani retribution against the families of the villagers.

I was then sent off to Brigade HQ where the entire debrief was repeated. Later, the G3 (general staff officer), Captain Trigunesh Mukherjee, said to me, 'You have got to be a mad chap! Who the hell told you to go for an operation like this on a full moon night?'

I looked at him: 'You know something, I didn't realize it was a full moon until we set out.' We both laughed, for it's amazing how the most basic details can sometimes escape attention. Tongue-in-cheek, I added that the orders emanated from Brigade HQ and it was presumed that they would have checked out the state of the moon. We had indeed been lucky. The ifs and buts were now behind me, all I wanted to do was return to my unit and go to sleep.

Battle of Chauddagram

Even as I got back to Battalion HQ, orders for the assault on Chauddagram had come in. Pakistan's 23 Punjab (minus one company) was holding a defensive position and, according to the original briefing, we were expecting to set up stops behind the enemy position and cut their retreat towards Parikot and Laksam once the main attack was launched. However, as the plans for the attack were received, we were surprised to see that the roles of 2 Rajput and 3 Dogra had been reversed. Brigadier Sandhu wanted us to take on the Pakistani positions while the Dogras were given the task of setting up blocks from the south. 8 Bihar would be held in reserve for any unforeseen eventuality. Though we all welcomed the opportunity to take Chauddagram head on, the rank and file was fully aware of the fact that the brigade commander, due to his own personal equation with the two commanding officers, had reversed the roles. This was another extremely important lesson that I filed away: never play favourites. Every man in the formation knows what is happening and though the troops may accept the good with the bad, nothing ever goes unnoticed, especially in the eyes of the men.

Now getting any rest was out of the question, for the CO asked me to do a reconnaissance of the dighi area around which the main defences of Chauddagram were centred. I was also tasked with finding a suitable location for the firm base to stage the battalion into FUP (forming-up point). The dighi was a large elevated fortified position around a water tank that dominated the entire area. Pakistani defences were barely visible behind the mound of earth that had been excavated when the pond had been dug.

A few huts and trees were visible on the bund itself, while the enemy bunkers were hard to pinpoint. Chauddagram village then extended to the south and west of the dighi. The position was held by approximately a company plus of 23 Punjab while their main Battalion HQ was situated further west along the road to Parikot.

By the evening of 2 December 1971, I had mapped the area. I reported back to the CO and suggested we use as a firm base—the L-shaped school building and its compound which was about two kilometres from the dighi. An elevated road on the bund, between the school and the dighi, shielded us from the Pakistani position. I was then asked to go back with the Alpha and Charlie Company commanders, Majors Raizada and Kukrety. The latter seemed particularly reluctant to follow me into enemy territory, constantly lagging behind and asking in hushed tones, 'Dushman kidher hai?' (Where is the enemy?)

Delta Company was also inducted into the holding area on the night of 3-4 December. At 1740 hours on 3 December, Pakistani fighter aircraft launched multiple pre-emptive strikes against Indian airfields in the Western Sector and Prime Minister Indira Gandhi went live on All India Radio to declare 'India is at war with Pakistan!' During the night we received orders from Brigade HQ to put in a daylight attack on 4 December to capture Chauddagram. The formal announcement of the war earlier in the evening had been greeted with a sense of relief, given the many months of build-up. There was no time to dwell on that, though, for as darkness fell, Delta Company was guided across the international border to the firm base location.

At the battalion level, we had no idea why we were being asked to attack during daylight hours. On the larger canvas, the main weight of the divisional attack was to be to our north. Chauddagram as a village was unimportant, but the Pakistani position overlooked the road that went to Parikot and then headed north towards Chandpur. It was imperative that the Pakistani position be cleared so that the route could be made operational for the sustenance of the division. The idea was to use this road as the division's main maintenance axis. Perhaps our earlier success against the Pakistani positions at Belonia and Parshuram had given the indication that the Pakistan Army was demoralized and would not put up much of a fight when attacked frontally. But whatever the state of their morale, the Pakistani company was cornered and the men of 23 Punjab had no choice but to fight. A daylight attack would be playing to the enemy's strength. Having seen the Pakistani positions on the dighi from up close, I protested to the CO, 'Sir, a daylight attack is suicidal. They can see us coming from across the border.'

'Those are the orders,' he said, as he pored over a map, going over each detail, 'we have to do as the brigade says.'

Major Raizada now came up and asked the CO to let the intelligence officer lead the way. In the eyes of the company commanders, I was obviously the most expendable person in the unit. 'You know the route,' the CO snapped at him, 'you lead.' But after repeated imploring, the CO told me to lead the battalion the next day via the firm base into the FUP for the attack. Bravo Company under Major Dharam Bhalla had a secondary objective to the south and was not part of the immediate Chauddagram assault. We set out in single file. The NCO from the intelligence section followed me; he in turn was trailed by Alpha Company, then came the Tactical HQ with the CO and finally, bringing up the rear, was Charlie Company under Major Kukrety.

No sooner had we stepped across the international border, than the shelling started. We were obviously visible to the Pakistanis who were on higher ground around the dighi and were calling in artillery fire from their 105 mm guns at Parikot. Despite my pinpointing the gun positions two days earlier, Brigade HQ had failed to call in air strikes to neutralize the guns. Air burst was followed by ground explosions, and then again an air burst, ground explosions and so on. We were buying casualties even before the attack had begun. I looked behind me, and realized that there was no sign of Alpha or Charlie Companies, with only the CO and Tactical HQ following me. Hugging whatever cover we could find, we used the road embankment and somehow made it to the firm base where Delta Company was deployed by then.

Once the firing had started, Alpha Company had veered off to the north, eventually getting to the FUP via a convoluted route. Of Major Dharam Pal Kukrety and Charlie Company, there was no sign. I tried raising them on the radio but got no response. The whole thing was very frustrating as the firm base was also being targeted by artillery fire. Our 76 mm guns, on the other hand, were not proving to be effective as a large number of rounds kept landing in the pond and not on the bund around which the Pakistani defences were located.

With both Alpha and Charlie nowhere to be seen, there was complete confusion. Our rear medical position (regimental aid post) was now three kilometres away and we had to turn our attention quickly to treating our casualties. There being no provision to evacuate any of the wounded, the casualties had to be given first aid in the school building at the firm base itself. My knowledge of first aid—gained primarily by sharing accommodation with the RMO in the past—came in handy as I was able to help our wounded. By this time, Tom Mathews' mortar platoons had also got into the act. Linear fire at the dighi was impossible as the earthen embankments coupled with the water body made our fire relatively ineffective.

Alpha Company, having taken a northern detour, arrived at the FUP but of Charlie there was still no sign. We would get to know later that the company commander had gone to ground the moment the Pakistani guns had opened up. Confused and leaderless, the men stayed put waiting to be told what to do. After a while, the brigade commander himself arrived at the scene and physically prodded Major Kukrety to move forward. They followed the northerly detour that had been taken by Alpha Company and eventually arrived at the FUP.

Charlie Company began to close in on the dighi, getting to within four hundred yards of the Pakistani position, thanks to the elevated road that ran north to south. A platoon from Alpha Company then made a straight run for the embankment. Every position on the dighi opened up and the Alpha Company platoon was decimated almost to the last man. Charlie Company tried to get over the embankment but the UMG (universal machine gun) and MMG (medium machine gun) fire made any movement forward impossible.

Artillery fire was still being called in by the Pakistani observers, which along with a hail of fire from their positions on the dighi was creating a wall of lead, and the toll was mounting. Apart from fifteen dead, almost three times that number had been wounded. In the heat of the battle, I found myself running with wounded soldiers slung over my shoulder in the classic fireman's carry. Yet, in spite of all this, the men were grimly dug in, waiting for an opportunity to present itself.

Back in the school building, I was helping with the casualties and also ensuring that the CO was kept abreast of the situation and contacting anyone he wanted to get in touch with. The casualties were being brought in at an alarming rate, and the dead were piling up. My medical skills were now being put to good use as I gave morphine shots and tried to dress the wounds as best I could. To make matters worse, the building had taken a direct hit, killing three Delta Company boys who, along with me, were next to the wall. It was a lottery—some of us survived while others didn't.

Charlie Company's MMG detachment commander, an NCO, had had his head opened up by the MMG burst. It was inconceivable that he would survive. Back at the regimental aid post, Captain Garg, the RMO, just looked at him, or rather what was left of him, and got down to work. Disregarding everything in the rulebook, he performed a surgery then and there. Garg's incredible performance that day saved many lives and it reinforced my belief that in the golden hour, RMOs had to be empowered to take whatever decision that needed to be taken to save a man's life.

Our attack having fizzled out, all we could do was wait for the cover of darkness before we could put in another attempt. Dharam Bhalla's Bravo Company had also been told to link up with us, for they had successfully executed their overnight task with just a couple of casualties.

The CO held a discussion with the officers and it was decided that we would regroup and launch the attack in the early hours of the next morning. As the sun went down, we pulled back Charlie Company and moved Alpha Company a bit further to the east. No sooner had these manoeuvres been completed when, under the cover of darkness, the Pakistanis sent out UMG and MMG jitter parties towards the road embankment from where they let loose with everything they could muster. The school building took a solid hammering and in the ensuing confusion it looked like we were going to be attacked. To me it seemed fairly obvious that the Pakistanis were trying to throw us off balance and I suggested to the CO we launch a full-fledged attack on the dighi. However, Bravo Company was still moving into its designated position, so it was decided to sit out the Pakistani onslaught and see if they would risk launching a counter-attack. After a while, the intensity of firing died down and there was only sporadic MMG fire.

As the evening became night, I was preparing to lead a patrol out. Captain Satish Vashist from Delta Company was lying on a ground sheet next to the room in which the dead were stacked. Looking at me, he got up and told me to get some rest. Ever since my Parikot patrol, there had been no time to grab any sleep, and three nights at a trot had obviously taken a visible toll. Disregarding my protestations, Vashist told me to shut up and take his place on the ground sheet. He volunteered to take out the patrol. Without much thought, I crawled into the space he had vacated and instantly fell asleep, oblivious to the dead men who were lying right next to me.

The CO, Dev Raj Dutt, was informed about the switch and he briefed the officer accordingly. Vashist then set off with a section of men towards the dighi, ignoring the firing by the jitter parties that were still spraying our positions with sporadic MMG fire.

A few hours later I was rudely awakened with the news that Vashist had been wounded and was being brought in. His patrol had explored an alternate approach towards the dighi from the west. After a while, one of the men told Vashist that it looked like the area was mined. The officer immediately told the men to get behind him in single file and continued to move forward. The inevitable happened. He was brought in unconscious with his foot blown off. It was left to me to dress the mangled stump. I was told later that I did a superb job for they only opened the dressing in the hospital after he was evacuated the next day. Vashist was subsequently awarded a Vir Chakra.

In the early hours of 5 December, we put in a textbook attack on the dighi and were met with limited opposition. These men were quickly overrun and the jitter parties in the area were mopped up. The bulk of the Pakistani troops had pulled out under the covering fire of their MMGs and UMGs. Once we crested the slope of the dighi, we were amazed at the network of elaborate bunkers, each connected with crawl trenches. Looking back towards Belonia and the direction from which we had come, it was a wonder we had not been decimated, for the entire approach was like a flat table top. Had we launched a night attack at the outset, we may have succeeded; a daytime assault was nothing short of suicide.

The Pakistani troops had begun to disengage around 2300 hours and had fallen back to their Battalion HQ, some five kilometres inland towards Parikot. From here the entire battalion began to withdraw towards Parikot but ran into the roadblock set up by 3 Dogra in the early hours. They had occupied the positions on the night of 3 December and had been waiting for the Pakistanis to run from Chauddagram. In fact, that entire day the Dogras had been intercepting the line communication between Chauddagram and Parikot and had monitored the forward observers calling for supporting fire while we were bogged down. As the Pakistani troops now approached, they were asked by the Dogra officer in command to surrender.

The Pakistani detachment closest to the Dogra position indicated that it was laying down its weapons. The company commander, Major Gahlot, then stepped out to tell the Pakistanis what to do, and was instantly shot dead. This treacherous act resulted in every weapon opening up on the Pakistanis. 3 Dogra had completely surrounded the Pakistanis and they now hit them with mortars and LMGs. On the Pakistani side, 23 Punjab suffered severe casualties as almost two companies were mowed down. However, under the cover of darkness and by taking a different route, their main Battalion HQ detachment managed to escape towards Parikot.

Mad Rush into East Pakistan

We moved further into East Pakistan, leaving behind a company to consolidate and secure the road axis. The Pakistani Battalion HQ was abandoned, but the documents recovered from the site confirmed that the battalion that had faced us at Chauddagram was indeed 23 Punjab. We pushed forward towards Parikot and, by the evening, had control of the hamlet. The Pakistanis had blown up the bridge where, a few nights earlier, I had contemplated taking out the Razakars. The guns had also been upstaged and were gone, and we crossed the river on country boats. With the bridge gone, none of our vehicles could go beyond this point.

No vehicles meant no supplies. And we were all constantly moving. Divisional HQ had come up and I saw the CO talking to the GOC, Rocky Hira (a Gorkha officer). The General's jonga had taken a direct hit, but he looked rock solid and exuded an aura of calm control that added to his reputation. The men felt the GOC was taking the same risks as them.

By the evening of 6 December, we had been without food other than a handful of shakarpara that each man carried as emergency ration. The cook with the Battalion HQ detachment, Mani Ram, was getting more and more distraught at the thought of all of us going hungry. Mani Ram was one of the survivors of Namka Chu, having been taken prisoner by the Chinese in 1962. Somehow, and in spite of the fact that we were mostly on the move, he had managed to get hold of a duck, unhusked rice and some unfamiliar vegetables. The duck made the supreme sacrifice towards the liberation of Bangladesh and we all got a fresh lease of life, thanks to the invigorating stew.

The next morning, elements of 23 Punjab who had survived the Dogra ambush were captured. The prisoners were herded on to a bridge and I saw a captain who was their adjutant. He was older than me and I asked him if he had eaten anything.

'No, we've been on the run for the last two days.'

'Here,' I reached into my bag and gave the captain a fistful of shakarpara. 'Have some,' I said, 'these are our emergency rations.'

He stood there looking most uncertain, almost frightened, but he made no move to eat the shakarpara. He was just staring at them.

The realization hit me suddenly: he thinks they are coated with poison! I reached out and took a couple of pieces from his hand and popped them into my mouth. The captain burst into tears.

The other prisoners and my men had all been watching this little drama unfold. Almost to a man, our boys dug into their kit bags and gave the Pakistanis whatever they could find, a few men even sharing their water canteens.

Their adjutant looked at me and said, 'Thank you.'

I turned to walk away, but he put his hand on my shoulder. 'You know, I was brought up to believe Indians were the biggest bastards—demons who were cruel and would torture us before killing us. Here you people are giving us your food and water.' Tears were still streaming down his face.

There was nothing to be said, so I moved away, leaving at least one Pakistani soldier to ponder the folly of it all. We were still to see the full extent of the brutality unleashed by the Pakistan Army although we'd heard numerous stories about it, the most recent one being the shooting down of the Dogra officer. Another report indicated that some of our engineers were stopped and killed by 15 Baluch. Cruelty and brutality would only result in further senseless retaliation. However, the biggest threat the Pakistani prisoners of war (POWs) faced was from the Mukti Bahini. One thing we knew was that no POW was going to risk escaping from us. The local population would have lynched them on the spot.

Division had established a POW camp, so we handed over our group for whom the war was now over. Another Pakistani officer at the camp, a lieutenant colonel, had grown up around Rewari and it was strange to have him talk of various familiar landmarks.

We were told to keep moving and to proceed to Mudaffarganj that was en route to Chandpur. On the larger canvas, everybody seemed to be on the move. The Indian strategy was to bypass Pakistani defences. The enemy, unsure of what was happening, would invariably upstage and try to head further inland where our ambush parties were waiting for them. Those who got away would keep moving. On the night of 7-8 December, the general feeling was that we were moving, the Pakistanis were moving and so was the Mukti Bahini.

We were told that 1/11 GR was in Mudaffarganj and that the Pakistanis had surrounded them on three sides. Our immediate task was to reinforce their position and break the Pakistani cordon. The intelligence officer from 1/11 GR, Captain Bhanwer Singh, married up with us and was soon leading us to the Gorkha positions through a route that was clear of mines. The company commander had been shot and the Pakistanis had eliminated a listening post of the Gorkhas. There was intermittent firing around us, but by daybreak we were in position. As usual, under the cover of darkness, the Pakistanis had broken contact and pulled out, leaving the odd jitter party to keep us on the hop.

With Mudaffarganj cleared, an air force Mi 8 flew in some supplies for 1/11 GR. Bread, eggs and all sorts of goodies were offloaded while we were living off shakarpara and the odd duck! There was a bit of leg-pulling, for 1/11 GR was the GOC's battalion and if they were getting priority as the supply chains were being established, so be it!

Taratari! Go, Go, Go!

1/11 GR was pulled out and redeployed elsewhere, so we occupied their positions. In the afternoon, another helicopter came in low, circled and landed next to our position. The rotors were still running when the door opened and a tall officer got off and began walking towards us. Lieutenant General Sagat Singh, the IV Corps commander yelled over the noise of the Chetak, 'Which unit?'

'2 Rajput.'

'Get Dev Raj Dutt here, now!' The CO was already sprinting towards the general. 'I've just flown over Chandpur,' said Sagat Singh, 'the Pakistanis are evacuating the town. You get your battalion across and occupy it.'

'We have no vehicles,' protested the CO.

'Well, get some! I don't care how you get there, but get there.' The general climbed back into the chopper, which lifted off and was gone.

We started commandeering everything that moved, from a broken down truck to cycle rickshaws. Suddenly, some men came upon a gleaming red fire engine. The CO jumped into the cabin while others clambered aboard and the mad rush towards Chandpur began, with the rest of the unit following in a chain of cycle rickshaws.

Chandpur was a mid-sized town on the eastern bank of the Meghna, a vast expanse of water that resembled an ocean at this point. The Pakistani retreat was more or less complete and the last ferry laden with their soldiers was pulling out. Those of us on the fire engine opened fire on the steamer, which soon sank. Our entry into the town was greeted by people pouring out on to the streets, shouting 'Joy Bangla'. They were laughing, crying, dancing and trying to thrust eggs, chickens and fish in our direction. We too were celebrating—for we were in a town with electricity and running water! We hadn't had electricity in months—since October, ever since we moved into Tripura.

The next day we were told to leave Chandpur and rejoin the rest of 83 Brigade that was somewhere between Comilla and Feni. I was told to collect some maps and then set off on the Comilla road in a jeep—the previous night we had commandeered a few Pakistan Army vehicles—with a driver and my intelligence team of two men.

In the forced march towards Chandpur, I had no idea what was happening to our north, and was certainly not aware that Comilla was still in Pakistani hands. The most obvious way to link up with the Feni road was to go straight through Comilla town. We came to a road junction that was manned by a military policeman. He had been placed there to guide people so that they could bypass Comilla.

The CMP (corps of military police) was a Sikh soldier who was unconcerned with the semantics of which side controlled which town. He had the air of a bored tourist guide and when I asked him if we could go straight through Comilla, he shrugged and said: 'Jana hai to chale jao.' (If you want to go, you go.)

We cheerfully waved to him and shot off towards Comilla, which we entered most confidently. At first, everyone stared at us and then the place erupted with a fusillade of Joy Banglas. Men, women, children were pouring out on to the street, again showering my lone jeep with a variety of goodies!

Comilla town was dominated by the Mainamati cantonment, into which the Pakistan Army had withdrawn and taken up defensive positions. Before a Pakistani patrol wandered in and spoilt our 'liberation party', it seemed prudent to keep moving. With a sigh of relief, we got out of the town, hit the Feni road, turned south and carried on to the brigade location, which was beyond Feni.

The rest of the battalion reached the road junction shortly thereafter. Kanwer Mohinder Singh, the adjutant, asked the military policeman if he had seen our jeep. He was told we had gone through directly to Comilla, which came as a nasty shock to the adjutant who was aware that the town was technically still not cleared of the enemy. After a hurried conference, the battalion decided to follow in our wake. As they entered the town, the local population went even more delirious with joy. Fortunately, the battalion too got through the town without any untoward incident. I, for one, knew that if they ever needed an epitaph for me, it would say: 'The Indian Army lieutenant who liberated Comilla!' What the Pakistanis thought of the incident has never been recorded.

By the night of 10-11 December, the battalion had joined up with the brigade after a long journey from Chandpur-Comilla-Feni-Haitkandi-Satbaria and on to Sitakunda. Our objective now was Chittagong. Most of the commandeered Isuzu trucks had by then had their clutches burnt out as our drivers were not used to such advanced technology. There was now a flurry of activity as the plans for the advance on Chittagong were drawn up.

The geography of the area ahead of us was now very different. The Chittagong Hill Tracts extended north to south on our left while the road followed the flat plains between the hilly terrain and the Bay of Bengal. The road was almost certainly defended by the Pakistanis, and that left us with no option but to try and find a route through the hill tracts, with the intention of getting in behind them. This was easier said than done, for the densely forested valleys actually ran east to west, which meant we had to go down, then up again, over and over. My reputation as the pathfinder had now preceded me, so once again I found myself leading a section along what was rather impossible terrain.

We started on the morning of 12 December and struggled through some of the densest vegetation we'd encountered so far. After a while we tried to move towards the slopes that overlooked the road and the coast and almost instantly drew enemy fire. We kept walking, going up and then down, until I decided to put a stop to the madness and settled down for some rest. One of the boys in my section was the long distance runner who had tried to take me for a ride when I had joined the battalion. He knew I had walked more than the rest and he offered to help me take off my boots. I told him to dry his own feet and make sure the men had a bit of rest before we began the tortuous journey back.

It was late at night when I reported back to the CO, and told him it was almost impossible to move a large body of men across such difficult terrain in a short time. The CO passed the message on to Brigade HQ, who promptly asked for me to brief them as well. When I walked in, Ajit Chopra, the CO of 3 Dogra was also present along with Brigadier Sandhu, and I repeated what I had said to my CO.

Ajit Chopra was of the view that I was not quite reading the terrain right. He pointed to a black dotted line that marked an inter-tehsil boundary running along the hill area and asked why I couldn't follow the track which was so clearly marked on the map. A lieutenant when asked such a question can only mumble that it is not a track. But has no choice when he's told that he is a novice who has no idea how to read a map. I was ordered to take another patrol and go find the damned track.

It was obvious I would have to go back yet again and I knew the geography wasn't going to change. 'Can I have some additional men?' I looked pointedly at the Dogra CO. 'Maybe the Dogra commando section?'

Ajit Chopra could hardly refuse. 'Yes, that's no problem. Captain Sirohi with ten men will join you.'

Sirohi was senior to me, which would give him operational command of the patrol. That was fine by me. If the Dogra CO eventually had to face the reality that his map-reading skills were off-track then I'd rather he didn't hear it from me. Two hours of sleep and we were off again. The jungle closed in on us and the endless up-down trek started yet again. We doggedly tried to follow the coordinates looking for the dotted line, but there wasn't even a game trail there, let alone a path for humans.

'You can tell your old man there's no track,' I finally said to Sirohi after we had spent a couple of hours in this futile search. He shook his head and grinned at me, 'You'll get me sorted out.'

We ran into some refugees who were hiding in one of the valleys. Once they realized we were Indians, they offered us whatever little food they had. We were more interested in information pertaining to the Pakistani positions, and they gave us a fairly detailed picture. When we tried to probe a couple of the positions nearest to us, we promptly drew fire. At sunset, we started to head back.

Elephant grass made it impossible for us to see anything and the enveloping darkness now completely disoriented us. It was critical that no man get separated from the main party either. Besides, the Pakistanis knew we were scouting the area and we didn't want to blunder into an ambush. We floundered around for a while and then Sirohi took a call for us to sit tight, for it was obvious we were lost. We couldn't light a fire so we cut some grass and huddled under it to keep the cold out. Come morning, we were on the move again, getting fresh bearings from the sun. By midday, we had made it back to Brigade HQ.

The next morning the brigade advance began with 2 Rajput clearing the way with daos (flat-bladed weapon of choice of the Mizo, Naga and Arunachal hill tribes). By now we knew the net was closing in on Dhaka, for despite the static and poor reception, transistors were picking up Manekshaw's appeal to the Pakistan Army to lay down their arms. Nevertheless, we continued to push forward. 16 December dawned and soon came the news of the ceasefire. For that moment, the euphoria of having won the war took a back seat to the fact that we didn't have to suffer the painful advance along the hill tracts. We literally came tumbling down the forested slopes on to the coastal road.

There we found a Pakistan Burmah-Shell complex that had a British manager who had served with the Gorkhas. News of the surrender had preceded us and a lavish breakfast for the officers was laid out while communication was established with the Pakistani garrison at Chittagong. Within a couple of hours, a detachment of the Pakistan Army came to receive us. Their khaki uniforms were starched and crisp while the entire lot of us looked like 'combat types'. The biggest difference, however, was that the Pakistanis were looking glum and defeated while we couldn't stop grinning. As we entered Chittagong on the shoulders of throngs of delirious Bengalis, we all were swept away with the emotion of the moment.

I was twenty years old and part of an army that, for the first time since World War II, had decisively changed the territorial boundaries of a country—and that too in fourteen days!

Pakistan's 97 Independent Brigade commanded by Brigadier Atta Mohammad Khan Malik held Chittagong, and though the harbour had taken a pounding from INS *Vikrant*'s Seahawks, the troops had not suffered excessive casualties. As per the division of responsibility, 2 Rajput was positioned at Fauzdar Haat Cadet College, while one company was deployed within the town. 3 Dogra moved into Chittagong Cantonment and 8 Bihar moved into the other part of town. There was the danger of the Mukti Bahini going on a revenge rampage and it was imperative that the situation be controlled. Further complicating the issue with the Mukti Bahini was the large Bihari Muslim population that had supported the Pakistan Army and even joined them in targeting their Bengali brethren.

On 17 December, two surrender ceremonies were held in Chittagong. A large number of troops, all part of the independent brigade, including 48 Baluch, 2 SSG Commando, 60 and 61 Wing Rangers, Brigade HQ, the logistic elements, the naval contingent and their anti-aircraft elements were marched in, the men and JCOs looking surprisingly smart and disciplined.

At Fauzdar Haat, our CO took the surrender, while in the cantonment Brigadier Sandhu presided over the ceremony. The Pakistanis laid down their weapons and side arms. Quite a few of their men were in tears. They felt they had been let down by the Pakistani military leadership. Time and again we heard the lament, 'If we had officers like yours, no one could touch us.' Almost 9,000 Pakistanis surrendered in Chittagong.

Later in the day I went with a couple of officers to the Chittagong Medical College. We walked into a nightmare. Around a hundred women, most of them pregnant, stared vacantly at us. It took a while for them to understand they were free, at which point they begged us to shoot them. Repeatedly raped, they had nowhere to go with their unborn children. One had read about the horrific Nazi deeds in World War II. The scene at the Medical College was just as shocking and unbelievable. After the surrender at Dhaka, similar reports of around 560 Bengali women being rescued from the Dhaka Cantonment also surfaced. They had been picked up by the soldiers either from the university or private homes and forced to work as sex slaves in military brothels. Many of these girls were now carrying 'war babies'.

What was shocking was that the United States, Pakistan's main backer at the time, was fully aware of these, and other, incidents. Thirty years after the war, US Archives declassified documents that clearly state that the Nixon administration was receiving detailed reports from their own people of the genocide that had been unleashed by the Pakistan Army. The fact that the United States continued to back Pakistan in Bangladesh and even sent their Seventh Fleet into the region in an attempt to influence the war underlines how deep-rooted US-Pakistan strategic ties are.

The worst part was that none of the Pakistani officers, who were otherwise terrified of falling into the Mukti Bahini's hands, showed even the slightest remorse for their deeds. While doing the documentation of the POWs, a Pakistani officer asked me if I knew how many Bengalis could be killed with a single bullet. Seeing me gape at him in horror, he cockily said, 'Twelve! I've actually tried it.'

Other than the adjutant of 23 Punjab who had broken down when I offered him part of my emergency ration, Pakistani officers were hostile, individually swearing that they would never forgive India for having 'intervened' in their 'war' and for having dismembered Pakistan. Had the roles been reversed, we were quite sure we wouldn't have been treated even remotely as well. Indian soldiers captured by the Pakistan Army during the last few days of the war had met horrific ends: boys of 22 Rajput who had been trapped in an ambush before crossing the Madhumati were tied to trees and had their eyes gouged out. In another case, two Kumaoni soldiers had been stripped and tied behind jeeps and dragged through the town at Laksam. Army HQ had acted with tremendous alacrity and immediately pulled the battalions out and sent them to the Western Sector. Any acts of revenge on the part of Indian troops would have probably led to the Mukti Bahini going berserk.

By then, most commanders were intent on limiting Mukti Bahini revenge attacks on not just the Pakistani POWs but also the minority Bihari community which had assisted the Pakistan Army with these atrocities. Nevertheless, and it rankles to this day, the Pakistani officers responsible for the genocide and rape of hundreds and thousands could not be tried for their war crimes.

At our level, we were obviously not privy to any of the thinking that shaped post-war events. As the COAS, I revisited the Chittagong area in 2010 and went over some of the old familiar ground. The Fauzdar Haat Cadet College was still there, while the area along the coastal road to the old Pakistan Burmah-Shell location was now a maze of shipping containers. The Bangladesh Military Academy had also come up in the area and the entire face of the region had changed, especially as shipbreaking became a major activity in Chittagong.

One could not help but think how short-sighted we had been as a country—the Belonia Bulge virtually extended up to Feni that was hand-shaking distance from Chittagong. The entire socio-economic reality and geopolitical scenario in our Northeast would have changed had we positively exploited this situation then. In pre-Partition days, the traditional trading routes from south Mizoram to Chittagong had run down the Karna Phuli River. Once these got blocked in 1947 owing to the new political boundaries, the entire Northeast got isolated from the sea, the closest port then being the looped route to Calcutta. The tragedy is that, at the time, these issues were probably not even considered and what-could-have-been remains part of the ifs-and-buts of history.

Chittagong

On the evening of the surrender, most of the officers congregated at the Chittagong Club which was jam-packed with people. A lot had happened since our desperate daylight assault on Chauddagram. The war was over and the battalion had done everything that had been asked of us. Hundreds of Indian soldiers had paid with their lives and now we basked in the glow of the birth of a new nation. The evening belonged to Mujibur Rahman, Indira Gandhi, the Mukti Fauj, the Mukti Bahini and the Indian Army. Everybody was laughing and crying. The atmosphere was euphoric.

Back at Battalion HQ, intoxicated, mentally and perhaps physically as well, I decided to test drive a sleek Toyota jeep—the cynosure of all eyes, including that of the CO—from the pool of captured vehicles. I was just getting into the groove when along came a railway engine! That was the end of my joyride. Shaken and badly bruised, I had to extricate myself from the car by climbing out *through* the windshield. The sleek Toyota was now a mangled heap. Fearing questions from the CO, I sought the help of a few of our boys and tipped the remnants of the Toyota off a bridge into the deep waters around Chittagong. With a deep gash on my head that would require stitches, I then headed to Garg, who too was suffering from the after-effects of celebrating the birth of Bangladesh.

'Stitch it here itself without anaesthesia,' I bravely volunteered.

I'm not too sure which one of us was suffering more as he broke three needles in the process of putting in the six stitches that were required.

Next morning, I don't know what story Garg told Dev Raj Dutt. I was too terrified to go anywhere near the CO. His enquiry about the Toyota drew sheepish looks and evasive answers, and coupled with a missing intelligence officer, he possibly drew his own conclusions. He didn't mention the Toyota again. No one else did either.

Revenge killings continued to threaten the fragile peace. In addition to 8 Bihar, two more companies moved into the town to control the situation. Documentation work was unending and batches of POWs were dispatched to Dhaka by sea. With most of the harbour no longer operational due to our air attacks, we had to use an improvised jetty, with the difference between high and low tides adding to the difficulties.

Most prisoners retained their military discipline, followed orders and cooperated with us. Major General Rahim Khan's 39 Ad Hoc Division had had its headquarters at Chandpur and their AOR included the brigades from Comilla and Feni that were also routed out of Chittagong. Comilla, the town which I 'liberated' with my driver and intelligence section, had been defended by 117 Infantry Brigade which was commanded by Brigadier Sheikh MH Atif, a former Pakistan hockey player who later went on to manage his country's national hockey team. Mainamati had perhaps the most formidable complex of defences in the entire region—low wire entanglements, a ditch and a strong network of bunkers that would have been difficult to capture without the attackers suffering huge casualties. IV Corps tactics are perhaps best illustrated by what happened to them. From Pakistani POWs we learnt that they saw the Indian brigade opposite them dig in, establish FUPs and go through the entire build-up of an attack. They waited for the assault which never came. Instead, the Indian Army bypassed them.

However, not all the prisoners were content to be cooperative. Major Husnain from 15 Baluch, also referred to as 'Para Baluch' by Pakistani soldiers, was identified as the ringleader who was trying to motivate and educate the prisoners on how to escape. This officer had been captured by us in 1965 but had successfully got away. We put him in solitary confinement, and Avinash Kapila, who was back with the unit and was now the adjutant (we always referred to him as the permanent adjutant because of his efficiency), threatened to hand him over to the Mukti Bahini. That promptly took the wind out of him and he started weeping with fear. Once he realized we were from 2 Rajput, he claimed he was a friend of Ashok Kalyan Verma, CO 18 Rajput. Both of them had been together at Fort Benning doing the Allied Officer's Infantry Course in 1969. He was among the last batch of POWs to be sent to Dhaka. True to character, he later escaped from the POW camp in Meerut as well and met his end at the hands of a Railway Protection Force constable who shot him as he tried to jump trains.

A few days later, I was told by the CO to take a platoon and escort civilian officers from the administrative set-ups who were going to disarm a Mukti Bahini outfit. We got to the location and I immediately deployed our boys around the armoury. Until then, I hadn't realized the seriousness of the situation. There had been a lot of tension between the Mukti Fauj, who were mainly elements from the EBR, and the Mukti Bahini, which was made up mostly of students. Quite a few incidents of settling personal scores and looting had been reported in the preceding days. If any semblance of law and order had to be maintained, disarming the Mukti Bahini was perhaps a necessary step.

As soon as we set up around the armoury, we noticed that the entire erstwhile Mukti Bahini cadre was extremely worked up. Suddenly there was a loud crash outside as first one and then another administration jeep was overturned. A hostile crowd closed in around us, I couldn't pull out, nor could we open fire without triggering a bloodbath in the confined area we were trapped in. I radioed the battalion for help and hoped for the best.

The next morning the Bangladeshi sector commander Major Rafique, who had been with us in Belonia, arrived and cooled down the Mukti Bahini boys. By now they had forgotten about the main issue and angrily held forth about the Indian Army pushing them into rooms and pointing LMGs at them. Fortunately, the officer who later served as a minister in the Awami League government, had the moral authority and, more importantly, the ability to handle the situation. Having worked with us earlier, he also knew that what we had told him was true and he could sift fact from fiction.

After a couple of weeks, the ships stopped coming to take the prisoners. We still had six truckloads of POWs, including civilian Pakistani women and children, in our charge. I was told to take the convoy to Dhaka and hand over the captives to 57 Division.

I have always felt that the higher the headquarters, the less chance there is that people are willing to take decisions. After an overnight drive from Chittagong to Dhaka, I was running around in the morning like a headless chicken, for no one was willing to take responsibility for my hapless prisoners. Eventually, Major General BF Gonsalves' ADC, the son of a Rajput Regiment officer, came to my rescue. He told me to let the prisoners out of the trucks and tell them to stretch their legs in a field opposite the GOC's office while I was served breakfast in the ADC's room. Shortly thereafter, the general came, he saw and he exploded! He wanted to know what was happening. He was told that an officer from 2 Rajput had brought the prisoners from Chittagong and no one was willing to take over. The GOC promptly blasted the divisional staff. Oblivious to all this, I was having a sumptuous breakfast while there was a hectic search on to trace me. The ADC had played his cards perfectly and it was hilarious. A detachment from 2 Jat then came at a gallop and I happily handed over the entire lot of captives.

During that period and after the war, there was a lot of talk pertaining to some senior Indian Army officers appropriating things for their personal benefit. Almost certainly there was an element of truth to this and a few senior officers were court-martialled. Some names were openly being bandied about. Just as some of our border guards and officials exploited refugees before the war, this too left a bad taste in the mouth. Each and every time it boiled down to the conduct of the senior officers, especially the COs, which influenced everybody else around them. A lot of the stories were exaggerated and the incidents were relatively few, but the fact is it happened.

These officers really let themselves and the Indian Army down, and this is a stigma we have to live with.

Back in Chittagong, the people literally opened their homes to us and we were overwhelmed by Bengali hospitality. One particular family was extremely fond of Trigunesh Mukherjee and we would play tennis at their home and be pampered with exotic dishes by the lady of the house. In between I managed to drive down further south to Cox's Bazar that was largely populated by Chakma tribals. Most of them worked in the cigar industry, rolling tobacco into leaves. Fortunately, Cox's Bazar had not been particularly hit by the war. On the beach there were two or three hotels and the place was known for its pomfret, reportedly the best in the world.

We were to stay on in Chittagong till February-end and were the last battalion of the brigade to pull out. We drove to Comilla where the officers were hosted to lunch by Zia, by then promoted to the rank of a brigadier. From there we proceeded to Karim Ganj from where we got on to a train that took us to Guwahati. Five months after leaving Tamulpur, we were back home to our dilapidated location.

PART II

THROUGH THE RANKS

4

GUNS AND ROSES

Eastern Bhutan

In Tamulpur, some dramatic changes had taken place; although we still had to make sure there was no snake inside our basha every time we entered, we now had electricity and, more importantly, clean running water. It took a major effort to clean up the area and cut the grass that was almost waist high. It takes time to get back into a regular routine after a battalion has been through a war. There were numerous things that had to be taken stock of, including an analysis of what we did and if we could have done it better. It was also time to reach out to the families of all those who were no more or were recuperating from their wounds in various hospitals.

The battalion also quickly got back to the business of training, dealing with the usual tasks that included a reconnaissance of flood-prone areas. The wartime complement of officers in the battalion was quite large, but this began to whittle down as some officers were sent to command POW camps while others went as instructors elsewhere. One of the annual tasks allocated to 83 Brigade was to send one of the infantry battalions to Bhutan for a three-month joint training session with the Bhutan Army. Most units were not too keen to uproot and head off into the mountains, for most of the on-ground facilities (especially the accommodation) were extremely basic. The men got no additional allowance either and, to make matters worse, the training was fairly tough. For a unit that had just got back from combat, the assignment was routine more than exotic.

The battalion rear was left at Tamulpur and the rest of us moved into eastern Bhutan through Samdrup Jongkhar to Yongphulla, which, at an altitude of more than 9,000 feet, was extremely cold due to the wind-chill factor. Situated close to Tashigang, which was the dzongkhag or district headquarters, we were operating in the region where a few survivors of the battalion's rear had withdrawn after the Namka Chu battle in 1962. Further to our north, along the old Monpa trails, one could re-enter India via Bleting and proceed to Lumla and Tawang. From Yongphulla, the companies fanned out to other locations, working in tandem with the Bhutan Army. The main objective was the integration of the two armies, and though the pace was hectic, it kept the boys combat fit.

Bhutanese officers would come on attachment and serve with the Indian battalions; there was a lot of bonhomie between the two groups. The afterglow of the Bangladesh War had its effect, for the Indian Army was held in great respect. We had quite a few officers whose association with individual units would continue over the years. There was Tashi Dorji with 2 Rajput and Batoo Tshering (the present Bhutan Army chief) who was also in the brigade with 8 Bihar. Overall, the Bhutanese were extremely dignified and a simple people who were wonderfully affectionate and warm towards us.

In early 1973, we were back in Tamulpur and, as usually happens in the army, there were plenty of changes in the formation. 3 Dogra moved out and was replaced by 3/5 GR. Major General BM Bhattacharjee, MVC, under whose command 4 Garhwal Rifles had put up a brave fight between Se La and Jung (now known as Jaswantgarh) against the Chinese in 1962, replaced the GOC, Rocky Hira. He did not stay for long though and was soon replaced by Major General SK Sinha, who was also from 3/5 GR. While all this was happening, I was nominated to attend the four-month Battalion Support Weapons (BSW) course in Mhow.

The nomination had come out of the blue and I had no time to prepare for it. When I reached Mhow, I was told there would be an entrance test. MMG was not a major problem for it was similar to the LMG which I was fairly familiar with; the RCL guns too I could handle. However, the mortar section was a problem as I had never effectively handled the weapon. A coursemate from NDA, Prakash Singh, from 6/8 GR, came to my rescue. Not only had he come extremely well-prepared for the BSW course but he had an added advantage—most of the instructors in the mortar wing at the time, from the NCOs to the divisional commander, were all from the Gorkhas. He told me to just follow his lead, while he spoke to them in Gorkhali. It obviously worked, for I wasn't put through too intensive a scrutiny and passed the entrance exam. It was a great relief.

We then boarded his red Enfield Bullet to head back to our quarters. As we turned towards the BSW lines, a motorcycle being driven by a civilian collided with us. As the pillion rider, I was thrown clear, but Prakash was knocked unconscious. We scrambled to get him to the hospital where the doctors said he was suffering from severe internal bleeding and a fractured jaw. By the evening he was on the 'dangerously ill' list and the situation was critical.

Despite the large complement of officers posted at Mhow in both the Infantry School and the College of Combat, the hospital had a lousy reputation. Hence, it wasn't surprising that the hospital authorities said that Prakash would need to be evacuated by surface transport to Jabalpur for further treatment. The doctor, a surgeon on temporary duty, said Prakash would die if he was moved. Prakash's best chance, the surgeon said, was to be operated on in Mhow itself, notwithstanding the lack of proper facilities. The authorities disassociated themselves from the decision and said the surgery could be done at the surgeon's 'own risk'. The doctor went ahead, and did a commendable job, with only a slight bump on Prakash's jaw as evidence of the hospital's infrastructural shortcomings. Prakash missed the ongoing course as he was recuperating. At his behest, I became the designated letter writer to his fiancée. I had the pleasure of meeting his wife years later when I was in Delhi as the chief.

After doing reasonably well on all the three legs of the BSW course, and armed with an instructor's grading, I returned to Tamulpur with the added responsibility of teaching others what I had learnt. Meanwhile, drawing lessons from our Bangladesh experience, Dev Raj Dutt had decided to implement a new doctrine with fresh standard operating procedures that would be applicable for training in both war and peace. The CO had accordingly got a detailed manual printed and he would quiz all officers at noon in his office. It was comical; once training hours finished, the bugler would sound the officer's call and all of us would rush to the CO's office.

Sometimes he would get mad at our response and throw the thick manual at offending officers who failed to satisfy him with their answers. 'I got this written for you people!' he would say in frustration. Around this time, the CO was detailed to attend the Senior Command Course in Mhow, which seemed quite amusing, for he had already commanded the battalion during the war. The brigade commander also changed around the same time and Brigadier 'Bob' Mahendra Singh from the armoured corps took over from Brigadier Sandhu.

The corps commander, Lieutenant General Inder Singh Gill, visited the battalion around this time. The usual preparations were made, and on the appointed day, he arrived with the GOC, General Sinha, in tow and was briefed by the CO. As was the norm, the CO then offered to take him to the battalion which was standing by in the training area.

'I don't need to go around the unit. I got an impression of the battalion the moment I drove in through the gate. We'll go to the mess and I'll talk to the officers and the JCOs.' General Gill's practical approach was reflected in most of his actions. On a subsequent occasion, we had an Artillery Practice Camp at the Daranga range. By then, I was given the acting rank of a major and was the Bravo Company commander whose job was to give out our fire support requirements and outline the tactical situation. The arrival of the corps commander in the midst of this setting was an event in itself, and we were extremely surprised to see the general walk up to a nearby stone on which he sat down, waving away the hastily arranged chairs, while telling all of us to get on with it. And when we broke for lunch, he just walked into the nearest cookhouse and sat and ate with the men. 3/5 GR, the GOC's own battalion, which had prepared an elaborate lunch, was left running around in confusion. Inder Gill was a leader who was adored by the men.

In those days, the artillery conducted the inter-battalion mortar competitions held within the brigade. We had an experienced JCO, Subedar Nawab Singh, who was our mortar expert and his handling of the 81 mm mortars (gifted by the US Army) was exemplary. These mortars had always been somewhat faulty, most weapons having a fair element of play between the base plate and the mortar tube. We would rectify this by pouring Araldite and other adhesives into the socket housing the tube. Nawab Singh didn't require any range finders or a sighting system; his estimations were always 'takreeban theek' which in practical terms meant 'bang on'.

On the other hand, the artillery officers were least interested in the 'bang on' approach, their sole agenda being to show up the infantry and prove that our boys did not understand the technicalities of mortar firing. Accordingly, they laid down impossible parameters, asking us to fire at an apex angle of 45 degrees. This created havoc with the length zone of the falling round, making corrections extremely difficult. The irony was that if the artillery themselves had to fire at an apex angle which was more than 20 degrees, they would throw a fit and refuse to undertake such shoots. Further, the gunners wanted us to first do a line correction, and then follow it up with a direction correction. This was tedious and time consuming, for most infantry units preferred doing a line and direction correction simultaneously to bring down fire on the target in the shortest possible time. As the artillery officers fretted and fumed, Nawab Singh and his mortar crews wondered what all the fuss was about when by just looking at the target they could generally hit it by the second or third round.

Bhup Singh had been nominated for Staff College after the war and Dharam Bhalla had taken over as the 2IC. Subsequently, Dev Raj Dutt had handed over the battalion's command to the officiating CO, Major Vijay Dhruv Verma. The battalion would do two more stints in Bhutan in 1973 and yet again in 1974 and we also hosted visits by IAS and IFS probationers. Most of these probationers were highly motivated and extremely keen to see how the army did things.

In January 1974, Major Verma sprung a surprise on me—I was to go to the Winter Warfare Course at Gulmarg. I protested, for there were many other junior officers available. However, I was curtly told that the CO had selected me. I was not at all happy about being sent at such short notice, for it was bound to affect my performance on the course that had already commenced. However, orders were orders! I reached Gulmarg almost a week late. Our platoon commander was an officer from the Rajput Regiment, Captain NR Naidu, a tough mountaineer who would climb the Khilanmarg slope in the wee hours and ski down to take the report at 0700 in the morning. His method of teaching skiing was to take on the most difficult slope and then order us to ski down. Many of the youngsters would have nasty falls leading to serious injuries. In Captain Naidu's book, those who survived were considered the right material for learning 'military skiing'.

We used archaic wooden skis with fixed bindings. This meant that if you went for a toss, your knee might get detached but the skis wouldn't come off. I learnt the ropes fast and was happy that my performance was good enough to be recommended to attend the Winter Warfare Advanced Course the next season. Just as I returned to the unit in mid-1974, I was posted to the Infantry School in Mhow, to the Platoon Weapons Division, as an instructor. Ever since taking over Bravo Company, I had been wearing the rank of a major, but was now back to being a captain.

My tenure with the Platoon Weapons Division barely lasted a few months, for an officer from the MMG Wing of the BSW course had been cleared to pick up his rank. There being no major's vacancy at the BSW, he was shifted to Platoon Weapons and I got sent to BSW as I had an instructor's grading. Even at that time I felt that the system of grading was somewhat flawed and that we actually needed to have a foolproof system in place. One couldn't help but notice that certain non-essential elements influenced the grading, the two biggest factors being the regimental affiliations of the battalion commanders and the commandant. If a student wore the same regimental badges as the men in charge, the grading seemed to favour the individuals at times. Despite these niggling issues, the Mhow tenures invariably helped to strengthen the regimental bonds at another level.

At the Platoon Weapons Division, I got to serve with Major (later Lieutenant General) Milan Naidu. Extremely soft-spoken, Milan was married to Neeharika, who was the daughter of Lieutenant Colonel B Awasthy who had been killed by the Chinese in 1962 at the Lagyala Gompa. Originally from 2 Rajput, Awasthy was moving to Mathura to take over the unit which had finished its NEFA tour of duty in Walong. Unfortunately, that was not to be. Neeharika was an extremely talented singer and was quite the star at most social gatherings.

▪

In 1975, my father was posted to Bhopal as a re-employed officer in the NCC. I got on to my scooter at night and made the four-hour journey from Mhow and was waiting at the railway station when the train pulled in early in the morning. After touching his feet, I got his baggage offloaded. Then he dropped the bombshell. 'You're fixed,' he said.

'What happened?' I asked.

'We have met the girl. You can now go and see her and decide.' The 'decision' was purely a matter of semantics and we both knew it. He filled me in on the details as we headed off to the place where he was to stay for a few days. After making my father comfortable, I began the journey back to Mhow with the thought that my days in the Bachelor's Colony were numbered.

Matrimony

Bharti's father, Kanwer Vijay Pal Singh, was a well-known lawyer settled in Gurgaon. More than his skills as a lawyer, his passion for hunting wild boar, nilgai, duck and partridge earned him the local sobriquet of shikari, a title that overshadowed everything else. The family was well-known to my mother's brother, Jangbir Singh, who in turn had written to my father suggesting the rishta and the two had gone together to meet the family.

Bharti was still in college. She came over to my mama's house along with her family. We were introduced to each other, and spoke briefly. We then told our respective families that we had no objection to the matrimonial alliance.

2 Rajput had by then moved from Tamulpur to Secunderabad, and Lieutenant Colonel Malik was commanding the battalion. As was the norm, I wrote to him requesting permission to get married. Back in Mhow I was

told that I was 'underage', and could not be allotted married accommodation until I turned 25. At best, I would be given a three-room set in Shangrila which were barracks earmarked for single officers posted to the Infantry School. The wedding was fixed for 25 June 1975, and I decided I'd go with the times and let my hair grow, so I wouldn't look like a typical cropped-hair fauji at least on my wedding day.

Given the scorching temperatures of a north Indian summer, most of the ceremonies were scheduled for the evening, and Bharti was to be 'given away' by her tauji (father's elder brother), a renowned veterinary doctor settled in Bareilly. Her tauji did not have any daughters, while my future father-in-law had four, so he could afford to be magnanimous.

As the evening progressed, there was a lot of tension in the air. The political situation in the country was extremely volatile with Prime Minister Indira Gandhi under pressure from Jayaprakash Narayan (better known as JP). My father-in-law was telling all the guests, many of whom were dabbling in the JP movement, to head for home immediately after dinner as 'something was about to happen' that very night.

Most of the guests were sceptical that anything would happen. As the marriage party left Gurgaon for Bhiwani in the morning, we ran into multiple police cordons. Emergency had been declared at midnight and the police had long lists of those who were anti-Indira or anti-government. Quite a few members of my wedding party found themselves on that list. They were charged under the Maintenance of Internal Security Act (MISA) and asked to disembark from the vehicles. For the next nineteen months, these people would remain under arrest.

The next two days were a whirl of post-wedding ceremonies at the village. Then, according to tradition, I had to accompany Bharti back to her parents' home. As that day drew to a close, my father-in-law produced a bottle of Chivas Regal and ceremoniously invited me to join him for a drink, his evening ritual. My comment that I was allergic to alcohol was met with complete disbelief. 'Nonsense!' he said. 'Alcohol cures allergies, doesn't cause them.' I suspect that my father-in-law thought I was being courteous. I was later to discover that Brigadier Kataria, a close friend of Bharti's family who was visiting his son, also posted in Mhow, had provided intelligence about my intoxicated look during Holi celebrations, which had included pakoras laced with bhang.

My protests were brushed aside and the drinks were poured out. True to form, within minutes I had an allergic reaction. The rest of the evening was spent trying to cure me. The next morning, Kanwer Vijay Pal Singh solemnly declared that he would never ask me to have a drink with him again.

In July, it was time to return to Mhow. By then, the Emergency was in full swing, and people were terrified of being arrested for any transgression. It was almost uncanny and unnatural—municipality workers were working, government staff was actually going to office on time and people were following rules! This state of affairs would last for a few months, before things again drifted back to normal. Just how terrified people were is best illustrated by the behaviour of a ticket collector as we boarded the Chetak Express that would take us directly to Mhow from Delhi on its way to Chittorgarh. My railway warrant was for the main route from Delhi to Ratlam, where in the early hours of the morning one had to change from the broad gauge to the metre gauge track.

I handed over my ticket and asked the official to let me know what the balance charges were, which I would pay in cash. Three hours later, with no sign of the official, I went looking for him. I found him poring over route charts, furiously working out the exact amount that I had to pay. Four rupees, he finally declared, adding that he had to be sure he was not making an error in calculations, fearing arrest. Amidst all the horror stories associated with the Emergency, this was the flip side that showed that things could be done in the country if the people were willing to implement them.

At Mhow, we were met by a large band of officers from both the Platoon Weapons Wing and the BSW. They had got a commercial wedding band and a horse-drawn tonga to take us to our new quarters in the Shangrila. Much to everybody's delight, we clip-clopped our way through Mhow, and Bharti got her first real taste of life in the army. Prabhod Bhardwaj's wife Deepa had done up the three rooms to look like home and even got all the rations and provisions stocked. Bharti was even more amazed at the spate of lunch and dinner invitations, which ensured that we were eating out most of the time. It was only after a few days that she would take stock of the kitchen and start cooking herself.

As was the existing norm, during the break between courses, all instructors headed for Goa. Married couples, bachelors and even the commandant's son and daughter, set off from Mhow for Pune where we were to stay at the College of Mechanical Engineering for the night. A visit to Khadakwasla the next morning was mandatory and Bharti got to visit the National Defence Academy for the first time. We then proceeded south to Belgaum via Kolhapur before cutting west through the Western Ghats, descending into the sun-soaked beaches of South Goa. We spent a week exploring the region, our base being Calangute, where we stayed in quaint little huts on the beach. In those days, South Goa was sparsely populated, with Calangute being the major attraction for western tourists.

The return journey was equally fascinating, as we followed the coastal route that took us through the Konkan region. Moving north, we made our way back to Pune via Ratnagiri, driving through the backyard of the great Maratha warrior, Chhatrapati Shivaji.

Later that year my father decided to visit us during Diwali, mainly to ascertain how we were coping with matrimony. Prior to his arrival, everything was spruced up and I received him at Indore railway station and escorted him to our modest digs. I had asked for a few days' leave, which was turned down on the grounds that I had been shortlisted for an overseas assignment: I had been selected to go to Fort Benning to attend the United States Army's Ranger Course. So I had to go into overdrive to get everything ready before I left.

To kit myself out appropriately, I headed to Balchand's in Mhow market. Known for his tailoring skills throughout the army establishment, the old man welcomed me with his customary smile. I told him I needed a suit stitched, ready and delivered to me the next morning.

'Aap ko aapka suit kal subah mil jayega,' (You will get your suit in the morning tomorrow) said the unflappable Balchand and proceeded to take my measurements.

At six in the morning, the suit was delivered to me and, needless to say, it was a perfect fit. The tailors of Mhow were in a class of their own. Some specialized in regimental uniforms, others in blue patrols. They rarely let anyone down and virtually clothed the entire officer cadre of the Indian Army.

I then went to Delhi which was a madhouse as I had only three-and-a-half days to get everything sorted out before catching the flight. 'Go! No go!' This Ranger terminology had its own connotation. Between Army HQ and the Ministry of Defence, the complete lack of cohesion kept everybody on tenterhooks. This was to be my first taste of what civil-military relations really meant! While running around for the passport and the various medical requirements, there were permissions and sanctions to be sought from the ministry. For some dastardly reason (and to a certain extent it continues to this day), these sanctions are always given at the very last minute. True to form, the civilian staff officer attached to MT-1 (Military Training), which was handling the case, had to run from office to office, getting the final sanction just a few hours before I was to board the flight. Despite the fact that most names are cleared for courses and delegations days in advance, bureaucrats always ensure that the sanctions are given only at the last minute. Military bureaucracy is no better, but in this case, the civilian bureaucracy has, for some perverse reason, resisted all attempts to change.

Bharti was to stay with her parents in Gurgaon while I was away for the next three months. Also earmarked for the course with me was Captain (later Major General) Manvender Singh Rathore from the Rajputana Rifles. He had just got married to Ranjana a month earlier. After hurried goodbyes, we boarded a Pan Am flight and took off from Palam early one morning sometime in mid-November. After a brief stopover in London, we flew to Washington DC, from where we took a connecting flight to Columbus, Georgia. We were met at the airport by a representative of the US Army and driven to Fort Benning where we got our first shock; someone in Delhi had mixed up the dates and the Ranger Course we had been earmarked for had already started.

There was nothing to be done but wait for the next course which was to start in three weeks. This was probably a blessing in disguise, for in a matter of four days we had been transported from the comfortable tropical climes of Mhow and Delhi to the bitter cold of Georgia. Apart from the weather, it also allowed us to get used to the social changes that included having 'supper' at six in the evening. With the Christmas break fast approaching, we were advised by the Morale and Welfare Department to take a break and visit Disney World in Orlando. There are special subsidized tickets for the armed forces, and we were given precise instructions, down to the last detail, as to where to go and what to do. The US Army then, and even now, takes great pains to look after its men and women.

Fort Benning: The Ranger Course

The sixty-one day combat leadership course oriented towards small unit tactics run by the Ranger School is given the highest possible status by the US Army. The Americans say it is the 'toughest combat course in the world which is by far the most physically and mentally demanding leadership school the Army has to offer'*. The students are drawn entirely from a list

*http://www.rotc.uci.edu/alumni/files/Newsletter04_UCIFirstRanger.pdf

of volunteers and each man has to pass a stringent entrance test. There are absolutely no exceptions—you could be the top honcho from the army, the marines or the navy, or you could be from the royal family of Saudi Arabia, the yardstick was the same for everybody.

Both Manvender and I knew the course would test us to our limits. Added to the physical and mental strain was the fact that the two of us were representing our country. However, with both the NDA and IMA training behind us, followed by the YOs and the combat experience of the Bangladesh War, we were both quite confident that we would survive.

The Assessment Phase was held at Camp Rogers. We set off on a five-mile run with one of the instructors setting the pace, the objective being to complete the stretch within forty minutes. This was followed by timed and numbered push-ups, sit-ups and chin-ups. Both Manvender and I had little trouble getting through this leg, which culminated with the combat water survival test. Here, we were assembled in full combat gear and pushed into a pool. As a significant part of the course would be conducted in the swamps of Florida, it was imperative that candidates did not display any signs of panic under water. We had to unhook our entire equipment and break water without getting flustered.

Having met the basic qualification standards, training at the Ranger School began in right earnest at Camp Rogers and Camp Darby, both part of the Benning Phase. Assigned to the Whiskey Company of the 75th Rangers Battalion, one couldn't help but wonder how many of us would actually finish the course. At another level, it was as if the clock had been put back and we were back at the NDA, with all the emphasis on blind physical obedience. With a feeling of déjà vu, I lined up for my US Army regulation haircut, which was rather an all-out attack.

'My name is Singh,' I said to Ranger Sergeant Peabody. 'It's against my religion to remove all my hair.'

The supervising NCOs all went into a huddle. I need hardly have bothered—the barber was allowed to leave half a millimetre of hair on my scalp. After that, it was: 'Hey, you hippie, give me a few more push-ups' and 'Hey, hippie, go do another extra mile'. I learnt my lesson fast; never draw attention to yourself if you could avoid it. The first week was the break in period where we were not allowed to walk but had to run for everything. To enter any barrack or dining facility, one had to do pull-ups, chin-ups and all sorts of physical tasks that reminded me of the first couple of terms at NDA a decade earlier. Each day would begin at 0230 hours, for we had to prepare for the first round of physical training that began at 0400 hours. With whatever little sleep that our exhausted bodies could muster, we had to not only get ready but make sure our beds were made, the toilets cleaned and the barracks were spic and span. For the next one hour we would be put through the paces—starting with the ritual of 'breaking the ice'—literally, as we had to smash the frozen sheet of water on the ground before spilling out into the training area. The bitter cold would soon be forgotten as we ran, crawled, jumped and slithered up and down ropes, ending with group runs that got longer and longer.

Filthy and dirty, it was back to the barracks. What followed can, at best, be described as a 'hose down' that included a washing of the clothes we were wearing. Within half an hour, the 'laundry' would be frozen solid. After a standing breakfast, the rest of the day would unfold at an equally dizzy pace. The emphasis at this stage was on the execution of Squad Combat Operations, which included instruction on troop leading procedures, principles of patrolling, demolitions, field craft, and basic battle drills focused on squad ambush and reconnaissance missions. We received instruction on airborne/air assault operations, demolitions, environmental and field craft training. We had to execute the infamous Darby Queen obstacle course, and learn the fundamentals of patrolling, warning and operations orders, and communications. The fundamentals of combat operations included battle drills—react to contact, break contact, react to ambush, platoon raid—which were focused on providing the principles and techniques that enable the squad-level element to successfully conduct reconnaissance and raid missions. It was, to put it very mildly, interesting.

One activity would blend into the other, and by sundown the body had had enough. Just then the NCOs would barge into the barracks and inspect the weapons, the beds, the toilets, anything they could think of. Sure enough, without fail, they would spot a tiny speck of dust, or a drop of oil and the entire squad had to move into the night for unarmed combat or crawl through the 'worm pit' which was nothing but freezing slush and mud under low strung barbed wire. The only way through it was either on your belly or on your back. Throw in the guard duties and the other routine tasks, and we rarely hit the sack before midnight.

The three weeks of the Benning Phase also included jumps from both fixed-wing aircraft and helicopters. Fort Benning's parachute training towers, visible for miles around, are a landmark of sorts, and soon, both Manvender and I were being taught how to land, roll on impact and the other rudiments of jumping. The US Army had written to Army HQ seeking permission to put us through this training, as our paperwork revealed that this had not been signed off. We were well on our way to getting our parachute wings when a signal from Delhi finally arrived denying permission on the grounds that we were infantry officers; not qualified to jump from planes.

Navigation and jungle training were two important aspects at Benning. This was one of the toughest assignments, for it involved both day and night navigation with the use of maps and compass. My successful foray behind enemy lines during the Bangladesh War once again gave me the added confidence to successfully tackle this leg of the training. The use of any lights to navigate terrain at night meant immediate dismissal. Any student, once declared 'no go' had to pack up and leave the course immediately and could never again apply to the school.

The grand finale of the Benning Phase was the water confidence test. This was similar to what we had done during YO training at Mhow, and I was confident that I would make it to the second phase. This phase consisted of three events which tested the student's ability to overcome fear of heights and water. We had to calmly walk across a log suspended thirty-five feet above a pond, then do a rope crawl before plunging into the water. Each student had to ditch his rifle and load-bearing equipment while submerged. Here onwards, the script changed from the event at Mhow, for we had to once again climb a ladder to the top of a seventy-foot tower and traverse down to the water on a pulley attached to a suspended cable, subsequently plunging into the pond at a given signal. This test was to be a watershed of sorts, for quite a few candidates were eliminated at this stage and unceremoniously dropped from the course. For those of us who survived, we had gained tremendously in tactical and technical proficiency and also confidence in ourselves. We now prepared to move to the next phase of the course: the Mountain Phase.

The most awesome aspect of the Ranger School was the limitless resources available to the US Army, and by extension, to the students. Everything and anything was at our disposal—weapon systems, ammunition, helicopters, dog-units. We just had to ask for it and it was there, the only catch being you had to carry the equipment around yourself. The realism was what made it special—every aspect of the course was a physical exercise, nothing was left at the theoretical level.

I had done some basic mountaineering training at the Himalayan Mountaineering Institute when I was in school, and had later operated with

2 Rajput and the Bhutan Army in eastern Bhutan in the dead of winter. The winter warfare stint now became an added bonus. To some extent, my earlier experiences gave me some idea of what to expect at Camp Merrill, which was in Dahlonega, a remote mountainous region within the state of Georgia. Fort Benning had been cold, but conditions here were much worse, the temperatures even lower. Almost instantly, we swung into action, learning the basics of mountaineering. This included learning knots, belays, anchor points, rope management, mobility evacuation, and the fundamentals of climbing and abseiling. Within a few days, we were confident that any of us could negotiate just about any mountain or traverse across any rock face. The training ended in a two-day mountaineering exercise at Yonah Mountain, and each student had to successfully complete all the prescribed activities to continue in the course.

Combat stimulation during this phase was even more realistic than before, with the 5th Ranger Training Battalion conducting the training. Time of day had little or no relevance; we would get orders to move at any point in the day or night. The squad would grab its gear and dash for the waiting helicopters which would drop us off at the designated zones. During this period, the stamina and commitment of the students was stretched to the maximum. To quote from the Ranger Manual, 'The rugged terrain, severe weather, hunger, mental and physical fatigue, and the psychological stress the student encounters allows him to measure his capabilities and limitations and those of his fellow soldiers.'

These missions included moving cross-country over mountains, vehicle ambushes, raiding communications and mortar sites, river crossings, and scaling steeply sloped mountainous terrain. We reached our objective in several ways: cross-country movement, parachuting into small drop zones, air assaults into small mountain-side landing zones, or a ten-mile march across the Tennessee Valley Divide. There were two more confidence tests during this phase: the first was a 240-foot rappel in the night. A moonless night is deliberately chosen and halfway down the cliff, in pitch darkness, you feel you're going nowhere at all. Far away in the distance, we could see some lights twinkling, but that was about all. The second test involved a slide and a winch that hurtles you towards a lake. The Ranger NCO brings down a flag and you're supposed to let go and plunge into the water. With correctly positioned feet, one could skim over the surface before hitting the water.

The next phase was in Florida. While the rest parachuted on to the airbase, a few of us 'non-airborne students' made a docile landing in C-130 aircraft after the others had captured and secured the airfield. The pre-course gen was that the moment we landed at Eglin Air Force Base in Florida for the third and final phase, we would be taken prisoner. But this didn't happen and instead we were plunged into basic boat training without any preamble. We were taught the basics of watermanship as a prelude to the twelve-day exercise which would be conducted in the swamps of Florida. This continued through the next morning, after which we hauled our exhausted selves on to trucks that would transport us to Camp Rudder where we were told we'd get a hot meal and could prepare ourselves for the main task ahead. Most of us were dozing when all hell broke loose. We were ambushed and taken prisoner by Russian-speaking soldiers.

This simulated exercise, called Survival, Escape, Evasion and Resistance (SEER, for short) is about as bad as it gets. Soldiers are subjected to it only once in a lifetime and the only thing that gets one through the POW inoculation is the knowledge that sooner or later the exercise will end. We were rounded up, bags put over our heads, our hands tied and we were thrust like animal carcasses into trucks. We were taken to a place where we were made to strip down, further abused and made to do all sorts of tasks. This was followed by interrogation sessions. The captors were quite brutal: kicking, punching and throwing us around in addition to the usual tricks of the trade. With our experience of the NDA, we brought into play some tricks of our own as well: once thrown, it made sense to writhe around in pain and stay down for those few extra seconds.

After a while it seemingly ends and your captives give you the good cop/bad cop treatment, suddenly offering you chocolates and other goodies while trying to get the same information out of you. Finally, we were all lined up and given some greenish slop to eat. Some of us managed to avoid eating the concoction, but those who did were violently sick. Eventually, the POW inoculation ended and we were put into trucks and moved to another camp where we were debriefed and then finally allowed to get some sleep. None of us had any idea where we were, which further added to the feeling of complete isolation.

The next day, the twelve-day exercise started. In those days, they had K-rations (daily combat food ration) that would sustain us for this period, but to our surprise, we realized we could carry food for only six days. There would be a resupply by helicopters at a designated point after six days, but one had to be prepared for contingencies. Throughout the exercise we were up against an 'aggressor force' that played the enemy, and God help those who got caught (we had already experienced being POWs and wanted to avoid repeating the experience).

We were ferried to mother ships from where we were transferred to LSTs (landing ship tanks), before switching to small rubber dinghies and then being rowed to shore. It was still extremely cold, the temperatures in Florida being only marginally higher than the mountains of Georgia. The water was freezing, and we were usually in chest deep. We would navigate our boats through the swamp, and then hide them. After hitting the targets, we would double back, recover the boats and move on to the next task.

The swamps were full of hidden threats, the worst being the alligators. We were moving through the swamp on the second day when suddenly there was an upward thrust and the entire section of ten men found itself in the water. Instinctively, we swam for the second boat but were stopped by Sergeant Browne on board.

'Get the hell back to your own boat,' he hissed, refusing to take any of us aboard. Swimming back, the dinghy was re-inverted and we clambered on. Two of the four tubes had been slashed and we were taking water, though fortunately, most of the equipment was still stashed away securely. The oars were gone, so we improvised and moved on to our next target, constantly bailing out water. After completing the task, the dinghy was repaired and we continued with it for the rest of the exercise.

On the third or fourth day, the Ranger officer who was with my squad said to me: 'Singh, you sure are smoking it out!'

Wondering what was coming my way, I was a little startled. 'I don't smoke, sir,' I replied. This brought the house down, for all members of my squad, including the sergeant, burst out laughing. I learnt later that 'smoking it out' was the term used for students who were doing well and setting the pace.

Most of the American students with us were not used to the deprivation we were being subject to and they all lost a tremendous amount of weight. I was quite happy to exchange the beef tins in my K-rations for 'pound cake' tins.

And then the course was over! We were given a day off, and flown back to Fort Benning. The graduation ceremony was held on a bleak day with a heavy drizzle. Everything was done on the run, and the reviewing officer joked that he was extremely thrilled at the fact that we had perfect 'Ranger weather'. The course had started with little more than three hundred students; only ninety had made the final cut. Along with an American officer,

I was graded an 'honour graduate' which meant that we had been graded at 80 per cent or more. We were the first to have our Ranger badges pinned on to our shoulders and, to top it off, I was awarded the class flag of Whiskey Company, 75 Ranger Battalion, by my peers as a keepsake. It was a singular honour.

Belgaum: Commando School

I returned to India via Washington and reported to the MT Directorate where we were debriefed. I had put in just over a year-and-a-half in Battalion Support Weapons and it was now decided to post me to the Commando Wing in Belgaum. All the three legs of the YOs course had initially been held in Mhow. After a couple of years, the YOs Wing had been shifted to Belgaum. The new establishment in Belgaum was placed under the Junior Leaders (JL) Wing and its scope was expanded over the years to include other courses for other ranks as well. Overall, the JL Wing continued to remain a part of the Infantry School, and the YOs being mandatory for all infantry officers, it meant all young officers had to go through the final thirty-odd days in Belgaum.

Bharti and I returned to Mhow where we packed our belongings into large wooden boxes that are a trademark of all army homes, loaded all our baggage on to a railway wagon and set off for our new destination. When we reached Belgaum, we found one of the boxes had been tampered with. It had a strange-looking lock that had to be broken open. To Bharti's horror, her entire collection of expensive sarees and accessories had been stolen. She was heartbroken and, to make matters worse, there was so much paperwork involved in filing a complaint that after a while it wasn't worth pursuing the matter.

We quickly settled into our regular routine. We were allotted a small apartment in a three-storied building called Jesse Mansion. Officers posted to the Commando Wing occupied all six flats in the building and we soon had a happy little social group of our own.

Belgaum is located close to the Western Ghats and the varied terrain with vast jungles combined with year-long good weather made it an important training locale even during British times. The Maratha LI (light infantry) Regimental Centre also being located in the city provided a distinct advantage. Brigadier Harbhajan Singh commanded the JL Wing while the Commando

Wing was the responsibility of Colonel PR Limaye who had done the Special Forces Course with the US Army.

Our Commando Course could be considered to be the equivalent of the US Army's Ranger Course, but with some major differences. First and foremost was the fact that the Ranger Course was voluntary while our Commando Course was mandatory for all infantry officers.

The second aspect was the philosophy behind both the courses: while the US Army prided itself on setting the bar at a level where they looked for reasons to disqualify a soldier-student, in the Indian Army, the establishment was terrified of failure, doing its best to make sure every young officer somehow got across the finish line. On the ground, this would play out in different ways. Let us take the example of a speed march that is common to both the courses. In Ranger's, we would walk as a squad, with rifles held out in front at the ready. The instructor, whose sole aim was to make sure some of the people failed to complete the exercise, would set the pace for the squad. So he would constantly vary his pace, making sure that no one blindly got into a rhythm. The norm was that you had to stay a step behind the Ranger in front. If anyone fell back even by a fraction, he would be given two warnings and then would be abruptly pulled out and that was that—it was ruthless!

In our own set-up, if we 'failed' a student, we knew there would be hell to pay with even Army HQ jumping into the fray. So in the speed march, the instructor would set the rhythm and lay out the guidelines at the outset: how many kilometres, at what pace, when to rest. The emphasis here was on the individual. This was wrong, for individuals don't fight wars, squads do. Eventually, it is all about teamwork—platoon level, company or battalion. The weak links, unless weeded out, will inevitably bring down the rest.

Third, in the case of the Americans, the emphasis was on realism, with combat conditions being created during virtually every sixty seconds of distance run. We, on the other hand, were administratively driven. As a result, we were far more liberal. We would ensure that an administrative vehicle would come at the right time during every exercise and people would be given a hot meal. Though our longest speed march is forty kilometres as against the US Army's maximum of thirty-two kilometres, our system lends itself to a certain amount of pampering—bringing the soldiers breakfast the next morning, allowing for massages, or simply letting the students sleep it off. The pressure that had been built up would dissipate, unlike in the Ranger Course where it was relentless.

The establishment would be very happy, claiming we had made the boys do forty kilometres, and on the charts another hurdle would be ticked off. The science behind each activity was unfortunately missing in our system. And the establishment didn't, and doesn't, take well to suggestions which might disturb the status quo.

We had a good bunch of instructors at Belgaum. Among the captains there was Subir Ahluwalia, who took premature retirement as a colonel; RM Barua from J&K RIF whose unit later converted to Mechanized Infantry; Narender Singh from Rajputana Rifles; Mohan Nikam and Mohinder Singh, both from the Mahar Regiment; Jasbir Singh from the Dogra Regiment; and, last but not least, Chandagi Ram from Sikh LI (who was my group commander for some time). An outstanding individual, he was also extremely fit. Whenever there was a shortage of instructors, he would be the first to volunteer, even if it was a speed march.

The Commando Wing being the last leg of YOs, the system by and large had a firm grip on the youngsters who were aware it was make or break time. We rarely had trouble, but every now and then a student would try to manipulate the system. Major General Shabegh Singh was commanding the ATK&K (Andhra Pradesh, Tamil Nadu, Karnataka and Kerala) area. The general had been one of the acknowledged driving forces behind the Mukti Bahini during the Bangladesh War—he commanded a sector on the eastern side and trained the Mukti Bahini in the art of combat. His son, doing the YOs, was in my group, and I was doing his fortnightly review. In the previous two legs, the officer had been given extremely high grades. Judging by his performance at Commando, I suspected he was being rated more on the basis of whose son he was rather than on merit.

'You better pull up your socks,' I concluded my review.

Deadpan, Papa's Boy said, 'I'm expecting an instructor grading. My father is the area commander.' I felt my temper rising—I wasn't even sure if he would make the grade, and this youngster was telling me blatantly he wanted the top-notch grading.

I told him to get the hell out of my office, wishing I had the authority to sack the officer then and there. Feeling physically sick, I almost wished he would complain to his papa, so I could be sent back to the unit. Unfortunately, the matter didn't end there.

The forty kilometre forced march was up next. Papa's Boy, along with another couple of accomplices, decided to get ahead of the competition. They arranged for a school bus to be stationed near a village, in one of the by-lanes along the main route. After going hell for leather initially, they slipped away to where the vehicle was parked. At this stage, fate intervened, for try as they might, the bus just wouldn't start. After an hour-and-a-half of futile pushing, they had to come back on to the main track and just sit down there. That fortunately put paid to the instructor grading, though the establishment didn't have the guts to fail him altogether.

▪

I was about to become a father! Bharti was expecting our first baby by the time we moved to Belgaum. As she prepared for motherhood, her maternal instincts began to kick in and she was constantly fussing over the young officers who she felt were being flogged to death, for she saw them constantly on the run. Given half a chance she would get together a small group, especially regimental officers, and lavish goodies on them. This would make me mad as hell, but she would simply ignore my protests.

The baby was due around Christmas. The anticipated arrival was still some time away and, as was our wont, we were driving everywhere on my scooter. Somewhere along the line, I forgot to be cautious and rode roughly over a speed breaker. The resultant jump created a problem and I had to rush my outraged wife to the civilian gynaecologist who was looking after her during her term. The doctor advised Bharti be taken to the Army Hospital, so I took her there and admitted her for the night. Making sure she was comfortable, I went home for the night.

The next morning I called to check if all was well. I was informed by the voice at the other end that I had become a father, and that both mother and daughter were doing fine. It was 2 December and the baby had arrived almost three weeks early. I was ecstatic, for I had always wanted a daughter. I raced to the hospital, virtually flying over the speed bumps that are a hallmark of all army establishments. We had already decided that should the child be a girl, we would name her Mrinalini, taking inspiration from the fact that Rabindranath Tagore chose to call his wife by that name after they were married. The word itself meant a bouquet of lotus flowers.

The demo company at the JL Wing used to be a Rajput Company. As was the custom, I had a large basket of laddoos sent across to the men. Soon enough, I was being asked, 'Kya hua saab?'(What happened?)

'Ladki hui,' I announced proudly. The men would mostly look astounded: 'Ladki hui aur aap laddoo baant rahen hai?' (You've had a baby girl and you're celebrating?) I couldn't care less what others thought or believed as that was their problem; I had got what I wanted and there wasn't a happier man who walked the planet.

Mrinalini's early arrival threw all our well-laid plans for the delivery out of the window. Both our parents had been planning to be around for the arrival of their grandchild, but now there was no point in their coming immediately. It was decided that after forty days, when the baby was fit enough to travel, Bharti and the baby would go to Gurgaon to visit her parents. I was also studying for the mandatory Part D exam, and although it was a chaotic period as we struggled to cope with the responsibilities of parenthood, it eventually worked itself out. The baby would stay awake the entire night, a habit that suited me fine, as it allowed me to study; but the flip side was that during the day I was a walking zombie as I went about taking classes for the course.

5

A DIFFERENT WORLD

The Revolving Door

Having completed my three years—Platoon Weapons, Battalion Support Weapons and JL Wing combined—I was posted back to 2 Rajput in Secunderabad in mid-1977. For Bharti, it was to be her first experience of life in the battalion. With Mrinalini, we moved into a single room in the officer's mess.

The next few days, the aabdar (barman), an NCE (Non-Combatant Enrolment), took charge of Bharti and marched her off to the mess. Painstakingly, he went over every bit of silver and other assets of the battalion, until she could rattle off in her sleep the history and importance of each item.

Having been away from the battalion for a fairly long period, I was looking forward to spending time with the men. Now I also had the seniority to command a company. The unit still had nearly seven to eight months left of its three-year peace tenure in Secunderabad, after which we would almost certainly move either to Jammu and Kashmir or go back to field deployment in the Northeast. Either way, it would almost certainly result in an enforced separation from my wife and the rapidly-growing Mrinalini, who was beginning to sit up without support.

Barely ten days had passed since we moved when the adjutant, Avinash Kapila, in his cheerful tone told me I was to pack my bags again and move to Mhow. 'You're going for the Junior Command Course,' he said, 'your name is on the list.'

The three-month Junior Command (JC) Course conducted under the auspices of the College of Combat was considered to be a major step as a career course in the army. All officers were expected to prepare fairly extensively for it. Not only had it not been anywhere on my radar, it put all my immediate plans into a tailspin. 'Course starts in a week, so you better get moving,' was the adjutant's helpful suggestion.

Leaving Bharti behind in the unit for three months to cope on her own in relatively unfamiliar surroundings, her knowledge of the mess silver notwithstanding, was not really an option. She had already done the parents and in-laws circuit with the new baby only a few months before, so we were not too keen on going down that road either. Hence, less than a month after leaving Belgaum, we were back in Mhow, bag and baggage.

There had barely been any time before we moved, but I had written to a friend to help arrange accommodation. Another crisis now loomed, for I was still nominally on the rolls of the Infantry School as a part of the JL Wing and could not, therefore, be allotted accommodation. I went and met the AQ, Infantry School, who then gave me a single room in the bachelor's barracks in Dhobi Ghat Lines for the family.

I had also been allotted a single room on the college premises and was to stay there. Unprepared as I was, the domestic chaos was only adding to my woes. There was nothing to be done but grin and bear it. The joke amongst my friends during the first few days of JC was 'With half the VK here, and half the VK there, what can the poor VK do?'

A week or so later the confusion was sorted out, but only just. We were shifted to a new house that was a part of the Tent Replacement Scheme. Despite its ominous sounding name, my new home was reasonably comfortable with a bedroom, drawing room, dining area and kitchenette.

Accommodation sorted, I could now get down to the business of training. We had some first-class instructors: Pankaj Joshi, who went on to be a three-star general and retired as the Chief of Integrated Defence Staff to the Chairman, Chiefs of Staff Committee (CISC); and Trigunesh Mukherjee, who had been the G3 in 83 Brigade during the Bangladesh War. Mukherjee eventually retired as a brigadier and continues to distinguish himself through his writing and lecturing. Others included Arjun Katoch from 1 Para who retired as a colonel and later served with the United Nations.

The course taught us a lot: starting from the basics to the more complex relations and functioning pertaining to company, battalion and brigade level operations. We would discuss realistic situations on the ground and go over various possible scenarios that evaluated various doctrines and concepts pertaining to tactics and logistics.

With most students—among whom were quite a few coursemates—fully prepared, I had to put in a fair amount of extra work. Fortunately, the eighty-nine days were so structured that the course allowed the unprepared stragglers to come up to par with the rest of the group.

Despite the intense study, this was a happy time. We had a male spitz at home who was somewhat regally named Caesar. Unfortunately, we soon discovered that Caesar was stone deaf! I would return home each day and would immediately set off to search for the dog who would invariably be missing in action. There was no point whistling or shouting, for one had to establish eye contact to bring him home. A gurgling Mrinalini further added to our happiness as she took her first steps and learnt how to walk. Evenings were exclusively reserved for her walks.

Despite my slow start, I got an A-I grading which was extremely satisfying. It was the best I could have done. With JC behind us, we returned to 2 Rajput in Secunderabad in time for Mrinalini's first birthday. Lieutenant Colonel Malik was still commanding the battalion. I was delighted when I was given command of a company, and I now looked forward to finally getting some uninterrupted time with the men.

▪

Within days, as a part of 54 Division, we were told to move to the Nagarjuna Sagar's left bank canal for a divisional exercise that involved crossing the water obstacle. The other two battalions in our brigade group were 18 Maratha LI—commanded by Lieutenant Colonel Vijai Oberoi, an extremely competent officer, who later rose to the rank of lieutenant general and retired as the Vice Chief of Army Staff—and 28 Madras under the command of another fine officer, Lieutenant Colonel Shanti Swarup.

Major General Ashoke Handoo, a Guardsman, was the GOC of the division. A flamboyant officer who later rose to a three-star rank and retired as an army commander, he was a hard taskmaster. The brigade commander was Brigadier S Tiwari from the Dogra Regiment and we officers were aghast to see the brigadier running around with us in full battle-kit. The battalion had moved from its launch pad through swampy terrain and was tasked with a canal crossing: the drill perfected was for two swimmers to cross with ropes which would then be used by the rest of the troops to get across with all their equipment. The general, however, was not happy with this. He wanted the water crossing to be done with all troops swimming across with their full complement of equipment. Accordingly, two of our boys from Charlie Company, which was the lead company, both outstanding swimmers, led the way into the water. Two strokes and they were gone, sucked under by a powerful current. The tragic turn of events left the unit stunned. What compounded the tragedy was the fact that it was all so unnecessary. As the shocked battalion proceeded with the exercise, the water was stopped and the bodies recovered after a couple of days. There was a court of inquiry subsequently and I feel matters were covered up.

Back in Secunderabad, I was in for yet another rude shock. Hardly had we returned from the exercise, I was called in by Avinash Kapila. 'You're off again,' he looked at me wryly, obviously convinced I was pulling strings to stay away from the battalion. 'Winter Warfare Advanced Course in Gulmarg.'

'I don't want to go for a course I should have gone for immediately after my basic course.' I could hardly believe my bad luck. The army was determined to train and drill me till I dropped. I had been with the unit now for barely two months.

'You've been detailed. We tried our best to get the orders revoked but they have not been cancelled,' he said with the resigned air of a harbinger of bad news. 'An order is an order. Now go get packed!'

I groaned inwardly. Ever since I had got the Dagger in the YOs, I felt I was looking at life through a revolving door, being shot off to training establishments at the drop of a hat, either to participate in a course or do tenures as an instructor. Doing well was beginning to feel like an albatross around my neck. The way things were progressing, I felt I would soon be the poster boy for training establishments. All I wanted was to spend some time soldiering with the men. And that just wasn't being allowed!

The High Altitude Warfare School (HAWS) runs the six-week Winter Warfare advanced segment. In our batch, there were seven officers, with the remaining being NCOs. The purpose of the advanced course was to groom us to become instructors, but I had no desire to get pulled into the mountaineering stream especially after having completed a three-year tenure that culminated with the Commando Wing. Fortunately, most of my instructors at HAWS were junior to me, so the first thing I did was to tell them not to give me an A I rating.

I had done the basic course four years ago when the battalion had been deployed in Bhutan. The immediate challenge now was to relearn the basic skiing skills that I had mastered then, particularly as most of the others in the batch were more adept mountaineers, given that they had done the basic course more recently.

Narinder 'Bull' Kumar was the head honcho at HAWS. He was a renowned mountaineer, having been a part of the first Indian Army expedition that had placed Major HPS Ahluwalia atop Everest in 1965.

His mountaineering and exploratory exploits, especially in the Karakoram region, were legendary, even though he was yet to venture on to the Siachen Glacier. And he almost didn't get there. For, during our course at HAWS, he almost got asphyxiated when he fell asleep in a closed cabin with a coal-lit bukhari. Rescued in the nick of time and none the worse for it, he then proceeded to cheerfully find additional ways to bump us off!

The best ski slopes were the extended runs from Jamia Wali Gali to the Loran Mandi area. However, giving credence to the fact that military intelligence is indeed an oxymoron, it was decided that the advanced course group should traverse the area between Gulmarg and Yusmarg. With the skis strapped to our backs, we climbed seemingly endlessly, virtually making a trail that led us through Pajan Pathri, Tosha Maidan, Raiyar and Kachhwar. To make matters worse, two of our group—Venu Gopal and Anil Malik—obviously under the mistaken notion that we were actually going to be skiing, had outfitted themselves with ski boots from the local civil outfitters. These moulded boots were absolutely useless for walking, and Gopal and Malik both developed frostbite! It was a nightmare rotating the ski boots amongst ourselves over the next eight days. Fortunately, the damage was contained and we even managed to do a bit of skiing towards the end.

Back in Secunderabad, towards the end of April 1978, there had been a change of command. Shailu Verma had taken over from Malik, and the unit was now headed for Poonch, which lay south of Gulmarg along the LOC, separated from the Kashmir Valley by the Haji Pir Pass. This meant we, as a part of 93 Brigade, would be holding the northernmost corner of 25 Division whose area extended from Naushera and Rajouri to Poonch on the Jammu axis. My excitement was two-fold: this would be my first tenure on the LOC and my first real stint as a company commander. I was looking forward to the move with a heightened sense of anticipation. But it meant that Bharti, with Mrinalini, would again have to move to Chandigarh to live with her parents since Poonch was a field area.

Three months prior to a battalion's scheduled move, an advance party of three to four officers is sent to the new location. Dharam Pal Kukrety, who was roughly of the same seniority as the new CO, was given charge of the advance party with two company commanders: Tom Mathews and myself.

Sometime towards the end of June, we reached Jammu where we were to establish our rear. Tom was preparing for his Staff College examination that required a lot of study. It had been decided that he would stay on in Jammu, while Kukrety and I started on the long road journey to Poonch.

Operation Pooching

As the road from Jammu heads into the hills, the terrain begins to change rapidly, with the plains of Punjab giving way to pine-clad hills. The advance party crossed the Chenab at Akhnoor, north of which the international boundary with Pakistan becomes the Line of Control. Driving parallel to the LOC which was to our west, we approached Naushera and Rajouri before halting at a transit camp at Narian near Bhimbar Gali where we spent the night.

Once all the men were settled, I sat outside my transit room and looked at the silhouette of the surrounding hills, drinking in the darkness. My mind drifted back to my village, Bapora, picturing my uncles living proud lives in the knowledge that they had served their country in trying circumstances. Two of my father's elder brothers, Honorary Lieutenant Devi Singh and Honorary Captain Ranjit Singh, had fought over this terrain in 1947-1948 as a part of 1 Rajput, inch by inch clearing out the entrenched tribal lashkars who were supported by the Pakistan Army. Simple souls, I had heard from them minute details of the fighting, and the siege of Naushera, Rajouri and Poonch.

I also thought of Naik Jadunath Singh who had been awarded the Param Vir Chakra at Naushera—he was the highest decorated soldier in our post-Independence regimental history.

It was a poignant moment, and I wondered what was in store for the battalion. We would be eyeball to eyeball with the Pakistan Army, and the prospect was oddly exciting. As a company commander, this would be my first real test. In the army you are constantly being evaluated: by your seniors, your peers and, more importantly, by the men. I had been looking forward to this for years. I war-gamed a few likely scenarios, attempting to cater to all possible eventualities. I was sure that we were fully prepared for whatever the enemy threw at us. Failure at the LOC was not an option.

I stepped into my room, took off my boots, changed and curled up on my cot. Somewhere in the distance a dog barked. In the adjacent room, Major Dharam Pal Kukrety was fast asleep. His snoring kept me awake for a while, before I too drifted off to sleep.

▪

We got into Poonch where 2 Rajput was to replace 1 JAK Rifles. The Betar Nullah drained the narrow Poonch Valley, running north to south at the base of the slopes on which our defences were situated. The Pakistan Army dominated the heights on the ridge flanking Poonch town. Our battalion position was on the northern fringe and Battalion HQ was at Gulpur. To get there, the nullah had to be forded at night, a tricky business given that it had to be done without any lights to avoid detection.

In Tom Mathews' absence, the painstaking and elaborate task of handing over-taking over fell to Major Kukrety and me. Unfortunately, the moment we entered Poonch, Kukrety seemed to be in a different world, behaving almost as if he wasn't there at all.

Before rejoining the unit in Secunderabad, Kukrety had been with the Army School of Mechanical Transport (ASMT) in Faizabad, Ayodhya. Some incident in the organization had resulted in Kukrety getting extremely upset, after which he had turned up at the quarter guard that was being manned by Garhwali troops. Speaking to them in Garhwali, he took the keys to the armoury and armed himself with a loaded weapon. He then tried to hold the guards as hostages. The resultant chaos only ended when the ASMT commandant, Brigadier Nandal, managed to cajole Kukrety into handing over the weapon and surrendering. Kukrety was arrested, tried and court-martialled. However, Kukrety had appealed to the Allahabad High Court and then the case had graduated to the Supreme Court.

On my return to the battalion in Secunderabad after completing the JC Course, he had called me to his office one day and asked if my father-in-law—who, apart from being a lawyer, was also the deputy speaker in the state assembly—could help him in getting the case resolved in his favour. I told him frankly that I had no clue about legal matters but would speak to Bharti's father. Accordingly I had briefed my father-in-law on the telephone and passed on to him the information that had been given to me by Kukrety. Having done the needful from my end, I had forgotten all about it.

In Poonch, Kukrety asked me again why nothing had happened to his case. All I could say was that my father-in-law had said he would examine the matter and see what could be done. Citing tremendous mental trauma, Kukrety refused to step out of the base, and under the circumstances, I could do nothing about it. I figured it was best to leave him alone with his own preoccupations. At a basic level, I knew the man had some problem. He had displayed his shaky behaviour on quite a few occasions during the

Bangladesh War. I think Kukrety was aware of my opinion of him, and that possibly also influenced subsequent events.

Not only was Major Kukrety's complete lack of interest in the proceedings proving to be a huge embarrassment for the advance party, it had also doubled my work. As the senior officer, he should have received Colonel Bhattacharjee's handing over briefing, and he in turn would have briefed our CO, Shailu Verma, once the main unit arrived. The JAK CO's eyebrows shot up when I arrived to take his briefing. After he finished, he then made me repeat the entire presentation three times to make sure I would miss nothing of critical importance when I passed on the necessary information to my CO.

From the battalion base, it generally took two to three hours to climb to the various posts. This was proving to be a nightmare as I was the only officer available for the task. Not only did I have to take over and understand the intricacies of each position on the LOC, I also had to check out the various linking paths between the positions. There was an upside, though. This exercise allowed me to completely familiarize myself with the battalion and the brigade's AOR by the time the main body fetched up.

It was with a sense of relief that I watched the battalion pull into Gulpur. In the steady drizzle, the slipping and sliding troops and our vehicles crossed the Betar Nullah in the dead of the night. Avinash Kapila was the 2IC and Dharam Pal Kukrety took over Charlie Company. Vijay Pillai (later a three-star) was the adjutant and it felt good to have our entire unit together again. Sharing Gulpur with us was 2/5 GR, which was being commanded by Lieutenant Colonel Chandana. The Gorkha unit was known as the Sarla Battalion while we were the Durga Battalion. These were the two main prominent posts in our respective AORs. I was given Alpha Company to command and Durga became my company location. Fresh out of the IMA, a Manipuri officer, something of a rarity at that time, also reported to the battalion. Konsam Himalaya Singh was to become my company officer at Durga.

From the Motimahal Palace in Poonch, if one looked northwards, on top of the ridge one could see Durga, just below a peak called Pritam. A three-hour steep climb from the base at Gulpur brought us to our post on the LOC. Beyond the ridge, there were spurs heading west, which linked with the Pakistani bunkers. Both sides could easily shout to each other across the pine- and fir-covered forest.

Each company commander was given a manual as thick as a telephone directory. Listed in extensive and minute detail were all sorts of probable situations and the dos and don'ts that were the SOPs. It was regularly emphasized to all and sundry right down the chain of command, that come what may, we were not to deviate from the prescribed actions.

The Pakistan Army obviously had no such restrictions. When any movement became visible to them, they might fire or not depending on their mood at the moment. More often than not, they would fire at random, just for the heck of it. It was much the same story all along the LOC, which extended for hundreds of kilometres on either side of us.

On our side, at least at Durga, there was no Indian civilian movement. The Pakistanis, on the other hand, would regularly follow a routine to mock us. There was one habitual offender who, weather permitting, would appear almost on cue at a given time. We had no option but to follow the laid-down SOPs. As company commander I would shout at the trespasser to draw his attention and blow a whistle three times in the form of a warning. When this was also ignored, I would move on to the next step—which was for the company commander to call the battalion base, seeking permission to fire a warning shot.

A call from the post would have the CO scrambling to the phone. 'Have you shouted and blown the whistle thrice?'

'Yes, sir!'

'Well, do it again!'

So with the CO listening in on the field telephone, we would shout, clap and blow whistles. He would make us do this four to five times.

'Wait on,' he would say, connecting to the brigade. The commander would say to the CO, 'Have you shouted, and blown the whistle thrice?'

'Yes, sir!'

'Well, do it again!' Now the brigade commander and the CO would be patched in and listening. After a while they would say, 'Okay...just wait a minute,' brigade would in all likelihood call the GOC.

By then the Pakistanis would be gurgling with delight. They would regularly shout across, 'Janaab, tumhara to order Dilli se aata hai.' (Your orders have to come from Delhi.) It was all very humiliating.

This went on for a few days. To add further salt to our wounds, the offending Pakistani would deliberately unwrap his lungi and flash us every time we whistled. Then, getting bored, he would cover himself, and sit and sun himself on a large rock. Two to three hours later, he would collect his motley cattle and leave. The length of his stay would determine the length and intensity of our hysterical telephonic tsunami.

At this rate, we were fast losing the battle for moral ascendancy. We decided that enough was enough. A sniper was positioned to zero in on the rock on which the good shepherd would eventually rest. 'Don't kill him,' I briefed the sharpshooter, 'just put a round through his lungi on the rock between his legs.' At the appointed hour the Pakistani appeared. I shouted, blew my whistle. He gave us his vulgar retort. I waited, then shouted, blew the whistle again. The Pakistani played his part perfectly, ignoring all our warnings. This went on for a while, after which he tired of the game and made a beeline for his throne, his legs straddling it like a saddle.

The thwack of the bullet and the resultant g-force generated by a high velocity round hitting the target sent the Pakistani vertically upwards. As the bullet ricocheted off the stone, the retort of the rifle reached him half a second later. By that time, he had already made it across the open ground, running at full tilt. That was the end of it, and we never had that problem at Durga again while we were there.

Nagar Khet was held by a platoon and I spent a few days living there with the men. This was one of the posts that was completely dominated by the enemy. We were tucked into the hill below the Pakistani positions. If they wanted, they could roll stones down and crush us. Langur was another unique post that was held by a neighbouring company. As one climbed up, there would be a series of false crests before reaching the flattish top.

Getting porters to bring fresh supplies was so fraught with danger that at times we just broke off raw wild peaches and made some edible concoctions.

One evening while giving the report to the CO on the telephone, I felt a severe blow to the back of my head. I must have lost consciousness for a few seconds. When I came to, I saw Lieutenant KH Singh sitting in front of me staring at me blankly.

'What the hell did you do?' I asked, incredulous that my own company officer should assault me.

'Sir,' he said, 'you were talking on the phone, then just went quiet,' he said. Lightning had struck the bunker. This was a fairly common phenomenon in the region, but neither of us had ever seen anything like this. Outside my bunker there had been a cut-out, then another inside. The entire telephone line had been charred along with the cut-outs and the telephone instrument. The cut-outs had saved me from being electrocuted.

The battalion slowly settled in at the new location. Shailu Verma visited Alpha Company at Durga. After speaking to the men, he asked me how best to approach the next post. 'Straight down and up,' I said. He thought I had lost my marbles. 'Sir, I go this way every other day. Whichever route we take, they can see us in any case.' If we wanted our men to go out of the posts and patrol the area, we simply had to take the same risks.

To keep the men entertained, one had to come up with all sorts of innovative ideas. One of the most tedious tasks involved going down to the Battalion HQ at Gulpur for any task. It would take two hours to go down, three to come back up. We would time ourselves and try and improve on previous records; those who came in later would serve the winner halwa.

My little world was complete at Durga. I was with my men, and every minute was pure heaven. Life was tough, but I was happy.

Jam Side Down

Shailu Verma, Avinash Kapila and Dharam Pal Kukrety had all been commissioned into 2 Rajput more or less at the same time. The dynamics of their relationship were hence quite different. Kapila was by far the steadiest of the lot, and his moving out of Poonch to take over 16 Rajput probably influenced subsequent events, for with Kapila went any semblance of reason. Kukrety, until then the de facto company commander of Charlie Company, also took over the 2IC's role.

Kapila was still in the unit when I was asked to come down from Durga and meet him at Battalion HQ. After meeting him, I went to have a word with the head clerk on some company documentation issue. He handed me a file with my name stencilled on the cover. Quite naturally, I started reading from the top, working chronologically backwards. Sometime shortly after the main body of the battalion had arrived in Poonch, Army HQ had written to the unit saying I was being shifted to 1 Para Commando. Shailu Verma, without breathing a word of it to me, had written back saying that the officer was unwilling. Army HQ had let the matter rest, but three months later they wrote again saying that I had been shortlisted for an instructor's appointment in IMTRAT (Indian Military Training Team), Bhutan. Again, the CO had written back to Army HQ declining the offer. This time, however, Army HQ wrote back stating that if the offer was being declined, the officer concerned must sign the letter personally.

This was unbelievable, but the evidence was all there in black and white. I started to reread the file but was cut short abruptly. 'CO will see you now.'

I entered, saluted and was asked to sit down. Without any preamble, the CO said, 'I want you to sign the refusal form for IMTRAT. You will get plenty of other opportunities in future. This is not important.'

This was ridiculous. I had obviously made the grade on merit and I was being ordered by my commanding officer to turn it down. If it had not been for Army HQ's insistence, I wouldn't even have known about these machinations behind my back.

The situation was tricky, and we both knew it. Acceptance didn't necessarily mean one would make the final grade. At best, the shortlist would only get narrower, so I could stand my ground with Shailu Verma, run foul with him, and still be at his mercy at the end of it.

'Sir, with due respect, if my name has come up on merit, I would like to give my acceptance.' Shailu Verma looked at me for a lingering second, after which he looked away. He was clearly not happy. I signed the acceptance form for IMTRAT, after which with my two men, I began the ascent back to Durga.

A month or so passed in the humdrum of our daily routine. The Para Commandos and IMTRAT had faded from my memory. I would regularly get letters from Bharti who was in Chandigarh. These invariably chronicled Mrinalini's headlong rush towards toddlerhood. The latest letter, however, was disconcerting as the child was not well. I decided to put in for a week's leave.

Shailu Verma himself was away, and Kukrety was the officiating CO. My leave was promptly sanctioned. Accordingly, I packed a bag for the trip, briefed KH Singh and the company JCO about the dos and don'ts and left for Gulpur, the rear location of the battalion, for the night. After a while, the battalion havildar major showed up with the leave certificate duly signed by OC Rear, Major Anand Verma.

My eyes widened when I saw I had been given ten days leave instead of seven. I went looking for Anand who said he had been told to issue a leave certificate for ten days. When I told him I had only asked for seven days, he telephoned Vijai Pillai, the adjutant, at Battalion HQ.

'I was told ten days,' he pointed out, 'VK says he asked for a week.'

'I had forwarded his leave application to the officiating CO, sir. He must have sanctioned ten days.'

'Can you ask him again? It's not like Uncle Kukrety to be magnanimous.'

'2IC is doing his pooja, sir, so he's not available for a couple of hours.'

It seemed a bit out of character for Kukrety to play Santa Claus but, as they say, it is better not to look a gift horse in the mouth. The standard drill for people proceeding on leave was to get to Jammu, which would take two days due to an overnight halt at Narain. The leave period was clocked once one left the transit camp at Jammu, with the same drill being followed on the return trip. In effect, a week's leave normally would mean being away for eleven days.

Though this was the procedure, most officers did not follow it. We would punch our cards the moment we left Gulpur, catching the much faster civil bus to Jammu, and then onwards. That was my plan too. So, after once again reconfirming the length of my sanctioned leave (and being reassured that I would be informed if it indeed was a clerical error), I crossed the Betar Nullah and, in the early hours of the morning, was on the bus to Jammu from Poonch.

There was no further news from the battalion, so on the tenth day, I reported back to the battalion at Gulpur. After completing the rejoining formalities, I planned on heading back to Durga in the morning. The few days at home had been wonderful, but I was also looking forward to returning to my post.

Within minutes of my arrival, I was handed over a sealed envelope that had been sent by the officiating commanding officer. In it was a formal letter stating that I had reported back on the tenth day, whereas I had been given leave for only seven days. This was unbelievable; not only was I being accused of being AWOL, it was also implied that I had fudged the leave certificate. I gave an angry retort in writing, fuming that my integrity was being questioned. The next morning I began the long climb to Durga.

My response to Kukrety's letter had its own repercussions. He immediately accused the adjutant and the OC Rear of being hand-in-glove with me and started claiming it was a conspiracy launched by the three of us against him. By the time Shailu Verma got back from his leave a few days later, this was the breaking news waiting to greet him. The very next day, I was hauled down from Durga and marched up to the CO.

I said my piece, going step by step over the sequence of events and handing over the leave certificate. But Uncle Kukrety's histrionics had obviously rattled the CO, who now berated me about my belt not being standard issue, my jersey pattern being different, my boots not being shipshape.

As far as I was concerned, this was downright silly; from the mundane we were fast entering the absurd. Shailu had earlier been the DQ and he now decided to get all legal with me.

'We will record an Abstract of Evidence,' Shailu Verma declared.

Even with my limited understanding of legal matters, I knew that in this particular enquiry the accused cannot question witnesses (whereas in the Summary of Evidence, the accused can question witnesses). This meant that Kukrety would have a free run with his version of events.

In my mind, I was absolutely clear; I had not done anything wrong and all the evidence was clear as daylight. I could also clearly see my career as a professional army officer eroding before me. Frankly, I was not too sure I knew what was really happening.

'Sir, I want to record my statement.' Under the circumstances, it was all I could do. I was told to come back the next day and that it would be done. I was dismissed. Back to Durga I went.

Through the next fortnight, this became the daily norm. I would make the long trek down from Durga, wait the entire day to get my statement recorded, be told it couldn't be done that day, then make the long climb back. The obvious intention was to have me put up my hands in despair and give up. All I could do was to try and improve my down and up timings. By the end of it all, I had set timings that the boys in the company would have a tough time matching.

Having failed to break me, Shailu Verma then decided to up the ante. I was to be produced before the brigade commander, Brigadier PN Kakkar. A Gorkha officer, he had seen me from the time I had arrived with the advance party. It was highly unlikely that he was unaware of the fact that Dharam Pal Kukrety, the senior officer in the advance party, had shown a decided disinclination to move out of his bunker at Gulpur. Kakkar gave me a patient hearing. Even as I was stating my case, I couldn't help but feel the absurdity of the situation—to a third party it would possibly seem as if two kids were stubbornly fighting over whose turn it was to bat!

The brigadier looked exasperated. He first turned to Shailu Verma, 'Look, I've gone through the entire evidence. The leave certificate is there. It isn't fudged, so where is the problem?' He then turned to me, 'Just apologize to your CO and get done with it.' I was dismissed. Outside the commander's office, I said to my CO, 'Sir, if you feel I've made a mistake, then I'm sorry. But I did not make a mistake.'

We returned to the battalion HQ. Shailu and Kukrety were locked in a conference while I waited outside. Not good enough, I was told; put it in writing. So I did, more or less repeating what I had told the CO verbally. No, not good enough—what do you mean by 'if' and 'but'. We were back to square one. At this point, Kukrety lost the plot completely. He got on the phone, called up the brigade commander and started abusing Brigadier Kakkar. Still not quite satisfied with his performance, he then called up the BM and let him have it in equally foul terms.

Brigade responded by sending the BM along with an ambulance for Kukrety, but Shailu Verma stepped in with the assurance that he could handle Kukrety. The ambulance went back to Poonch without its patient.

The drama of the absurd was to continue. The CO now decided that it had been a technical mistake to have me marched up to the brigade commander as I was wearing the rank of a major. Legally, he declared, I needed to be brought before the GOC. Major General Narender Singh, an armoured corps officer, was commanding 25 Division and when he heard of Shailu's plans, he let it be known that this was a regimental matter and need not be brought before him. However, by then, no one was listening to reason, regardless of where it came from. Legal clauses were quoted, and a date was fixed. Once again, I was hauled down from Durga and found myself standing outside the GOC's office in Rajouri.

The CO was conferring with the general, and I could hear every word of what he was saying. 'He's hot-headed and needs to be taught a lesson. When the colonel of the regiment had visited, he was wearing a non-standard issue belt.' He went on in that vein for a while, finishing with a dramatic, 'Sir, I recommend that you at least give him a severe displeasure.'

Then I was marched in.

'I've been through your statement and I am not satisfied. You asked for seven days leave, you should have reported back in seven days.' I stood there at attention, looking straight ahead, wondering just how ridiculous things could get. 'Based on your CO's recommendation, I've decided to convey my displeasure to you verbally. Nothing is to be recorded in your dossier. Now get the hell out of here.' I must have gaped at him like a gold fish, then saluted and backed out of his office. In spite of the CO's passionate recommendation for my crucifixion, this man was trying to build bridges. The CO and I drove back to the battalion in absolute silence.

My orders for IMTRAT had already arrived and I was ordered down from Durga after a couple of days and told to move out on posting as all this nonsense had already delayed my move. By then we were into December.

This, however, was not the end of the story.

Dharam Pal Kukrety ranted and raved about my having got away, in what, according to him, should have been an open and shut case. He claimed that political pressure had been brought to bear and continued to abuse the brigade commander and everyone else who he felt needed a dressing down. A few days later, he ventured out of the battalion base for the first time and 'captured' a company position, a la Faizabad. There was absolute chaos. Shailu Verma went into the company position to reason with him; they both sat together, swapped stories and actually wept; the CO came out minus Kukrety, who had by then got into a bunker with a couple of grenades. More drama ensued. An assault on the company position was contemplated, but fortunately wasn't carried out. The corps commander then flew in by helicopter, went into the company locality and personally arrested Kukrety and brought him out. Shailu Verma was moved out from command for his leadership failure and was subsequently reduced to the rank of a major. Lieutenant Colonel CM Chaudhury from 18 Rajput took over the battalion and so ended the amazing saga in Poonch, one that, to this day, continues to amaze me for its absurdity.

Dragon Kingdom

I left Poonch determined to put the highly unnecessary drama behind me. At the time a part of me was bewildered at what had happened, for each day I would wake up expecting the so-called issue to resolve itself. My departure from the battalion, minus the irons I was to have been clamped in, was seen by many as the last straw that broke the camel's back that lead to Kukrety's commandeering the company post and his subsequent breakdown. Fact of the matter was, Kukrety should have been sent home after his failure to advance during the Chauddagram battle. Every man in the battalion knew what had happened during the war and it was an open secret that 'Uncle Kukrety' would develop blood pressure problems if he was given even the simplest of tasks that required any physical exertion, however mild. The tendency in the army to repeatedly cover up for deadwood throws up situations that need never have happened. If Bangladesh was not bad enough, his performance in Faizabad should have nailed him. The Poonch fiasco was a virtual replay of the quarter guard drama.

After a couple of days in Chandigarh, I proceeded to Bhutan. The plan was that Bharti and Mrinalini would join me later.

The Indian Military Training Team (IMTRAT), headquartered at Haa Dzong, was under the command of Major General IJ Khanna from the Brigade of the Guards. The G1 was Lieutenant Colonel AM Mullick from the Madras Regiment while the AQ was PS Sandhu from the Dogras. As far as the military training was concerned, officers of the Royal Bhutan Army were more or less dependent on their Indian counterparts. IMTRAT prepared them for the courses they would attend in India.

Though I had been wearing the acting rank of a major in Poonch, in Bhutan I was back to being a captain. Most of us at Haa Dzong were designated Instructor Class C, which required the basic minimum qualification of having done the JC Course in Mhow. A small band of thirty-five officers, we lived cheek-by-jowl in a small cluster of houses. A couple of my coursemates were there too: Captains Arun Yadav and PV Reddy; NK Rai from the Artillery, AS Bakshi from Signals, Subir Ahluwalia from Mahar in Det East. The more senior of us included VK Rai from the Dogra Regiment, Deore from Mahar, Sudhir Sharma from Guards, VK Kapoor from Armoured Corps, Lalit Malhotra from Engineers, Arun Roye from the Brigade of the Guards (and also the Rajput Regiment), KK Khanna from Jat, SRR Ayengar from Signals, Manvendra Rathore and NB Singh, both from the Rajputana Rifles. With limited options available to us, social interaction often bordered on the hectic, with frequent comings and goings between officers' houses.

I was allotted a small wooden house that consisted of a bedroom, study, a small dining-cum-drawing room area, the kitchen and a small sit-out. Situated at around 9,000 feet, our location was in a valley that was drained by the Haa Chu River. To one side was a mountain range that separated us from the Paro Valley while on the other flank we had the range that linked up with the range of mountains that marked the border with Tibet. The valley was more like a funnel, and in the evening the howling wind would rip across at a tremendous velocity. It was extremely cold and each room had to be equipped with a bukhari on which we had to heat water every morning, for everything would be frozen solid. After a fortnight, I was given some leave so I could go and fetch my family to Bhutan.

Given the limited facilities, we were encouraged to take up golf. The course consisted of nine browns that were tucked away in the barren and rocky outcrops. One's scorecard at the end of each round was dependent on 'lucky' and 'unlucky' stones, for anything could happen to influence the natural direction of the ball once it hit mother earth. Though golf was the craze, it was usually a saner option to go to the squash courts for a workout. Apart from that we had a small movie theatre which played Hindi movies on 35mm projectors once a week.

Life at Haa Dzong was extremely tough, especially for the families. There being no local produce available, everything, including fresh vegetables, had to be ferried up by road from Siliguri in India. The single biggest problem was milk, with each family being rationed three tins of Amul milk per month, along with three tins of Lactogen, for a family with small children. There was no electricity; generators provided some relief for four hours in the evenings. We would sometimes get assigned to the board that went down to get the various provisions for the officers, which in turn would be rationed and sold to the families. During the summer, locally-produced asparagus would be bountiful, so much so that with every purchase, it was mandatory to take a kilogram of the stems free whether you wanted them or not.

In spite of the tough conditions, both Bharti and Mrinalini adapted fairly quickly. There was a small Garrison School into which the three-year old Mrinalini was enrolled. Her class teacher was Ruby Sharma, whose husband later retired as the QMG (quarter master general), Lieutenant General Sudhir Sharma. A month or two into the toddler's education, I found a distraught Ruby seeking me out. 'VK,' she said, 'I'll pay you the fifty rupees you pay the Garrison School each month for your daughter's education. Just keep her at home!'

I knew Mrinalini could be classified as a naughty child, but for Ruby to get this rattled, the provocation must have been severe.

'What happened?'

'I went to the restroom and your daughter locked me in,' she exploded, 'and then...' Ruby gulped in a lungful of the fresh mountain air, 'she told all the other children to go home!' I apologized sincerely and told her that I would discipline Mrinalini.

The silence at Haa Dzong, especially in the hours before the wind picked up in the evenings, underlined the pristine beauty of the region. I would walk Mrinalini around the golf course, drinking in the silence.

As a part of our duties, we would also be sent on long-range patrols with the Royal Bhutan Army so that we were familiar with the terrain and the day-to-day functioning of Bhutanese troops. The start of such days was almost ritualistic: the muleteers accompanying us would report in the morning, only to tell us that the mules had run away during the night. 'Woh to chala gaya!' the muleteer would look you straight in the eye and just stand there.

One would then take out a bottle of the potent Bhutan rum and pour out two large pegs for the muleteer to knock back in a single gulp, the liquid hitting the back of his throat with the tilt of the head. He would then wipe his mouth with the back of his hand, salute and walk ten steps away. Taking a whistle from his pocket, he would blow a couple of loud blasts. Soon the mules would trot, in their master's demands having been met and Indo-Bhutanese relations having grown even better than before!

On one of these high-altitude patrols I saw a musk deer at very close quarters. Unlike most deer, the musk deer does not grow antlers, but the male has an enlarged front canine that protrudes like a small tusk pointing downwards. So unused to humans, and hence possibly devoid of any fear, this animal allowed me to watch him for quite some time. Unfortunately, this dainty animal is extremely sought after by poachers who hunt them for their scent glands as it can fetch up to $45,000 per kilogram in animal trafficking markets. It was believed that ancient royalty wore the scent of the musk deer and that it is an aphrodisiac. Some others believe that if a dying man is made to inhale the substance, he will revive miraculously. Whatever the reasons, the Bhutan Army was under orders to protect the animal, and patrols would regularly be launched to deter poachers.

The area was teeming with pheasants and other high-altitude birds. The most spectacular of the lot was the male multicoloured monal pheasant that stood almost two-and-a-half feet tall. The region was known to have snow leopards, but I wasn't fortunate enough to run into these elusive cats. However, one of the patrols stumbled on to a huge black bear that was, amazingly, dragging away an equally huge yak bull. Before anyone could react, a Bhutanese soldier opened fire, pumping in round after round into the magnificent animal, stopping only when his entire magazine had been emptied. The yak, though badly mauled, was thus rescued.

The bear was skinned and the joyous troops then hacked it into portable pieces and brought it down to the IMTRAT camp. After treating the pelt, the black bear was presented to the IMTRAT officers' mess. The meat of the bear was allowed to putrefy until it could be smelt hundreds of yards away. Only after it was suitably putrefied was the meat divided into lots and taken away by the local Bhutanese troops to be devoured as a delicacy.

We were constantly playing host to various senior officers who would visit IMTRAT. As is the norm in the Army, we would all line up to be introduced to the visiting dignitary. Two visits stood out for their contrasting styles; the first was Lieutenant General Eric Vas. Before we could be introduced, he announced that there was no need for introductions as he had read the individual dossiers of each officer the previous evening and was sure we were all highly qualified for the jobs we were assigned to. He then proceeded to talk to us about our varied interests. General Vas was an old Bhutan hand who later went on to write a book on the Dragon Kingdom. The second visit was that of the then deputy chief, Lieutenant General (later General) Krishna Rao. He went down the line, talking at length to each officer, asking them what courses they had done and how qualified they were to be in IMTRAT.

▪

In 1980 some of us were detailed for the pre-staff session in Missamari. After the cool confines of Bhutan, the sweltering heat of the Assam plains was crippling. Missamari, a short distance from Tezpur, was a one-horse military cantonment that straddled the Assam railway line on the north bank. The army had just constructed new quarters that had servant rooms into which we were crammed for the duration of the session. From there we were to move back to Bhutan via North Bengal; again we were stuffed into a railway bogey where there was but one window seat while the rest of us were standing in the corridor. To get some fresh air, we were taking short turns at the window. It happened to be my turn when the train approached the North Bengal border.

Pulling the chain to activate the emergency vacuum brakes, someone on board started to slow the train down. Before I could realize what was happening, my watch had been flicked off my wrist with a hook, while a large number of travellers in the train lost their valuables as well. The coordinated robbery perhaps lasted just a few seconds, after which the train began to gain speed. At the next stop, as angry passengers flooded into the police control room, we were told that our complaints could not be registered as the robbery had happened outside the jurisdiction of the West Bengal police. We were to learn later that this was a daily occurrence on this stretch.

In June, a telegram arrived for me. In those days, there was no provision for wires to be sent to Haa Dzong (from Phuntsholing, where it had been received), and the accepted practice was for the message to be read out over the telephone. The telephone operator at the other end slowly and clearly read out the message: my father had passed away.

The shock of the news—my father was only in his mid-fifties, with no health problems—was compounded by the remoteness of my location. All the officers rallied around: Arun Roye and his wife helped us pack while Major Katoch, the new commanding officer of the school, arranged for a jonga to take us down to Alipur Duar. We had no train reservations, but the railway officials were extremely helpful, arranging for one seat on which Bharti and Mrinalini could travel.

The cremation was over by the time we reached Bapora. Stunned relatives surrounded me. My father had had a massive heart attack while bathing. Ironically, on that very day, he was preparing to take his elder brother to the hospital to get his routine cardiac check done.

I went through most of the post-funeral ceremonies in a daze. As the eldest sibling, the entire family responsibility was now mine. Being posted in Bhutan now complicated matters, for my sister was to be married in December. With the help of the extended family, we somehow managed to deal with the domestic issues as well.

Mrinalini was not told about her grandfather's passing; she was told that he had gone to Kashmir for a holiday. In fact, for a while, I even wrote letters to her in his name—until she was old enough to comprehend the loss.

The two years at IMTRAT soon came to an abrupt end, almost a month ahead of schedule. The early arrival of my relief at Haa Dzong created its own problems, for we were mentally not prepared to move out. However, with no choice left in the matter, I had to run around and get all our baggage sorted and packed. We then said goodbye to Haa Dzong and Bhutan and made our way down again to Alipur Duar. Immediately, we were faced with the TINA factor (There Is No Alternative) and had to agree to pay the stipulated number of rum bottles to get our luggage loaded on to the brake van of the Tinsukia Mail. As the train steamed across the Gangetic plain, I looked at the passing countryside and wondered where I was headed to now. I had been told to move back to 2 Rajput, which was in Keri, still a part of the Rajouri Division and was scheduled to move to a peace station shortly. My immediate concern was what to do with the luggage upon our arrival in Delhi.

6

IN HIGH PLACES

A Brand New World

In Delhi, I went and met Major Kanwer Mohinder Singh, my unit officer, who was posted in the MS (Military Secretary) Branch. My tryst with the haphazard and ad hoc functioning of this wing of the army was just about to begin.

'You're not going back to the unit,' said KMS. 'Go see Bhopinder, he's dealing with your posting.'

Not knowing what to expect, I made my way to Bhopinder, who later was to become a lieutenant general, and after retirement served as the lieutenant governor of the Andaman and Nicobar Islands.

'Why have you moved out of IMTRAT?' he asked, incredulous that I should be standing before him in Army HQ, roughly 1,600 kilometres west of where I should be.

'My relief arrived, what else could I do?'

'We have just issued your posting order for Fatehgarh—25 Rajput.' This was a double whammy—not going back to 2 Rajput was a shocker, but now I was being sent to a new raising. PV Reddy, who was with me at IMTRAT and who was of the same seniority, was also being posted to 25 Rajput. I pointed this out.

'Colonel of the regiment's orders; all officers outside their units are to be sent to new raisings.'

I promptly put in a request for an interview with the Additional MS but was told to see the Deputy MS, Brigadier Sood. Since he was on leave, I was told that the interview would be with Colonel Karmbaiyya instead. The colonel told me clearly that the new policy was inflexible. 'Report to the new battalion, then put in an application and we might consider it.' I walked out of Army HQ knowing it would be impossible for me to put in a request to move after I had reported to the new unit. With a stroke of the pen, I had been moved out of the rolls of one of the oldest infantry battalions in the world and would be joining a brand-new unit.

After installing Bharti and Mrinalini in Chandigarh for her brother's wedding, and spending a few days in Bapora, I reported to Fatehgarh on 1 March 1981. If ever there was a one-horse town, it was Fatehgarh. Situated in the heart of the Gangetic belt on the south bank of the Ganga, the town was named after an old fort and was the administrative headquarters of Farrukhabad district. The cantonment housed the Rajput Regimental Centre (RRC) that, at the time, had complete monopoly over the area. A decade later, the Sikh LI Centre was also shifted to Fatehgarh. That move alone would have at best elevated its status to a two-horse town!

My new commanding officer was Lieutenant Colonel Jimmy Abraham, a veteran of the 1971 Bangladesh War from 18 Rajput. During the war, he had commanded Charlie Company, being among the first Indian Army officers to walk into Dhaka. The son of a railway officer, two of his brothers had also been in the army. His wife, Usha, was a doctor, and also from a services family. Having been a part of 18 Rajput when it was raised in 1965, Jimmy had a realistic idea of what to expect from a new raising and from Fatehgarh. Extremely enthusiastic, the CO's motivating mantras were from films like *The Dirty Dozen* and his pet phrase 'good man the lantern' was the catchword in the battalion. Jimmy Abraham was to give 25 Rajput a solid foundation.

For most of us, coming from well-established units with regimented drills in place for even the smallest detail, this was a cultural shock! Here, there was absolutely nothing. We would sit under a tree on a pakhal with a mat spread over it, interviewing men sent by other units so that we could pick suitable manpower for the new raising. It was almost impossible to concentrate on even the simplest of tasks as the relentless heat and the Ganga sand, which covered everything with fine powdery grit, made life extremely uncomfortable. To make matters worse, there was also an endless stream of flies.

Life for us lesser mortals may have been hellish and uncomfortable, but there were other denizens of Fatehgarh who were obviously having a ball. Our second-in-command, Major AK Singh, was part of a board that was looking into the mysterious draining of countless bottles of vintage scotch from the cellar in the officers' mess. As the court of inquiry progressed, the investigating officers were treated to what has to be one of the most colourful explanations ever for any 'act of crime'. The Fatehgarh rats that dated back to the days of the Raj, they were told, were extremely clever. They were pukka little sahibs who knew how to break the bottle's seal, then

General VK Singh
Photo credit: Kunal Verma/KaleidoIndia

My father (extreme left) with his elder brothers Hon Lt Devi Singh (second from left) and Hon Capt Ranjit Singh (fourth from left), both of whom had also served in the Rajput Regiment

With my parents, circa 1952

Pre-boarding school, circa 1955

On a trek from school. (In the centre, leaning on a walking stick)

An aerial view of the Sudan Block, the imposing hub of the NDA, Khadakwasla

Battalion Cadet Captain, Hunter Squadron, 1967

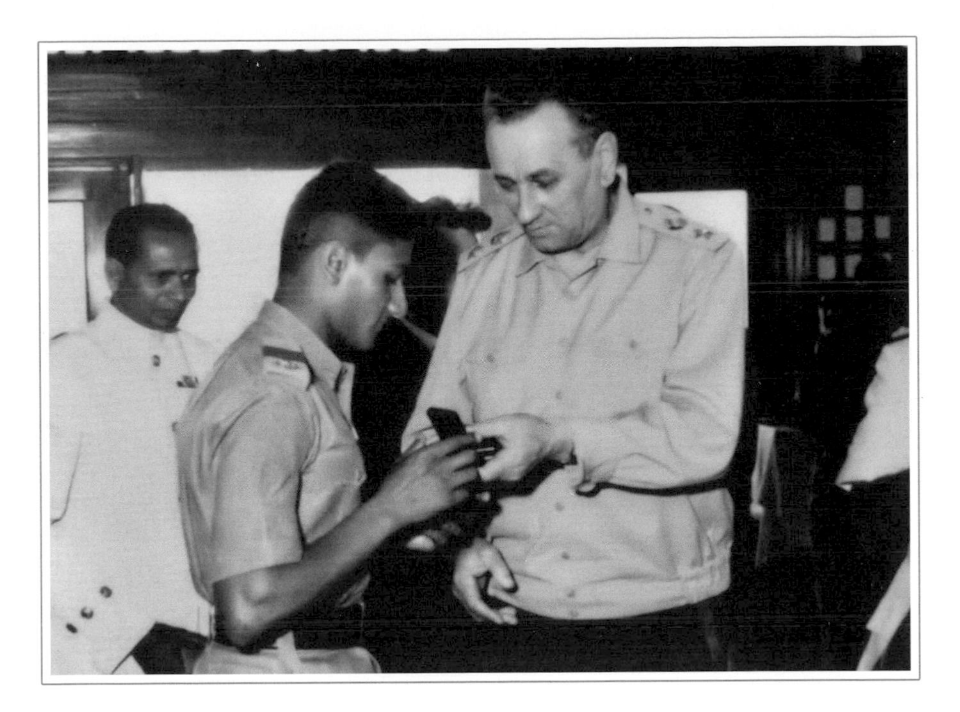

Soviet Marshal Grechko presenting me with a medal at NDA, 1969

On an exercise, second from left, NDA, Khadakwasla, 1969

Receiving a trophy from the Commandant, IMA, 1970

As an Under-officer, second row middle, IMA, 1970

As the Intelligence Officer of 2 Rajput at Belonia during the Bangladesh War, 1971

Chittagong Harbour after an air attack by Naval Sea Hawks that operated off INS Vikrant *during the Bangladesh War*

Portraits taken during our wedding in Gurgaon, May 1975

Ranger Course, Fort Benning, Georgia, USA, 1976

Playing cricket at IMTRAT, Bhutan, 1980

Mrinalini in Bhutan, 1980

With Yogja in Wellington, 1983

On board a naval ship during the Staff College study tour, 1983

With battalion officers in Sri Lanka as a part of the IPKF, 1989
Lt Alankar Bhardwaj, Major AK Singh and Capt Rakesh Dwivedi

Flanked by Mrinalini and Yogja in Faizabad, 1993

Graduating from the US Army War College, Carlisle, USA, 2000

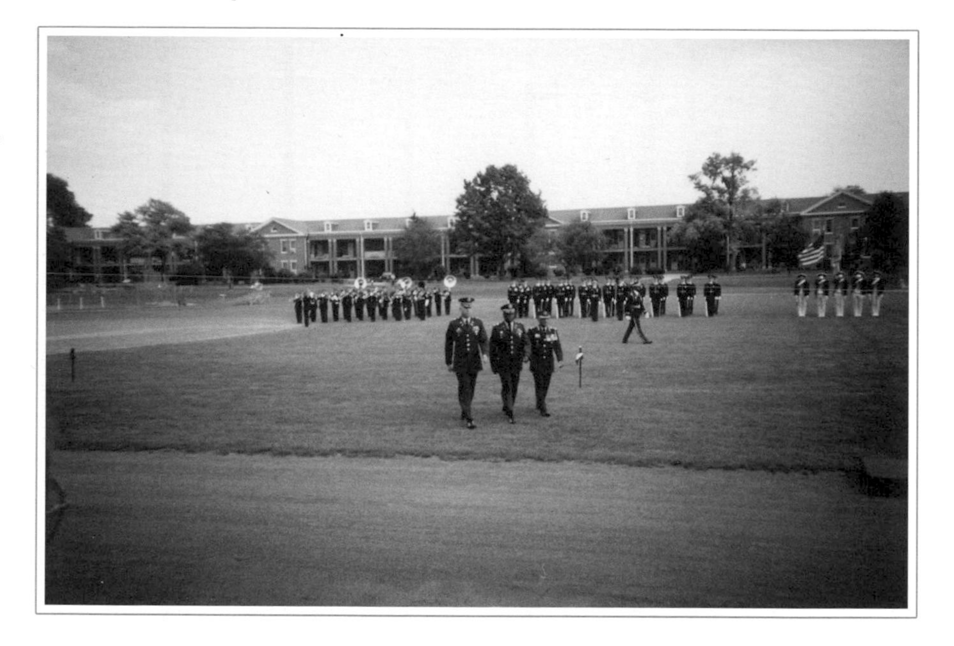

Graduation Ceremony, Carlisle, USA, 2000

As the GOC II Corps visiting 14 Rajput in 2007.
To the extreme right is Lieutenant General Milan Naidu

A gathering of former GOCs of Victor Force.
With Gurdeep Singh, RK Kaushal, Shantanu Chaudhary, RS Jamwal,
Prakash Menon and Anil Nandal

General officers from the Rajput Regiment, 2008
With VS Tonk, Mukesh Sabharwal, Tom Mathews, Milan Naidu, RK Karwal and Anand Verma

Talking to Gorkha troops after taking over as GOC-in-C Eastern Command, 2008

Vijay Diwas, Fort William, December 2009

With Major General Ashok Kalyan Verma (second from left) and General Shankar Roychowdhury (sixth from left)

With Bharti, Kolkata, 2010
Photo credit: Kunal Verma/KaleidoIndia

With our four cocker spaniels in Senapati House, Kolkata
Photo credit: Kunal Verma/KaleidoIndia

one would use its tail like a dipstick and others would proceed to suck off the scotch! Countless bottles had apparently been drained in this manner!

These were probably the worst days the Regimental Centre would see, for things started to get a lot more professional. Brigadier Prem Kukrety was the centre commandant and, gradually, over the next few years, lots of hard work was put in by regimental officers to make Fatehgarh a well-run centre. Over the years, even our approach towards new raisings has changed; we now give them a lot more freedom and resources. The one room we had that served as our battalion mess had a rickety old sofa that needed bricks to be placed under it strategically to prevent it from toppling over. After much persuasion, the centre allowed us to buy a carpet that was purchased from Shahjahanpur. However, that too lost its sheen pretty soon for it was communicated to the battalion that the centre commandant was unhappy about the amount of money that had been spent on it! The carpet had cost us ₹10,000!

Along with 24 Rajput, we were the first totally mixed battalion to be raised, in itself a major departure in recruitment policy that had been in place ever since the British raised the Bengal Army on strict caste lines. In earlier units, at the company level itself, it was either a Rajput or Gujjar or Bengali grouping. In the case of these two new battalions, even though the class composition was 30 per cent Rajput, 30 per cent Gujjar and the remaining 40 per cent Brahmins, Jats, Muslims and Bengali troops, the men were mixed up to the section level.

I was assigned Delta Company that was the last to be raised. By then, the other companies had absorbed most of the good draftees from other units and I was left to separate the wheat from the chaff. Quite a few men were unfit and failed to meet the basic QR of qualifying standards. As we regularly kept rejecting potential candidates, the centre commandant started getting annoyed. His ire notwithstanding, we were unwilling to lower the bar set by the centre commandant himself. Finally, it was decided that I would be given 50 per cent new recruits. By any yardstick, this was an extremely tricky situation.

Jimmy Abraham was fully alive to the challenge and the suggestion that we take Delta Company out on a mini-exercise away from the confines of Fatehgarh met with his immediate approval. After twenty days of working together in the field, I felt we had a cohesive group of men who were well on their way to becoming a fighting team. Shortly after that, when the battalion was put through certain manoeuvres, Delta Company proved to be up to the task.

By June, we received orders to move to Alwar in Rajasthan. I was selected to move with the advance party and was extremely relieved to leave Fatehgarh behind. The rest of the battalion soon followed and we were in our new location by September. The entire place was green in the aftermath of the monsoons and some of our vehicles were stuck in wheel-deep slush—hardly the reception we expected in the dry, arid state of Rajasthan!

Alwar: The Gateway to Rajputana

We arrived in Alwar and were assigned to 20 Brigade that was part of 18 Division commanded by Major General 'Baba' Giri from JAK RIF. The brigade was under the leadership of Brigadier Sukhdev Singh, a fine gunner officer, and we shared the new location with 16 JAK RIF (which was converting into a mechanized battalion at the time) and 3/11 GR. We were told to take charge of Itarana Cantonment, which was dominated by an abandoned palace. The Itarana Palace had served as the shikargah (hunting palace) for the Alwar royal family. An architectural marvel, the palace had never been used, as it was considered inauspicious after two ships carrying furniture for the palace from England sank during their voyage.

When news of the second disaster came through, the Maharaja decided that the Itarana Palace was an inauspicious building and that it must be razed to the ground immediately. However, that was an impossible task; so the king's advisor suggested that the facade be destroyed and the palace be abandoned. Subsequently, when this area was allotted to the army, it was obviously thought that we were hardy enough to overcome whatever bad luck fate might have in store for us. Anyway, owing to the damage done to the building, we now had to negotiate steep steps that had been put in place once the army took over.

The 'bad luck' factor almost had serious consequences for me. The area had, over a period of time, become home to the animals in the area. Teeming as it was with peacocks, partridges, a multitude of screaming parakeets, tree pies, babblers and bulbuls, not to mention the cattle and a large number of nilgai, the area was almost like a mini wildlife sanctuary. One day, I was riding my scooter when a cow tried to leap over me. Not as agile as a nilgai, it failed to get high enough and ended up dragging me a fair distance.

Battered and bruised, but none the worse for my tumble, I had difficulty convincing people that I had been hit by a cow.

In a land of kingdoms and princely states, Alwar is perhaps one of the most picturesque regions of them all. Situated close to Delhi, it bordered my own ancestral region to the south and acted as a gateway into Rajputana. Apart from the fort, the City Palace was a beautiful and imposing building in amazingly good condition. The Government Museum of Alwar has some fine exhibits including rare ivory miniature paintings. The quaint railway station amidst the Aravalli Hills also added an old-world charm to our existence. 25 Rajput, determined to make the best out of its first location, was soon a happy cohesive battalion under the hard-working and fun-loving Jimmy Abraham. Itarana was a new location with only tent replacement huts and with very little tree cover, even though the place was a scrub jungle. The accommodation could get extremely uncomfortable, but with the winter months ahead of us, we hoped to be reasonably well prepared by the time the summer heat descended on us the following year.

At the time of raising the unit at Fatehgarh, Jimmy Abraham decided the battalion must have a proper mascot, and we soon got hold of a beautiful male nilgai. The unit pundit did a proper pooja and the animal had its ears pierced and was adorned with golden balis to help identify it among its wild cousins. A delightfully frisky and friendly animal, it soon had everyone tearing out their hair in frustration for it would eat anything that was planted within the unit lines. It was also growing into a huge beast and soon it was rather reluctantly decided to take him to a new location and release him there. No sooner was the translocation party back, the young fellow was back too, his quivering nose drawing him like a homing pigeon to the unit langar. A standing conference of the officers was held, with an emotional Jimmy Abraham finally decreeing that this time the mascot must be left in a secure forest some hundred kilometres away.

▪

Along with HN Sharma and Devinder Atri who were also company commanders, I travelled to the Rajputana Rifles Centre in Delhi to sit for the Defence Services Staff College (DSSC) entrance examination. Even though the examination was being held at the Rajputana Rifles Centre, Atri and I moved to Haryana Bhavan courtesy my father-in-law. While going over various case scenarios, Atri would sometimes go off on a tangent.

'Forget it,' I said, scanning through previous question papers, 'this type of question never comes up.'

'Yes, but what if it does?' So we would diligently discuss it. Rather amazingly, quite a few of those (or similar) questions actually featured in the examination.

On the morning of a particular exam he did it again. He wanted me to run him through an appreciation on infiltration. 'Forget it,' I said. 'It's come four or five times in the past. The law of probability rules it out.'

'Sir, tell me anyway.' So we went over the entire appreciation. Lo and behold, the question was staring us in the face a short while later. After the exam I asked him how he had done. 'Couldn't finish it,' he grinned. Atri got very good marks but failed in Tac B (paper on Tactics).

Towards the end of 1981 we went out for a four-month divisional exercise called Shikar held at Jhakrawali near Hanumangarh. By then we were functioning reasonably well as a unit and the battalion did exceedingly well, performing with a lot of josh. For a new unit fresh off the blocks, it was extremely commendable. The battalion level exercise was then upgraded to a brigade level, until it culminated with a full division affair with armour and BMPs (armoured personnel carriers). The adjutant, Virendra Gulia, devised our own battalion code, as we knew everyone else would be listening in. For example, if we captured the objective, we were to flash a message: 'Jawani dhal gayi' (My youth has fallen away). Quite naturally, no one wanted to say that on the air, so Gulia would repeatedly ask, 'Jawani dhali ki nahi dhali?' The men would be tickled pink with this brand of unit humour and would laugh their guts out.

I was sitting on the sand dunes with some of the others on the last day of the exercise when a telephone call was patched through to me over the radio set. It was Bharti, telling me that I had passed the Staff College examination. Later, as we began the move back to Alwar, I got the news that I had made it in the competitive vacancy.

The move to Wellington was still nine months away, so we got back to the usual unit activities. By then, Bharti was expecting our second child, and after the Belgaum experience, I was not willing to take any chances. She shifted to her parents' place two months ahead of the delivery, while Mrinalini, who was at the time studying at the Alwar Public School, suffered my cooking skills—which started and ended with eggs. Just before the new baby was due, I took leave, and the family was together when Yogja, my second daughter, was born. I was overjoyed. By December, Bharti and the children moved back to Alwar and we got down to the serious business of packing.

DSSC Wellington

In every professional soldier's life, the year-long course at the Defence Services Staff College is a watershed of sorts. For the first time since NDA, one is back in a tri-service environment. The DSSC and the Madras Regimental Centre together make up the Wellington Cantonment that sits astride the Nilgiri mountains of Tamil Nadu. Also known as the Blue Mountains, the Nilgiris are part of the Western Ghats. The area, home to the indigenous Toda tribe, remained completely unexplored until 1810 after which the British began to probe the area from Coimbatore. It took another decade for the English to discover that the upper reaches of the Nilgiris were not only habitable, but possessed a 'European climate', a discovery which led to a large number of them building their homes around Coonoor and Ooty. Later, the practice of moving the government to the hills during the hot summer months began and by the end of the century, the entire region was completely accessible with the laying of roads that was also supplemented by a narrow gauge railway line.

After the heat and dust of Fatehgarh and Alwar, a hill station was a major relief, especially for Bharti and the new baby. From Alwar we went to Delhi with all our baggage, and then proceeded to Chennai, a forty-eight hour journey. Madras Central was a hub of activity as officers who had qualified for the course made a mad dash for the Nilgiri Express that chugged through the night to Coimbatore. After a brief halt, the train moved north along the base of the Nilgiris to Mettupalayam where we finally disembarked from the train after almost four days. After that, the college took over our lives.

As was to be expected, the Staff College was a model of efficiency—as the officers arrived, they were allotted their accommodation, which was based on seniority. The big daddies, the senior students, were accommodated on Nilgiri Hills, closest to the college buildings. The second lot, which included me, were given the newly constructed quarters on Gurkha Hill.

The juniors were given the older houses at Circle Quarters, furthest from the college. As a result of this policy, most of my coursemates—there were around fifteen of us—were all living in the same row.

The college did a thorough job of mixing up the three services. Your own coursemates who had been with you in NDA, and were now part of the air force and the navy, were coloured by the thinking and the ethos of their service. It was soon obvious that three officers looking at a problem through the prisms of their service often had extremely divergent approaches and viewpoints. Each service had its own systems that were deeply ingrained in their officers. I always felt that the systems in place in the army were far more grounded and solid. For example, army officers had to compete their way to the Staff College, while naval and air force officers were simply nominated.

The commandant of the Staff College was Major General Balaram from the Signal Regiment. On the directing staff (DS) was Lieutenant Colonel Ravi Eipe (he retired as an army commander), a Namka Chu survivor who had gone on to command 18 Rajput. On the third day, the entire college, including the wives, assembled for the commandant's lecture. General Balaram had taken over towards the end of the previous course and he frankly shared with us the problems faced by the students.

The main issue on his mind was the hectic socializing that seemed to completely exhaust the already overworked students. Some student officers were even known to have sold off some of their assets to meet the financial demands of keeping up with the Joneses. 'Students are supposed to study,' he intoned, 'and the directing staff are supposed to correct their work, which means you all have to put in a lot of work. Therefore, you don't have to go to any DS's house; let them work and you do your own work.' This near-ban on running around after the directing staff had an extremely positive impact on the conduct of the course. The general concluded his talk with words that have stayed with me, and which I have often passed on to other officers: Don't think of the future—where you will go, what you will become—just stay focused on today and do the work that has been given to you to the best of your ability. No one has seen the future, and all you will succeed in doing is ruining your today if you follow that path.

As the commandant, he then ensured that we had a lot of work, which effectively meant we had to do a lot of writing assignments. The DS then would have to spend double the amount of time correcting our work and would, in turn, have to write copious notes as the commandant would then look at the corrected copies. This would often lead to hilarious situations, for, at times, there would be almost three to four pages of observations in red ink on your work. When we would look at the DS questioningly, he would say, 'This is not meant for you. It's meant for somebody else!'

We had an excellent team of officers supporting the commandant. The chief instructor (army) was Brigadier 'Guddi' Grewal who was an armoured officer. The division I was a part of had Brigadier Guru Bakshi from JAK RIF who was a professional soldier and a first-class officer.

Through discussions and the work allocated to the syndicates (classes), student officers were brought to a level where they could comprehend possible operations that went well beyond the battalion level. In every given situation, it was then our job to figure out the staff work that was the matrix around which everything else would function. As a result, each syndicate was worked to the bone as the students were groomed to be good military leaders at the higher level. Exercises were always critical, but so were the sand model discussions and various other tasks performed by us. Interaction with one's peers, including students from foreign countries and the constant stream of intellectual guest speakers culminated in the college having an aura of intellectual evolution. In a nutshell, the Staff College virtually opened up our horizons as future military commanders. Though the immediate job was pitched more at the brigade level, we learnt how things were interlinked and were now quite competent to discuss staff work and other scenarios up to the divisional and corps level.

With an extremely down-to-earth commandant at the helm, it was but natural for others to imbibe some of his values. Some officers felt he carried things a bit too far, even going vegetable shopping with his wife on his scooter. Another Balaram dictum was that all the work had to be done within the college itself. No work was to be taken home, so as to ensure the integrity of family time. There were times when we worked till late in the evening, but that was that. No one was burning the midnight oil to meet the morning deadline.

One of the highlights of the course was the Ooty Hunt, the annual ball. As the date for the ball drew closer, the student community was abuzz with the latest news that the commandant had decreed that all DS would travel to the Ooty Ball in buses along with the students. The DS who bristled at the thought of using the same mode of transport as the student body decided to take lighter vehicles. It was amusing to see their discomfiture when the commandant himself alighted from a bus.

Another highlight of the course was the ten-day industrial tour. It was extremely interesting as we travelled through Bangalore to Hyderabad and Pune before heading back to the Nilgiris. We had with us a railway officer who was a fellow student and he ensured the railways did us proud, which included serving food on proper china.

The Staff College was also a great place for families; in between breaks, student officers would collectively hire a mini bus and we explored as much of south India as we possibly could. Madurai, Cochin, Trivandrum, Guruvayur were on almost every student officer's agenda. We also managed to explore the wonderfully scenic landscape of the Blue Mountains, frolicking with our families in Pykara, Mukurthi and the Upper lakes.

For service officers' children, Wellington had a lasting impact: many of them start their education there, the beauty of the place and the friends they make stay throughout their lives. Mrinalini studied at the Holy Innocents High School while Yogja's first birthday was celebrated on Gurkha Hill with reasonable aplomb. All student officers with little children had been sent scuttling to a homeopath at the beginning of the course and had been given a dose to make them immune to chickenpox. Unfortunately, we were not told that a booster dose had to be given after six months. Mrinalini was the first to get affected and was isolated to protect the baby. It was a futile exercise, for Yogja soon got her infection at the fag end of the course.

Though our performance at the Staff College was graded, there was no merit list as results were never declared. However, rumour had it that the serial number on the posting orders of departing students reflected one's position on the merit list. I was pleasantly surprised to see that I had been posted to the Military Operations Directorate at Army HQ, an honour usually reserved for one of the top three. The majority of army student officers were posted as brigade majors (BMs) and, not surprisingly, the entire talk in Wellington during that period was BM-centric. With the posting orders being published, the bush system of communication had all the wives buzzing, each one revelling in her husband's new posting. The significance of my new job had not yet gained any traction in the gossip mills, so Bharti was quite oblivious. The reality of the situation only dawned on her when my friends started congratulating her and jokingly offered to exchange their BM postings with me.

Battle of the Roses

This was the first time I was being posted to Army HQ, the sanctum sanctorum of the Indian Army—and within that, the Military Operations (MO) was the operational hub around which everything revolved. As GSO2 in the MO3, we were expected to handle virtually everything that came our way.

Accommodation in Delhi for a junior officer was always a nightmare, as the wait for a flat in the cantonment area could be two to three years. As was the usual practice, I looked for a place from within the accredited pool that usually had flats belonging to serving army officers. I was offered a DDA flat near Tihar Jail in East Delhi in what was then known as the G-II Area (and is today called Maya Enclave). Cupboards and basic woodwork had not yet been done in the flat, and the landlord—a colonel from the mechanized infantry—said we should move in, after which he would get the work done.

We moved in, but the promised work just didn't start. I finally went to see the colonel who rudely said he had no money to start the work. I suggested he at least buy a couple of cupboards for the flat so that we could at least put away our clothes that were still stored in wooden boxes. He promptly started throwing rank at me—and that really infuriated me. I took out the keys to the flat and tossed them on to his table, telling him the flat would be vacated in the next few hours.

I came home and told Bharti to shift the refrigerator to a neighbouring naval officer's residence; the rest of the baggage was shifted out and deposited on the road. I got a large tarpaulin to cover it, after which Bharti, Mrinalini and Yogja went to her parents' house. My week-long search for accommodation ended not far from the recently-vacated flat. An IIT professor who had a duplex in the same colony then offered his place. After sitting on the road for a week, our possessions were moved into our new home.

On a cold foggy February morning, I made my way to Army HQ on my scooter and reported to Major Udai Bapat (later major general), also an infantry officer from the Kumaon Regiment, whom I was slated to relieve. My immediate boss was Colonel Ajinder Singh 'Ginger' Bal, who was an armoured corps officer from the Deccan Horse. Ginger Bal, in turn, reported to the DDG (deputy director general), Brigadier (later Lieutenant General) DD Saklani, who was from the Kumaon Regiment and subsequently served as the security advisor to the Governor of J&K. Next in line was Major General VK 'Tubby' Nayar, another outstanding officer who retired from the army as the Western Army Commander and then went on to serve as

Governor of both Nagaland and Manipur. A paratrooper, 'Tubby' was the straight-talking, no-nonsense type. Presiding over this empire was an equally impressive guardsman, Lieutenant General CN Somanna, who in true regimental tradition, kept a comb and a brush handy to keep his moustache immaculately combed.

As Bapat initiated me into the job, I was also introduced to the entire chain of command. Eventually I found myself facing the DGMO who gave me a warm handshake and a quick introduction to what was then the prevailing philosophy at MO: 'Son, you've come here as a GSO2. The work culture at MO is that you are free to give your opinion even if it is shitty! It will then be my job to figure out if your opinion holds water or not! So do not be afraid of giving your opinion.'

General Somanna was from Coorg, the region that had given India some of its finest generals, including the first Indian commander-in-chief, General (later Field Marshal) KM 'Kipper' Cariappa and, subsequently, General KS Thimayya. Somanna ran an effective team, where the emphasis was on handwritten notes, typed documents usually only being reserved for the COAS's briefs. This open system of communication was extremely effective, particularly as we were dealing with a wide range of subjects: from the JSQR (Joint Service Quality Requirement) of a weapon system to nuclear policy! Each subject required a reasonable amount of study and one had to be extremely careful in putting up one's comments. The joke doing the rounds in Army HQ was that any and every issue, which no one knew where to slot, would eventually land up in MO3 (this probably even happens today).

MO3 dealt with the entire Western Sector, stretching from the extreme north of Kashmir to Punjab, Rajasthan and Gujarat. MO1 looked after the Eastern Sector while MO2 handled all internal security issues.

The buzzword in MO at the time was 'Siachen' and it was demanding most of our attention. The trigger point for our interest in the area was the discovery of US Air Force maps that amounted to cartographic aggression on what was essentially our territory. On the American maps, the boundary from NJ 9842 (roughly the location of Chalunka near Turtuk) ran almost in a straight line to the Karakoram Pass on the eastern edge of what is known as the Aksai Chin region. Until 1972, most maps from Pakistan, the United Nations and other atlases depicted the ceasefire line more or less correctly, but then the United States Defense Mapping Agency (later renamed the National Geospatial-Intelligence Agency) began to tamper with the boundary on their Tactical Pilotage Charts. Taking their cue from the American maps, various other agencies began drawing the same lines on their maps. This effectively meant that the entire area north of the Nubra-Shyok junction, including the whole of the Siachen region, adding up to approximately 5,000 square kilometres, was shown as being under Pakistan's control.

Subsequently, Colonel Narender 'Bull' Kumar had led a probing army expedition across the glaciated region, going up to Indira Col at the extreme northern edge of Siachen beyond which lies the Shaksgam Valley. He had found significant evidence of expeditions from various countries that had been sent in with support from Pakistan, and at a particular point, Colonel Kumar's expedition was even buzzed by Pakistan Army helicopters. At this stage, the decision was taken to get on to the glacier and occupy the two main passes—Bilafond La and Sia La—which allowed ingress across the north-south Saltoro Range that flanked the western edge of Siachen.

Lieutenant General ML Chibber, a Gorkha officer, was the Northern Army Commander, and was universally respected for his professional acumen. After retirement, he was awarded the Padma Bhushan, and his books on leadership have been a welcome addition to our own home-grown military literature on the subject. At the time, XV Corps, headquartered in Srinagar, was looking after both the Kashmir Valley and the entire Trans-Himalayan zone (which included Zanskar, parts of Baltistan, Ladakh, the Nubra Valley and the area up to the Karakoram Pass where we had a presence at Daulat Beg Oldi (DBO). Lieutenant General PN Hoon, a Dogra Regiment officer, was the corps commander and his Colonel MS (military secretary) was NC Vij, also from the Dogra Regiment, who later rose to the rank of general and was the Chief of Army Staff.

During the previous year, a team led by the corps commander had begun shopping for alpine and arctic equipment in Europe so that we could reassert ourselves by sending troops into the area usurped by Pakistan. This team reported from Europe that the Pakistanis were also looking for similar equipment, which indicated that they were planning to come across Bilafond La and Sia La on to the glacier itself so as to block off any attempt from our side. This added a sense of urgency to the whole affair.

By February-March 1984, plans were being prepared for Operation Meghdoot which got its code name from the cloud messenger of the fourth-century play by Kalidasa. The first big problem was the lack of information about the area, as the maps were extremely sketchy. I went about collecting all the old journals of the Indian Mountaineering Federation (IMF) to see what information could be garnered from the various expeditions that had gone into the region. Until then, the plans on our side were only for the occupation of the two main passes, but as I leafed through the IMF journals, I came across details of expeditions that had crossed over from other passes as well. The expedition that caught my attention was that of the American mountaineer and cartographer, Fanny Bullock Workman, who in 1912, had come down the Lolofond Glacier through Gyong La on to the main Siachen Glacier. This expedition included the British surveyor, Grant Peterkin, who did an extensive study of the upper section of the glacier. Workman was responsible for naming Indira Col and also for bringing to the fore the local name 'Siachen' (derived from the wild roses found near the mouth of the Nubra River). In the Balti language, 'Sia' means rose and 'Chun' means abundance.

I prepared a handwritten note based on this study and sent it up the chain of command, pointing out that the occupation of Gyong La should also be vectored into our plans. XV Corps said that, as the people on the ground, they had a better appreciation of the region and they brushed this suggestion aside.

The entire plan was then presented to Prime Minister Indira Gandhi. Also present were Defence Minister R Venkataraman (later President of India), Defence Secretary SK Bhatnagar (later one of the accused in the Bofors case, where it was alleged that he had swung the deal in the Swedish firm's favour; he went on to be Governor of Sikkim) and the JS (G), Ajai Vikram Singh. The prime minister approved the plans and sanctioned the operation. There were no long notes, no endless debates, just a very focused briefing where a decisive prime minister took a firm decision and gave the go-ahead. This was Indian territory and, as far as she was concerned, that settled the issue. Accordingly, the date for launching Operation Meghdoot was then decided—D-day for airlifting troops on to Siachen was 13 April 1984.

The Pakistani side was expecting us to make our move, and they figured we would follow the same time-span as had been followed by the probing expedition of May/June in the previous year. Our main concern was the weather and the level of fresh snow over the ice, but, as it turned out, the initial operation was extremely successful. Helicopters could lift only one or, at the most, two soldiers at a time with their equipment and ammunition, and our boys moved on to Sia La and Bilafond La. Each pass was to be held by teams of sixty men, but, in the final analysis, not more than half that number could be sustained at any given time.

The Kumaonese and Ladakhi Scout troops pulled off what seemed at the time an impossible task. Colonel DK Khanna was commanding 19 Kumaon while Major RS Sandhu was the officer in charge of operations on the ground. Captain Sanjay Kulkarni had the honour of posting the tricolour on Bilafond La. With the heights secured, the rest of the men moved forward under the command of Captain PV Yadav. Many men suffered from frostbite, and the helicopters, unused as they were to flying at those heights, did an incredible job. A small five-man team was even dropped at Indira Col. At the time, the road link to Siachen along the Nubra River was virtually non-existent, the track terminating well short of the mouth of the glacier. On the main body of the glacier a DZ (helicopter drop zone) was established and this was to become the rear that would sustain the troops at both Sia La and Bilafond La. It was then known as the advanced camp but was later named Kumar in honour of Bull who had led the army expeditions into the region during the previous years.

As previously decided, Gyong La was to be bypassed by us, but as D-day approached, it became obvious that it could prove to be a costly mistake. Further, it soon became apparent that the Pakistani side was trying to occupy the pass. This resulted in a change of plans and Gyong La was also included in our list of objectives at the last minute. All available helicopters, however, were earmarked for the other two passes and it was decided to take the objective by walking up to it. Tragically, an avalanche wiped out a platoon as they advanced during daylight hours. Subsequent troops could not advance across the crevasse-infested snowfields leading up to the pass, as Pakistan's Burzil Force had occupied the area by then, and machine guns had the area covered from positions that were later labelled as OP1 and OP2. To this day, we haven't recovered this area. Almost thirty years on, the Pakistanis still have domination to deny us the use of Gyong La, which is the closest they come to the Siachen region today. Other than that, the entire Saltoro Range was then with us.

The failure to take Gyong La impacted our lines of communication to the central part of the glacier, and we had to develop an alternate approach through an area that was extremely unstable and treacherous in terms of avalanches and crevasses. This was unfortunate because we suffered quite a few casualties in that region. Sia La and Bilafond La, on the other hand, quickly became well-established posts. By the end of April/early May 1984, the first attacks were launched by the Pakistanis, but they couldn't dislodge us from there.

The performance of the Indian soldier had, once again, been outstanding, almost unbelievable, and it is a pity that many of the outstanding actions never got the recognition they deserved due to the shroud of secrecy. Operation Meghdoot clearly highlighted that, given political will and careful planning, our troops could deliver even the impossible.

Because Siachen was treated as a 'national cause', a lot of things fell into place which might have not otherwise happened. One of the immediate requirements was for an over-snow vehicle (OSV)—a huge contraption that could go over the glacier. Colonel APS Chauhan, who later retired as a major general, headed the MO4. An engineer officer, he had considerable high altitude experience, having also been an instructor at the High Altitude Warfare School. An extremely practical, down-to-earth officer, he immediately did a paper analysis which involved looking at all available equipment. He narrowed down the options to an Austrian OSV which he felt had the appropriate power ratio best suited to the requirements. It was procured without any delay.

The next problem was transporting the OSV to the glacier. Here again, the Indian Army did what it does best: a three-ton vehicle was modified with planks to increase the width and was hoisted across some of the most hostile terrain in the world without any fuss and bother. Later, quite typically, all sorts of nonsense came up. Some people from the Ministry of Defence wanted to procure German OSVs that had performed well in the Antarctic regions. We had to tell them quite firmly that the conditions in Siachen were quite different. It wasn't just the temperature; it was the terrain that we had to look at. For most of us junior officers, the lesson was clear—it was necessary to staff the Ministry of Defence with bureaucrats with military knowledge; failing this, we would never be able to attain the type of synergy we needed.

At one level, I felt like I was back at the NDA, for I was constantly on the move. The Siachen Operation was to be totally under wraps, and every report would come as a 'top secret SITREP'. As the GSO2, I had to personally receive it, take it by hand, show it by hand, and finally file it by hand. In the meantime, we were continuously updating our own database with whatever information we could garner, for we were now getting aerial photos and all other hitherto unavailable information. It was quite a busy period and an extremely interesting one.

Demilitarization? Sentimental Hogwash

Post-retirement, the army and corps commanders Lieutenant Generals Chibber and Hoon published articles that expounded their views on Siachen. Quite naturally, over the years, these have had a bearing on the ongoing discussions, with proponents of demilitarization often quoting both these officers who were involved in the initial operations.

Why did we go into Siachen in 1984? This was crystal clear: Siachen was a part of our territory and US cartographic aggression could not be tolerated without it impacting our claim over the entire state of Jammu and Kashmir. As far as Mrs Gandhi was concerned, that was the beginning and the end of the debate. Given the conditions and the available information, I think it is fair to state that Northern Command, in its appreciation of the situation, planned on occupying the two possible major routes of ingress during the summer months, pulling the troops back once the weather closed in (as was the norm along most of the LOC beyond Zoji La). In 1983, the XV Corps commander, General Hoon had done a threat assessment from Pakistan that had exaggerated the opposing side's offensive capability at the time; the exercise finishing with a flourish in which Khardung La and Leh were threatened.

The US interpretation, it needs to be understood, went against the grain of the Shimla Agreement that clearly stated that the boundary was demarcated up to NJ 9842 and 'thence north to the Glaciers'. Two factors influenced our approach: first, as stated earlier, we were looking to establish our claim line and then man it only during the summer months; second, not wanting to go against the spirit of the Shimla Agreement, we were not looking at occupying Dansum which would have been the most logical objective for the Indian Army. All the three major passes, Sia La to the north, Bilafond La in the middle and Gyong La in the south, converge at Dansum, which is a flat valley roughly at the same height as Leh, and ideal for heliborne operations. This would have cut Pakistan off from the Saltoro altogether and also threatened Khapalu. Incidentally, Dansum was to become the headquarters of Pakistan's 323 Brigade subsequently. The option of occupying Dansum, however, though discussed and debated, was ruled out because the area lay distinctly to the west of NJ 9842.

At the time, quite naturally, our policy vis-a-vis Siachen was completely Pakistan-centric and our stand was in keeping with our legal and moral stand on Kashmir, ever since the state had become a bone of contention between India and Pakistan in 1947. Prime Minister Indira Gandhi was a good decision maker, with the ability to get to the crux of the problem immediately. A couple of perceptive questions, and she would know what the larger issue was. She had the feel—and this, combined with her ability to take the decision, was a great asset.

Subsequently, Siachen developed a momentum of its own—8 JAK LI captured Qaid Post (at 22,000 feet) from Pakistan. This was an incredible action in which Naib Subedar Bana Singh was awarded a well-deserved Param Vir Chakra, and since then the post has been renamed Bana Top. Eventually, though they continue to claim otherwise, Pakistan does not have any influence on the Siachen Glacier, all their positions being well below the western slopes of the Saltoro Ridge. In subsequent talks with Pakistan, we pointed out that even in the old princely demarcation of regions for revenue within the state of Jammu and Kashmir, the Saltoro was the dividing geographical feature that separated Baltistan from Ladakh. The Shyok and the Nubra rivers had always been considered to be in the Ladakh region while the area where the Pakistanis are today was always considered Baltistan.

Leave alone Siachen, in the larger context of Jammu and Kashmir, Pakistan never had a case. The sooner our people realize this, the better. In 2007, in a bizarre move, under the aegis of an American agency, two brigadiers—one from India and the other from Pakistan—worked out a knock-kneed plan which focused on the demilitarization of the Siachen Glacier.

Shaksgam Valley had been ceded by Pakistan to China in 1963 and the understanding between Pakistan and China was that the agreement would be reviewed once the status of Jammu and Kashmir was finally decided. This tacitly indicates that China recognized that the area was in dispute, and that Pakistan had no right to give away the Shaksgam Valley.

Then there is the Aksai Chin that is to the east of the Karakoram Pass that is the boundary with the Chinese. KK Pass is just above DBO as a part of the Karakoram watershed, dividing Sinkiang and J&K. This was the old pass that linked the two countries. DBO was the place where caravans used to halt—Daulat Beg died there. Today DBO is held by our troops—mainly Ladakh Scouts and ITBP (Indo-Tibetan Border Police).

In the larger sense, if you leave Siachen unoccupied, it has a major impact for then it gives the levy for interpretations which is something the United States did in the late 60s and early 70s which resulted in Pakistan upping the ante by very cleverly sponsoring expeditions into this area. If we are indeed asked to 'demilitarize' and pull our troops out of what is our own area, then Pakistan and China have complete freedom to move where they want and we will be in no position to oppose this. We may not even get to know about it, as happened in Kargil, for we will not have any eyes on the ground. Once they come into this area, the whole of the Nubra Valley is vulnerable—for the enemy can outflank Turtok and come straight down the glacier. Not only that, but when facing eastwards from Siachen, there are routes available through the Rimo group of glaciers to cut through to the Karakoram Pass. Tomorrow, if there is a confluence of interest between China and Pakistan to move into Ladakh, then it will be very difficult to stop them. The recent ingress by the Chinese into the DBO area on the eastern flank of Siachen underlines the fact that with improving technology, there is no area in the region which cannot be accessed.

Today, Siachen is completely stable, and with the ceasefire in Jammu and Kashmir, the situation is holding up. Logistics have improved by leaps and bounds, and we have enough clothing and material support for a large number of troops. The roads are reasonably good; the induction routes are clearly defined; and the troops are in much better condition today. Twenty-five years of data over a period of time is also allowing us now to tackle problems associated with extreme high altitude.

A withdrawal from the positions on the Saltoro and the glacier would also require a fresh line of defence, which perforce would have to be south of the Shyok River along the Ladakh Range. All sorts of figures have been bandied about the 'economic cost' of Siachen over the years. These figures will mean next to nothing if this fresh defensive line has to be drawn up. Basically, we'll be right back to the US-sponsored pre-1984 line that was propagated by American mapping agencies.

The other factor that pro-demilitarization groups have been implying is the 'human' factor, saying it is inhuman to have troops deployed in these areas. However, we must remember that our troops elsewhere also face the same conditions: Turtok, Chorbatla, Batalik, Dras, Guraiz, even Bum La and North Sikkim are just a few locations with similar problems. As a nation, we have no choice but to guard our borders, however difficult and challenging the conditions. This sentimental nonsense has to be put aside for good. CBMs (confidence building measures) with Pakistan are fine, but not at the cost of our national security.

The General K Factor (The First Big Blunder)

In 1947, the Punjabi Suba Movement under the aegis of the Akali Dal demanded a Punjabi state on linguistic grounds. The States Reorganization Commission, however, felt that there was very little grammatical difference between Punjabi and Hindi and thus dismissed the demand. The issue continued to fester and, in 1955, the demand for Punjabi to be recognized as the official language led to the issue spilling on to the streets. The police were ordered to control the situation and several Akali Dal leaders—including Tara Singh, Gurcharan Singh Tohra and even the Jathedar of the Akal Takht, Achchhar Singh—were arrested. As the police closed in on the protestors, the crowds fell back towards the Golden Temple, seeking sanctuary in the holiest of Sikh shrines.

The original gurdwara was constructed in 1574. A small lake amidst scattered brush country, so typical of the Punjab, surrounded it. Subsequently, the third Sikh Guru, Guru Amar Das, was visited by the Mughal emperor Akbar, who gifted a jagir to the Guru's daughter on her wedding to Bhai Jetha, who later became the fourth Sikh Guru, Guru Ram Das. The lake was enlarged, but it was left to the fifth Guru, Guru Arjan, to build a full-fledged gurdwara. Construction started in 1588 and it was finally completed in 1604. The architectural features of the Harmandir Sahib (as it is known to the Sikhs) were designed to represent the Sikh world view. Instead of the established custom of building a place of worship on high ground, the gurdwara was built at a lower level than the surrounding area so that the devotees would have to descend steps to enter the temple. It was also open from all four sides. Guru Arjan then installed the Guru Granth Sahib in it and appointed Baba Buddha as the granthi. In 1764, Jassa Singh Ahluwalia and other Sikh misls got together and rebuilt the gurdwara. However, it was left to Maharaja Ranjit Singh in the early nineteenth century to cover the upper floors of the Harmandir Sahib with gold.

Following the 1965 India-Pakistan war, the state of Punjab was further split to form Himachal Pradesh and the new state of Haryana. And, Punjabi was finally recognized as the official language of the truncated Punjab.

The dividing line between the religious and the political has always been a bit blurred in Punjab. In 1971, an advertisement appeared in *The New York Times* proclaiming the formation of Khalistan or the Land of the Khalsa. Millions of dollars were collected during the next few years and, eventually, in 1980, Jagjit Singh Chauhan, the chief proponent of the movement, was granted an audience with Prime Minister Indira Gandhi. Shortly after that, at Anandpur Sahib, Chauhan declared the formation of the National Council of Khalistan with himself as the president and Balbir Singh Sandhu as its secretary general. In Amritsar, postage stamps and currency notes proclaiming the state of Khalistan were issued, while the Government of India watched nervously from the sidelines. The Akali Dal, under the leadership of Harchand Singh Longowal, attacked the Congress after accusing it of being hand-in-glove with the Khalistani.

By the end of May 1984, the situation in Punjab was becoming extremely tense, with the Khalistan movement at its peak. Pakistan was having a field day, not only fishing in troubled waters but also doing its best to stoke the fires of a secessionist movement that sought to create a separate Sikh country within the Punjab region of India.

With Pakistan's open and blatant support, some of the proponents of Khalistan turned to militancy, with the most prominent among them being Jarnail Singh Bhindranwale, a religious leader whose tough stance against the government was attracting a large following.

In 1982, Harchand Singh Longowal, the leader of the Akali Dal invited Bhindranwale and his followers to take up residence within the Golden Temple, hoping to use the firebrand leader as a weapon against the government. Accordingly, accompanied by a group of heavily-armed followers, Bhindranwale moved into Guru Nanak Niwas, the Shiromani Gurudwara Prabandhak Committee's (SGPC) guesthouse within the temple complex. The die had been cast, and the situation continued to worsen. By December 1983, Bhindranwale and his entourage had moved into the holy Akal Takht in spite of the objections of the head priest, Giani Kirpal Singh. The Punjab Police and the government watched from outside the temple complex as a stream of self-loading rifles and light machine guns were smuggled in, helping not just to fortify the temple, but create a volatile situation that would blow up sooner or later.

The deteriorating situation in Punjab was being closely watched at the MO Directorate. Various scenarios were discussed and contingency plans drawn up, to tackle any untoward situation that might suddenly develop with Pakistan an active partner. All sorts of intelligence was coming in, some of which surely would have had an impact on the government's thinking. One can only presume that there was additional information that convinced the prime minister that the time had come for the army to be brought in.

In May 1984, Indira Gandhi called for a conference at her residence. It was attended by the COAS, General Arun Shridhar Vaidya, the DGMO, General Somanna, and the Western Army Commander who had come down from Chandimandir, Lieutenant General Krishnaswamy Sundarji. After the conference, a somewhat subdued and despondent General Somanna returned to the MO directorate. Details of the meeting with the prime minister soon trickled down the chain of command. Indira Gandhi had discussed the situation within the Golden Temple, and asked the Western Army Commander if the entire group of militants could be flushed out. General Sundarji had responded positively, reportedly saying that if there was a requirement to clear the Golden Temple, he would have it cleared in no time. If the situation warranted, he would put his troops through. There was no problem.

Sundarji's belligerent stance put the COAS in an awkward situation. Nevertheless, General Vaidya stuck to the logic that had been given by the MO Directorate and suggested a 'wait and watch' policy. As the chief, with General Somanna by his side, began to explain the reasoning behind this advice, Indira Gandhi impatiently cut him short and asked him why he was anticipating problems when the army commander on the ground was confident of resolving the issue.

General Sundarji always looked to be a man in a tremendous hurry, and it was felt that he was too willing to do things without getting into the details of the matter. Mrs Gandhi had faced a similar situation in 1971 when, early in the year, she had wanted the army to plunge into East Pakistan. The army chief then, General Sam Manekshaw, had firmly stood his ground and advocated that we wait, build up our own positions and then move in when the time was right. At that time, Mrs Gandhi had no option but to follow Manekshaw's advice. On this occasion, the army commander was far more confident, articulate and positive, while the chief was pointing out the negatives that the prime minister did not want to hear, so she decided to overrule the COAS. Sundarji's optimism carried the day and a decision was taken to commit the army.

This set the ball rolling for what was to be one of India's darkest chapters—Operation Blue Star.

There were two fundamental violations, and these were to stay deeply imprinted in my mind. In the history of independent India, this was the second time that a prime minister had gone over the head of the army chief and taken a decision based on a subordinate officer's advice. In 1962, Indira

Gandhi's father, Prime Minister Jawaharlal Nehru, had done much the same thing, relying on inputs given by Lieutenant General Brij Mohan Kaul who was then the chief of general staff, overriding the chief, General PN Thapar. In general, the army chief's advice to the government is based on the studied and evaluated inputs provided by the MO Directorate, and is rarely based on personal opinion. The chief's input and advice would no doubt shape and influence the decisions, but once these had been recommended by the MO, the matter usually ended there. The very fact that General Sundarji was present at the meeting was in itself a blunder.

The second issue was even more basic and it impacted most of us to our very core: the use of the army as an offensive weapon against our own people has always been traumatic, be it in the Northeast, Jammu and Kashmir or Punjab or elsewhere in the country. One of the army's mandated roles in independent India has been to come to the aid of civilian authority whenever called for, internal security being as important as combating external threats. This topic was the subject of much debate within Army HQ; calling for the army to tackle internal law-and-order issues implied the failure of the police and the paramilitary forces. Calling for the army to prevent anarchy was always an option available to the government, but its ramifications were huge; and in the case of Punjab, even with terrorism rampant in the state, calling the army to clear out the Golden Temple was akin to plunging a dagger into one's own breast.

Indira Gandhi also unwittingly created a situation where Army HQ now had to play a secondary role to Western Command in planning the operation. Even then the warning signs were clearly present. The army commander's bravado having set the ball rolling, Command HQ now went into a tailspin, the staff realizing that they actually had very little information on the temple complex. Amazingly, there wasn't even a tourist map or chart of the place that could be made available. MGGS Western Command called the MO Directorate and asked for photographs of the Golden Temple complex. We told them we didn't have any. He called back shortly asking for aerial images. The request was immediately passed on to Air HQ who launched a Jaguar sortie.

Western Command drew up the operational plans. The chief of staff was Lieutenant General Ranjit Singh Dayal, an excellent sportsman and a paratrooper. Humane, approachable, big-hearted and a popular figure who was held in high esteem by both officers and men, he had distinguished himself in the 1965 war (he was a major then) when he led a night assault and captured the important Haji Pir Pass that separated Poonch from the Kashmir Valley. He was awarded a well-deserved Maha Vir Chakra for this action. That he himself was a Sikh was to play an important part, as he was instrumental in helping to defuse and control the emotions around Amritsar as events unfolded.

The army commander continued to take decisions that were surprising. 15 Division, based in Amritsar with some local knowledge of the temple complex, was commanded by Major General Jamwal, but the task was given to the Meerut-based 9 Division. Accordingly, a brigade was hurriedly moved into the city. Major General Kuldip Singh 'Bulbul' Brar, a second-generation Sikh officer, was picked to lead the assault on the temple complex. Commissioned into the Maratha Light Regiment, Brar had commanded his battalion during the Bangladesh War and had been awarded the Vir Chakra for the battle of Jamalpur, where his battalion had faced the same 31 Baluch whose offensive language had stalled the Mukti Bahini attack in August 1971.

Could Blue Star have been handled differently? Those are the 'ifs and buts' of history, but to us in Army HQ, it seemed that the Western Army Commander, having forced the situation, was relying heavily on the militants inside the Golden Temple surrendering the moment they saw the army.

Major General Shabeg Singh (of Bangladesh fame) who had joined Bhindranwale had supervised the entire defences; the Akal Takht and the surrounding buildings had been completely sealed off. All the defending weapons were sited just a few inches above the ground, which meant that not only would any attacking force get swept off their feet, the men could not even crawl forward towards the objective without getting shot in the head. Frankly, General Sundarji was in a terrible situation: he had told the prime minister that he would clear out the temple complex in no time; but the assaulting units still didn't have any basic intelligence of what to expect within the temple.

On the eve of the attack, 'Bulbul' Brar decided to take a walk around the Golden Temple in civilian clothes. Shabeg Singh immediately recognized him but he was not confronted by any of the militants. Brar recognized the enormity of the task at hand, but it was too late, for the events had been set in motion. To complicate matters further, the sanctum sanctorum (which houses the Guru Granth Sahib) in the middle of the temple complex would have to be protected at all costs—orders were given to the men that no one would fire in that direction regardless of the provocation. The only hope for avoiding a bloodbath was that the militants holed up inside the Akal Takht would see reason and surrender.

On the night of 5 June, the tension at Army HQ was palpable. Two huge blunders would complicate the already extremely delicate situation. First, it was the anniversary of Guru Arjan's martyrdom, which meant that in the days preceding the attack, a large number of pilgrims were inside the Golden Temple. Most of the devotees had been herded into the various rooms and were not allowed to leave, effectively serving as hostages. Second, and this was bizarre, it was a full moon night! The white marble parikrama of the Golden Temple complex was lit up like a shooting gallery!

Sundarji's bluster now had to face the realities on the ground. The plans for the attack were ad hoc, and virtually all basic tenets of fighting in a built-up area were ignored. 1 Para Commando was to lead the assault from the western entrance, but a team from special forces, armed with gas canisters, arrived and insisted they had been tasked by 'madam' to gas the militants out. Frantic calls eventually resulted in an An-32 flying in gas masks for the supporting commandos so that they weren't put to sleep as well. The gas canisters had been rushed in from the BSF training centre at Tekanpur near Gwalior and stencilled on each was the horrifying message 'Do not use after 1978'.

It took a lot of courage on the part of the soldiers to go in for what was virtually a suicidal frontal attack, made deadlier still by the complicated orders of not using rocket launchers or firing in the direction of the sanctum sanctorum. Not surprisingly, the gas canisters failed to explode and a carpet of light machine-gun fire meant that we were buying casualties by the dozen. Both the Akal Takht and the Dakshini Deori, the two objectives on the northern end of the complex, were almost unapproachable. With the special forces and the Para Commandos unable to move, elements of 10 Guards were pushed in from the west, 26 Madras from the south and 15 Kumaon from the eastern entrance.

Eighty-three men of the Indian Army died that night while another 220 were wounded, a horrific number by any standards. Added to this was the tragic loss of a large number of hostages, including women and children. Eventually, from not letting his advance elements use even basic weapons like RLs, Bulbul Brar had to call in tanks and BMPs that eventually neutralized the Akal Takht.

As a major in the MO Directorate at that time, my perspective was obviously limited, but the lessons of Operation Blue Star deeply influenced my thinking. And these lessons got entrenched over time.

The most obvious lesson was: never bypass the chain of command. The genesis of the entire problem lay in the prime minister inviting the Western Army Commander to her residence when the decision to involve the army was taken. The events that were set in motion that day eventually cost the prime minister her own life.

The moment General Sundarji pulled the carpet out from under the feet of the COAS, military logic had been compromised and each subsequent decision was guided by political rather than operational logic. It also underlined the fact that someone somewhere along the line had to have the gumption to point out that the situation was being handled wrongly. This never happened and Army HQ effectively became a spectator. At the end of the day, I realized it is imperative that we speak up and point out a mistake even if it is an unpopular thing to do. The casualties, both of the army and the civilian population that got caught in the crossfire, were just not acceptable.

Last, but not least, the fact that the army had the fallback option of using tanks probably acted as a huge negative. Western Command would have, in all probability, planned and executed the entire operation far more methodically, with less collateral damage, had the option of using armour been removed completely from General Sundarji's table.

One unfortunate fallout of Operation Blue Star was the assassination of the prime minister, Indira Gandhi. Two Sikh members of her own security detail gunned her down at her residence on 31 October 1984. As she was rushed to the All India Institute of Medical Sciences, MO started monitoring the situation. By the evening, BBC and All India Radio had announced that the prime minister had breathed her last. Almost on cue, riots erupted across Delhi, as hundreds of Sikhs began to be targeted and butchered in the most heinous manner.

In my opinion, complete policy paralysis had set in. The army should have been called in almost instantly, but this was not done, and forty-eight hours were to go by during which time there was absolute mayhem on the streets. Through that fateful night, our black-and-white television screens were reporting events via Doordarshan, but the reports were mainly confined to beaming tributes and funeral music. The next morning, I made my way from my residence near Tihar Jail to Army Headquarters and there was a pall of smoke hanging over the city, with vehicles having been burned along with people who had been dragged out of their homes. Delhi's police force had in effect abandoned the city to political goons who were on a savage rampage.

This complete failure to act was shocking—a more pragmatic chain of command would have acted swiftly. To add to the horror, a lot of our own Sikh troops and officers, who were in transit, travelling on trains, were hunted down and killed. A situation like that should never be allowed to develop again, not just in our cities but anywhere in the country. Yet, sadly, refusing to learn from history, similar situations have repeatedly erupted.

In the MO Directorate the immediate concern was the welfare and safety of the troops, especially since there were a few mutinies that took place. The most notable was the shooting of the commandant, Brigadier SC Puri, and some other officers at the Sikh Regimental Centre in Ramgarh, Bihar. Fortunately, by and large, the situation within the army remained under control. Somehow, one couldn't help but feel that the leadership quotient had failed us when there had been trouble. It was a tense and grim period—the most important lesson one learnt at the time was that the political leadership was not without its own cracks. Even the most revered leaders often developed feet of clay when the chips were down.

This had a direct impact on national security, for in the civil-military command and control structure, the security forces, despite having the resources to deal with a situation, just sat back on their heels waiting for orders. Firm, decisive leadership in times of any crisis is an absolute must. Situations had to be anticipated and if possible, a problem had to be tackled even before it began to germinate and developed multiple tentacles of its own.

Emotions were running high, yet, on the ground, most units with Sikh troops held firm. The credit for this has to go to the commanding officers who were pragmatic in their dealings with both the men and officers. In a volatile situation, it takes very little for troublemakers to drum up support on religious matters. Ever since June when Blue Star was launched, we felt we were sitting on a tinderbox. Something had to happen and when it did, we as a nation were found wanting. *The anti-Sikh riots should never have happened.*

1984 came to an end and the nation heaved a collective sigh of relief. Towards the end of the year, the Congress Party, riding on a sympathy wave, had swept back to power giving Prime Minister Rajiv Gandhi an unprecedented majority of 411 seats out of a possible 542 in Parliament. At forty, Indira Gandhi's son and heir was the youngest prime minister the country had ever had, bringing with him a wave of fresh hope and new ideas that promised to put the years of 'licence raj' behind us.

7

IPKF AND THE UNCONVENTIONAL WAR

General K's Folly: The Second Big Blunder

Towards the end of 1986, India had begun its preparations for Exercise Brasstacks that was due to run its course the following year. The war game was one of the largest ever to have been planned, involving thousands of troops and armour, and it extended well beyond just the army. Various new concepts were to be tried out under simulated battle conditions and the scope and scale of Brasstacks was massive by any standards. Being held on the Pakistan border in Rajasthan, it was imperative that, we did not spook the Pakistan Army into doing something silly. Accordingly, as was the norm between the two countries, the Pakistan Army high command was notified of troop movements relating to the exercise.

After the usual hectic day in MO3, I packed my bag and headed home, where Bharti was waiting impatiently to attend a social engagement. I had hardly entered the house when the telephone rang, and I was asked to return to Army HQ. Leaving my annoyed wife behind, I got on to my scooter and drove back to South Block.

The MO Directorate, which had been virtually deserted when I left earlier in the evening, was abuzz with activity. Officers from Military Intelligence were also there, but looked perplexed, wondering what had warranted such a scramble. With everyone in, we were briefed by Colonel Ginger Bal: 'We've been asked to take a look at all the activity across the border, training or otherwise. Our job is to go through all the information we have about the Pakistani formations and see if there is any change or unusual pattern emerging from their behaviour.' For the next four to five hours, we diligently pored over every bit of information we had and came to the conclusion that all was quiet on the western front. Accordingly, a brief was prepared for the DGMO to take to the COAS.

Lieutenant General RN Mahajan from the Kumaon Regiment had taken over from Somanna. He was the first DGMO to have come from Perspective Planning, and he took the brief prepared by us to the COAS,

General K Sundarji, elevated to the top job after General Vaidya retired. Sundarji, talking technology and modernization, had a personal equation with the prime minister and the political decision-making body, which was quite admirable.

Mahajan finished briefing the chief, stating categorically that there was nothing discernible which suggested any problems. Sundarji, however, was not convinced. 'Look at their 10 Corps again,' he insisted, 'why is it moving troops to the north?' This Pakistani formation was based around Murree and movement to the north would particularly impact the border in Jammu and Kashmir.

We re-examined every piece of information from every possible angle. Again, the same conclusion. No matter how we looked at it, there was nothing that suggested even the slightest deviation in the Pakistani position that could be viewed suspiciously. Once again, a brief was prepared stating that all was quiet. It was presented to the chief who was still not convinced. Until the previous evening, the entire focus had been on Exercise Brasstacks. This new development was not making any sense.

'Let us suppose,' said the chief, changing tack, 'that there is movement. Then what?'

The question was hypothetical and it could not possibly have any logical answer. It was true that for Brasstacks every Indian formation was moving into its designated place, leaving Punjab somewhat exposed. However, when the chief had planned the exercise, surely that aspect had been taken into account.

It almost seemed as if he was now second-guessing himself and in the process losing his nerve. Musing to himself, the chief intoned, 'With all our troops and attention in the Rajasthan area, we are wide open to any thrust by Pakistan in Punjab. They could move 10 Corps and declare Khalistan.' He then issued an order that stunned the DGMO and everybody else in the room. 'Move one of Army HQ's reserves opposite the 10 Corps area.'

As the implications of this development became clear, I walked into Ginger Bal's office. 'Sir, for two days we have gone over every bit of information and we are convinced that the Pakistanis are doing nothing untoward. Not just me, but all of us who have been tasked to look into this are convinced that there is absolutely nothing happening on the other side. But if we move our reserves, they have no option but to react to our move as a quid pro quo, then we'll react to that and they will move against that and soon we will be mobilized on the border.'

Bal looked at me with a resigned look, 'Yes, but you've heard the chief. Orders are orders.'

'I've heard the chief and I know what he's saying, but as a staff officer, it is my duty to point out the pitfalls of this order. I'm going to initiate a note to you, sir. You can tear it up or you can send it further up the chain, that's your call.'

I promptly prepared a handwritten three-page report saying much the same thing and handed it to Bal as was the prevailing culture at MO. I have no idea what happened to that note. The next day, I was called and told to start issuing instructions for the movement of the Army HQ reserves. Orders were accordingly drawn up and the reserves were mobilized over the next few days. Operation Trident had been launched willy-nilly.

Approximately ten days were to pass before the call came from Pakistan's DGMO on the hotline to his Indian counterpart. The Pakistani general said that while India had notified Pakistan about all Brasstacks-related troop movements in Rajasthan, there were other movements that did not fit into the overall profile. General Mahajan was non-committal, saying he wasn't aware of any such developments. The Pakistani general then signed off, saying that if the Indian position was that there was no deployment beyond Brasstacks, so be it. A few days later we started getting information of Pakistani formations taking up defensive positions in Jammu and Kashmir. Lieutenant General Ashoke Handoo was the Northern Army Commander and, in response to the Pakistani movement, he moved his artillery guns and some units forward towards the LOC. With Jammu, Akhnur, Rajouri, Poonch, Uri and the entire region in a state of high alert, we then got further information of Pakistani movement of troops in Punjab, where their Army Reserve South (ARS)—the 1st Armoured Division and 37 Infantry Division based in Multan—had a brigade move north into the corridor between the Sutlej and the Ravi. It soon became obvious that Pakistan was also reinforcing Army Reserve North (ARN) with formations from 11 and 12 Corps otherwise situated at Peshawar and Quetta respectively. A note was accordingly prepared for General Sundarji and the information was passed on to him.

'There,' exclaimed the chief, 'I told you people; they are moving in Punjab.' Unfortunately, it was going to get even worse. 'They're up to tricks! This is a zero warning situation.'

The chief wanted to know where our defensive formations were so that they could be mobilized. DGMO didn't know what exactly he was expected to say, 'They're deployed in Rajasthan for Brasstacks, sir.'

Sundarji now stared at his DGMO, taking in the information as if he was hearing of Brasstacks for the first time. 'Move them back. Post-haste.' The new orders led to a mad scramble as formations now rushed madly this way and that. Owing to Operation Trident, Brasstacks was effectively reduced to half the exercise it was supposed to be. It seemed to me that the disastrous consequences of Blue Star were as nothing when compared with the drama that was unfolding in Brasstacks and Operation Trident. The situation was soon so volatile that any trigger-happy officer or soldier on either side could have started a full-scale war. Fortunately, the junior leadership showed a higher degree of maturity than their senior officers in Army HQ.

With war hysteria building up all around, hundreds of thousands of people evacuated the area. War seemed imminent, with both the Indian and Pakistani prime ministers issuing threats to each other. In this grave scenario, Lieutenant General Hanut Singh (he had been the ADGMO earlier), who was commanding the elite II Corps, asked the chief a pertinent question. 'If we go to war, what do I tell the men? What are we fighting for?' The otherwise extremely articulate and suave chief had no answer.

The biggest casualty was Brasstacks itself. The armoured concepts that were being advocated by General Sundarji were to be checked on the ground but that never fully happened because the COAS seemed to have shot himself in the foot by launching Operation Trident in the interim. This would soon become a discernible pattern—rush in with little or no heed to the actual situation on the ground! It was later to transpire that Sundarji's source of information about 10 Corps' initial mysterious movement north had been an intercept that had been put up to the chief without going through proper procedures. It should have been routed through the DGMI to the DGMO, been assessed and if found to have weightage, only then been put up to the chief. In this case, an over-ambitious officer, seeing he had the chance to get the chief's attention, had circumvented the entire system with disastrous consequences. There can be no doubt that General Sundarji's was a brilliant mind with some very good ideas. Yet, he seemed to regularly get into a mess. Anyone who disagreed with him would face his wrath: 'You chaps cannot think big. Your brains are suited only for tactical appointments.'

The Dragon Stirs

Rajiv Gandhi had retained the defence portfolio. Even though he had the able Arun Singh as his minister of state, the prime minister, like his mother, repeatedly gave in to Sundarji's bluster. However, the fallout of Sundarji's belligerence was not always necessarily negative.

The Indo-Sino boundary dispute has been a lingering and vexing issue. The focus on Pakistan coupled with the remoteness of the boundary with China tends to push the problem away from the public gaze. Despite many rounds of talks, a solution to the problem does not seem imminent. On the contrary, China has had a tendency to subtly and surreptitiously move into unclaimed areas; these tactics were first evident during the Zhenbao incident and have also been a regular feature in both the Western (Ladakh and Lahaul Spiti) and Eastern (Arunachal and Sikkim) sectors. Any perceived sign of weakness on India's part, the Chinese are likely to become that much more assertive and overbearing.

Since the 1962 defeat at the hands of the PLA (People's Liberation Army), the Indian Army had not returned to the Namka Chu, stopping short on the Hathung La ridge that overlooked the ill-fated river valley from the south. The northern side of the valley led to the Thag La ridge, which was the demarcation of the McMahon Line that had been ratified by the British, Indian and Tibetan governments in 1914. Until the 1980s, the army had decided that in the event of another conflict with China, Tawang would be the forward line and the main line of defences would be along the Se La pass to its south. During General Krishna Rao's tenure, the thinking had changed, with the forward line once again being the Hathung La ridge.

Since 1983, IB (Intelligence Bureau) expeditions had probed into the Sumdorong area, which lies to the northeast of the confluence of the Namka Chu and Nyamjang Chu, but on the Indian side of the McMahon Line. Similar patrols had gone into the valley in the following few years as well and the Chinese had reacted by remonstrating through diplomatic channels. Though the army had repeatedly advised against going into the valley, the IB continued to send expeditions that would stay in the Sumdorong pastures and then fall back during the winter months. In 1986, when the IB team reached the valley, it found the Chinese had preceded them and the patrol almost got surrounded. The army had to send troops to bring them back safely.

Lieutenant General NS Narahari, a big, strapping engineer officer, was commanding IV Corps at the time. In a bold move, 9 Guards quickly occupied all the high features around the Chinese position while, at the same time, extracting the IB team from the area. Reinforcements were also pushed up to Zimithaung, south of Hathung La. Though this escalated tension all along the border, the Chinese eventually withdrew from the Sumdorong area though they established a small post at the mouth of the valley. So isolated had they become that one of their soldiers was reported to have committed suicide.

Similarly, in Ladakh, it had been felt that our positions were too far within our own area—both along the Indus River and across Chang La. Plans had been drawn up by Ashoke Handoo, when he was the BGS (brigadier general staff) XV Corps, to fix the situation, but no one seemed to want to alter the ground positions for fear of annoying the Chinese. In 1987, Operation Kartoos followed Exercise Checkerboard that had analysed the existing line of defence in Ladakh against the Chinese. Operation Kartoos was designed to implement Handoo's plan and push our positions forward, right up to the actual ground positions, thereby eliminating the gap between the LAC and our actual defensive line. All the commanding heights that had been ignored were therefore occupied. Post Checkerboard, even BMPs were inducted into Ladakh, a direct result of the chief's broader vision. General Sundarji needs to be given accolades for this.

25 Rajput

After two-and-a-half years in the MO Directorate, almost towards the end of my tenure, I had been allotted accommodation in Dhaula Kuan, and we moved from our quarters near Tihar Jail to the serene surroundings of the cantonment. This allowed Yogja to begin her academic career at the Delhi Area Primary School (DAPS). Two of Bharti's brothers, Sandeep and Vikrant, were also living with us, and they, along with Mrinalini, went to Army Public School (APS). It used to be a happy gaggle of children that hopped across the road to and from school.

I was posted back to 25 Rajput that had moved from Bum La in Arunachal to Pune, and was now lodged at Meerut. The battalion was in Pune just around the time when Operation Trident had been let loose and like most Indian Army units, had been all over the place during the next few months. They were cooling their heels on the Meerut firing ranges when I got my joining orders in January 1987. Colonel MC Nanjappa was at the helm and the 2IC was Venkat Ramanan. With seventeen years of service, a senior major, I was now back in the battalion as a company commander.

We stayed in Meerut for a few months, finally moving back to our lines in Pune in May where everything was a mess by then. It required a lot of cleaning up to get things back into some sort of working order. Around then, Major General VK Singh handed over charge to a new GOC who decided to inspect the brigade while we were doing our field firing. I was detailed to handle the general's visit.

Major General Harkirat Singh was a guardsman and there's nothing more terrifying than having a senior officer from the Brigade of the Guards come on an inspection—you never quite know what'll be the flavour of the day. The GOC decided to first visit our sister battalion, 12 Garhwal, and, true to form, he went into their officer's mess and inspected their refrigerator. There he found all kinds of problems; unauthorized items placed in a haphazard manner that did not conform to Indian Army regulations. Our sources were giving us feedback on the visit practically as a running commentary and we braced ourselves for our turn. Shortly thereafter, leaving a shell-shocked Garhwali battalion in his wake, Harkirat arrived at our location. He immediately recognized me, for I had been a student at the Staff College when he had been an instructor. 'I've taught you, so everything must be perfect with the unit,' said the general, paying himself a backhanded compliment.

'Yes, sir, everything is fine with the unit,' I echoed.

'Wonderful,' beamed the general, but years of being a guardsman leaves an indelible mark. He just couldn't help himself, for he compulsively pointed to a wire that was hanging somewhat loosely from a tree. 'Fix that, won't you?' and he was gone.

Along with 12 Garhwal and 2 Maratha LI, we made up 76 Brigade that was being commanded by Brigadier IM Dhar, who was from the Rajput Regiment. Towards the end of June, we knew something big was afoot, for we were placed on short notice to move into Sri Lanka. There had been a flurry of activity in the recent months that included the Indian Air Force air-dropping supplies to the Tamils in the northern part of the island. Reading the news and watching the reports on television, I could well visualize the buzz in MO3 that would have been akin to a beehive by then. However, at the unit level, one had to focus on working out load tables for a variety of aircraft types and get all the equipment packed accordingly.

Blissfully unaware of the geo-political developments, Bharti, after deciding to give up the Delhi accommodation, arrived in Pune with the girls just then. To her horror, she found everything packed or being packed at a frenetic pace. According to army regulations, we could not tell our families where we were going, so I beat around the bush in an effort to evade her questions.

A futile exercise, for she found out from the brigade commander that we were earmarked for Sri Lanka. The definition of 'short notice' kept changing; sometimes it was seventy-two hours, sometimes more, other times less, as all sorts of mobilization signals flew around in a flurry. In the meantime, a lot of telephone time was taken to ensure that the Delhi accommodation was not handed over and the transfer certificates from school returned.

The agreement between Sri Lanka and India was signed on 29 July 1987. The Indian intervention, meant to be a peacekeeping mission, was intended to end the war between the LTTE and the Sri Lankan Army. It got off to an inauspicious start with a Sri Lankan sailor from the Guard of Honour taking a swing at Prime Minister Rajiv Gandhi with his rifle butt in Colombo. The same night we were told to move—so we headed for Lohegaon, which is the Pune air force base. At the airport, there was complete chaos; all Indian Airline flights had been cancelled and aircraft after aircraft diverted to airlift troops to Chennai from where Indian Naval ships were being detailed to sail us across to the Emerald Isle. Most aircraft that landed in Pune had no idea of what was happening either—they were arriving with their full complement of airhostesses and in-flight food. They, in turn, were gawking at the boarding troops that had all sorts of equipment with them, including thunder boxes!

My company had already loaded on to two separate aircraft when there was a lot of commotion around one of the planes. I was watching from a distance when the brigade commander appeared and asked me to find out what was happening. I walked across to find the battalion havildar major (BHM), Tej Singh, an old paratrooper, in an animated state, confabulating with various members of the Indian Airlines ground crew. 'What is the problem?' I tentatively enquired.

'Saab, yeh quarter guard pole load nahin hora,' said the BHM. (Sir, the quarter guard pole is not loading.)

I asked them to tell me what had been tried until then. First, they had attempted to push the pole into the fuselage but had failed to get past the initial bend near the entrance where the airhostess usually stands, greeting passengers with hands folded. Then they had tried to tie it to the top of the aircraft, but the captain of the plane had freaked out, muttering some incomprehensible stuff about aerodynamics before running off into the dark in the general direction of air traffic control. So now they were trying to tie the pole to the bottom of the aircraft.

'Don't be daft,' I said, telling the BHM to get the pole to Chennai by train along with the vehicles of the battalion. My order was greeted with incredulous stares. How on earth could the battalion move without its quarter guard pole! Fortunately, an order is an order and the matter was settled without further debate.

I turned my attention to the second aircraft that had a lot of equipment waiting to be loaded into the cargo hold. The luggage area seemed jam-packed already, which was a bit surprising considering we had done all our weight calculations in advance. I poked my head into the aircraft's hold and gaped at the king-sized utensils that were occupying all the space.

I extracted my head and bumped into the company JCO, Girdhari Singh. I asked him what would happen to the rest of the baggage.

'Bade patile rakh diye hain,' he announced. (We've loaded the large utensils.) 'What about the forty-man sets?' I asked. 'Usme unit ka khaana nahin ban sakta,' said the subedar saab. (You cannot cook for the unit in those.) I decided to choose the path of least resistance, and ordered the men to stuff the rest of the baggage into the main cabin. By then the airline crew was far too horrified to complain any further, so the doors were shut with the giant cookware firmly in the hold. As a result of this, we were perhaps the only battalion that had the ability to feed our men when we landed in Sri Lanka.

The drama of loading was far from over. My men came and told me that the entire first line and second line mortar ammunition had been loaded in the aircraft I would be travelling in. 'Good,' I said, 'where?' 'In the hold, under your feet,' they proudly informed me. Mortar ammunition being fairly compact, though extremely heavy, had fitted neatly into the hold. The civil loaders had been contemptuously shooed off, and what had to be done had been done. There were fifty-five men in my aircraft. I told them to fan out so it looked like we had a full load of troops, hoping to compensate for the extra weight of the ammunition. The pilot came on board and asked how many men were 'manifested'. Ninety-five, he was told. They did a head count and finished with over a hundred; then did another and came up short with a figure around forty. Two, three more attempts and the crew gave up and announced that they would assume the strength of the passengers was one hundred. They shut the doors and the aircraft took off into the night sky, heading for Chennai.

As we approached Meenambakkam airport, the pilots were struggling, the aircraft obviously being overloaded. Their flying skills were fully tested and they did a superb job putting the aircraft down smoothly on the runway. Once the unloading began, the curious crew came around to the hold to see what came out. Three truckloads of compact cases were taken out, after which the senior pilot asked what was in the boxes. 'Mortar bombs,' he was told.

'Live?' he asked tentatively. 'Haan saab, bilkul live,' he was informed. The crew took a solemn oath never to fly the Indian Army again.

We parked ourselves near the airfield for the day. In the evening we were told to move across through the city to Madras Harbour and board the INS *Magar*, a newly-commissioned vessel, an LST, that would ferry us across the Palk Strait to Sri Lanka.

The *Magar* was a good-looking ship. However, having barely been at sea for a month, it had a lot of teething problems, the most critical of which, from a troop carrying point of view, was the non-functioning of the exhausts in the cargo hold. I had had some experience of sailing with the navy, having been on a naval goodwill cruise. Being the first battalion on board, I opted for the men to be accommodated around the helideck while the officers were to be billeted in the sick bay. 12 Garhwal was the next battalion to arrive and they were given the cargo hold for the men and the officers. By the time the Marathas boarded, space was scarce and they had to squeeze in.

The LST is a flat-bottomed ship and, at sea, it pitches and tosses wildly. The officers in the sick bay had stabilized cots on which to sleep, but everyone, especially the Garhwalis and the Marathas, were soon green in the face. Even our CO, who had been given a cabin, was sick throughout the crossing, which lasted two nights and a day. The crossing took even longer than usual because our eventual destination was Trincomalee that was reached after taking a slight detour.

Situated around 250 kilometres northeast of Sri Lanka's capital, Colombo, 'Trinco' was a major port city with one of the finest natural deep-water harbours. The city lies on the east coast, around 182 kilometres south of Jaffna, and is the administrative capital of Sri Lanka's Eastern Province. Though the countryside was extremely picturesque, the heat and humidity were at their peak in the month of July. In any case, the troops were so relieved to be on terra firma that no one was complaining.

In the army if you excel at a particular job, chances are you'll be detailed for it again and again. The brigade staff had been most impressed with 25 Rajput's ability to load equipment on the LST and we were now tasked with unloading everything. The boys quickly improvised a ramp on which they began rolling down the awkward two-hundred-kilogram fuel drums. The moment they had that set up, brigade staff jumped in and handed over the task to the Garhwalis while the Rajputs were told to figure out a way of unloading the mounds of atta that were being carried in the hold. Once again, our innovative JCOs worked out ingenious ways of shovelling it off the ship without any of it falling into the water. Soon, we had the entire brigade's wares offloaded and were sitting around awaiting further orders.

The first order we got was that all officers and men should put on their combat helmets. For most of us Bangladesh veterans who had fought the war mostly without reinforced headgear, this seemed a ridiculous order, especially in the hot and humid conditions. So helmets would appear the moment any brigade staff happened to be in the area, and promptly disappear as soon as the staff officer went away. After a while the brigade commander himself put in an appearance. He was received by the CO on the docks and, within a couple of minutes, served tea by the mess waiter.

Brigadier Dhar's eyes narrowed in disbelief, 'You chaps are serving tea in china cups?' He took the tray from the serving soldier and threw the entire lot into the sea. We watched the cups go down in dismay. Tea was promptly served again in tin mugs. The brigadier was mollified and a happier man.

A couple of hours later, we were ceremoniously received by a small detachment of the Sri Lanka Army who escorted us to a location known as the Monkey-bridge Camp. This was a Sri Lankan army base that had been vacated to accommodate us. There was proper accommodation for the entire brigade, with bunk beds and actual mattresses. Two Sri Lankan officers had been assigned to look after the Indian Army personnel. Just then, brigade got into the act again, and orders were passed that no Indian soldier would sleep in the huts and that we should put up our tents and live in those. The Sri Lankan officers were in tears, saying they had vacated their camp for our troops and it was their job to look after us. Brigade remained unmoved and all three units spent the night under canvas, a few hundred yards from the tantalizing bunk beds.

Girdhari Singh's king-sized pots and pans that had occupied the entire aircraft's hold now came to the rescue. Not only 25 Rajput, but even the men of the other units had hot steaming food to eat. No military manual in the world would ever advocate carrying those monstrous utensils, but eventually they made the difference between well-fed troops and hungry men in a new environment.

The next morning there was a flurry of activity as news came that the Sri Lankan army chief was coming to visit the camp. Brigade staff came sprinting into the unit location asking us for a proper tea set. We couldn't resist replying, 'But the commander threw it into the sea!'

Ethiri Yar? Enge?

Despite the lighter moments, the battalions had done their homework well and the troops were combat-ready and morale was high. Throughout the next day, additional ships kept arriving, some of them bringing in mechanized units with BMPs. No sooner had the ships disgorged their cargo, orders were issued that 25 Rajput, along with a mechanized company, should move inland and proceed north towards Vavuniya (straddling the Kandy-Jaffna highway). We moved out of Monkey-bridge Camp, most of us riding on the BMPs, and got to our new location in a few hours. The battalion immediately got down to the serious business of siting our companies, preparing the defences and setting up camp. Soon some LTTE representatives (at this point, we were not at war with the LTTE) arrived and offered to assist us in settling down. Our biggest asset was our 2IC, Venkat Ramanan, who was a Tamil himself and extremely good with dialects. He was soon able to establish a rapport and we started finding out what we could about the LTTE, about whom we actually knew very little at that point.

After three days in Vavuniya, we were told to proceed further north to Elephant Pass via Kilinochchi. This move pitchforked us into the Jaffna region, for the Elephant Pass was a thin strip of land between the Jaffna Lagoon on the west and the Bay of Bengal towards the east. The area is quite marshy with extensive mangrove vegetation. We were deployed between the Sri Lanka Army and the LTTE positions, the latter being extremely well sited and superbly camouflaged. In fact, though we knew the LTTE was dug in around us, we had no idea where they actually were until some of us went out looking for wild boar. Only when we were almost on to their camp did the LTTE cadres show themselves. We realized that the gap between the LTTE and the Sri Lankan Army positions was less than a kilometre, and we were sitting bang in the middle.

Our local knowledge of the ground at that stage was next to zero. We were using old vintage maps of Ceylon and, administratively, we were stretched thin. 76 Brigade continued to be headquartered in Trincomalee with 12 Garhwal while the Marathas were deployed somewhere further south near Batticaloa. There was no communication with home—forget telephones, there was no provision to even send letters back. Apart from a vague brief that we were in Sri Lanka to enforce 'peace' between the Sri Lankan Army and the LTTE, we actually had not been briefed as to what the role of the IPKF (Indian Peace Keeping Force) was supposed to be.

So far what one had seen of the Sri Lankan Army indicated that they were a mixed bag. At Elephant Pass their troops seemed isolated and hemmed in by the LTTE, who not only had superior positions flanking them but also had the ability to melt away through the lagoons. The army's main task was to check each and every vehicle that moved up north into Jaffna. This was an extremely tedious process for it entailed unloading every bit of cargo, checking it and then reloading it before waving it through. Further south, at Vavuniya, the Sri Lankans had a brigade, commanded by Brigadier Parami Kulatunga (he was subsequently assassinated by the LTTE). The troops stationed at Vavuniya were alert and sharp, as were their other detachments in Trincomalee.

Having placed ourselves between the two sides, we awaited further orders. Information, especially pertaining to our role in Sri Lanka, remained sketchy and nebulous. To put it mildly, it was an odd situation; the Sri Lankan Army was polite, yet distant, for they felt we were there primarily to protect the Tamils and curtail their operations. At the unit level, though, it didn't take long to break through the reserve, for most Sri Lankan Army officers had some experience of our training institutions. On the other hand, the LTTE, whose area of influence extended from Jaffna all along the Eastern Province to Batticaloa, was also trying to size us up. Their networking and administrative control throughout the Tamil areas was extremely impressive.

A week after our deployment at Elephant Pass, one company was ordered to proceed to the west coast and report once it had established a base at Mannar. Barely ten days had elapsed since our arrival at Trincomalee and this was already our fourth move. Mannar is located on the northwest shoulder of Sri Lanka and is linked by a ferry to Rameshwaram in India. Before coming under Portuguese, Dutch and then British control, Mannar was an integral part of the old Jaffna kingdom. It was one of the major strongholds of the LTTE.

On reaching Mannar, we were told by the Sri Lankan Army unit garrisoned there that we could set up our base in an old abandoned fisheries building. Not only did the location smell extremely fishy, it was also in ruins. Nevertheless, the men rolled up their sleeves and immediately got to work to make the place habitable. The next morning, our unguided tour of the island continued—we were told to abandon the fisheries location at Mannar and move to Mullaittivu. Our outdated maps were adding enormously to our problems as new landmarks in terms of roads and other recently constructed features were missing from them.

We were still in a state of incredulous shock at the frequency of our movements and had just pulled out of Mannar when we received orders to disregard the previous instructions and stop where we were. It seemed the GOC had landed at Elephant Pass where he found the rest of 25 Rajput. 'What the hell are you doing here?' he wanted to know. 'Trincomalee is on fire and you chaps are sitting here. Pull back to Trincomalee immediately.' Radioing me, the CO ordered me to make my way back to Trincomalee and marry up with the rest of the battalion. Out came the maps again, and I looked for a suitable route. Having found a road that cut across Sri Lanka, we set a course for Trincomalee via Anuradhapura. This was a different route as it went south of Vavuniya, an area we had already seen on our whirlwind tour of Sri Lanka. Anuradhapura looked extremely inviting to us with its monasteries, besides, it was a new route.

Our move subsequently created a big uproar in divisional headquarters; unknown to us then, there was a ban on entering Sinhalese areas. Since the fourth century BCE to eleventh century CE, Anuradhapura had been the capital of the Sinhala kingdom. There was a famous Bodhi tree at Anuradhapura where the entire company stopped and took a few minutes off to pray, surrounded by gawking monks and Sinhalese people who had not yet seen any Indian troops in their area. The ancient city, considered sacred by Buddhists, was the hub of the Sinhalese people. The trouble was no one had bothered to tell the lower levels of command that we were not supposed to go there.

What prompted the withdrawal to Trincomalee will always remain a mystery, for things seemed fairly normal when we got there. We were now allotted space between the airfield and the sea. The entire area was covered with scrub, which we began to clear in right earnest during the next forty-eight hours. To our surprise, we began to uncover a series of concrete plinths that dotted the entire location. Obviously, the same area had been used by troops earlier during World War II when Trincomalee had been an important naval base for the Royal Navy. Soon we had our entire unit set up, with even electrical connections in place.

Since our arrival in Sri Lanka, we had been using an assortment of vehicles. The battalion's entire surface transport had followed by rail to Chennai after the troops had been airlifted from Pune. These vehicles had then been drained of all their fuel according to regulations and were loaded on to various ships that ferried them to Trincomalee where they arrived along with the unit quarter guard flagpole (which we hadn't managed to fit on to any aircraft). Now that we had our own transport, it was but a matter of time before the higher-ups would move us; sure enough, we received orders to head immediately for Ampara, which was south of Batticaloa from where one climbed into the hills. This was predominantly a Sinhala area.

The vehicles were far from ready, for there is a procedure that has to be followed to flush the tanks before they are roadworthy. There were howls of protest to the CO, but the usual lament that 'orders were orders' sealed the issue. At 2000 hours, the battalion convoy began to snake south. Within a couple of hours, vehicle after vehicle had sputtered and stopped. There was no option but to wait for first light and then move forward again, somehow nursing the groaning vehicles along. We reached Batticaloa at mid-day where we were met by the Marathas, and then headed on towards Ampara. I was in an RCL jeep that was the last vehicle to give up the ghost a couple of kilometres short of Ampara. Behind me, the entire battalion was stretched out, each group huddled around its broken-down transport. The locals were amazed especially with the Nissan one-ton trucks that were stranded in a line at the side of the road with their bonnets open. They would stop, shake their heads and laughingly say, 'Saar, Nissan vandi.' (Sir, this is a Nissan vehicle.)

The unit deployed at the new location in a tactical manner. We had hardly settled in, when the GOC paid us a visit and told the CO to redeploy ourselves as a proper camp, with neat rows of tents as was the norm in NCC units. Before we could implement that order, fresh instructions were received to move the battalion, less one company and platoon, east to Akkaraipattu. In what was fast becoming a daily occurrence in Sri Lanka, 25 Rajput wearily clambered aboard its vehicles, the men weighed down with equipment and steel helmets, we roared off to yet another location. From what would now be the headquarters of a company plus, I watched them go—we were yet to complete three weeks as part of the IPKF and we had already seen a fair bit of the country.

I turned my attention towards getting to know my area. Ampara had an airfield and the surrounding forest had a large population of elephants.

Though the area was Sinhalese there were some pockets in the east where the LTTE was known to operate. I also developed excellent relations with the Sri Lankan Army garrison that was commanded by an armoured corps officer, Lieutenant Colonel Kalupahana, who was also our coordinating officer. His adjutant, Captain Chitraranjan, was a signals officer who had recently done a course in India. To my utter delight, I managed to obtain excellent, updated maps from them, which was a huge boon, considering we were otherwise completely dependent on our extremely poor charts of the region.

In the beginning of September, we had a platoon of BMPs arrive in Ampara, adding considerably to our strength. I would often go down to Kalmunai, which was the main junction on the Akkaraipattu and Batticaloa road, and liaise with the LTTE, trying all the time to increase our knowledge of the area. Towards the end of the first week, we suddenly got word that a civilian bus had been hijacked by the LTTE with thirty-seven people on board. We were tasked with assisting the local police to find the bus and rescue the passengers.

Mounted on BMPs, we thundered off at top speed towards Mile Post Junction 69 on PBC Highway even though it was already dark. It was a long drive and, suddenly, hidden behind a bend, a Sri Lankan Army checkpoint loomed out of the darkness. The only option available to the BMP driver, if he wasn't to overrun the Sri Lankans, was to veer sharply off the road. The tracked vehicle literally flew over a ditch, landed across it, and somehow managed to get back on the road with no casualties. I had no option but to grab the turret and hang on for dear life. I am sure the Sri Lankan personnel were suitably impressed with this demonstrated capability.

We found the abandoned bus soon enough, but of the passengers there was absolutely no sign. We searched around it but there was no trace of them. The next morning, we went down to our LTTE contacts and tried to get some information. It would transpire later that the bus had been 'captured' by local criminals and the passengers had been herded into a building a kilometre away. Fearing for their lives, they had not dared make a noise even though they could hear the local police searching for them.

During the interaction with the LTTE over the bus incident, I started to get the feeling that there was a perceptible difference in their behaviour towards us. Until then, the LTTE had been extremely forthcoming, be it at Trincomalee, Vavuniya, Elephant Pass, or Kalmunai. Whatever information we asked for—buildings damaged, areas occupied by the Sri Lankan Army—would be given to us promptly, more often than not presented as neatly typed, multiple copies. The bus incident itself was of no major importance, but the impression one got was that the Tamils were definitely taking a step back. 'Something is going to happen,' I told the CO while filing my report.

Headless Chickens or a Sinister Plot?

Ever since Ceylon, as Sri Lanka was then known, was granted independence by the British in 1948, there had been simmering discontent between the majority Sinhalese and minority Tamils. At the very root of the issue was the passing of certain laws by the Sinhala majority government (that included the Tamil Congress) that were seen to be discriminatory. In the 1970s, two major Tamil political parties united to form the Tamil United Liberation Front (TULF) that agitated for a separate state of Tamil Eelam in north and eastern Sri Lanka, for greater autonomy within the federal structure. However, the sixth amendment to the Constitution of Sri Lanka, enacted in August 1983, classified all separatist movements as unconstitutional. Alternate Tamil factions, including the LTTE, advocating a more militant course of action, soon emerged, and the ethnic divisions eventually led to violent civil war. Historically, the conflict between the two communities was almost three thousand years old. With the benefit of hindsight, one feels that the solution, at the time, needed much more deliberation than what was being attempted.

Initially, successive Indian governments sympathized with the Tamil insurrection in Sri Lanka because of the strong support it received within the Indian state of Tamil Nadu. Supporters in Tamil Nadu provided a sanctuary for the separatists and helped the LTTE smuggle arms and ammunition into Sri Lanka, soon making them the strongest force on the island. India's regional and domestic interests wanted to limit foreign intervention on what was deemed to be a racial issue between the Tamils and the Sinhalese. To this end, the Indira Gandhi government sought to make it clear to Sri Lankan President Junius Richard Jayewardene, that armed intervention in support of the Tamil movement was an option India would consider if diplomatic solutions should fail.

The Black July riots in 1983 resulted in the first round of civil violence where the killing of thirteen soldiers of the Sri Lanka Army sparked anti-Tamil pogroms in which approximately four hundred Tamils were killed. Militant factions, mainly the LTTE, bided their time before launching an attack on

Anuradhapura in 1985, attacking the Bodhi Tree shrine. An estimated one hundred and fifty civilians died in the hour-long attack.

Subsequently, the Indian government cut back overt aid to the Tamil fighters while playing a more proactive role in finding a political solution. The Sri Lankans, noting the decline in support for the Tamil rebels from within India, stepped up their anti-insurgent activity with material support from other countries, prominent among whom were Pakistan and Israel. Apart from the political ramifications of these developments in south India, the Indian government could hardly afford to have Pakistan fishing in the troubled waters of Sri Lanka.

By May 1987, the Sri Lankan Army had laid siege to Jaffna with large-scale civilian casualties; over 4,000 troops supported by helicopter gunships and ground attack aircraft were pounding LTTE positions. With the mounting threat of a Tamil backlash at home, India sent a convoy of unarmed ships with humanitarian aid to Jaffna. The convoy was intercepted by the Sri Lanka Navy and forced to return home, after which, on 4 June, Indian Air Force An-32s dropped twenty-five tonnes of supplies under fighter escort. More than the aid itself, the Indian action demonstrated the seriousness with which it viewed the situation and reaffirmed the option of armed intervention in the island country. So far so good, but from here on the script seemed to go horribly wrong for India.

The Indo-Sri Lanka Peace Accord of 1987 was signed to help resolve the ongoing civil war. Colombo agreed to the devolution of power and the withdrawal of its troops from the Northern and Eastern provinces while the Tamil rebels were to surrender their arms. The first sign of trouble came when, after disembarking from ships at the Sri Lankan naval base at Kankesanthurai, the northernmost harbour on the island, the Indian mechanized columns began to head towards Jaffna. The Tamil civilian population spilled on to the streets to block the way, and a young girl hit her head against a BMP, leading to a lot of blood and drama. In the ensuing chaos and impasse, no one seemed to know what to do.

The uncertainty stemmed from the nebulous and undefined nature of the peace accord itself. The agreement had been signed between the Government of India and the Government of Sri Lanka with the LTTE not being a party to it. The LTTE chief, Velupillai Prabhakaran, was fully aware of this lacuna and he adopted a wait and watch policy, testing the waters to see how far he could push the limits of tolerance with India. We, on the other hand, were completely bound by the agreement. We were supposed to protect the Tamils who were not under our control, and yet we had an agreement with the Sri Lankans. Whoever had been the diplomatic brains behind the agreement had failed to understand the situation on the ground. It was a complete failure of statecraft to say the least.

In my opinion, three people influenced the situation: JN Dixit was the Indian High Commissioner in Colombo and he was known to have a severe dislike for the LTTE. President Jayewardene, working with the Indian diplomatic corps in Colombo, succeeded in selling to Rajiv Gandhi an agreement that could never have worked. The third person in this chain was General Sundarji, the army chief, who, in my opinion, had demonstrated time and again that the more complex and dangerous the situation on the ground, the greater the chances of the army charging in with bluster and bravado. It had happened in Blue Star, and during Brasstacks and Trident, and, from day one, it was happening in Sri Lanka.

Within the first month, we had demonstrated to ourselves and also to the LTTE that we had no clear-cut objectives, and were just rushing from one location to the other. If indeed our objective was to act as a peacekeeping force, we should have been deployed as a buffer between the Tamil and the Sinhalese along the border of the Eastern and Northern provinces and the rest of the island, somewhat akin to the UN deployment between the warring factions in Cyprus. Instead, we were running around all over the place, pushing into virtually every Tamil stronghold. It made no sense whatsoever and by early September most of us were completely bewildered about our purpose in Sri Lanka.

For a force that claimed it received its basic military training in India and most of its material backing from Tamil Nadu, to have taken up arms against the Indian Army does not make any sense. From our point of view as well, the IPKF had arrived in Sri Lanka with the avowed intention of protecting the Tamils. For the LTTE to be in our gunsights within a couple of months speaks volumes for the policies we follow.

In the subsequent months, when the fighting with the LTTE would assume serious proportions, many senior commanders would try to obfuscate by shifting the blame to the junior leadership and, in some cases, to the troops. That unfortunately was the biggest cynical lie that could have been perpetuated—the failure was at the highest levels, and no amount of whitewashing can change the fact that it was the junior level of leadership and the performance on the ground that eventually saw us through. The first couple of months of mad merry-go-round, the complete lack of coordination, the absolute lack of information about the objectives of the IPKF, all reflected terribly on our senior commanders. The fact that the battalions were still combat-worthy is actually a testament to the resilience of our men and their training.

Back in Ampara, with the LTTE clamming up, I turned my attention to getting to know the Sinhalese people and the area. We made a lot of friends, amongst whom was the eighty-year-old head priest of the eastern region who lived in a monastery situated to the west of us. He once complained to me of severe pain in his knees, so on a subsequent visit I took the RMO along. The doctor examined him and told me that nothing could be done as it was a problem of old age. All this while, the head priest was looking at the Indian Army doctor with reverent hope.

'Put your stethoscope to his knee,' I told the doctor, who started to protest when I repeated the order. He dutifully put the gadget to the knobby knee and listened intently, his head tilted to a side. The exercise was then repeated with the other leg. We then huddled in a corner, our heads together while the priest continued to watch us in awe.

'Give him some coloured pills and a vitamin B complex injection,' I told the RMO, who nodded sagely and proceeded with the job.

The vitamin obviously had some effect, for the old man looked delirious with joy. In all his subsequent discourses to his disciples he would start by saying, 'Indian Army doctors are very good... They even checked my knee with a stethoscope and gave me an injection.' The amount of goodwill we earned can be gauged from the fact that when President Jayewardene visited Ampara, he talked in glowing terms of the relationship between the Sinhalese population and the Indian Army in the region. He was generally rather critical of the Indian Army in Sri Lanka.

Jayewardene's speech had further ramifications. The High Commissioner, JN Dixit, promptly called the brigade wanting to know what we had done at Ampara that was so different, and scheduled a visit. I told him about the goodwill we had earned with the head monk, and then requested him to gift a carpet to the monastery. The head priest, who had the ear of the president, was even more thrilled and added yet another line to his discourse, 'This wonderful carpet I am sitting on was gifted to me by India.'

Meanwhile, the situation on the ground was changing fast. On 4 October, the Sri Lankan Navy intercepted an LTTE boat off Point Pedro. Colombo claimed the LTTE cadre was smuggling weapons across the Palk Strait, and were hence denied immunity. The LTTE denied the charges of gunrunning, instead claiming that their men were in the process of shifting documents from Madras to Jaffna in accordance with the truce. The prisoners included some high profile Tigers—Pulendran, Kumarappa and others wanted in connection with the Bodhi Tree massacre in Anuradhapura a few years previously—and the Sri Lankans were determined to bring them to trial.

The LTTE appealed for the enforcement of protection to the IPKF who were holding the rebels in custody at Palaly air base. The Sri Lankans, on the other hand, were adamant that the prisoners be transferred to Colombo. As a peacekeeping force, there should have been no debate on the matter, but JN Dixit was inclined to hand the LTTE prisoners over to the Sri Lankan Army. There were furious parleys between him and New Delhi. The moment it became obvious to the prisoners that the Sri Lankans would prevail, they committed mass suicide by biting into cyanide capsules hidden inside their mouths. Their death had an electrifying effect on the situation, which now spiralled out of control. On the night of 5 October, there was a large-scale slaughter of Sinhalese people in Jaffna and that of eight Sri Lankan prisoners who were then being held hostage. There were also reports of armed skirmishes between Indian troops and the LTTE around Jaffna.

Three days later the LTTE opened fire with mortars on Indian positions. The Indian defence minister, Arun Singh, and the army chief, General Sundarji, were in Colombo when Jayewardene threatened to redeploy the Sri Lankan Army if the IPKF failed to retaliate. As the country watched in horror, it became clear that we were now to fight the very people we had come to protect. The IPKF was now to fight the LTTE.

Code-named Operation Pawan, the Indian Army launched its first assault on LTTE broadcasting stations at Tavadi and Kokkuvil and also destroyed the printing presses of two LTTE-sponsored newspapers. Almost two hundred LTTE operatives were captured. The LTTE retaliated with an ambush on a CRPF convoy near Tellippallai, in which four jawans were killed. They also launched an attack on an IPKF post and later captured a 10 Para Commando jeep, killing all five occupants.

On the morning of 10 October, 91 Brigade, commanded by Brigadier J Ralli, began its push into Jaffna with three infantry battalions and BMPs. The plan was to neutralize the LTTE's operational capability in and around the city by capturing or destroying the LTTE's chain of command—hence leaving the Tamil movement directionless.

Come October, in the south, at Ampara and Akkaraipattu, our LTTE contacts and point people seemed to have melted away. On the day our sister brigade moved into Jaffna, the CO's jeep was blown up by an IED. Colonel Nanjappa was fortunate to walk away with minor injuries, but one of our boys suffered spinal damage. We reacted quickly and effectively, rounding up a key LTTE Eastern Province military commander, David, along with other male members suspected to be LTTE cadres. The men were segregated from the breast-beating and wailing women who were putting on quite an act, and made to sit in the open ground adjoining the place of the blast.

'Our CO's jeep has been targeted,' they were told, 'and we can go on a revenge rampage, just as the Sri Lanka Special Task Force has been doing. But we are not like them. Let this be the first and the last incident of its kind. If something like this happens again, we may not be able to control tempers.'

We let everyone go. At first, the local population just gaped at us, not quite believing that we hadn't rounded up some people and shot them. This act of 25 Rajput paid huge dividends, for we always had information available to us whenever the LTTE cadres moved in our area. Subsequently, my column did get blown up, but it was our own fault, for we failed to interpret the information that had been given to us. Had we read the situation correctly, three of my boys would not have been killed.

The fighting between the IPKF and the LTTE intensified on the night of the 12-13 October with the heliborne assault on the Jaffna University headquarters of the LTTE. A detachment of Para Commandos and Sikh LI troops executed what was to be a quick in-and-out operation. Indian intelligence agencies had placed the top LTTE leadership in the university and the operation was expected to put a swift end to the Jaffna fighting. Even as the helicopters approached, the LTTE, having intercepted IPKF radio transmissions, was waiting in ambush. The Sikh LI boys were virtually wiped out while the Para Commandos lost another six men. Eventually, detachments of an armoured regiment managed to extricate the survivors from their besieged positions.

By then, minor skirmishes had erupted between the IPKF and the LTTE all along the east coast. Almost immediately, sensing their opportunity, rival Tamil groups like PLOTE and EPRLF began coming forward with information about the LTTE. We welcomed these groups who not only provided intelligence but also helped identify key hostile personnel. We were, however, still far from adept at telling friend from foe. Having got some information, I launched a quick operation using civil vehicles. Undetected, we soon had two operatives in our custody, one being a high-ranking

LTTE honcho from the region. To our consternation, no sooner had we caught our quarry than women began to pour out of the surrounding huts, wailing and weeping, claiming that our captive was either their son, brother, husband or friend who had nothing to do with the LTTE. 'Sir, I think we should leave this guy. Looks like we got the wrong chap,' said my company officer. I decided to let him go, and had the women shower us with blessings. Later, the same LTTE operative masterminded an attack on an Indian column. We soon realized the weeping and wailing brigade didn't even know who the captive was. It was quite a convincing nautanki that had been perfected over a period of time.

The battle for Jaffna had been fiercely contested by the LTTE. With all approach roads laced with deadly Claymore mines and remote-controlled IEDs, the Indian side suffered significant casualties. Snipers armed with sophisticated rifles and infrared telescopic sights specialized in taking out Indian officers and radio operators. Added to this was the muddled thinking of the Indian high command, initially handicapping its own troops by imposing a blanket ban on deploying heavy weaponry. Within days, it became obvious that reinforcements were required, especially in the face of New Delhi's insistence on the capture of Jaffna without bypassing pockets of resistance.

After a fortnight's lull, the advance was resumed using T-72 tanks, BMPs and Mi-35 gunships along with Naval Marine Commandos. Ultimately, Jaffna Fort fell on 28 November, with the LTTE simply melting away from Jaffna. Their hard-core fighters moved south, to the safety of the jungles around Vavuniya and Mullaittivu, by skirting the coast from Point Pedro to Elephant Pass, sheltered by the crisscross of waterways in the impenetrable Nittkaikulam region. And, although the LTTE had lost Jaffna town itself, it continued to harass 54 Division's efforts to consolidate its positions—by using IEDs and anti-personnel mines.

By the end of 1987, 36 Division, commanded by Major General Jameel Mahmood, had also landed in Sri Lanka. While 54 Division was now fully occupied with Jaffna, 36 Division had operational control of the area south of Trincomalee. 76 Brigade was shifted to the new formation. General Mahmood was an artillery officer and had been the military assistant to General Sundarji. I had met him a few times during my time at the MO Directorate. As a part of his familiarization, he soon came to Ampara. I drove him around in my broken-down RCL jeep, having padded the passenger seat with an extra blanket. General Mahmood had the ability of making everyone comfortable. He looked at the blanket and grinned. 'VK, this is perfectly fine. It's nice of you to put an extra blanket for me!'

After I drove him around, we headed for my Company HQ for a briefing on the general area. Jameel Mahmood was barely listening; he was staring at the maps pinned on to the boards. 'What maps are these?'

'Sri Lankan Army maps,' I said. He walked up to them and took a closer look. I suddenly realized that he had the same antiquated maps we had when we got to Sri Lanka. I picked up the phone and spoke to the Sri Lankans asking them to send me two sets post-haste for my GOC. By the time I had completed my briefing, the maps for the GOC had arrived, but it was quite bizarre, and I could hardly believe it. We had been in Sri Lanka for four months and the Indian Army had not even obtained these updated maps, so vital for any operation. I just could not understand why we were refusing to accept any help from the Sri Lankan Army. Starting with the refusal to billet our men in the barracks at Monkey-bridge Camp, we seemed hell-bent on doing things the difficult way. To further compound the issue, some of the orders issued by the higher headquarters during those days were downright ludicrous.

A typical order would read, 'Get into the jungle and clear it up!' No one seemed to realize you don't get into terrain dominated by the enemy and try to wipe them out. All too often the LTTE would see us coming and just melt away through the swamps and lagoons that were their backyard. In the jungles, they could pick the spot and ambush us at will. That there would be IEDs and booby traps should have been anticipated and the information passed down to the formations. Nothing of the sort happened; we just kept getting orders to move from one place to the other. The very fact that 25 Rajput had not been moved from Akkaraipattu, and I had been allowed to stay on in Ampara for a reasonable length of time was a miracle of sorts. It was no major wonder that we were buying casualties by the dozens in other sectors.

By February 1988, 57 Division also arrived in Sri Lanka, and once again we stayed put as the rest of 36 Division moved up. 76 Brigade, for the second time in quick succession, was transferred to the new division that was being commanded by Major General TP Singh, a Rajputana Rifles officer. 57 Division was inducted into Sri Lanka from the Eastern Theatre where it was engaged in Counter Insurgency (CI) operations. This division had its SOPs clearly worked out, with a GOC who was crystal clear about how to tackle the LTTE. There would be a marked difference in the fighting.

Until then, the LTTE was actually toying with us. I remember spending a night at Brigade HQ in Batticaloa. As darkness fell, a Tamil Tiger randomly fired a burst at an ASC (army service corps) location. Immediately, the post retaliated and soon others in the vicinity also opened up. Eventually, even BMPs joined the fray and there was hot lead whistling all over the place.

One of the first things the new GOC did was to visit Batticaloa where the 76 Brigade commander received him. 'I want to see the city,' said the general. As Brigadier Dhar hesitated, the general decided to drive himself, star plate, flag et al. 'Let's make it clear to everyone—it is we who control the town, not the LTTE.' This had an electrifying effect on the troops, who finally had a general they deserved. 'The LTTE dominates the jungles; so let them. We will control the towns and population centres. Sooner or later, if they have to have the support of the people, the Tigers have to come into the urban areas. When they do that, we'll be waiting for them.'

The Eastern Province

Throughout 1988-1989, the Indian Army was engaged in a grim battle of attrition, dealing with an enemy that was especially adept in the use of IEDs and Claymore mines. A far cry from the days of 'go here' and 'go there', we were now extremely chary of any movement. 25 Rajput's Battalion HQ remained at Akkaraipattu while the other companies were stretched out between Kalmunai and Pottuvil (that was next to the Lahugala National Park that extended north up to Ampara).

Because of IEDs, often remote-controlled from a distance of over a kilometre, orders had been passed that all movement of troops would be on foot. It was a good order that certainly saved lives, but it was a nightmare for us when we were asked to conduct an operation around Akkaraipattu, a distance of thirty kilometres from Ampara. Walking was never an issue, but it was impossible to go undetected over such a distance. With information of our passage, the chances of being ambushed were extremely high. Taking a decision to disregard the SOP, I requested the Sri Lankan Army to provide me with a civil bus. I loaded two platoons on to the bus and, along with the company one-ton and my ramshackle RCL jeep, we dashed off for Akkaraipattu.

25 Rajput had two officers who were considered by the men to be 'lucky' and 'unlucky' respectively. Vikas Uppal was a youngster who invariably brought with him good luck, for wherever he went, the battalion would

meet with success. Diametrically opposite was 'Kutty' Sharma, for his presence (though it had absolutely nothing to do with him) meant that the target would invariably run away or the battalion would draw a blank. Anyway, I was glad to see Vikas Uppal waiting for us at Akkaraipattu and, sure enough, we conducted a successful operation during which we got three LTTE Tigers. Flushed with the successful chase, we were then heading for Battalion HQ when I felt something was seriously wrong. 'Is it always this quiet around here?' I asked as we passed through the small township of Akkaraipattu.

'Yes, sir,' confirmed Uppal, 'yahan par aisa hi hota hai.' (It's always like this here.) We were passing through an open area along the road between Akkaraipattu town and the Battalion HQ location.

At the unit, the newly-married RMO threw a small party, which meant an extra sweet at best. During dinner, I told Colonel Nanjappa that I would like to leave immediately for Ampara, for all the company support weapons and ammunition were under the guard of just one section. Just then, we received intelligence that there was an old IED buried somewhere along the main road between the unit and the town. Our source, a postmaster, was generally very reliable. He also told the CO that the IED was quite old and that the LTTE had not managed to recruit any villager to trigger it off.

We took this information at face value. Hoping that the postmaster was right and that the IED would not be triggered, we decided to move. The bulk of the men took off in the bus. I followed in my RCL jeep which did not have any headlights, and was thus navigating with the one-ton's lights behind it. As we came to an open patch, I once again got the eerie feeling that something was desperately wrong. By then we were at the centre of this flat area, and I remember thinking to myself that this was an ideal place for an IED. Instantaneously, there was a low blast and I spun around to see the one-ton lifting off the ground. In the ensuing darkness, small arms opened up and the area was sprayed with bullets. We fired back towards the gun flashes. Hearing the blast, the bus had stopped ahead and men were fanning out trying to engage the enemy. The one-ton lay in a smoking heap in a deep pit, the wounded groaning in pain. Within a few seconds, the LTTE had melted away into the night and we took stock of our casualties. One JCO and a couple of men were dead, others seriously wounded.

The blast had been heard at the battalion location, and soon we had troops rushing in to help evacuate the wounded. Sri Lankan Air Force helicopters were asked for and they came in extremely quickly, homing in on the mini flares we fired once we could hear them.

Within a few minutes, the brigade was on our case. 'Why the hell were you in vehicles when orders were to walk?' came the inevitable question. I felt a surge of anger. There was no doubt in my mind that had we walked back, the LTTE would have ambushed us somewhere along the thirty-odd kilometres. Being insensitive was one thing; being altogether removed from reality was another matter. However, with Colonel Nanjappa standing like a rock behind me, brigade had no choice but to drop the matter purely on the grounds of common sense.

I continued to operate with Alpha Company from Ampara. Around that time, 25 Rajput was formally transferred from 76 to 24 Brigade, which was a part of 57 Division. Initially, the brigade moved into Ampara, and set up its HQ next to the airfield. On the first night, the entire brigade was up and about, making a terrible din, the men beating tin plates and shouting at the top of their voices. There was such a racket going on that one felt that even the LTTE listening posts in Jaffna, some two hundred kilometres north, would have picked it up.

Having spent a sleepless night as a result, the brigade commander, Brigadier Loganathan, was furious the next morning. The CO of the brigade camp comprising Assam Regimental troops, was hauled up, for his unit had been making the maximum din. 'Elephant, sir,' he said, explaining the commotion. Convinced that the Sri Lankan elephant would only understand Tamil, the Assam troops had been practicing their limited vocabulary, shouting 'Po, po.' The JCO had told the CO the next morning, 'Saab, Tamil haathi hai. Sirf Tamil samajte hai.' (These are Tamil elephants. They only understand Tamil.)

24 Brigade eventually set up its headquarters at Kalmunai. The deployments for 25 Rajput also changed, and I moved down to Karaitivu, on the road from Kalmunai to Akkaraipattu. Here we occupied an abandoned government building. One company was at Akkaraipattu along with Battalion HQ and other supporting elements, one company was at Thirukovil, and one south, at Pottuvil, with one platoon at Komari. One of our companies eventually moved alongside Brigade HQ at Kalmunai replacing elements of 13 Guards after a communal incident in Kalmunai.

Shortly after that we captured a local militant and succeeded in extracting information from him that led us to a camp in the jungle. I had with me the hardworking Kutty Sharma and some cadres from other militant groups who were working against the LTTE. In the jungle, I always preferred to have the 'friendlies' lead the way, for they were extremely well-trained and moved like ghosts through the vegetation. I would come in next, staying close to them while the rest of my men, not so adept at moving silently, would be stretched out behind me. In fact, the LTTE would always say that Indian troops moving in the jungle were at par with a herd of elephants moving through bamboo!

The clearing in the camp had two clusters of huts; one on relatively low ground while the other was situated above it. I estimated that the LTTE would occupy the higher ground for tactical reasons and decided to tackle that cluster myself. Kutty Sharma was to move into the lower huts. We deployed accordingly, and began to close in on our objectives. Suddenly, I heard music, so I sent a scout to take a look ahead. He found a Tiger on guard and, in his excitement, the scout opened fire and killed him. This alerted the rest of the LTTE cadres who were having their meal, and they promptly took off like jackrabbits and made good their escape with their weapons. It was one of those things.

We were too far from Battalion HQ and the LTTE now knew we were in the jungle. Had the dead man been one of ours, there would have been no question of leaving the body behind, but there was no way I could jeopardize the safety of my own team by lugging a dead Tiger back. Without any further ado, we quickly buried the dead sentry, searched the camp, destroyed the remaining rations and beat a tactical retreat from the area.

The brigade commander wanted to know why we hadn't brought the dead man back. A paratrooper, he was a fine officer who would not hesitate to fly his flag when he moved about the area. A few days later, the brigadier asked me to fly with him in a helicopter as he was going to visit the Rajput Company at Pottuvil. As we flew over the dense jungle, I showed him the clearing with the huts. Seeing the terrain, the commander agreed that it would have been suicidal to try and extract ourselves with a dead body, especially as it wasn't one of ours. That was the end of that matter.

By the middle of 1988, I was promoted to the rank of a lieutenant colonel and took over as the 2IC from Venkat Ramanan. This entailed moving out of Karaitivu where Virendra Gulia took over the company from me. I had a wonderful working relationship with the CO; he told me that I should continue looking after the operational side while he looked after everything else.

Intelligence-Based Ops

The thin line between 'triumph and disaster' is intelligence. 57 Division, under General TP Singh, understood this very clearly and there were SOPs in place to minimize one-upmanship. Previously, while operating with 76 Brigade under 54 and later 36 Division, we would be obliged to forewarn a neighbouring battalion in case we thought we might stray into their AOR. Sometimes, out of sheer enthusiasm to beat you to the draw, the local CO would churn up the region and we would draw a complete blank. TP Singh was pragmatic enough to understand the fragility of human egos. New orders were accordingly issued. We no longer needed to forewarn the battalion whose turf we were heading into; rather, we could inform them once we were already there. This simple change in policy paid extremely handsome dividends.

The emphasis was entirely on 'intelligence-based operations'. At the top, there was deep distrust between the R&AW (Research and Analysis Wing) and other 'higher level' intelligence groups. We would quite often receive information from Delhi to check out X, Y or Z location. More often than not, our own sources would have already led us to those locales well before this information trickled down to us, but given the 'top heavy' nature of this information, we often had to go through the motions all over again. In the Eastern Province of Sri Lanka, there was little mixing between the communities, and even within the Tamil community Hindu villages and Muslim villages would be segregated. The Tamils studied in Tamil schools, the Sinhalese in their own Sinhala institutions while Tamil Muslims made sure their children were educated in their madrasas. This type of division only enhanced differences amongst communities. In such a divided community, our best sources of information were invariably rival Tamil groups and locals who were fed up of Tamil Tigers enforcing the writ of LTTE on them.

Sometimes we really got lucky. 13 Guards was based around Kalmunai and they were conducting a large cordon and search operation. As Colonel Ram Singh, their CO, wanted additional troops, 24 Brigade allocated one company from 25 Rajput to provide the Guards battalion with support. My task was to deploy my troops on two exit points in case anyone made a break for it. Just then, one of my sources gave me information about a LTTE recruitment drive in a nearby area. I contacted the 13 Guards CO and told him I had what I considered solid intel about the LTTE.

'You get on with your task. You are attached to us,' said Ram Singh, preoccupied with the job at hand.

I thought about it for a few minutes and then decided to take a calculated risk. I thinned down my stops and culled out a platoon worth of manpower. The men quickly changed into civilian clothes while three local vehicles were commandeered. Though I was convinced my source was solid, there was a possibility of looking quite silly if this turned out to be a red herring. We roared into a local sports stadium where five senior officials of the LTTE were on a scouting mission. The element of surprise was absolute, and the five LTTE men began to run helter-skelter. Two of them were tackled and brought to ground in front of the entire stadium, while the remaining three were grabbed as they tried to escape into surrounding houses. I knew two of the captured Tigers—one of them had been the senior military leader who used to liaise with me in Kalmunai before hostilities broke out. The other was the military leader's second in command. The others included the 'political boss', the 'financial boss' and the leader of Beirut Base—which was their training base and also served as a major arms cache. The news of their capture was flashed all over the world by the international media, with the BBC running a special report on the operation.

In the meantime, the cordon and search had drawn a blank. I called Nanjappa and told him we had busted five top leaders. Colonel Ram Singh, whose telephone I was using, was most morose. 'We got nobody,' he said sadly.

'I didn't think you would,' I replied frankly. 'The larger the operation, the lower the chance of nabbing these guys.' The Indian Army took a while to learn this valuable lesson. I, for one, never forgot it, and passed it on to whomsoever I could. Work on your intelligence sources and stay sharp and focused. This was to be my mantra even when I was to command Victor Force in the Kashmir Valley many years later.

It did not always work though, for luck played a major part. The other big fish we were after was Karuna, one of Prabhakaran's key lieutenants who would make waves later when he defected from the LTTE. The GOC, General TP Singh, was frank to the point of bluntness. 'Forty-eight hours. I want you to get me Karuna.'

I grinned. Karuna wasn't exactly a coconut hanging from a tree waiting to be plucked. Besides, the entire Indian Army had been looking for him for almost a year. 'You find that amusing?' growled the GOC.

'No, sir,' I quickly put on my 'I'll get Karuna' look.

I almost had him, not once but four times. His karma on those days was good, my luck wasn't quite holding. 'Well?' asked TP, when I ran into him next, well past my forty-eight-hour deadline. I told him the facts pertaining to all the narrow misses. In turn, I got a lecture on how to conduct successful operations and carte blanche to encroach on any unit's AOR in my quest for Karuna. Alas, it was not to be.

25 Rajput's hold on its AOR was fast approaching legendary status. For eight months, ever since we took out the five head honchos of the LTTE in the sports stadium, we had the upper hand within our AOR. Any movement on the part of the LTTE would result in them buying casualties. The LTTE high command, sitting in Jaffna, was obviously aware of this. Determined to make a splash, eleven hand-picked Tigers slipped into our area. Six Tigers from Akkaraipattu joined the party and, together, they decided to hit us at our southernmost point. The party set up an elaborate ambush between the platoon locality at Komari and the company position at Pottuvil.

For three days, the Tigers lay in deadly wait; finally they ambushed a vehicle headed to Pottuvil for rations. The LTTE ruthlessly gunned down the JCO and three other three men on board, after which they fled from the scene, as was their style.

It was a gruesome sight; our boys never stood a chance. The officiating company commander at Pottuvil almost broke down when the bodies were brought in. I had to shake him by his collar, for you cannot break down in front of the men. The funeral ceremonies over, we stood there looking at the burning pyres for a very long time, the face of each dead man haunting every one of us. Rarely had I ever allowed rage to take over in the field, but I swore we would get the perpetrators who had done this.

Back I went to the ambush site, looking for tell-tale clues. Every blade of flattened grass, every spent shell casing, every scuffed mark around the blood-soaked earth was of interest. It was then that we found a small piece of paper—actually the inside flap of a cigarette packet—that had the duty roster of the ambush party. From the roster we deduced that the Tigers had been lying in wait for three days. We also learnt that six of the killers were from the Akkaraipattu contingent of the LTTE.

Back at Battalion HQ in Akkaraipattu, I pulled in all my informants. Thirty thousand rupees, I told them, to anyone who gave me a definite lead on the six assassins. Where the money would come from, I hadn't a clue.

Almost fifteen days later, Nanjappa had called a meeting for the mundane task of auditing the battalion accounts. As the meeting progressed, I got word that one of my sources was waiting outside. In his broken English and my equally broken Tamil, information that the six men were together, in a house in Akkaraipattu was passed on. I stuck my head back into the meeting, telling the CO I'd be back soon as some urgent work had come up. Nanjappa, dulled by the monotony of accounts, hardly noticed. I grabbed an AK-47 and started collecting whoever was around. The 'lucky' mascot, Vikas Uppal was there, so was the JCO adjutant. A couple of boys on regimental police duty, two signal platoon boys and runners quickly made up a team of ten men. The house with this group was identified; it was approachable from two sides. Uppal, in one vehicle with four men, would take one flank. I would take the other.

Less than fifteen minutes had elapsed since I had got the initial intel. The two civil vans roared in, blocking off any exit route. A lone sentry opened fire. We fired back. Another Tiger stuck his head out to see what was happening—we dropped them both. Now I was stuck—I had no heavy weapons, not even grenades. Even as I wondered what to do, the Tigers rolled a couple of grenades out of a window. Using hand signals, I indicated to Uppal that we were going in. Just then, three Tigers came rushing out with blazing guns. We shot them. The momentum had to be kept up, so I smashed the door and went in. The last Tiger was wounded, but he was hiding in a corner, trying to raise his weapon. We shot him too. It was over, and within an hour of having left Nanjappa alone to do battle with numbers, we were back at Battalion HQ.

Nothing we could do or did would ever bring our dead back to life. In Sri Lanka, 25 Rajput under Colonel Nanjappa had played the game as fairly as we could, ever since the first incident where we let everyone go. To my acute embarrassment, for I was after all his 2IC, the CO recommended my name for a Yudh Seva Medal.

The battalion (keeping the brigade and the division in the picture), managed to adjust the accounts so that we could pay the promised ₹30,000 to my source. This was another key lesson that would stay with me. If you want information, you sometimes have to pay for it. Subsequently, I always made sure that units operating under me always had this freedom.

General TP's tenure saw the IPKF in eastern Sri Lanka at its most effective. It underlined how critical the higher level of command is for smooth functioning at the lower level. To attribute the initial days of chaos to anything other than poor leadership would be to add credence to the lie that has been floated by certain quarters to exonerate themselves.

TP Singh moved out after completing his command, and was replaced by Major General Ashok Mehta from the Gorkhas. Like General Harkirat, he too had been on the DS body at the Staff College when I was a student there.

A few days after the change of command at the divisional level, my sources coughed up some interesting intelligence. In a camp bordering the Sinhalese area, sixty Tiger recruits were undergoing training with ten instructors. I had very little time to act, and I planned a surprise attack with five friendlies and another nine men. Having decided on a plan of action, I briefed the CO accordingly.

'You're a lieutenant colonel, you cannot go,' said Nanjappa. He insisted we needed to brief Brigade HQ.

'We don't have the time for that,' I said, but things were different under the new GOC. Brigade huffed and puffed, refused to sanction the operation and kicked it up to the Division. Ashok Mehta did a double take when he saw the projected force levels. 'No way. This has to be a battalion plus attack.' The 'jam side down' syndrome had already kicked in. 'Fine,' I told Nanjappa in my I-told-you-so voice, 'I'll be your 2IC.' Elaborate, coloured maps were prepared (they looked very impressive and would have given the brightest a run for their money at the Staff College) and as the plan went through the wringer, additional troops were allocated. Artillery guns were positioned to provide support fire and Mi-25 attack helicopters were thrown in for good effect. Not just the GOC, but also the force commander of the IPKF would view Operation Golden Katar. As 2IC, I got myself a vantage point from where I could see the events unfold. I also had the mortar platoon deployed nearby.

The guns opened up and they must have spooked the daylights out of the wildlife in the surrounding area. The LTTE, having realized something was up, had melted away ages ago. Attack helicopters then buzzed the abandoned camp, adding their little contribution to the hullabaloo. The GOC and the force commander now decided to land there in a helicopter. Overzealous escort parties sprayed the jungle with gunfire just in case the LTTE had survived the initial onslaught. On hearing the gunfire, the approaching helicopters with the top brass took evasive action and scooted from there. The end result was a lot of jungle bashing and tons of shredded vegetation.

When put to the test in Sri Lanka, Ashok Mehta as a commander was bookish and uninspiring and 57 Division lost its sheen under him. Shortly after his IPKF tenure, General SF Rodrigues, who had taken over as the chief from Sundarji, asked Mehta to put in his papers on moral grounds, and he made an inglorious exit from the army.

By April 1989, 25 Rajput had completed its tour of duty in Sri Lanka and orders were received for us to move to Bombay. The advance party had already preceded the main body, and in June we began our journey from Akkaraipattu to Trincomalee. To our absolute shock, we found the streets between Akkaraipattu and Kalmunai lined with the civilian population—Tamils, Muslims and Sinhalese—begging us to stay. It was a proud moment, and a fantastic tribute to Colonel Nanjappa and the simple men of the Rajput Regiment who had had such an effect on the people of the Eastern Province. The unit, barely a decade old, had done India proud. I, for one, was humbled to be a part of this wonderful bunch of men.

8

A KING'S LIFE

Bollywood

By 1989, President Jayewardene had been replaced by Ranasinghe Premadasa, and he wanted the IPKF out. He even went to the extent of actively supporting the LTTE in its fight against the IPKF. VP Singh had replaced Rajiv Gandhi as prime minister and he too wanted to bring the IPKF home. The sentiment in south India was negative, so much so that the Tamil Nadu chief minister, Karunanidhi, even refused to visit the wounded in military hospitals in Madras. We had walked out of Sri Lanka as a battalion with our heads held high; almost all Indian Army units that had fought on the island had performed well on the ground. While we had gone to Sri Lanka to protect the Tamils, what we actually ended up doing was on no one's radar.

Over 1,200 pyres had consigned the mortal remains of our fallen officers and men to the flames. The Sri Lankan Army's offensive against the Tamils was halted in 1987 by India, which held all the cards at the time, including the option of armed intervention in support of the Tamil population (which, we must understand, was not all a part of the LTTE). Shortly after 25 Rajput de-inducted, the rest of the IPKF soon began to extract itself out of the island and the process was completed by March 1990. For India and Indians, Sri Lanka became our Vietnam, perhaps not so much physically, but certainly mentally.

A decade-and-a-half later, when President Percy Mahinda Rajapaksa decided to resume the offensive against the Tamils and began the final push, India assisted him covertly. Even William Shakespeare, master of irony, would have been baffled by the developments. With no checks and balances, the Sri Lankan Army decimated the LTTE and, with it, the Tamils. Today, we find ourselves in a real dilemma: do we alienate the Sri Lankans by condemning the massacre and risk them opening their door to the Chinese (remember the paranoia about the presence of Pakistan and Israel in Sri Lanka in 1987); or do we not condemn the Lankan Army's genocide and risk alienating the whole of Tamil Nadu?

For people who remember those who laid down their lives in the island country, it will be comforting to know that Sri Lanka built a memorial in 2008 for our martyred soldiers who fought as a part of the IPKF. In India, the names of our fallen men are etched in granite only at memorials within army locations. The rest of India, especially the political class, just does not care. Unfortunately, for those who died, they have been long forgotten by their own country.

There was insufficient post-critical analysis of the Sri Lankan episode even within the Indian armed forces. During a visit to the Higher Command Course in Mhow, General Rodrigues (who had been vice chief for a fair period of the IPKF's deployment) got into a terrible tangle when questioned on Sri Lanka by officers who had finished commanding their units as a part of the IPKF. Roddy's spectacular walk-out of the talk, and his subsequent actions to try and convert the Higher Command into a 'graded' course sent out a clear message: criticism was not acceptable. After Roddy, it was the turn of General Bipin Joshi to become the chief. He too had been the DGMO, and a part of the chain of command. As middle-ranking officers who had fought through most of the period, we watched all these developments and resolved, if for nothing but the memory of our fallen comrades, that when, and if, one got a chance to set the record straight, one would do so.

We had arrived at Trincomalee two years ago, most men miserable from the crossing. The battalion now ascended a steep gangway and boarded a Shipping Corporation of India passenger ship, MV *Akbar.* The giant ship eased out to sea, sailing southwards away from India, rounded the southern tip of the Sri Lankan island and then turned north into the Arabian Sea. Two days later, we closed in on land, passing multitudes of blue-coloured fishing trawlers, each flying a medium-sized Indian flag. Then, suddenly, in the morning glare of the sun, we saw the Bombay skyline.

We disembarked at the harbour and roared out of Lion Gate in a convoy of vehicles, shouting 'Bharat Mata ki jai' and 'Indian Army ki jai'. As we moved into the city, we could only gape at the multitude of people milling around, and the ambient noise levels after the silence of the Sri Lankan countryside were shockingly high. On the other hand, we never felt safer. We could drive along Marine Drive or any part of the city not having to worry about Claymore mines and remote-controlled IEDs. We were home, we were alive, and we had done our duty. We felt good about ourselves!

Major Virendra Gulia, who is no more, had come with the advance party, the battalion taking over from 20 Rajputana Rifles. We now came under the Maharashtra, Gujarat and Goa Area which was being commanded by Major General Harkirat Singh, our old 54 Division GOC. Initially the men found it extremely difficult to adjust, for, in Bombay, we had a myriad duties, most of them administrative in nature. We were the only infantry battalion catering to Area HQ's varied demands, and as a result we were soon stretched thin. While we were stationed in Colaba, we had a small detachment in Juhu as well. The tasks could range from providing blood to hospitals to providing officer or NCO escorts to transiting and visiting dignitaries. Our AOR extended way beyond Bombay: we were charged with the security of the Bhabha Atomic Research Centre (BARC) and the Tata Thermal Power Station at Trombay; the IAF airfield in Barmer, Uttarlai; the Rajasthan Atomic Power Station in Kota, along with a host of other critical locations.

Colonel Nanjappa's nomination for the Higher Command Course at the College of Combat in Mhow came as a huge boost, adding greatly to the esteem of 25 Rajput. The entire unit revelled in his selection, which was looked at as an acknowledgement of the excellent work done by the battalion in Sri Lanka. Overall, Nanjappa had had an extremely successful command tenure. As the CO of a battalion during combat, his relationship with the troops was special. My job as the 2IC was to give this fine officer a fitting farewell from the unit.

The various goodbye ceremonies culminated with Nanju being towed out in a flower-decked jeep, after which some of us officers went to see him off at Santa Cruz airport.

'Vee Kay!' a familiar voice boomed in my ear. 'What are you doing here?' I turned to find Ajit Chopra, the former CO of 3 Dogra, our sister battalion during the Bangladesh War, standing next to me. I had also briefly served with him in the Commando Wing in Belgaum. He was now a major general commanding the JL Wing in Belgaum.

'I'm the second-in-command of 25 Rajput, sir,' I said. 'Our CO has been nominated for the Higher Command Course.'

'You're just the chap. I want you to come to Belgaum as the chief instructor (CI) in the Commando Wing.' I protested, saying we were just back from Sri Lanka, and also that it was imperative I stay on with the unit, particularly as the incoming CO would most likely be from outside the battalion. None of this had any impact on Ajit Chopra, who waved cheerfully and disappeared.

After returning from Sri Lanka, I had informally checked with the MS Branch about what was in store for me, and had been assured that I would stay on with 25 Rajput until my board for full colonel was held. A few days later, much to my horror, I received a signal saying I had been posted to Belgaum as the CI in the Commando Wing and should report for duty by 29 August. This cannot be true, I thought to myself. I went running to the area commander and apprised him of my impending move. 'This is not right,' he agreed. 'The battalion gets a new CO and he's an outsider. It's imperative that you stay. I'll take up the case.' Assured of the area commander's support, I got on with the task of running the battalion. Within a few days, the new CO arrived and I got busy with his familiarization. In fact, I quite forgot about the posting.

With two days to go for the reporting deadline, I got a telephone call. It was General Harkirat Singh. 'VK, it's off to Belgaum with you.'

This led to a real scramble. Bharti and the girls were in Bombay. While Mrinalini was admitted to the Kendriya Vidyalaya, I had, with great difficulty, got Yogja admitted to St Annes in the Fort area. One of the first things I had to do was get transfer certificates for both the girls. 'Colonel,' said the exasperated Mother Superior at St Anne's, 'this is very irresponsible of you.' She went on to give me a long lecture about parenting. I interjected weakly about my country and my duty, but she wasn't listening. I'm still not sure what was worse—the months of struggle to get the admission or this hour-long lecture.

In Belgaum, I reported to the commandant. He beamed at me, 'I told you that you never quite know how things turn out.'

'I didn't want to come here,' I decided to be upfront about my feelings on the matter.

My sentiments obviously didn't concern the general. 'Being the 2IC of a battalion is no job,' he said, dismissing my protest. 'I need you to run this place efficiently. You know the setup. I know you.'

I would later learn from my friends in the MS Branch about what had transpired. The day after my chance meeting with General Chopra at Bombay airport, he had breezed into the Colonel MS 2's office at Army HQ. After the usual pleasantries, General Chopra had looked around disconsolately at the rather sparse and somewhat shabby office. 'Hmm, you could do with some new curtains. And this upholstery...' He let that hang. 'I could sanction ₹5,000 from my funds'. By this time, Colonel MS 2 had abandoned his chair and was 'cosying up' to General Chopra on the shabby visitors' chairs.

The prospect of new curtains and fresh upholstery was the man's mortal weakness, and having identified the chink, General Chopra had struck. 'What can I do for you, sir?' The blatant 'official' bribe had squarely hit its mark.

'Oh, nothing much,' said Ajit Chopra, 'just give me a Ranger qualified CI for the Commando Wing.' My fate had been sealed.

The Confidence Jump

For the first time in my army career, I was repeating a location. The MS Branch had been very thoughtful with me and had ensured I never repeat a station. Even though I felt a bit cheated, I decided to make the most of the opportunity, drawing on my experience of the Ranger Course and my stint as an instructor in Commando Wing, and to try and make a few meaningful changes. For starters, I was fortunate to have some of the finest officers in the Indian Army on my team—almost without exception. The entire lot has done brilliantly and continues to be among the best the army has to offer. Among them were MR Babu, CP Cariappa, Santosh Kurup, Pem Tshering, Shivender Singh, AK Singh, Anuj Bhalla, Daya Chand. I can go on and on, as all of them excelled professionally.

As the CI, I could now actually bring about changes. Work in the Commando Wing was extremely intense and a lot would be happening at any given time. Though all instructors and staff were supposed to be adept at doing all the things YOs were expected to do—for example, tradition had it that no one would shake your hand when you got posted to the Commando Wing until you did the confidence jump—in reality, we had our 'specialists'. There was always an officer who would be a natural when it came to handling snakes; another would become the showpiece confidence-jump specialist, his body and feet ramrod straight as he dropped off the tower into the water below.

A month or so after arriving in Belgaum, the DS Coord called up in a panic. There was to be a high profile visit and our confidence-jump specialist, Captain Rawat, was on leave. We could hardly have an instructor falling through space with arms and legs flailing!

'We've got to recall him,' said the DS Coord, 'the others are, well...'

'OK, recall Rawat,' I said, 'but this is the last time something like this happens.' I issued orders that from now on, with the chief instructor leading, all officers would do the confidence jump once a month. I certainly didn't want instructors demanding and evaluating student officers on events where they themselves were not 100 per cent proficient.

We also started working on a book that was modelled along the lines of the *SAS Survival Guide*. The editorial team working on the content really got into the project big time, collating information on various aspects relating to survival, be it edible plants, poisonous snakes, navigation by the stars and a host of other issues. Captain Pem Tshering, who was from Kalimpong, produced some excellent illustrations. All in all, we were extremely pleased with our effort, which we were convinced would greatly reinforce what the YOs took away from the Commando Course. General Chopra leafed through the fat manual and was extremely pleased with it too. He even recommended me for an award, while forwarding the manuscript to Army HQ for publishing it in the same format as the SAS book.

Army HQ gave a lukewarm response, saying they would publish parts of the work as a pamphlet. We were all tremendously disappointed and I think the army missed out on what potentially would have benefited the young officers considerably. A pamphlet is a pamphlet, a book is a book!

Life in Belgaum was extremely busy, the regimented schedule keeping us on our toes from morning to evening. Both Mrinalini and Yogja had settled into Kendriya Vidyalaya, their new school. Towards the end of the year, I received word that my father-in-law had expired in Gurgaon. His end came while he was narrating a joke to some of his friends. He was laughing loudly when he collapsed. At first, his companions thought it was a part of the act, but to their horror, they realized he was gone. I quickly shepherded the family to Delhi via Bombay.

▪

My endeavour in the Commando Wing was to try and make it as realistic as possible. We combined 'survival' with 'navigation' and laid a lot of emphasis on 'escape and evasion'. We picked new locations in the jungles of the Western Ghats, taking existing roads and tracks out of the equation.

During the Ranger Course, there were a lot of aspects that had struck me as being extremely practical and vital for overall training. We therefore introduced the advanced mountaineering segment (which involved balanced rock climbing using pitons) into the training. Pitons would be driven into a crack or seam in the rock with a hammer. Pitons have an eyehole through which we would attach a karabiner that would then be linked to a nylon rope. In the adjoining Ghats we found a sheer rock face that was perfect for our training. The view from the top, looking down at the depression below, was enough to make anyone feel fearful. To get over that fear, student officers were made to abseil or rappel down.

Exercises would combine navigation and practical survival. Chickens would be let loose and the student officers had to set up traps to catch the birds. If they succeeded in snaring a chicken, well and good; if not, they simply went hungry. Finally, we had a free-for-all exercise at the small Kalandigad Fort. The rules and parameters for the exercise were set by the students themselves, with the DS body being bystanders whose only job was to make sure that safety was not compromised. More than anything else, this exercise tested the ingenuity of the youngsters.

By the end of 1989, my board had been held and I was now cleared to command a battalion. Soon, placements started and some of my peers were already getting their commands. As congratulatory letters started pouring in, I got a DO (demi-official letter) from the 26 Rajput CO telling me that I would be taking over from him. Other similar letters had me being posted to various other units. I then received the communication that mattered: the colonel of the regiment, Major General Ashok Kalyan Verma, wrote saying he had earmarked me for 24 Rajput.

I had left 2 Rajput, my parent battalion, exactly a decade ago. I had hoped to return to the battalion after my IMTRAT stint in Bhutan, but the colonel of the regiment at the time had decreed all officers away from their units be sent to new raisings. Since then, I had been a part of 25 Rajput. I had fought in the Bangladesh War with 2 Rajput, and then performed as an integral part of 25 Rajput in Sri Lanka. Having just moved to the JL Wing in Belgaum, I could afford to wait for either of these two units to fall vacant.

Having himself been commissioned in 2 Rajput, General Ashok Verma, then a captain, had been posted as a platoon commander at the IMA during the 1962 China War. After the Namka Chu debacle, he fought tooth and nail to go back to his battalion. He had instead been sent to a new raising, 18 Rajput, a battalion he went on to command during the Bangladesh War. As the colonel of the regiment, he was not at all happy with my request that I be given either 2 or 25 Rajput. I added gingerly that I was prepared to wait.

'It doesn't happen that way,' he said firmly, 'you're going to 24 Rajput.'

To my mind, if I went to 24 Rajput, I would be completely rootless in the regiment! On the other hand, if I pushed too hard, I might just get into conflict with the colonel of the regiment. I sought an appointment and went to see the Additional MS, Major General CK Kapoor from the Grenadiers. I soon realized I wasn't cutting any ice with him either.

'You understand the implications of your request? You're being adamant and obstinate, going against your colonel of the regiment's wishes. You do not even understand what you will lose if you wait.' I held my ground as unobtrusively as I could. For me, the high point of my army career was to command *my* battalion.

I was sent to Colonel MS, Colonel Kaushal (who retired as a major general) to put it in writing. Kaushal, though from the Kumaon Regiment, had come to the MS Branch after doing the Higher Command Course where General Ashok Verma had been his commander. It had been under his watch that officers of the Higher Command had questioned General Rodrigues and the Chief of Air Staff, Poly Mehra, about the aims and objectives of the IPKF. The incident had sealed General Verma's career, but he still had an iconic reputation and a following among infantry officers. 'You're going against the wishes of my guru,' said Kaushal as I wrote out my letter. Once I had finished it, I signed it and gave it to him. Kaushal grimly read it, sighed and added, 'Okay. Now that you've put it in writing, I'll see that you get neither 2 nor 25 Rajput.'

I returned to Belgaum, not sure if I had shot myself in the foot, but was convinced that if one is right then something good will eventually happen.

Around that time General Ajit Chopra retired and was replaced by Major General PC Puri, also from my regiment, having commanded 19 Rajput. He was an excellent officer and had earlier commanded 3 Division in Ladakh. I was officiating as the commander of Commando Wing as Colonel Jerry Gonsalves was on leave. Somehow, General Puri had come with a preconceived mind set against the way training was being conducted at the Commando Wing. His main bugbear seemed to be that we were going too far and pushing the young officers unnecessarily. The first conflict involved the age-old issue of haircuts.

'Why are you chaps insisting on these atrocious haircuts?' he wanted to know. 'These boys are no longer in the NDA or IMA.' The haircuts were indeed quite drastic, even though by the time the YOs moved out, they did have a thin veneer of black on their heads: 'Sir, it's because of all the sweat and grime, crawling through pits and the undergrowth. They find it very hard to maintain their hair.'

General Puri wasn't convinced. 'I want to talk to the YOs. Let's see what they have to say.' The course was rounded up and produced before the general, who told them they looked like convicts. Having given them a broad hint about his own leaning on the subject, he then asked them for their point of view. YO after YO said more or less the same thing, 'Sir, all the sweat and grime, crawling through pits and the undergrowth. We find it very hard to maintain our hair.'

PC Puri turned and, without saying anything, looked quizzically at me. I knew he was convinced that we had coached the YOs.

He turned his attention to the syllabus. 'Why are you teaching them navigation? You are just repeating what they've learnt at IMA.'

'Technically, yes, sir. But we find the YOs to be completely deficient in the subject.'

'How can that be?'

'We have an exercise coming up tomorrow on navigation where we give them five points of reference. They are expected to cover three during the day and two during the night, but few get beyond one or two during the day.' I pulled out a map and pointed out the grid points, each approximately five to six kilometres apart. 'They cannot follow each other, as there are approximately ninety-two permutations and combinations.'

The next day, I drove PC Puri to the first point. We waited until the first buddy-pair arrived. They were given the grid references that they had to plot on the map. The DS had clear instructions not to interfere; only if the students were more than the stipulated degrees off course, were they to be advised to re-calculate before proceeding. The first pair got it wrong. After a while, a second, then a third, buddy-pair arrived, miscalculated, and were asked to do it again before being allowed to carry on. Even by normal standards, these guys were all left feet! The general was now even more convinced we were conspiring to prove our point. He sat there with a shocked look.

'Can't be,' he finally said, incredulously shaking his head, 'IMA can't get it this wrong. I want to go to another point.'

The situation did not look good. Many a career had been cut short for smaller provocation. I spread out a map which had all the points clearly marked on it. It was like Russian roulette, 'Pick the point, sir.'

To my horror, PC Puri's finger came to rest on a point somewhere in the dead centre, a point that was not approachable by road and one which involved a tough climb. I told the general it was a difficult area. He said, 'No problem, we'll walk.' The approach was extremely tough even for the YOs; for a senior and older officer, no matter how fit, it was going to be a good cardiac workout. PC Puri fell three times, but he simply got up and kept going. To make matters worse, the sun set and soon after, we were enveloped by darkness. Just then, from a nearby hill came the echoing shout, 'Commando! Commando!'

'Why are they shouting?'

'They're lost,' I said.

PC Puri shook his head in disbelief. 'You chaps are taking me for a ride. Let's zero in on this pair.'

After a while we found the two student officers. 'Why are you shouting?' asked the general. They said they were lost. 'Look at the stars, the moon...'

'We've tried all that, sir, but we are still lost.' Eventually, we led them to the centre point, where the DS gave them their fresh coordinates. They calculated, we watched. Then the DS curtly said 'Do it again, gentlemen.' After a while, another buddy-pair came in. Same result.

We walked back in the dark, the general once again losing his footing a couple of times. We drove back to Belgaum in deafening silence. It was four in the morning by the time we got home.

The next evening, after I got home, the doorbell rang. Bharti went to open the door and I heard PC Puri's voice, 'How about a cup of tea for me and VK?' Nothing more was ever said about the suitability of including navigation in the syllabus again. What really struck the commandant was the level of teaching at the Academy, which was unconcerned with ground reality. My own experience in Bangladesh had equipped me better: behind enemy lines, we had worked out a testing navigational course over fifteen/sixteen kilometres. Once a YO had gone through such training, he wouldn't need a DS to guide him.

Time passed and I kept myself fit, running and keeping up with the YOs. Having given it in writing that I was prepared to wait, there was nothing I could do but wait and see which way the coin would fall. I then received word that Colonel Kaushal from the MS Branch was coming to the Infantry School and that he wanted to see me. Not knowing what to expect, I went to see him. He looked at me and said, 'Well fought, blue. Red is the winner,' and handed me an envelope. I opened it to find my posting order. I was to take over 2 Rajput!

At the time, I had no idea what had happened behind the scenes. Later I was to learn that my CO during the Bangladesh War, Dev Raj Dutt, and Tom Mathews, who was commanding the battalion at Naushera, had both made a strong pitch to the colonel of the regiment to get me to 2 Rajput. 'Remember your own case, Ashok,' Dev Raj Dutt had said. 'You fought and fought to get back to your parent battalion. VK is doing much the same thing. He'll be good for the battalion.' The last line probably sealed the deal in my favour. Everyone in the regiment knew that though Ashok Verma had commanded 18 Rajput, his heart had never left the Kali Chindi.

Naushera

The girls were growing up fast, and Mrinalini, in particular, needed stability as she was entering her crucial school years. We decided to apply for separated family accommodation in Belgaum. The family would be extremely far away from Naushera, but that was a small price to pay for academic continuity.

I was already a year behind my immediate contemporaries who had by now been commanding battalions for over a year. I was taking over with almost twenty-one years of service. I was still wearing the rank of a lieutenant colonel when I got off the train at Jammu railway station with the intention of making a quick trip to Vaishno Devi. At the station, the 2 Rajput adjutant, Captain Anurag Chauhan received me. I had to forget about my pilgrimage, as we were required to make an immediate dash to the battalion. There had been a change of plans and Colonel Tom Mathews was to leave in two days.

I had left the battalion more than a decade earlier while it had been in the same sector. It had returned to Naushera and was now deployed along the LOC as a part of 80 Brigade, the first of the four brigades that made up 25 Division whose AOR extended north along the border to Poonch and its surrounding areas. The handing-taking over from Colonel Tom Mathews was a hurried affair, and even before one could take a deep breath and look around, he was gone. Like almost every young officer who joins the army, my ambition in life had been to command the battalion I was commissioned into. Now that I had got what I wanted, I was determined to do my best. It was perhaps the most emotional moment of my life, the CO's baton being handed over to me.

Despite the time lapse of a decade, the 'feel' of old infantry battalions more or less remains the same, even though quite a few faces, especially among the officers, were relatively new. My 2IC was Vijay Lal. Alpha Company was being commanded by my old company officer, Konsom Himalay Singh; Bravo was under Amulya Mohan, Charlie and Delta were under the command of Yogesh Taragi and Sulakhan Singh Sandhu respectively. The subedar major, Zalim Singh Tomar, was a military transport specialist who hailed from the area around the Chambal Ravines in Madhya Pradesh. KH Singh and Amulya Mohan moved out a few months later on posting and Sharad Kapoor came back. My team of officers and JCOs was about as good as it probably gets.

All companies of 2 Rajput were deployed along the LOC with the Battalion Rear at Rumlidhara. Besides us, 11 Dogra, 11 Jat, 17 Punjab, 5 Bihar and a BSF battalion together made up 80 Brigade. Our brigade commander was Ugrasen Yadav from the Kumaon Regiment. I had known the commander from my days at Platoon Weapons in Mhow and subsequently from Poonch where 8 Kumaon had been with us. The GOC commanding 25 Division was a gunner, Major General KS Sethi, who was known to ambush new COs in his division by sending his visit programme to the battalion within a few days of taking over. The GOC was reputed to go through the unit brochures, pick up some trivia and, after the briefing was over, ask a couple of questions. For example: 'How many grenades are there in your battalion inventory?' The hapless CO had two options: if he said he didn't know, the GOC would give him a public dressing-down for not knowing what was happening. On the other hand, if he said '480 grenades' or whatever the correct answer was, the GOC would look at him with contempt and say, 'As a CO don't you have anything better to do than sit around counting grenades?' Maybe it was his way of keeping the new COs on their toes or scuttling any inflated egos. At that point of time, I knew I had at best a week to visit all my posts before the old man came calling.

The moment Tom left, I headed out for the nearest company posts. I had no choice but to cover as much ground as possible and get conversant with the lie of the land before the GOC's visit programme arrived. 2 Rajput was stretched out along the ridgeline that guarded the approach to Naushera town. The AOR was fairly large, spread across some extremely tough walking terrain. In all, we had some twenty-odd posts and the number did not take into account some of the smaller listening and observation posts that kept changing.

Primarily, 2 Rajput was guarding the Sadabad Gap that leads via Adiana Gala to Bhimber. It was also the historical Mughal route. Opposite us was the Samahni Valley in Pakistan Occupied Kashmir, which was dominated by us to quite an extent. Facing our positions were a Baluch and a Punjab battalion of the Pakistan Army. Ravi Rikhye's book, published in 1982, *The Fourth Round: Indo-Pak War 1984 (Future History)* opened with the Pakistanis launching an attack through the Sadabad Gap. This had also been the major route of ingress for the kabailis (tribal lashkars) during the 1947 conflict.

True to form, HQ 25 Division sent the visit programme on the fourth day, and two days later the GOC descended on the unit. From the battalion's point of view, his visit was not a burning issue, for the real worm on the hook was me. As he settled down for my briefing, General Sethi conversationally asked me, 'Have you been around the posts?'

'Yes, sir.'

'Well?' he enquired.

'There are a few places where we need to redo a few things. Some defences need repair,' I said.

Fortunately, he never asked me my trivia question. However, within an hour of his departure, I had the brigade commander on my case. Even the ring of the telephone sounded angry and shrill. The general had told him I was making changes to the defences along the LOC as I felt they needed to be redone. He asked furiously: 'What changes are you making?'

'Changes? I'm not making any changes. I just told the GOC that we needed to redo a few things in some places.'

'You mean to say people before you were not working?' The sarcasm was audible in his voice. It was obvious that I had to do some quick thinking, for it was evident I had the onerous task of cooling down my immediate boss and proving to the chain of command that I wasn't some self-styled smarty-pants CO.

Within a month of my taking over, an NCO from the Intelligence Section committed suicide. Once the shock of the incident ebbed, I called for the man's records. He had joined the battalion just three years ago. This was perplexing, for the established norms of the unit were that no man, regardless of who he was, would be assigned to a specialist platoon unless he had at least five years of service. I couldn't find anything in the deceased man's papers that explained this abnormality. I sent for the senior JCOs of the battalion and asked them how this had come to pass.

'Saab, woh pada likha tha aur achha likhta tha. Is liye usko Int mein dal diya gaya.' (He was an educated type who could write well. So it was decided to put him in Intelligence.)

Infantry battalions, especially old established units like 2 Rajput which had two centuries of history, thrive on SOPs and norms that should never be violated. Unit tartib, the unwritten rulebook, is the bedrock on which things function. In this unfortunate man's case, its violation had manifested itself as a tragedy. As an educated person, the pressure on the deceased to make it through the ranks and become an officer had eventually been too much for him. Fast-forwarded into Intelligence, he never had the opportunity to build relationships with the other men that might have otherwise carried him through. Unfortunately, over the years, unit tartib had got diluted to some extent in 2 Rajput. Subsequently, as I gained seniority, I always spoke to the battalions about unit tartib and just how important it was for established norms and SOPs to be followed.

The Pakistanis across the LOC were, as usual, up to their nonsense, always trying to go one up on us. News of a new CO taking over 2 Rajput soon got to them. Almost compulsively, they started aimlessly firing at Charlie Company positions. Yogesh Taragi immediately picked up the phone and sought permission from me to fire back. 'Go ahead,' I said, 'but I'll be there at 0530 hours tomorrow morning to see the damage inflicted on the other side.'

The whole night the LOC echoed with gunfire. It was still dark when I made my way up to the Charlie Company position. In the early morning light, I scanned the Pakistani bunkers through field glasses. There was no obvious damage on their side. I asked Taragi how many men he had dropped on the other side. He said he had no clue. From where I lay at the observation post, the one big danger was that Pakistani tracer rounds would ignite the surrounding grass. Containing the resultant blaze would be a nightmare, with the choking smoke and the danger of the flames spreading into the post that was stacked with live ammunition.

I told the company commander that there should be no more tit-for-tat firing, and that in fact there should be no more firing by us. One by one our posts fell silent. The Pakistanis initially stepped it up, firing even more the next night. After a couple of days, they realized they were wasting their time, and there was no fun shooting endlessly at someone who wasn't responding, so they just shut up and that was the end of that. Our dominance over the Samahni Valley was such that we could just lob a few rounds into their area and the entire civilian population on the other side would get after the Pakistani military. My instructions were clear; we would retaliate only for maximum effect and not get involved in any frivolous shooting incidents. We had no major incident in my remaining two years in Naushera.

Some elements of the battalion took part in the Kirni Operation in the Poonch sector. The Pakistanis had constructed a couple of bunkers on our side of the LOC and these had to be eliminated. Kirni was situated east of Point 405, also known as Raja Rani, towards the Shahpur post. Fire support platoons from 2 Rajput assisted 19 Punjab and 15 Rajput in flattening out the Pakistani intrusion. The enemy suffered heavy casualties during the course of the operation.

The entire LOC, extending from Akhnoor to Gurez, has its myths and legends, most of them relating to pirs. Our area was under the protection of Khori Baba. The word 'khori' in the vernacular means 'cave' and it was believed that when the kabailis came through the Sadabad Gap in October 1947, they zeroed in on the pir living in the area, as he was the most influential man in the region. The kabailis asked the pir to tell the people to support and join Pakistan. As the learned man refused to do so, the kabailis rounded up his family and shot them in front of him. The tribal raiders then again asked him to do their bidding. The pir said he needed time to think and entered a cave, from which he failed to emerge. Despite the kabailis looking high and low, they were not able to find him. The bodies of Khori Baba's family were buried near one of our posts. It was a revered place and people made offerings there every Thursday. As a rule, no one drank liquor or ate meat on Thursdays and Fridays as a mark of respect for Khori Baba. The men, regardless of faith, revere these pious men and adhere to local customs.

The Sadabad Gap had another interesting story associated with it. During the days of the Mughals, the road went through an area known as the Haathi Paon Gap that was in a defile. According to local legend two elephants had been sculpted on either side of the cliff through which the road passed; the elephants were so life-like that the approaching Mughal caravan came to a halt thinking they were facing wild elephants. The Mughal emperor was extremely angry when he realized stone elephants had stopped them. In a fit of rage, he ordered their destruction. Most of the elephant parts were strewn all over the area, while of the original art only the feet remained—hence the name.

▪

The brigade commander moved out after four or five months. His relief was Brigadier Jitender Singh from the Dogra Regiment. The battalion soon received word that the new commander wished to visit Haathi Paon. I received the brigadier and drove him to the road head from where we had to walk. A pony had been arranged with a saddle, but Jitender Singh waved it off. We began walking. After half an hour, the commander looked most puzzled. 'How much further?' he asked. I said it was still quite a distance.

The track was not only steep, but it was a good three to four kilometres before we got to the gap. Even as the brigadier looked at the broken sculpture, his appreciation of the artist's skill was tempered by the daunting walk back. When he had asked his staff at Brigade HQ how much of a walk it was, he had been told that it was a mere fifty metres—which is why he felt insulted at the offer of the pony as transport. The important lesson here was that, quite often, officers sitting at the rear are quite removed from the reality on the ground.

A short while later, in early 1992, General Sethi also moved out, and was replaced by yet another Dogra officer, Surjit Sangra, as GOC 25 Division. There had been a change at the corps level as well, with Lieutenant General Shankar Roychowdhury taking over the White Knight (XVI) Corps. An armoured corps officer, he went on to take over as the army chief subsequently (when General Bipin Joshi died in harness). He visited the battalion which he knew quite well because of Tom Mathews. While he was going around the posts, he suddenly decided to enter a bunker. Seeing the tense faces of the company commander, he affably said, 'I'm not inspecting the bunker. I'm a tank man. I have never been inside a firing platform that is more than six feet off the ground. I'm just going in to get a feel.' An extremely down-to-earth man, he had the knack of putting people at ease. Yet he managed to take a look and see if the men could fire comfortably from their confined positions, not relying on the opinions of others.

An unconventional man, the corps commander always wanted to see how things looked on the ground rather than go with war game scenarios. A corps level exercise was being held in Nagrota, in an area that was the AOR of 2 Rajput. No officer from our battalion or any other unit in the brigade was present. An attack on one of the posts by the opposing force was declared a 'given' by the war game umpires. General Roychowdhury stopped the exercise and decided to come to the actual post and see the terrain for himself. Once there, the general went around the defences. Then, like a JC discussion, he called the JCO, the company commander and other officers and discussed the theoretical situation on the ground. Soon it became obvious that the direction from which the attack had been launched during the corps exercise was a sheer cliff and there was no way any sizeable force level could have been brought to bear on the particular position under discussion. He turned to his staff and said, 'Declare the attack a failure.'

▪

In 1992, we experienced torrential rains. Even the bridge (lower in the plains) over the Chenab was washed away. In our area, the approach track to one of our posts had been completely decimated. The brigade commander called me and told me that the corps commander was coming to the post in the next forty-eight hours. 'But there is no road,' I said to the brigadier, 'it has been completely destroyed by the recent rains.'

'Just do what you can do,' said the commander.

I gathered up 2 Rajput, the JCOs, and every man I could lay my hands on. 'Paltan ki izzat ka sawal hai.' (It's a matter of honour for the battalion.) The magic words having been uttered by the CO, it was a magnificent sight; for forty-eight hours we worked ourselves to the bone, no one taking a break—officers, JCOs, sweepers, cooks, et al. I'm quite sure if the wives had been present, they would have joined in too.

At the appointed hour, the corps commander arrived and I drove him up the steep track to the post. He was suitably impressed to see that the post looked good in spite of torrential rain, and the rank and file knew their job. After the corps commander left, the brigade commander turned to me, 'I thought you said there was no road the day before.'

'There wasn't,' I said, extremely proud of my battalion for having pulled off what seemed an impossible task.

'I thought as much. It was much too smooth a track to have been an old road,' mused the commander.

There was a lot to learn from General Shankar Roychowdhury. Perhaps being an armoured corps officer, he was frank and open enough to question what most others would consider to be a given. A few years earlier, a Sikh LI officer, Major (later Brigadier) Navin Maini, had written an innovative paper 'Attack in Skirmish Order'. Maini had obviously served with Shankar Roychowdhury earlier and the general decided to hold a seminar in Jammu to discuss what Maini had advocated. During the seminar, the corps commander decided that he would like to see the theory put into practice and the task was assigned through 80 Brigade to 2 Rajput.

The demonstration involved live ammunition with fire-and-move tactics, homing the attacking troops on to the target. The men had to be oriented accordingly and the risk of any accident eliminated. As is the norm with most units when conducting a demonstration, we had done a bit of sprucing up of the area. Roychowdhury arrived and made it clear he wasn't interested in any of the cosmetic work but in the exercise itself. Fortunately, the demonstration went off like clockwork and the general left quite satisfied with what he had seen on the ground. He moved out in 1992 and was replaced by HS Bedi from the Dogras.

In Belgaum, while in the Commando Wing, I had privately done a course in basic computer applications. In 2 Rajput, we ceremoniously went and purchased a computer for Battalion HQ and started looking around for someone to operate it. It took a lot of coaxing to convince one of the battalion clerks to take on the task. Once the computer got going, things started happening. All that the operating clerk now had to do was work out a few formats and start loading data into it. Every time the 'print' button would be pushed, an admiring lot of men would watch the paper effortlessly slide out with everything neatly laid out in ink. It was nothing short of a miracle. By the time we moved from Naushera, the rest of the clerical staff wanted to dump the typewriters and were all collectively clamouring for computers.

Visiting various battalion posts was an extremely dangerous business. At each location, regardless of the size and the number of men it held, I was greeted with a mug of tea. The word 'tea' doesn't quite give an accurate picture of the concoction that was one-third sugar and two-thirds milk, with a sprinkling of tea leaves to give it colour.

Zalim Singh Tomar, the SM, was in my office, concern written all over his face. 'Aaj post par aap naraaz they kya?' he asked. (Were you angry about something when at the post today?) Seeing my blank look, he said I had refused the tea that had been offered to me. I explained to him that the endless cups of tea with endless amounts of sugar were not good for my metabolism.

He looked even more concerned. Left to the SM, he would have yelled for the medics by now. 'Aapko sugar ka problem hai kya?' (Do you have a problem of high sugar levels?)

The next day, to prove to him that I was fit as a fiddle, I took the SM along with the unit panditji. Knowing how the grapevine worked in the unit, I knew each and every man was watching my every step, convinced I had a 'sugar' problem. A few days of zipping around combined with my steadfast refusal to drink 'tea' in each sub-unit was soon put down as one of my idiosyncrasies.

I like to think that my two-year command tenure in Naushera was a happy period for the battalion. The men were extremely upbeat, especially after their excellent performance on the LOC and in the fire-and-move demonstration that had been laid out for the corps commander. Major General RS 'Munna' Taragi had taken over from Ashok Kalyan Verma as the colonel of the regiment and he visited us during this period. Munna Taragi had been a subaltern in 14 Rajput and had served with my father.

Towards the end of 1992, we received our orders to move to Faizabad (Ayodhya) where we were to replace 1 Maratha LI who were doing a one-to-one changeover, moving into Naushera to take over from 2 Rajput. By the time we moved, we were into April of 1993. The bridge over the Chenab damaged in one of the earlier rains still had not been repaired, and the battalion de-inducted using the Kruppman Bridge further towards the LOC. We came down to Bari Brahmana , which was the railhead from where we were to embark on to a special train that would take us to Faizabad, the military cantonment near the city of Ayodhya. There was a delay of a fortnight as the railways needed more time to marshal the rolling stock to take us to our new destination, and my job was to somehow keep the men occupied, fit and out of trouble. I decided to bring spirituality into the equation, so we had an inter-company competition to see which company could run up to Vaishno Devi and back in the shortest time.

Special train journeys are always that—special—and we finally set off in regal style, with morning halts for battalion PT. While going through the unit's digest of service on the train, I found we were returning to Faizabad after 101 years. In 1892, 2 Rajput had been stationed in Faizabad to tackle the dacoit problem in the Azamgarh area. After 6 December 1992, when the Babri Masjid had been demolished, Faizabad was no longer a laid-back, peace location in the heart of Uttar Pradesh. It was now a live wire station!

The Hornet's Nest

Once we knew the battalion was moving to Faizabad, I had written to the MS, Lieutenant General VK Singh, requesting that I be given a three-year tenure as Mrinalini was now in her final school year. Not too many COs were keen to stay in their unit that long, so the MS Branch assured me I'd stay the course. Once we moved to a peace station, I could not retain the separated family accommodation in Belgaum. Even as the battalion's advance party moved to Faizabad, I took leave and drove the family to Ayodhya where they were to stay in temporary accommodation until the unit moved in from Naushera. Both the girls were transferred to the Kendriya Vidyalaya in Faizabad. For them it was a culture shock; the school in Belgaum had had excellent faculty, while in Faizabad, I suppose I'd describe it as a very laid-back, betel-chewing environment.

On 6 December 1992, the Babri Masjid was demolished in an attempt to reclaim the land as the birthplace of Lord Ram. The demolition sent shock waves through the subcontinent. And, while the city remained tense, there was no ban on the movement of army vehicles. With Bharti in tow, I decided to visit the location of the masjid, not more than forty-eight hours after the demolition. I expected to see a mass of rubble, some damage and destruction. Instead, it was almost impossible to tell if anything had happened at all. A neat parapet had replaced the earlier structure and there was nothing there that gave even the slightest hint that the landscape had been different just a few hours before. Absolutely nothing. Some bored security personnel who were on duty barely cast a glance in our direction, while under a cloth canopy there were a couple of idols that had been installed to mark the Ram Janmabhoomi.

After the battalion had arrived from Naushera, we had gone over the events with an eye towards tackling any fallout from the demolition. As the kar sevaks had proceeded towards the masjid, the entire local population had clogged the narrow approach streets with whatever furniture they could find. With the streets blocked, movement of any security forces would have been a nightmare. Coupled with this the fact that the people who brought down the structure had left behind not an ounce of rubble, it was pretty obvious that whoever had planned the demolition, had planned it meticulously down to the smallest detail.

Another notable feature that could hardly escape any of us who served in Faizabad during that period—army, paramilitary or police forces—was the complete lack of animosity between the Hindu and Muslim communities. Left to their own devices, both sides would have probably sorted out the issue within a day. However, as invariably happens in such emotive issues, passions and hardened stances were imposed by people who had their own personal and political agendas. To garner support, these individuals who were otherwise nowhere on the scene, would become more and more strident.

We were now once again part of 7 Brigade; thirty years earlier, the battalion had fought and was decimated at Namka Chu in NEFA (Arunachal) as a part of the same formation. Brigadier Mahabir Singh from the Madras Regiment commanded the brigade, which also included 7 Kumaon commanded by Soli Pawri and 2 Bihar under CS 'Cherry' Sandhu. The brigade continued to be a part of the Red Eagles (4 Division) that was being commanded by a gunner, Manjit Singh Dugal, Vir Chakra.

Within a few days of our arrival at Faizabad, we were told that the I Corps GOC, YM Bammi, would be paying the battalion a visit. My commander briefed me that Bammi was a real stickler for detail and he was extremely keen on inspecting the unit's training facilities. The proposed visit programme suggested that after visiting 2 Rajput, the corps commander would proceed to 2 Bihar for lunch. This seemed a bit odd, so I suggested that the lunch should also be held in our officer's mess. Preparations then began on a war footing; the area needed to be cleaned up and made habitable as it had been unoccupied ever since the Marathas had moved to Naushera. The older the unit, the more stuff it has accumulated over the years and settling into a new location takes time.

On the nineteenth day of our arrival at Faizabad, the corps commander arrived. By then we had succeeded in bringing some semblance of organization to the unit lines and the Battalion HQ outwardly looked as if it was up and running. I finished my briefing after which the corps commander asked a lot of questions pertaining to the battalion's performance in Naushera. Once the briefing was over, I then told the general we were ready to take him across to the battalion's training area. General Bammi looked at me incredulously, 'Training? I haven't come here to see training. You chaps have just reached here after four years in the field and modified-field areas. Once you've fully settled down and the unit has stabilized, I'll come and see your training. I want the boys to settle down in a peace environment and get on with administration before you all put your heart into training.'

I looked at the brigade commander, but he was deliberately looking elsewhere. We moved for lunch, during the course of which Bammi looked around the mess approvingly. 'Your boys have certainly worked hard to settle down. How many days since you moved in?'

'Nineteen.'

A Gorkha officer, the general had commanded a battalion that had moved from one location to another under his watch. Even during the briefing, his questions and observations were extremely logical and sensitive towards the unit. After lunch, as we prepared to see him off, he turned to the brigade commander and told him he was a bit taken aback as to why he, as the commander, had put so much pressure on the battalion. 'The least you could do was to host the lunch in the brigade mess.' As the corps commander's car moved forward, I could see the brigade commander from the corner of my eye. I instinctively knew I was in trouble.

As one of his COs, Mahabir Singh expected me to spend more time socializing with him. A couple of days after General Bammi's visit, we met casually and he asked me what was happening in the other two battalions. I looked at him and said I could answer any question that he had pertaining to 2 Rajput, but anything he wanted to know about the Kumaon and the Bihar units, he would have to ask their respective COs. Rather patronizingly, the commander then lectured me how it was important for an upwardly mobile officer to keep his eyes and ears open. At the end of his discourse, I don't think I earned any brownie points by repeating that I was only concerned with what was happening in my house.

Mahabir Singh had been an instructor at the MT (Military Transport) School earlier. He then decided to inspect the battalion's vehicles. He poked his finger into the radiator of a parked vehicle and said the water level was too low. Any person with even a basic knowledge of engines could have told the commander that in parked vehicles, the water level does not brim to the top. As he went down the row of vehicles making trivial observations, I had to keep saying, 'Sir, we will rectify the mistake.'

A month was to pass without any major incident. Then I received a telephone call from the BM, a very fine officer from the Sikh Regiment, JP Santhanam. He told me the commander was not happy with the battalion.

'Sir, commander feels your unit is not doing enough BAUT (Boat Assault Universal Type) practice. Commander has noted that the battalion plays games in the evening while the other two units are training through the day. 2 Rajput is hardly putting in any time.' The role of our new formation was centred on the crossing of rivers and canals. For this purpose, the army relied on flat-bottom aluminium contraptions that were known as BAUT. These were extremely heavy and part of the drill was for the men to lift them and cover distances ranging from one-and-a-half to two kilometres.

Frankly, I wasn't surprised to receive the call, for, increasingly, Mahabir Singh seemed to believe that 2 Rajput was trying to get the better of him. The last thing any CO needs is a hostile commander. I chose my words carefully and deliberately, explaining to the BM that my boys were doing BAUT practice from morning till noon. Training period ended at noon, after which unit tartib demanded that the men follow the established routine. It was also important as the unit had been in field and modified field areas for four-and-a-half years. It was vital for the men to play games where they could mingle with the officers and JCOs, strengthening the bonds between them through various inter- and intra-company matches. I concluded by telling Santhanam to convey to the commander that my boys were sturdy, extremely fit, and that 2 Rajput would not let him down. If the commander felt unit tartib was not important, he was free to say so.

The refusal to run around with boats over the battalion's head through the day may have aggravated matters, but in my book, unit tartib was something that could not be compromised. There was no further communication from Brigade HQ on the subject. We continued BAUT training, and I was convinced we could easily outlast any other battalion, regardless of how much they practiced.

Whatever subtle hostility existed prior to the phone call now became more overt. The commander would, almost routinely, call up every evening and ramble on about the need to have a conference early in the morning the next day, or talk of some other trivial matter. The next morning there would be no conference, nothing, just business as usual, almost as if the previous evening's conversation had not taken place.

Matters came to a head after a few days. After dinner, Bharti and I decided to stroll down to the Saryu Ghats. Hardly had we left that than commander called. Mrinalini, then studying for her final school exam, answered the phone. 'Uncle, they've gone for a walk,' she told the commander, only to be questioned further. The bewildered child answered as best as she could. By the time we got home, she was almost a quivering wreck. After calming her down, I picked up the phone and called Mahabir Singh.

I politely asked him if a war had been declared and if any urgent action needed to be taken. He mumbled something about wanting to hold a conference at seven in the morning.

I was seething by then. I told the commander that from now on, if there was any need for the brigade to communicate with me past seven in the evening on routine staff matters, then the call must come in through the battalion exchange. I then wished him goodnight firmly, put the receiver down and disconnected the phone. The unit telephone, connected to the 2 Rajput exchange, remained operative in case there was any emergency. After that, we turned in for the night.

Hardly had I gone to sleep, than the doorbell rang. I opened the door to find the Sparrow (brigade signals officer) standing at the door, looking bleary-eyed. He had with him two linemen who were carrying their usual testing equipment.

'Sir, your phone is faulty. Commander personally called me and said to rectify it immediately,' said the Sparrow, a young captain, who was looking frightened at having to wake up a CO. I looked at my watch. It was almost midnight. I told the captain there was nothing wrong with my phone and that I had deliberately disconnected it, and he could convey to the commander that if he wanted to talk to me, he could get me through the unit exchange. I got back into bed, wondering if I could have handled things differently. One thing seemed certain: I had achieved my ambition to command and reach an equivalent rank as my father so there were no worries for the future despite a hostile commander. I really couldn't see a way out of my predicament in dealing with an irate superior.

Sure enough, the pinpricks started and two days later Mahabir Singh wanted to test the unit in Battle Physical Efficiency Tests. The unit did well with 80 per cent of its personnel finishing in the 'excellent' grade. In the evening we were told that the commander felt that the distances were not correct and the run would be held again. I invited him to witness the run on a distance personally measured by him. Before we started I told the boys, 'Paltan ki izzat ka sawal hai aur mujh se peechhe koi nahin aana chahiye.' (It's a matter of honour and I don't want anybody to finish after me.) This time there were 96 per cent in the excellent category. Units are very conscious of their izzat.

The divisional exercise for the canal crossing was soon held. Mahabir Singh decided that 7 Kumaon and 2 Bihar would be the two assaulting units while 2 Rajput, a recent addition to 7 Brigade, would be the reserve battalion. As was his wont, the commander trusted no one and refused to delegate anything, personally rushing around the exercise area making sure everything was the way he wanted it before the top brass arrived. His own BM was left sitting idle without any instructions from the commander. Major Santhanam was trying hard to work out the orders that the commander was to give, but Mahabir Singh was out of communication, busy with officers from the two units marking out the assaulting routes.

Once the division staff arrived and took their appointed places, the exercise began and ran smack into trouble. The BAUTs had to be carried through an area covered with sarkanda. The clumps of elephant grass soon threw everything out of gear, for the men could barely move along the marked routes. Soon there was absolute chaos and the GOC who was walking behind the BAUT parties was making his displeasure quite obvious. Somehow, the two battalions struggled across to the banks of the canal, which was, at that point of time, without water.

We were following the developments on the radio. As the first boats hit the dry embankment, Mahabir Singh ordered us to move as well. The order made no sense, for only when the assaulting battalions have captured their objective and consolidated the ground can the reserve battalion go through. If we were to follow the order, we would all be milling around the canal embankment. Given the existing relationship between the commander and myself, I knew the entire blame for the unfolding fiasco would be laid at my doorstep. The last thing I wanted was to get into professional trouble.

'Please authenticate,' I radioed back, desperately buying time.

Authentication is a procedure that requires the officer issuing the orders to give out a certain code word that confirms that he is indeed the person who has issued the order. With his BM sitting far away under a tree, Mahabir Singh was in no position to authenticate anything. It took almost forty minutes for the authentication to come through, during which period the two assaulting units had performed some of the required actions. Even though it was still a little early for the reserves to be launched, 2 Rajput's arrival on the embankment couldn't be faulted beyond a point. My professional standing had been saved, but relations with my immediate boss soured further.

There is a universal rule that applies not just to the Indian Army but to all organizations across the globe—don't rub your boss the wrong way. I could feel the noose tighten around my neck. To be fair to my commander, he continued to throw me lifelines, telling me to conform to his rules if I wanted a bright future. I simply could not understand the commander's mental make-up and the rules of engagement in his book were just not acceptable to me. I had no choice but to do what I thought was correct and somehow shield the battalion from any collateral damage, given that the situation seemed to be getting increasingly personal. At that point of time, I had no idea that things were only beginning to heat up and the worst was yet to come.

I had taken a few days' leave and was away from the battalion when Brigade HQ tasked 2 Rajput with conducting the inter-brigade boxing championship. At that stage, even the 2IC was not available. Nevertheless, the officers quickly got down to the task of making all the necessary arrangements. I returned from leave a day earlier than scheduled and my officers reported to me saying the boxing championship was underway. Referees and umpires were drawn from the three battalions, but almost all bouts involving boxers from 7 Kumaon were running into problems as all decisions against the particular unit were being fiercely contested.

Being on leave, perhaps I shouldn't have gone, but since the officers had said they were having problems, I decided to attend the finals that were being held that evening. Matches in various weight categories started, and the support for each battalion from their respective corners and the audience got more and more voluble as the evening progressed. Soon, we were witnessing a bout between a 2 Rajput boxer and a 7 Kumaon opponent. The fight was extremely intense, with both opponents fighting not just for themselves but for the izzat of their battalions. Gradually the Rajput boxer started forging ahead. The Kumaon opponent, perhaps getting a little desperate, fouled his opponent and the referee immediately cautioned him. It happened again, and yet again the referee issued a caution. At this stage, one of the men from the Kumaon section in the audience, got up and hit one of the referees, Anurag Chauhan, on the head with a bamboo stick. Chauhan, who was one of my officers, collapsed.

The blow resulted in complete mayhem. The arena exploded resembling a bar brawl in a Wild West movie. Rajput and Kumaon troops went for each other, flattening out whoever they could from the other battalion. The chaos must have lasted a few seconds, for I leapt up into the centre and physically started separating the brawling troops. Some other officers joined in while others quickly shielded the women and children. In the process, I probably manhandled a couple of my unit chaps, roughly pushing them to calm them down. Interestingly, the senior officer from 7 Kumaon was the battalion's 2IC. Throughout the fight, he just kept sitting on a sofa along with the ladies, calmly watching the action unfold.

Men from 7 Kumaon then realized they were cornered, for they were on our territory. Quite a few of them broke out of the boxing arena and made it back to their lines. The incident was easily the most shocking breakdown of military discipline that I had ever seen in my professional career. Bar fights between exuberant young officers who would get all worked up over regimental and service issues were known to happen; hockey, football and basketball inter-unit and unit competitions were always prone to high emotion, sometimes resulting in people being pushed around. Now we had boxing added to the list. I was furious with my men for having got provoked and had every intention of cracking down hard on the culprits. Unit discipline was entirely my responsibility and unit tartib demanded I sort it out. Exactly the same thing would apply to Colonel Soli Pavri and the men of 7 Kumaon.

The Dogra Regimental Centre Commandant, Brigadier Sachdeva, also doubled as the station commander. As the free-for-all was a discipline issue, I filed a detailed report of events with Sachdeva, with a formal copy to 7 Brigade HQ and all other concerned units. Anurag Chauhan, who had received the blow to the head, was fortunately not grievously hurt. This in itself was a blessing, for he had been felled by the full swing of a bamboo stick.

Brigade HQ soon got into the act. Both the subedar majors were promptly attached (removed from their units and placed at Brigade HQ) and an inquiry ordered. The summary of the incident prepared by brigade squarely put the entire blame on 2 Rajput. The inevitable call from Mahabir Singh followed. His voice was oozing sympathy: 'VK, give me three or four names from your battalion and I'll save you.'

I put the phone down. In the afternoon, Brigade HQ followed up with a letter on similar lines—give us some names. I took a sheet of paper and picked up a pen. If the commander wanted names, I had every intention of giving them to him.

Brigadier Mahabir Singh blew a gasket when he got the list. There were three hundred names on the paper, all 2 Rajput officers, JCOs and men who had been present at the boxing arena, serially listed as per seniority. As the top cat in the unit, the first name was naturally mine. I Corps and 4 Division HQs, getting the reports of the incident through 7 Brigade HQ, were also likely to put the entire blame on us for the incident. With the subedar majors of the two battalions attached, even though the inquiry was still on, there were even murmurs of disbanding 2 Rajput. The situation could not be grimmer.

The entire cantonment was abuzz with the incident. Being a small station, everyone knew what was going on, being perhaps even aware of Brigade HQ's bias against 2 Rajput. Brigadier Sachdeva, with whom the battalion had filed the first report of the incident, called me and advised me to talk to the army commander and give him my side of the story, which he felt would not see the light of day given the current mood in 7 Brigade HQ. The general was due to visit Faizabad in the following couple of days. Commissioned into the Grenadiers, Lieutenant General YN 'Yogi' Sharma had lost a leg during the Bangladesh War. Despite the physical handicap, the general had emerged as the Douglas Bader of the Indian Army, rising to the top ranks, eventually retiring as the vice chief.

I decided my going to the army commander alone would not be right. I called Soli Pavri. Together, we asked for an appointment with the army commander, which was immediately granted by his staff officer. Like two errant schoolboys, we told the general what we knew of the incident. Soli had not been present at the boxing arena on the fateful evening. We collectively conveyed to the army commander that what had happened should never have happened, even though tempers do run high in most inter-battalion competitions. Secondly, as COs of the two respective battalions, the onus and responsibility was ours to take the necessary disciplinary action. By attaching our two subedar majors, Brigade HQ was only making a bad situation worse.

General Yogi Sharma looked at us carefully and then called his staff officer to get the brigade commander immediately. He told Mahabir Singh to note down his directions: (a) immediately send the two subedar majors back to their respective units; (b) finish off the inquiry within fifteen days; and (c) leave the two commanding officers to take necessary action. He made it clear that no one should be victimized unneccesarily and the matter should then be closed.

Division and Corps HQs were not pleased at this development, but since Soli and I had both gone to the army commander on the advice given by the station commander, they could not nail us for having leapfrogged the chain of command. Individuals from both units were subsequently identified and punished and the matter ended there as far as the boxing incident was concerned. However, ever since we had moved to Faizabad, I had been in the gunsights and it was now time for the commander to pull the trigger. Though Brigadier Mahabir Singh had been posted out, he still got to write my Annual Confidential Report (ACR). As is the norm, reports have to be personally shown to the officer being reported on and his counter signature is essential. The commander's hands were shaking uncontrollably as he gave me my report. He wouldn't look at me directly, muttering that the ACR was 'not that bad'. I did not want to give Brigadier Mahabir Singh the pleasure of watching me read his comments, so I just signed it. 'You do realize I will be contesting your ACR, sir,' I said, signing it and giving the file back to him.

Later, I did read the ACR, which amounted to hitting a drowning man on the head with an oar. That report would surely be the end of my career. Given the biased feeding of information to the division and the corps, the report was likely to be dittoed by the higher HQs. To me, however, what was important was that I had not succumbed to the pressure to give an incorrect version of the incident to save myself. The unit had also realized this, and I could sense that they were happy that no innocent man had been punished despite the pressure from the higher authorities.

Over the years, the army has handled equally bad cases of momentary breaches of discipline on the sports field by simply sending errant units on a long march together. Usually, by the end of the slog, most of the animosity is buried.

9

RESURRECTION

Fear and Panic

In mid-1993, 4 Division saw a change at the helm, with Major General DS Chauhan from the Madras Regiment taking over. The GOC had earlier commanded a brigade in Sri Lanka as part of the IPKF. 7 Brigade also got a new commander, Brigadier VP Malhotra from the Sikh Regiment.

The new commander, like most officers of his seniority in the Indian Army, was a professional soldier with little time for theatrics of the kind that seemed to obsess his predecessor. The brigade gave the unit plenty of professional tasks and these were performed with quiet efficiency. It doesn't take a senior officer long to gauge a battalion's worth, and 2 Rajput passed muster on all counts despite small niggling issues faced by almost all units. We settled down quickly and were soon working in close coordination with Brigade HQ, evolving new techniques for an attack across a canal obstacle, the project culminating with a smart demonstration on the ground. After these last few months, it was good to be back to professional soldiering. Overall, the brigade did well during that period, with the commander getting the best out of all three battalions.

Throughout my three-year tenure, officers had been coming and going from the unit. Major KH Singh was back after having left the battalion in Naushera. As a senior company commander, he had been assigned the task of preparing the NCOs for their cadre review which would decide who was to become a JCO. One of the subjects taught was administration and morale. KH—who had done his schooling in Sainik School Goalpara, Assam—was labouring to explain the nuance between 'fear' and 'panic' to the trainees sitting in front of him.

On a blackboard under a tree, Shantiniketan style, KH had written the two words boldly with chalk. While driving around the unit, I decided to visit the class and see how things were progressing. I asked one of the soldiers to explain what he had understood so far.

'Saab, phear dar hota hai! Yeh hamare level pe hota hain.' (Fear means being frightened, at our level.) So far so good, after all no human being can go into battle without some element of fear. 'Panik,' he continued, 'unche darje ka dar hota hain jo officer level pe hota hai.' (Panic is also fear but it is only applicable at the higher level, to officers.)

I looked at KH, said, 'How true,' and moved away quickly, somehow getting back to my vehicle before exploding with laughter, much to the astonishment of my driver. The good NCO didn't know it, but he had just spouted words of wisdom that would have given Socrates a run for his money.

The line between fear and panic was to get blurred, for as a family we were in for a massive shock around that time. Bharti started complaining of serious back pain. The army doctors in the small Military Hospital in Faizabad did not have the required specialist and they referred her to a civil orthopaedic doctor. At first, Dr Atul Verma treated her with diathermy for a fortnight or so, but the pain did not abate. Looking perplexed, the doctor ordered a second round, saying he had never ever had to do two sessions of diathermy. Almost as an afterthought, he ordered an X-ray. A short while later, he looked at the films and kindly asked us both to sit down. 'I'm happy I have detected what the problem is,' he said, 'and it is extremely serious but curable.' The X-ray showed that Bharti was suffering from a serious condition: medically referred to as Koch's Spine, also known as spinal tuberculosis. Basically, the bone tissue in the L3 and L4 vertebrae had disintegrated due to an infection. By the time it was detected, there was only a thin piece of bone connecting the two vertebrae. The moment that gave way, which could be at any time, it would mean a complete collapse of the entire spinal column. In most cases, this would be fatal.

Dr Verma wanted to put Bharti in a full body cast while, at the same time, treating her with a four-drug regime. The thought of being in a body cast was terrifying. The other option was even more complex; she would have to lie absolutely still for seven months. At the time, even the idea was incomprehensible. Nevertheless, after taking a solemn commitment that she would abide by the doctor's instructions, come what may, Bharti was brought home and made to lie down in one posture, without any movement or thought of getting up. The 210-day vigil began. The doctor would come almost every day to check on her and the girls and I made sure she did not move.

After a couple of months, the brigade commander commented that he didn't see Bharti at any of the social functions. I invited Brigadier Malhotra home and he was shocked to see Bharti's predicament. I also decided to brief him fully on her condition and explained to him in detail what the problem was. Slowly, agonizingly, Bharti clawed her way out of danger. The seven-month nightmare of lying absolutely still was to be followed by intense medication over a period of time, but at least she was out of danger and eventually able to walk around on her own. The help and support the family received from the battalion and the brigade during this difficult period is something one can never forget. It underlines the bond that exists within the army, which makes it one large family, a fact that always comes to the fore when the chips are down.

Then it was the turn of the MS Branch to spring a surprise, for I suddenly received posting orders for Mhow. At the end of my Naushera tenure, the MS had agreed in writing to give me a three-year command and given the situation at home, my moving now would have led to absolute chaos. I had no choice but to seek an appointment with the Deputy MS, Brigadier Keshav Singh who was from the Sikh Regiment. I explained my predicament to him, and also drew his attention to the fact that the MS, Lieutenant General VK Singh, had agreed that I would be given an extended command.

Keshav Singh was unmoved, 'We have to manage the officer cadre. There is another officer waiting in the wings to take over from you.'

At that time, Vijay Lal, who was to take over from me in Faizabad, was posted in Mathura, and he was equally keen that he not be moved for another six months as his children's education would have been disrupted. He had told me he was quite willing to wait and I informed Keshav Singh about this. With Bharti in no position to be moved, I was desperate. After a while, Keshav Singh looked like he would throw his paperweight at me, 'You've wasted two hours of my time,' he growled. Seeing that I was in no mood or position to budge, in exasperation he said, 'Will Vijay Lal give it in writing that he is willing to wait for six months?'

'You'll have his letter on your table tomorrow morning, sir,' I said, seeing a ray of hope.

'Okay, go to Colonel MS 2 and give him that letter. Now get out of my office!' MS Branch rarely, if ever, gave an inch. I knew I had been more than lucky. I raced back to Faizabad, relieved that we wouldn't have to move Bharti after all and Mrinalini could also finish her final year in school, undisturbed.

Around this time, Mrinalini did something that would transform our lives. I had always been extremely fond of shooting, rarely missing out on the chance to bag a partridge or two for the table. One day after school, she handed me a letter, asking me to read it before sending it on. It was addressed to Maneka Gandhi. It began, 'My father is a poacher…'

I tried to explain to her the difference between shooting as a sport and poaching. It made no difference. The fact that I always obtained a license for any shikar was of no consequence to her.

'Okay, let's do one thing,' I said. I belonged to the old school of thought that one must hunt for one's food whenever possible. 'There will be no more meat or fish or eggs in the house if there is no more shooting.' The compromise was agreed on, on a trial basis, for a month. The letter to Maneka Gandhi was put on hold for the time being. Vegetarianism became the watchword, and we were amazed with the ease of the transformation, and we subsequently just continued with it.

The next round of inter-battalion boxing was soon on us. 2 Bihar were to host the event, and there were some suggestions that referees should be brought in from outside the brigade. All three COs reacted most strongly to this suggestion, saying that one could not breed distrust and suspicion. In any case, with everybody else watching the event, it was highly unlikely that any biased decisions would be meted out. There was a massive build-up though, with all eyes on 2 Rajput and 7 Kumaon boxers who had a healthy rivalry going. The event was, as usual, keenly fought, with 2 Rajput emerging clear winners by a handsome margin.

A few months after my interview with the Deputy MS, the list with the names of officers who had been selected for the Higher Command Course in Mhow came out. I was delighted to see that both Soli Pavri and my name figured among the nominees. At that time, though I had represented against it, Brigadier Mahabir Singh's report was still very much on the record. It would only subsequently be expunged when it was judged by the competent authorities as not being in keeping with my overall service record. At the same time, Vijay Lal also received his posting orders for 2 Rajput, designated to take over the battalion from me in June 1994. The handing-taking over ceremonies completed, I moved with the family to Mhow via Delhi.

Dr SM Tuli, one of the foremost orthopaedic doctors in the country, reviewed Bharti's case. Some of the drugs she needed to take were extremely toxic, which meant she needed constant tests to watch for further complications, especially blindness. He was evidently quite satisfied by her progress, but he cautioned Bharti that the recovery would continue to be slow. The next eighteen months would be particularly crucial. Even though the bone eventually healed, even now, some residual pain continues to bother her every once in a while.

The MS Branch Never Forgets

While in Delhi I visited Lieutenant General Ravi Eipe, who had taken over as the MS. As one of the senior ranking officers, I had often invited him to visit 2 Rajput while we were in Naushera and Faizabad, but his visit never materialized. I briefed him about the battalion and the main events that had occurred during my tenure. He was delighted that three Rajput officers had been nominated for the Higher Command Course and yet another had made it to the College of Defence Management in Secunderabad. The Higher Command Course being a ten-month affair, he then pointedly asked me where I would like to be posted after Mhow.

I told him about Bharti's problem and requested that I be posted to Delhi so that the final stages of her recovery could be under the best possible medical care.

'That's no problem,' he said immediately, adding that there were always plenty of vacancies for an officer of my seniority in Army HQ.

The family quickly settled in Mhow. Yogja was admitted into the Army School in Mhow while Mrinalini was a bit of a free bird, doing her BCom through distance education with Delhi University. This allowed her to dabble in all the things that army wives and daughters are encouraged to do in Mhow, ranging from baking and bread-making to attending classes on welfare activities via the Army Women's Welfare Association (AWWA). I prepared to attend the Higher Command Course along with fellow officers who had also finished commanding their respective battalions. We had a sprinkling of naval and air force officers as well. The Higher Command is an excellent course. As middle-ranking officers, we were expected to question things. As we were no longer attached to any formation, we were encouraged to analyse everything, giving our opinions without any reservations while imbibing the views of our peers who had just recently commanded units in diverse conditions across the country.

As a part of our study, we were to visit each command and see for ourselves the ground reality in each region of the country, operationally and otherwise. These aspects would then be war-gamed, studied and discussed in detail. As a result, we were in a position to imbibe a lot, enhance our knowledge base and expand our horizons considerably. Over the years, the Higher Command Course has emerged as one of the most vibrant professional courses in the Indian armed forces. The commander of the course was an engineer officer, Major General RN Chadha, a thorough professional and a gentleman. During the next eleven months, we were visited by guest lecturers from various walks of life. Equipped with a well-stocked library, the course allows officers to de-stress considerably after the rigours of having commanded a battalion.

During our stay in Mhow, we were expected to submit a dissertation on a subject of our choice. The Higher Command Course is affiliated with the better known as Indore University, and officers attending the course are awarded an MPhil in Defence Management, based on their dissertation. I opted to do a detailed study on 'Relations Between the Military and the Police' and wrote the entire thesis by hand. There had been instances of conflict in the past between the army and the police. As a part of my thesis I wanted to study the reasons for the conflict and understand why the two sides could not work together. Part of the study focused on ways to make the relationship more harmonious and synergize the efforts of the two so that, in the overall national setup, both organizations could be optimally made use of.

After having completed the study, I decided not to apply for the MPhil; somehow, it seemed rather odd to be awarded a degree on the basis of a single dissertation. It was perhaps one of those quirky things, but I felt some of us needed to do things differently. I was not alone in my thinking, for two or three other officers also opted out. However, certain ideas and the thought process behind the study continued to germinate in my mind. Some of these concepts would be integrated into the Transformation Study that I initiated subsequently as the Eastern Army Commander more than a decade later.

Lieutenant General NK Kapoor, also from the Rajput Regiment, was commanding the College of Combat, now known as the Army War College. Major General RS Taragi had been his deputy, and he retired from Mhow, handing over to 'Nikki' Kapoor the baton of the colonel of the regiment. Milan Naidu was the commandant's MA at the time, but he was moving out on promotion. Towards the end of the course, in April 1995, Nikki Kapoor wanted me to sidestep into Milan's job. Earlier, in December, as a matter of course, we had been asked to give our various posting requests. Having already appraised the MS, Ravi Eipe, of Bharti's medical requirement and having got his assurance, I confidently filled in as my three options: (a) Delhi (b) Delhi and (c) Belgaum, knowing fully well that there was no post in option (c) for an officer of my seniority.

When we had arrived in Mhow, General Taragi had introduced us to Dr Harish Sahni at the Choithram Hospital & Research Centre in Indore. Bharti had since then been under his care and had been progressing well. Had I not had the MS's assurance that I would be posted to Army HQ in Delhi where I hoped to bring Bharti under Dr Tuli's care, I would have jumped at Nikki Kapoor's offer. I explained my predicament to Milan Naidu. There were two more Rajput officers doing the course. They were sounded out, but both had pressing reasons for not wanting to stay in Mhow. PV Reddy wanted to go to Bangalore and Raj Karwal was keen on being posted to Delhi. This created an awkward situation. I suggested to Milan Naidu that he sound out DS Attri who was from 25 Rajput and who was attending the corresponding Defence Management Course at the College of Defence Management, Secunderabad.

Two months before the course ended, Colonel Mandhata Singh, the Colonel MS 1 from Army HQ, visited the college and announced the postings. I did a double take when he told me I was to proceed to Jodhpur where I was being posted to 12 Division as Colonel GS. For a moment I thought he had got it wrong, and told him the MS had assured me I'd be posted to Delhi.

'Well, you are his regimental officer, and I'm not privy to what was discussed. However, I can assure you, these postings have his approval.'

The Colonel MS traditionally precedes the MS, who is one of the last bigwigs to address the Higher Command. After Ravi Eipe had finished his talk, all officers moved to the adjacent tearoom for the informal interaction. In the confined circulating area, I was soon face-to-face with the general.

'Are you happy with your posting?' he asked. I looked at him with questioning eyes but before I could speak, he added, 'So, you have accepted it like a good soldier?' Till today, I have no idea what that was about.

Jodhpur is the second largest city in Rajasthan and is the gateway to the Thar. The closest I had come to serving in the desert was in Alwar, where 25 Rajput had moved after its raising. As a part of various study groups, I had visited the region on a few occasions, and being stationed within Jodhpur, one was still somewhat shielded from exposure to the harshness of the terrain. The bulk of the division, whose AOR was spread across the Thar Desert, was however living and operating in conditions where the all-pervasive sand created an environment like nothing I had experienced before.

Bharti had her final check-up at Choithram Hospital with Dr Sahni. She was now on a two-drug regime and still had at least six months of medical treatment ahead of her. I sent the girls to Delhi for a break and moved our luggage to Jodhpur, driving down alone in my car. To further complicate matters, there was a major shortage of accommodation in Jodhpur. The Colonel A of the division was himself living in temporary accommodation. On medical grounds, I would be lucky to get allotted family quarters, leapfrogging over a large waiting list. When we got to Jodhpur in May, after a brief holiday, we were given two rooms in the officers' mess. The MES, which since Independence has shown singularly poor taste in its housing design, had also thrown logic out of the window. Following the Western style of architecture, the rooms were small and felt like tin boxes, making the temporary residence an oven during the day. We were moved to Shaitan Singh Enclave where the biggest problem was the brackish water that was piped into the houses.

Yogja was admitted into the Rajmata Krishna Kumari Girls' Public School where we hoped she would get an uninterrupted run till she graduated Class XII, a luxury in the nomadic existence of the armed forces. Mrinalini gave up on the idea of a long distance degree and joined the Kamla Nehru College in Jodhpur. It would be almost six months before we would get a house on Rasala Road. Not only was the house independent, and hence a delight, the quality of water also improved tremendously.

The GOC of 12 Division was a Maratha LI officer, Major General Karthikeyan. During an Op discussion a month earlier, the army commander, Lieutenant General Moti Dhar, had pulled up the GOC in no uncertain terms. A few days later, Karthikeyan had taken sick and had to be hospitalized. The Deputy GOC, Brigadier HS Narang from the mechanized infantry (Garhwal), had been officiating ever since. The deputy was an excellent amateur photographer who went on to publish a superb pictorial book on the Thar Desert.

The formation had two infantry brigades in Jaipur and a third infantry brigade, along with the artillery brigade, in Nasirabad near Ajmer. However, the entire ORBAT (order of battle) was being restructured. From Nasirabad, the infantry brigade was moving to Pune, doing a one-on-one exchange with another infantry brigade, which after coming to Nasirabad was to convert into an independent mechanized brigade. This would function under the corps, and the infantry brigade at Udaipur was to come under the command of our division. Amidst all the moving of troops across Rajasthan, the Division HQ had no infantry troops in Jodhpur, only an armoured regiment and a mechanized unit. HQ XII Corps, under the command of Lieutenant General HM Khanna, was also located in Jodhpur, and they would pass on all sorts of odd jobs to us for which we rarely had the manpower. It was all quite complex, and the officiating GOC hoped that I, the new Colonel GS, would get up to speed quickly for a war game was imminent.

Our operational area was hard-core desert and we were responsible for the entire area north of Shahgarh, extending up to Kishangarh. As a result, we were responsible for the historical cities of Jaisalmer, Ramgarh, Longewala, Tanot and Kishangarh. With the shadow of the previous disastrous Op briefing hanging over Division HQ's head, we now got cracking, going over every minute detail. Fortunately, I had a good head for names and had squeezed in a few reconnaissance trips that allowed us to conduct a fairly good war game. The army commander went away satisfied and, though I was barely a month old in the job, we were now confident that, as a team, the divisional staff knew its stuff.

Four months later, we got a new GOC—Major General Keshav Singh (earlier the Deputy MS) who was known to be a stickler for detail and lost his temper easily. I was first in line to be introduced to the new GOC by Brigadier Narang.

The general shook hands and then growled, 'So you're going to be my new Colonel GS?'

'I don't think I have a choice in the matter, sir,' I said, meeting his gaze squarely.

We settled into a professional routine quite easily. A month or so later, I was called into the GOC's office in connection with a matter which had nothing to do with the GS Branch. Keshav Singh was seething, his famous temper having snapped. He threw a file in my direction. Papers flew and landed awkwardly on the ground. I stood there looking at him, not moving an inch, trying to keep my face impassive.

'Who'll pick up the file?' he spoke at last.

'I suppose your runner will.'

I came back to my office, trying to breathe easy and control my own temper. I must have sat there for a while, when suddenly the GOC entered my office and sat down. He came to the point of the visit, and apologized for having thrown the file.

Finally, I got a chance to speak. I told my general that, in my book, throwing files was not acceptable under any circumstance. Even more so because the matter on which he had exploded had nothing to do with the GS Branch or me. The GOC had not only apologized in words, but the gesture of stepping into his Colonel GS's office said everything. Though Keshav Singh was known to blow a fuse every now and then, it was also acknowledged that he rarely carried a grudge beyond his office. In fact, whenever anybody visited him at home, the general would personally look after his visitor as if he were an honoured guest, even though it was rumoured that he also ran his household like a tyrant. Our lines were clearly drawn and the matter ended there. I enjoyed working with this professional soldier through the rest of his tenure. After the successful conducting of a war game and various Op briefings, I think the GOC also started viewing me as an asset who was there to support him.

There was a flip side to the GOC's growing confidence in my abilities. Not too happy with some issues pertaining to A Branch, Keshav Singh announced I would be handling them from now on. I protested, for G Branch was always flooded with work. Similarly, later when the GOC was not too happy with the work being done by AWWA, it landed as an additional responsibility in my lap. My protestations were again brushed aside.

Corps HQ would also bat everything that needed to be done across to us; a major problem in the absence of any real manpower in Division HQ. The Chief of Army Staff, General Shankar Roychowdhury, was from 20 Lancers (earlier called Jodhpur Lancers). He was visiting Nepal and wanted to present a sword fabricated in Jodhpur to the Nepalese army chief. Army HQ called up XII Corps; the BGS, Brigadier Ashish Dubey called me and the next thing I knew I was running around the city looking for a sword maker. Eventually, I had to design a sword, sit through its fabrication, and then finally ship it off to Delhi. Since no one ever said anything about it again, it must have passed muster.

That year, out of the blue, Jodhpur was lashed by three days of continuous rain creating unexpected floods. This created another emergency situation that had to be dealt with. In the evening, the electricity was cut off and, as I opened the door to approach the shed that housed the generator, I was surprised to find water lapping around the steps of the house. We spent a couple of hours trying to block the rising water from entering and moved everything on to tables. By morning, we were knee deep in water inside the house. Even before I could deal with my own domestic crisis, XII Corps had contributed to the situation by summoning me to the corps commander's residence that also had to be drained of water. So off I went, with my uniform on a hanger and shoes in hand. I managed to change in the vehicle and organize damage control.

As the CO of 2 Rajput, my mantra had been to follow the unit tartib. As Colonel GS of the division, I tried to make sure the GOC would leave the office by midday, so that the rest of the staff would get a clear two hours to wrap up the day's work, avoiding, if possible, late hours in the evening. We also constituted a divisional team for most games and would take part in various competitions, making sure that all formations under our command also followed the regime of working hard and playing harder. I like to think all this contributed positively to the functioning of 12 Division.

However, in the division, the Colonel GS is virtually the principal staff officer and it was my job to make sure things moved smoothly. In Wellington, there was a saying: 'Everybody blames the staff officer, and the staff officer blames everybody else'. As a rule, people who complained bitterly about staff officers throughout their career promptly forgot what it was like on the other side once they became staff officers. Ever since I left DSSC, I have always carried this with me; on staff, my job is to help people and not create obstacles. Once a requirement was projected by the field formations, we would ensure everything happened post-haste; legalities and other formalities could always be sorted out later. As I rose in rank, it was my endeavour to make sure units and troops came first. Whatever objections there were, could be dealt with subsequently.

We were to have a large demonstration for the Fifth Pay Commission for which we had to lay the groundwork. That was the time when we began to realize that our inventory of ammunition was nowhere close to what it should have been. Missiles, armoured and artillery shells, small ammunition—there were serious deficiencies everywhere. Surface transport, with most units facing high attrition rates in the desert, was also inadequate.

The catch-22 was our inability to actually face up to these serious problems of shortages. Somewhere along the line, the army had started taking pride in being able to manage with what we had in terms of resources. Once the exercise was over, things would once again get swept under the carpet. At our level, we would constantly put up notes highlighting this, but would get vague replies from the corps that the matter was being looked into. Corps, in turn, was in all probability getting similar replies from command who, in turn, were at the mercy of Army HQ who would be bashing their heads against the various departments in the Ministry of Defence. It was quite obvious that no one in our current system of command and control was in any position to actually pin anyone down or get real answers out of anyone. Add to that the bureaucracy within the army, and we had a situation where we not only create problems for ourselves, but also tie ourselves in knots when it comes to looking for solutions. At our level, we could only hope that in the eventuality of a war, the shortages would be made up; improvisation and innovativeness can only get you thus far and no further.

The exercise almost ended in disaster. The Member-Secretary of the Fifth Pay Commission was MK Kaw, and the entire Combat Group was fielded. Corps HQ was deployed, while 12 Division depicted how defences were occupied. Armour was to demonstrate how they would move at night, and Kaw was sitting on top of a BMP with the army commander, Ved Malik, who advised the star guest to hold on tight. Obviously the advice had not been taken, for when the BMP hit a dune at high speed, Kaw went flying through the air. Despite landing on his head, the soft sand luckily cushioned his fall. Miraculously, the immediate order for the entire formation to hold and halt where they were also went through. The shaken Member-Secretary was none the worse for the fall, but despite the armoured column's efficiency in coming to a grinding halt (which probably saved his life), the Pay Commission did little for the Indian Army.

A year-and-a-half later, Keshav Singh moved as chief of staff to III Corps in Nagaland. Most unfortunately, the Indian Army was to lose a good officer in a tragic air crash when he, along with two other officers, went down in a Cheetah. Major General Ram Subramanyam from the engineers took over from him. Around the same time, Lieutenant General Ved Prakash Malik moved to Army HQ and HM Khanna replaced him, while Lieutenant General PS Joshi replaced Khanna as the corps commander.

Ram Subramanyam was a professional with desert experience, since he had commanded the brigade in Suratgarh. A good sportsman, he was always willing to play in the divisional headquarter teams. He had been to the Staff College in the United Kingdom and was an excellent squash player and golfer. The division benefitted immensely from his professional acumen. I think I met his standards of professionalism and have been lucky to stay in touch with him.

The First Star

After two years and nine months, it was time to move from Jodhpur. Having made the grade for brigadier, once again I was asked by the MS Branch where I'd like to go. If past experiences with the MS Branch were any criteria, I should have scrunched up their letter and thrown it in the nearest wastepaper basket. Nevertheless, like a moth drawn to light, I once again hopefully gave my three choices as (a) Siachen (b) Bhimber Gali in the Rajouri Sector and (c) anywhere in the 'field'. Once again the feedback was extremely positive. SK Singh, the civilian staff officer in MS Branch, who handled postings at this level, said he foresaw no problem, for very few officers opted for a field tenure. Yet, I might as well have waved a red rag in the face of the MS Branch, for, true to form, I was posted to a 'peace station'. I reread the signal when it arrived to make sure: I was to be the next brigade commander of 168 Infantry Brigade in Samba. Until recently, Samba had been classified as 'modified field', but a few years earlier, someone had changed its status to that of a 'peace station'.

Apart from the fact that Jodhpur had also been a peace station, I was keen on a field tenure, as I would then be eligible for separated family accommodation in either Jodhpur or Delhi. This I wanted for two reasons: though Bharti's spinal problem was under control, she had had to undergo a hysterectomy at Ram Manohar Lohia Hospital in Delhi, where her younger brother was a surgeon. She was still medically on somewhat shaky ground. The second reason was Yogja's Class X board examinations that were still a few months away. I tentatively tried to find out why I had been earmarked for Samba.

'You were handpicked by the Additional MS,' I was told. He himself was going as GOC 29 Division, and I would be operating under him. I had no option but to grin and bear it. Major General Pawan Chibber from the Kumaon Regiment had barely taken over the division when I arrived in Samba.

The town was notorious for the 'Samba Spy Case' that had scandalized the country in the late 1970s. Virtually the entire officer cadre of 168 Brigade, along with a host of JCOs and men, had been implicated on charges of spying. The Directorate of Military Intelligence had based its case investigation on the statements of two self-confessed Pakistani spies who had enlisted as gunners in the artillery. Twelve years later, one of the gunners, Aya Singh, had been shot while trying to smuggle himself across the India-Pakistan border. In 1994, the second gunner, Sarwan Das, in a sworn affidavit, admitted that he and his companion, Aya Singh, had falsely implicated the men. It was probably a case of 'too little too late' by then; a classic instance of misplaced justice, where countless careers and families were destroyed, their lives and their honour irrevocably scarred. The commander of the brigade at that time, Brigadier DP Nayar, was also from the Rajput Regiment. A fine officer and a gentleman, he too, along with all his battalion commanders and other officers, was a victim of injustice.

Not much had changed since 1978 when Samba had been unfortunately thrust into the limelight. It was still a one-street town that was always a tinderbox because of its close proximity to the border. The brigade was tasked to look after the international border from the Punjab-J&K boundary till the Devak River, beyond which lay the jurisdiction of 26 Infantry Division. I had four infantry battalions and two-and-a-half BSF units under my command. 5 Grenadiers was commanded by Colonel Rakesh Saxena; 19 Kumaon by Prabodh Kayastha; 10 Sikh LI by Adolf Pinto (they were replaced by 20 Raj RIF commanded by Khevinder Singh thereafter) and 24 Rajput, who were in reality attached to 25 Division for CI Ops and therefore only technically on my nominal roll. There was also the 13 Armoured Regiment being commanded by Rajiv Manali and 15 Field Regiment (subsequently replaced by 165 Field) in a direct support role. In addition, there were a few static units and a large ammunition depot also under my charge. Our accommodation was still that of a 'modified-field' formation, something that put a lot of pressure on all units across the board, and the area itself was extremely challenging.

My tenure at Samba was to begin with a mundane issue. I was taking over the brigade from Brigadier BR Wadhawan who was from the Gorkhas. After going around the area and attending multiple briefings, my predecessor dropped a bombshell as he was leaving: the cinema in Samba, which was run by the brigade, had invited an audit objection. In our system of red tape, this is generally a harbinger of doom. Before this bit of information could sink in, Wadhawan was gone.

A week passed before I could turn my attention to the vexing problem of the audit objection. As is usually the case, the behind-the-scenes story was far more interesting than the bland figures and sentences on paper. A local auditor had gone to see a movie and the NCO in charge of the cinema had asked him to purchase a ticket. The subsidized ticket amounted to just six rupees, but the auditor had no intention of paying. There was a bit of a fracas, after which the auditor hit back at the brigade by promptly raising an audit objection amounting to a couple of lakhs.

Completely at the mercy of such petty sniping, most army units eventually find a way to deal with such problems. However, being a Brigade HQ issue, the problem got bigger and bigger, so much so that my predecessor had sprung it on me only once he had one foot out the door! Anyway, there was nothing to be done but take on the auditors. However, an unfortunate fallout of the situation was that we had no choice but to close the cinema to civilians, who were mostly ex-servicemen for whom the little theatre was a connect between their present and their past. The Samba region has one of the largest densities of ex-servicemen in the country. During my entire two-and-a-half year tenure, the audit objection continued to generate its own paper trail. Eventually, the dramatis personae either got transferred or just became too old to care; the matter died a painful death with some sort of a compromise.

Small stations are particularly vulnerable to this sort of bullying. Local audit authorities are notorious, as are some defence accounts personnel, especially in regimental centres, for turning the screws just because they are in a position to exercise authority. This sort of perennial sniping at the army has been eroding the entire social fabric of the institution. More often than not it is the infantry that has to bear the brunt of this sort of behaviour. As a result, units then develop their own SOPs to deal with these irritants.

A typical case was of an EME (Electronics and Mechanical Engineering) officer on an AIA (Annual Inspection of Arms). Supposedly an expert on weapons, he kept looking down the barrels of the rifles of the unit.

'Corroded,' he announced, barely looking at the inside of the rifle. The next weapon was handed over. 'Corroded.' This went on and on until the EME officer casually enquired about some blankets that had recently come to the unit canteen.

After a while, the JCO accompanying the EME officer said to him in a low voice, 'Saab, kambal aapki gypsy mein rakh diya hai.' (Sir, the blankets have been kept in your vehicle.) On hearing this, despite having repeated 'corroded' ad nauseam, the officer promptly declared, 'All okay!' The AIA was over!

With people like these supposedly on one's side, one wonders how we keep the morale of our troops high and maintain ascendancy over our adversaries. Unless and until these maladies are addressed and ruthlessly snuffed out, we can never expect things to function smoothly during crises. The army is always expected to deliver in a scenario where failure to perform is not an option. Yet, we as a country have completely failed to insulate ourselves from incidents like these which get only worse as the same officials climb the ladder of success. The higher they go, the more they demand for themselves. It is like a cancer.

▪

The defences in Samba were based on the DCB (ditch-cum-bunker) concept. The linear stronghold had primarily been built to create obstacles in a terrain which was all flat ground. The DCB had been designed to infuse a time penalty on to any attacking force, and also to give the infantry a fighting chance against armour.

It is questionable as to how successful the concept of the DCB really is; by creating linear defences, we have no choice but to have the manpower to defend them. Linear defences can be breached; it is really a matter of resources and there are multiple methodologies to get past fixed obstacles. Earlier, the concept was to defend areas that would be self-sustaining. There would be gaps, but each strong point would give a suitable fight. This debate has been vexing commanders for a long time; yet there may not be any hard and fast answers, for there are certain areas where you definitely need to create obstacles, for which we need more troops.

The other three brigades in 29 Division were stationed at Mamun and Pathankot. Samba was situated roughly halfway between Pathankot and Jammu and our operational area was a hop, step and jump away from Brigade HQ. In addition, the two-and-a-half BSF battalions under my command were guarding the entire frontage of the division, making me responsible for any incident on the international border. This was an extremely odd arrangement, for part of the frontage was the operational AOR of the other brigades. I had my hands full with such a large area, while the BSF were stretched thin on the ground. Every night, the BSF boys would physically man nakas in pairs. BOPs (base ops) would be reduced to a handful of men; sometimes the strength would barely be three or four. Somewhere along the line, someone felt the BSF jawans sitting in the nakas needed protection from snakes, so tiny parapets were made. A couple of years later, overhead shelters were constructed to provide protection from the elements. Physically, however, it was not possible for any human being to stay sharp and alert, especially if they rarely got more than three to four hours of sleep a day. The Basantar-Devak river area was particularly vulnerable to infiltration. Having got past the cattle fence that separated the two countries, the terror parties would crawl beyond the fixed nakas undetected. Once the line had been breached, the militants would simply stroll into the rear.

Area domination has always been my mantra. I began to focus on known routes and safe houses used by militant parties, putting together a grid of ex-servicemen and informants who were to be our eyes and ears on the ground. I also knew quite a few Gujjars and Bakarwals who transited through from these areas to Naushera in the summer to graze their animals. They too were a valuable source of information. Working swiftly on local intelligence, the units started laying ambushes and traps well inside our own area. For the first time in decades, 168 Infantry Brigade started chalking up a number of kills and regularly recovered a large number of arms and ammunition.

Though Samba was known to be an infiltration zone, until then incidents had been restricted to the border, with the BSF getting into occasional firing skirmishes. Just how well-trained the terrorists were and how well-established the actual network was can be judged by this incident involving five Afghan militants. A local shikari reported their presence but by the time we zeroed in on the party, darkness had enveloped the countryside. In the ensuing firefight, it appeared as if all five militants were engaging our boys. In actual fact, three of them had slipped out even as the army closed in. The two Afghans who had been left behind were taken out, and the next morning the troops went after the remaining three, among whom one had been badly wounded. Though the troops dropped one more of the party in the ensuing chase, the remaining wounded militant and his companion managed to slip across the border.

▪

By the middle of 1998, Mrinalini had graduated from college and Yogja had finished her Class X exam. They promptly joined me in Samba, where the modified-peace residence of the commander had two tiny rooms. The only consolation were the spacious grounds within which flagstaff house stood in splendid isolation.

Yogja's education continued to be a problem. The Army School in Samba only went up to Class VIII and was considered to be quite sub-standard. On the other hand, the Ratnuchak Army School was under the stewardship of Mrs Vijaya Puri and was considered to be extremely good. Yogja was admitted into the Army School at Ratnuchak, an hour's journey by bus or a three-ton, from where she eventually was to finish her board exams.

I was particularly impressed by one of the teachers on the staff in the Army School at Samba. Mrs Rao was the wife of the TA (Territorial Army) Battalion CO. After consulting the staff, I felt that she would make a good principal for the Samba Army School. She was interviewed by the GOC, passed muster and was given the task of reorganizing the Samba school. The results were electrifying—by the time I left Samba, the school had gone up to Class XII. New premises had been identified, and today it is reputed to be one of the finest schools in the region. The school's evolution and growth gave me tremendous satisfaction. Though I was just a facilitator in its growth and the credit must go to others for the work they put in, I consider my contribution towards the development of the Samba Army School one of the high points of my career.

I had been the commander for more than a year when Pakistan intruded into the Kargil region—Operation Vijay was launched. All along the border, formations were immediately put on stand-to, and like the rest of the army, my brigade also moved into its operational location, which happened to be right next door. After a while, when it was obvious nothing was happening, we allowed our troops to fall back to their unit lines during the day, walking back to man the defences at night. For the first time, men posted to the 168 Infantry Brigade began to realize it wasn't such a bad deal after all to be in Samba.

Sometime in 1999, the Government of India decided to increase the retirement age by two years, leading to a standstill on postings. As a result, this would prove to be my longest serving tenure under any one boss. Pawan Chibber had taken over a month before me, and he was to move a month after I relinquished command. Though an extremely hardworking GOC and a good professional soldier, Chibber had the habit of constantly dressing-down people around him, always looking for minor details to pick on. Having served as the BGS in XVI Corps before being posted in the MS Branch, the GOC knew the worth of 168 Brigade's work in mopping up terrorists behind our lines, so much so that the 29 Division AOR was no longer considered a worthwhile infiltration route by the Pakistanis. Being some distance away from Mamun was a huge advantage, for in many ways one got to function almost like an independent brigade. I also always had an hour's notice whenever the GOC set off for my location.

By the end of 1999, Mrinalini was engaged to an ordnance officer, Captain Sangram Singh Katoch, and the wedding was planned for 17 January 2000. Sangram's father, Colonel RS Katoch, was from the Assam Regiment and at the time was re-employed and posted in Pathankot while Mrinalini's fiancé was posted at 1 FOD, also in the vicinity. On 14 January, I called the GOC and asked for a day's leave so as to conduct the engagement ceremony. 'There's an important conference and a discussion,' said the ever-pragmatic GOC. I was advised to conduct the ceremony after the conference.

A month after the marriage ceremonies were over, I was called to Army HQ in Delhi for an interview. I had no idea what it was about, but soon learnt that five of us were being screened to select the candidate who would go to the US Army's War College. Among the candidates were Rakesh Loomba and Balraj Nagal.

'I hope you are current on current affairs,' I was told by a staff officer, as I was ushered into the interview room. The vice chief along with the MS and the DGMO asked questions on a range of topics. After the interview, we were told that we would be informed in case any of us qualified; we then returned to our respective formations.

Towards the middle of June, my relief, GJ Singh from the Sikh Regiment, had been announced, but where I was going only the MS Branch knew and was keeping it a closely guarded secret. This time around, they had even dispensed with the practice of asking me for my three preferences. On 20 June, with barely ten days left for the course to begin, I received a signal saying I was to proceed forthwith to Carlisle in the United States. Nothing had changed since the mid-1970s, when I had scrambled at the last minute to get to the Ranger Course.

The Higher Direction of War

Yogja was already in Delhi, running around for her admission to college. She was in for a surprise, for we had decided to take her with us for the year-long course. In effect, this meant we would have to foot the expenses for both Bharti and Yogja, a decision that would drain us of virtually all our savings. Nevertheless, it seemed to be the most appropriate thing to do. It would also give her the opportunity to study in the US, an experience which we felt would benefit her enormously, especially as she had had to do her final years of schooling in relatively obscure places.

We landed in Harrisburg in Pennsylvania in July and were received by Professor Martin Cook, who, apart from being on the War College faculty, was also to be our official sponsor (liaison person). Situated on the 500-acre historic Carlisle Barrack, the college is the senior-most educational institution of the US Army. While most of the American students are handpicked and nominated from within the army, others from the US Navy, Air Force and Marines are further supplemented with civilian officers from the Pentagon, State Department and the National Security Agency. In addition, students from forty-two other countries joined the 290-odd American students.

'We've identified a house for you which was occupied by a foreign student earlier. We can take a look at that. If you like it, great, otherwise we can look further,' announced the professor as he drove us into Carlisle.

The house was extremely modest, with one small bedroom supplementing the slightly larger master bedroom, the two sharing the single bathroom. But it was just a ten-minute walk from the college premises. With a monthly rental of $900, we knew we had little choice but to accept the house.

'We'll take it,' I said.

Not very far from the historic town of Gettysburg, where one of the bloodiest battles of the American Civil War was fought in July 1863, Carlisle itself is a post that dates back to that period. The commandant was a two-star appointment, who had two deputy commandants; one a colonel while the other was of the rank of an ambassador. Most serving army instructors were colonels, with a large number of retired officers who had earned doctorates in various fields on the staff. There was also a large complement of civilian instructors who together with the other two categories, made up the faculty. The first month was exclusively meant to help orient the foreign students, bringing them up to date with current US affairs. Some officers, not very proficient in English, had been in Carlisle for a few months already. The main course was to start at the end of July.

The course itself is very well designed with the single purpose of converting selected officers into strategic leaders for the future, so that they can fill higher leadership slots. In the initial phase, all students go through human resource and leadership theories—how they work and how they are related—there are certain psychological and physical tests to enable higher leadership to stay mentally and physically fit. Then come the discussions and

With the Chinese commander Lt Gen Shu Chi, Lhasa, 2009

With General Deepak Kapoor and Major General AK Chaudhury, IGAR South in Imphal during a visit to the Assam Rifles HQ
Photo credit: Assam Rifles

Chief of Army Staff
Photo credit: Shri Gurudev

Arriving at South Block to take the Guard of Honour
Photo credit: Kunal Verma/KaleidoIndia

2 Rajput (Kali Chindi) Colour Party outside South Block
Photo credit: Kunal Verma/KaleidoIndia

61 Cavalry mounted review, 2010
Photo credit: 61 Cavalry

Visiting Victor Force in the Kashmir Valley, 2010
Lt Gen SA Hasnain and Maj Gen Gurdeep Singh
Photo credit: Victor Force

Inspecting captured weapons with the Special Forces

With Special Forces in 2011

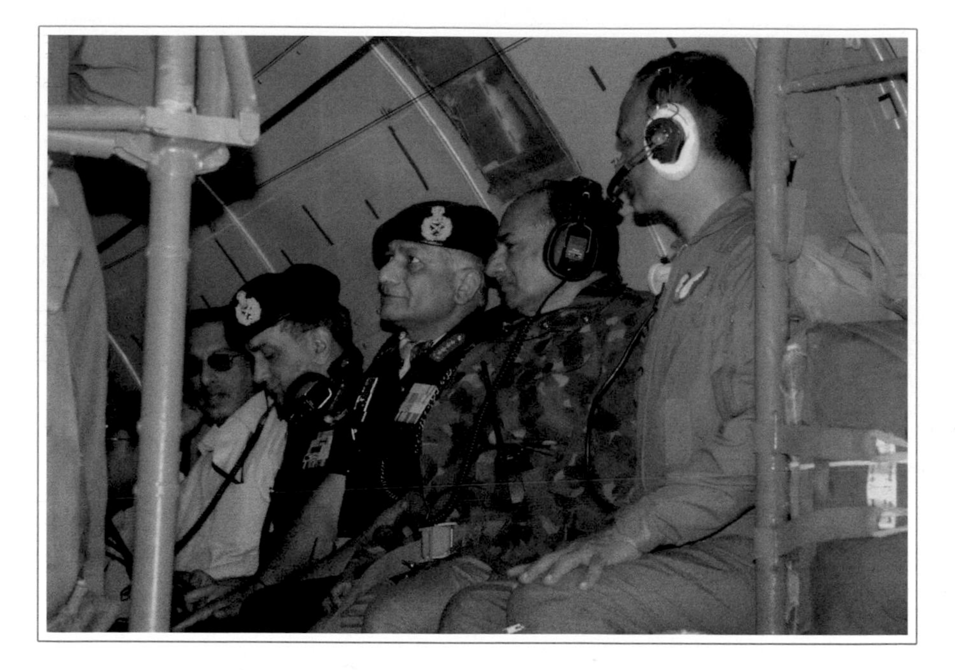

On board an An-32 with Raksha Mantri AK Antony

Inspecting the NCC detachment of the Daly College in Indore, 2011
Headmaster Sumer Singh on the extreme left
Photo credit: Daly College/Indore

Arriving at Leh airfield—Lt General KT Parnail, Lt General Ravi Dastane
Photo credit: HQ XIV Corps

Siachen Base Camp
Photo credit: HQ XIV Corps

With troops in Siachen
Photo credit: HQ XIV Corps

At Daulat Beg Oldi
Photo credit: HQ XIV Corps

Signing the visitor's book in XIV Corps
Photo credit: HQ XIV Corps

Inaugurating the Officers Training Academy in Gaya, 2011
Photo credit: OTA/Gaya

On a visit to Vietnam, 2010

Inspecting a Guard of Honour on arrival in Tajikistan, 2011

Test firing weapon at US Special Operations Command, Fort Bragg, North Carolina
Photo credit: US Army

Taking a breather on the golf course

Tomb of the Unknown Soldier, Arlington, 2011
Photo credit: US Army

With General George W Casey, Jr., Chief of Staff United States Army, March 2011
Photo credit: US Army

In the Pentagon
Photo credit: US Army

Meeting Michelle and Barack Obama

Releasing the Northeast Trilogy with Admiral Nirmal Verma and Air Chief Marshal NAK Browne, January 2012
Photo credit: Army Liaison Cell

Final visit to the National Defence Academy, May 2012
Photo credit: National Defence Academy/Khadakwasla

Track 2 in Democratic Republic of China (post retirement), October 2012
Photo credit: Kunal Verma/KaleidoIndia

Addressing a kisaan rally in New Delhi, 2012

With Anna Hazare at the launch of the Jantantra Morcha, 2013
Photo credit: Kunal Verma/KaleidoIndia

Launch of the Jantantra Yatra from Jalianwala Bagh, 31 March 2013
Photo credit: Kunal Verma/KaleidoIndia

classes on strategy and tactics where the ambit is expanded considerably. The college then tasks the students to convert theory into tactical application in certain exercises. This eventually culminates with the selection of four electives. There are ninety-nine subjects to choose from, and an elective is approved only if there are at least ten students opting for it.

I chose advanced war fighting, negotiations, planning and budgeting, and military and media as my four electives. In addition, we had to submit a strategic research paper that was graded. In fact, throughout the course, we were constantly being graded in three areas: participation, oral and written work. Any student dropping below the required standards was shown the door a la Ranger style, and told to go home.

We visited quite a few places of strategic interest within the US, while also traveling to Mexico, Nicaragua and Brazil, with a stopover in Panama. These visits were related to the studies we were doing and they were extremely fruitful, for they allowed us to interact with the strategic think tanks in these countries.

Back in the college, we had to submit a detailed paper on the existing systems we had seen during our visits and how these compared with the existing systems in the US. It was all extremely intense. In New York, Mayor Rudy Giuliani gave us a detailed talk on how the city had tackled organized crime, and turned things around. The city's crime rate had fallen by an incredible 57 per cent using new methodology, and eventually the FBI rated New York as America's safest large city. Using his past experience as a public prosecutor, Giuliani had also eradicated the influence of organized crime from the city's commercial life.

For my strategic research paper I was to have a guide from the faculty. I was told in rather hushed tones that the person was 'from the Agency'. When we met, my future guide looked at me quizzically.

'You know I am from the Agency.'

'Yes, I know you are from the Agency,' the conversation was progressing at the breath-taking pace of a John le Carré film. After a long pause, I told my would-be mentor that since ours would be a purely professional relationship, it didn't matter to me if he was from the Agency or any other organization. I told him that in the academic environment of the War College he had to render advice professionally and if he felt he could not do his job properly then he was free to suggest someone else. This set the rule for our future meetings.

•

'Good, then that little business is settled,' he said and I got on with the job of writing my paper. I was fairly critical of US policies, which my man from the Agency would ask me to water down every now and then. When it came to the role of the CIA, we would have even more heated discussions. Eventually, I produced a paper that satisfied us both. At the end of the course, I was graded 'Exceptional' and I'm told my paper was among those recommended for additional study in subsequent years.

For Indian students doing any course in the US, the biggest drawback was the lack of funds to meet our basic expenses. Everything in the college had a charge, including social functions. Even while doing the Ranger Course, we barely managed to keep our heads above water. In Carlisle, foreign students would throw a bash for their national days. Propriety demanded we reciprocate, but we never had the requisite funds. On my return to India, in my report to Army HQ, I strongly suggested that if we could not afford to pay our officers appropriately, we might as well not send them at all. Having visited the War College again in the recent past, once as the COAS and then again on an official invite after retirement, I can state that today things are only marginally better.

Additionally, officers who come back from War College are not utilized properly. A case in point is the United Kingdom, perhaps the closest strategic partner of the US. A British officer, on completion of the course, usually sidesteps into his country's embassy in Washington. This allows him to build on his experience and build his contacts. In our case, we are pulled back and, generally, the MS Branch decides where to send us without any analysis of how the knowledge gained can be utilized. At this level of seniority, it is highly unlikely that the officer will ever go back to build on the contacts and friends made in the US.

Protecting their turf fiercely, Ministry of External Affairs seems to have a major chip on its shoulder. Equally bizarre is the fact that all defence attachés posted to Indian embassies across the globe are not accorded the status due to them as per their rank. The reason given is that if the defence attaché is not downgraded, he effectively becomes the highest-ranking officer after the ambassador. The Government of India has been doing this sort of thing ever since the country became independent. The constant erosion of the army's status within the country will sooner or later boomerang on us as a nation. One fails to understand the logic in all this manipulation.

Brigadier Isfandiyar Ali Khan Pataudi was the Pakistani officer attending the course with me. He was from Probyn's Horse, and the first cousin of

Mansur Ali Khan Pataudi. He subsequently rose to the rank of a major general and later commanded the Pakistan Army's 25th Mechanized Division before becoming the deputy director-general of Pakistan's Inter-Service Intelligence (ISI). An aristocrat and the son of a Pakistani general who had served as his country's MA in the United States, he was also a fine polo player. His liberal lineage and outlook made him an ideal candidate for the War College, for Pakistani officers had earlier been barred from attending US courses. As I mulled over the problem of shipping my books back to India, Isfandiyar gave me some free advice. 'Kya problem hai? Embassy ko bolo, woh sara samaan pack karke ghar bhej denge.' (What's the problem? Tell the embassy and they'll ship it home.) He further added helpfully, 'Humne toh bahut samaan kharida hai.' (We've bought a lot of things.) He then gave me a sly smile which implied that he knew our embassy would not entertain such a request.

All in all, the US War College was a terrific experience that certainly widened my horizons considerably, even though it left us nearly bankrupt. In recent years, the strength of foreign students has been increased at the War College. Though the US Army has regularly been pressing the Indian government to increase India's quota to two, (since they feel Indian officers have a lot to contribute to the course), the Ministry of Defence has steadfastly resisted this.

Once we got back to Delhi, to my utter surprise, I received orders posting me as the BGS to XI Corps in Jalandhar. After having done the War College, I expected Army HQ to look at the electives I had taken and utilize my services accordingly. With a resigned air, I headed off to meet the MS, Lieutenant General Chauhan who had been my GOC and corps commander earlier. The general consented to see me.

'So you are going to Jalandhar?' he said, after quizzing me in some detail about the War College.

'That's what I've come to talk to you about,' I said, getting straight to the point. 'Why can't you utilize me in Delhi in areas where I can be more productive?' I was told he had handpicked me for XI Corps and that was that. There was no scope for any more discussion and I knew that MS Branch has a dictum: 'You show us the man and we will show you the rule'.

Yogja had been enrolled at Shippensburg University in Pennsylvania where she had completed a year of her Bachelor's degree in Psychology. Having got an 'A' in her first year, she had qualified for a scholarship, but we were in a quandary over her visa extension. According to the rules conveyed by the embassy, she needed to come back to India and reapply for a student visa. By then, she would have lost her scholarship, without which there was no question of staying on, for we simply did not have the money. Now she was back to square one, running around trying to get admission to Delhi University where admissions for the year had all but closed. A few colleges who were willing to consider her case said she needed to get a minister to recommend her case. I knew no minister, so that option was closed. With the situation getting desperate, a relative in Chandigarh used his networking skills and got her admission sorted out for the Government College for Girls in Chandigarh. She was told that she could be admitted to the second year provided she agreed to do both the first and second year papers together. This would have been tough on her, so we decided that she should get into the first year and not take any chances with the honours course. Though admissions into schools and colleges are a problem for all levels of society, in the case of the army, the situation gets magnified because of the nomadic existence of its personnel.

College settled, I joined the formation in Jalandhar. The corps commander, Lieutenant General Shantanu Chaudhary was an artillery officer. He had been a battery commander with 57 Mountain that had been in direct support of 2 Rajput during the Bangladesh War while we were deployed in Meghalaya. He was by far one of the finest commanders I've ever worked with, and a wonderful person to boot. Every morning we would meet and the corps commander would let his thoughts on relevant issues be known. He would never make us wait for a decision. Having said his bit, he would leave it to me as his principal staff officer to run things to his standards. There was absolutely no tension in XI Corps HQ during his tenure.

On 9/11, as the twin towers were hit, I called him on his hotline. 'Sir, switch on CNN.'

'What has happened?' he asked calmly.

'Twin towers are down. There has been a terrorist strike on New York.'

'Aw, shit!' After a while he called back, letting loose on the telephone with some choice Allahabadi abuses. Instinctively, we knew that Pakistan would, in all probability, be directly or indirectly involved in the terrorist strike. It was imperative that XI Corps be put on high alert even before any alarms sounded from Army HQ. Sooner or later, the developing situation could result in our deployment. If and when that happened, we wanted to be ready to move.

XI Corp's AOR was the entire Punjab border up to the Chand Bhan Drain that separated the Fazilka-Abohar area from Ferozepur. 15 Division, based in Amritsar, was being commanded by Ashok 'Tarzan' Kapoor (named thus ever since he performed the role of the ape man in a skit at NDA) who had also been a brigade commander in 12 Division when I was Colonel GS; 7 Division was in the charge of Major General Nandrajog, who had commanded 4 Guards (1 Rajput); and 9 Division was in Meerut with Major General Arun Chopra from the Madras Regiment as its GOC. Our chief of staff at the time was Major General Nargorwala from the engineers.

Having taken a few pre-emptive steps, all we could do was to wait and watch, fine-tuning our reaction times in case we were asked to deploy. Around this time the corps war game was also due and as the BGS, it was 'my baby'. I decided to code name it 'Exercise Aridaman'. As part of the setting, I scripted in an attack on the Indian Parliament as the trigger point.

The Western Army Commander, Lieutenant General Surjit Singh Sangra was, at the time, on a visit abroad. Since the Red Land (enemy) activities were being conducted by ARTRAC (Army Training Command), Lieutenant General Shamsher Mehta, an armoured corps officer and army commander, was to be the senior officer present. Though we constantly had differing opinions that generated plenty of heat on the deployment of Red Land forces, matters progressed reasonably well. It was interesting to see Shantanu Chaudhary in all this, for he had to officiate as Western Army Commander and also give decisions pertaining to his own corps. He maintained his calm in all the tension that the exercise generated.

As we entered the last phase of the exercise, the stunning news of an actual attack on Parliament came in on 13 December. 'How the hell did you know?' became the constant refrain, even as we quickly took stock of the developing situation. Soon the joke doing the rounds was that the corps exercise setting had been leaked to the ISI, who had promptly decided to give us a real-life scenario. We had been prepared for such an eventuality ever since the twin towers had been brought down. Now we put into effect the preparatory actions as part of our training unit deployments to cater to any emergency.

Operation Parakram

General Sundararajan Padmanabhan had taken over as the COAS from General Ved Prakash Malik in September 2000. An artillery officer, he had been at the helm of affairs for just over a year when five terrorists entered the compound of Parliament House using a car with labels of the Ministry of

Home Affairs and those of Parliament. For nearly half a century, starting with the kabailis in 1947, Pakistan had been abetting and encouraging various terror groups to help fight a jihad against India. Apart from trying to create mayhem through bombings and suicide attacks on military and civilian targets, Pakistan's state-sponsored terrorism also served another purpose. It allowed them to periodically use regular troops in their endeavour to make a dent in Kashmir, while always claiming that they were kabailis or mujahideen over whom they had no control whatsoever. Kargil had been the last such blatant transgression, and the country was still recovering from having lost over five hundred brave souls who had had to pay the supreme price while evicting the Pakistan Army from the heights around Kargil.

Even though India had displayed limits of tolerance that had it labelled a 'soft state' in the eyes of the world, the attack on Parliament could not be countenanced, especially as it came within months of 9/11. Fortunately, all five terrorists were brought down by security personnel before they could actually get into the Parliament House, but it had been touch and go. Seven Indian lives had been lost and another eighteen security personnel, policemen and others had been wounded in the ensuing gunfight.

With Home Minister LK Advani publicly announcing that the attackers had Pakistani links, the writing was on the wall. Pakistan promptly put its army on high alert, and a few days later, orders were issued by the Army HQ to mobilize. At that time XI Corps was without a chief of staff; Major General Nargorwala having moved out a few days earlier while his relief was yet to arrive. Shantanu Chaudhary now was the picture of a calm, rock solid and stable commander, letting both the General Staff and Adm branches handle the situation with complete freedom to execute their tasks. The Brig Adm (brigadier administration) was Brigadier Opinder Singh from the Mahar Regiment, and together we set the ball rolling along the lines that we had prepared for.

However, when troops actually start moving on the ground, all sorts of shortages began to surface, especially when it comes to road vehicles that are required for mobilization. The Adm Branch tackled all the problems admirably, and XI Corps was in its designated position well within the stipulated timeframes despite foggy weather conditions. Our deployment was based on the premise that the Indian Army was going into Pakistan to sort out the perennial problem of state-sponsored terrorism. Looking back, now I am 100 per cent certain that had we pushed forward then, we would have achieved all our objectives. Unfortunately, the script didn't quite play out that way.

Maintaining the country's fighting forces is akin to paying one's insurance premium, and a better policy demands a higher price. For years now, it was fairly obvious to most officers who had served in the field that things were nowhere near what they should have been. As Colonel GS in Jodhpur, I had felt completely helpless and impotent, for all I could do was report the shortage of missiles, ammunition, vehicles and war stores. We always got soothing replies that matters were being looked into. No matter what level of command one was at, 'the system' simply hemmed you in. Even in Kargil, we had managed to gloss over our shortcomings mainly because it was a localized affair. Everyone talked of the various hands that were working on the problem but that was it. No one seemed to be in a position to do anything about it. The insurance premium was not being attended to and the policy was becoming defunct.

Now the pigeons were coming home to roost. At that point, I don't think we had quite hit the 'scandal-a-day' scenario that exists today, with comparatively milder issues like Bofors still grabbing the headlines. Now, as we waited for other key formations to arrive, we found they were in no position to meet their schedules. With every passing hour, the situation was getting more and more critical, for the delay was allowing opposing Pakistani forces to prepare their positions. Though subsequently there would be additional reasons identified for the delays, the fact of the matter was that when push came to shove, key elements were not in a position to deliver. The very first few days of Operation Parakram exposed the hollowness of our operational preparedness.

Key elements of Western Command were getting delayed (eventually an armoured brigade reached the Indira Gandhi Canal where it was halted). Northern Command further compounded the problem by declaring that it needed time for the troops—who were mostly deployed in a counter-insurgency role—to re-orient themselves. Bizarre developments were further closing our options; Lieutenant General Kapil Vij, commanding the critical armoured strike corps, told the Western Army Commander that he suspected he was being drugged in his HQ and asked to go on leave; and a major ammunition column transporting missiles and tank ammunition went up in flames near Bikaner.

Schedules having gone out the window, the US started exerting pressure, saying India must await General Pervez Musharraf's statement, which was delivered in the second week of January. Having got a breather, thanks to the Americans and the delayed mobilization by some key elements of the Indian armed forces, Musharraf did what he specialized in: side-stepped the issue after making some half-baked promises.

The logical thing that needed to be done at this stage was to cut our losses and pull back the bulk of the troops, but by then tensions on the border were escalating along completely different lines. With the army literally sitting on the border, we were now in a face-to-face confrontation; frankly neither side knew what to do next. Army HQ then came up with orders that at the field level were referred to as the 'mine panic'. Lieutenant General NC Vij, until recently the DGMO, had moved as the vice chief, being next in line for COAS. Frantic orders now came at us in a torrent, telling all formations to start laying both Priority 1 and Priority 2 mines.

Field formations could hardly believe what was happening. Suddenly from a proactive role, we were going into a defensive posture. There was a scramble for mines that hitherto had not been on the agenda. Then the problems started, and it soon became apparent that there had been no check on quality control. A large number of mines had fuses that wouldn't fit and, in true Indian Army style, the men would try and force the fuse in. Mine after mine exploded, killing men in numbers that were shockingly high.

Helplessly, the army kept sitting on the border, its men and equipment both victims of attrition. Training schedules had gone out of the window and after a while we seemed to be at war with ourselves. Casualties continued to mount as we watched in frustration. Most areas where mines had been laid had sprouted sarkanda and there was near-total chaos as mines had shifted and were going off at regular intervals, adding to the death toll and the list of wounded. Soon, there was a huge demand for mine shoes. Though the old mine shoe in service was a very well-designed boot, it was quite an outdated design and the available numbers were inadequate. The hunt for mine shoes in the global market now began in right earnest.

These were still not the days of web portals and the internet; information travelled at a slower pace than today. Yet, we almost fell off our chairs when we were told that a Jalandhar-based shoe manufacturer was the official supplier of mine-shoes to the US Army. Casualties from mines were beginning to match the overall Kargil figures; not only was no one seemingly responsible for the situation, the apparent apathy of our procurement system was staring us in the face.

We approached the shoe manufacturer at the corps level, but for them to set up production for the Indian Army required fresh moulds. Acquiring the raw materials required funds, which were way above our pay scale of decision-making. All we could do was refer the matter to command and make a lot of noise. Needless to say, nothing happened.

Shantanu Chaudhary moved out on posting and was to be relieved by Lieutenant General K Nagraj from Maratha LI. By then, Major General Arun Pathak from the armoured corps had also taken over as chief of staff. An extremely sharp and intelligent officer, he had a laid-back style of functioning. The army commander had also changed, with Shamsher Mehta moving from ARTRAC to replace Surjit Sangra. Command HQ promptly announced that the new army commander would be visiting XI Corps for a briefing. General Nagraj, who was to move from Northern Command where he was the MGGS, promptly let it be known that he was busy and would arrive only after the army commander's visit. I went to Arun Pathak and told him that he would have to do the briefing as the officiating corps commander.

'I'm the chief of staff,' he announced, 'I am not supposed to do the briefing.' I gaped at him. Surely as the BGS, I could hardly be expected to hold the can. To my horror, I realized Arun Pathak was dead serious.

This was to be Shamsher Mehta's first visit as Western Army Commander, though he had been part of Exercise Aridaman as the boss of ARTRAC. He had not forgotten the difference in opinion between the Red Land force and us. As I started to brief him on XI Corps deployment, he kept stopping me, repeatedly asking me if we had learnt our lessons from Aridaman. I finally stood at attention and told him we had learnt many lessons from the exercise and had implemented them all.

'Have you read the Indus Waters Treaty?'

I was beginning to feel like I was back in school again, facing an angry master who was determined to trip me up in front of the class. 'Yes, sir, I have a copy on my table. I have gone through it in detail and am aware of the implications.' At this point Shamsher Mehta fortunately decided that I could hold my own. Ever since then we have shared an excellent relationship.

Unlike his predecessor, General Nagraj loved tension. The corps commander had brought with him a young, smiling captain as his ADC. Halfway through his tenure, the poor boy couldn't have managed a smile even if one physically pulled at the corners of his mouth, for the corps commander was constantly on his case. Under these circumstances, no one could arrest the slide from a happy headquarters to an extremely tense outfit. To make matters worse, Operation Parakram was going absolutely nowhere.

'Where is our TAC HQ? Why are we not operating from there?' asked the new corps commander.

We were operating from Jalandhar due to connectivity and ease of communications. We had also constructed a brand-new underground complex for the headquarters. We had found parts of an old iron rail bridge lying around in the engineer stores depot and had used the iron girders to construct this underground complex. It was so solid it could have withstood even a direct hit. General Nagraj, however, thought it was necessary that we move away from Jalandhar. So we moved the TAC HQ to Kapurthala. Even before the rest of the Corps HQ could follow, the general realized that all he had succeeded in doing was in cutting himself off from the rest of the world. He ordered us to fall back, having realized the advantage of Jalandhar as a communication node and nothing more was said of moving again.

General Nagraj had a peculiar habit. He would come into his office and go about rearranging everything for a few minutes each morning. If he was disturbed during that process, his mood for the day would spiral downwards and woe betide the 'disturbing' party. After a few days, I received a file with a note from the general saying 'discuss'. I walked into his office with a notebook in my hand.

'Where is the file?' asked the corps commander.

'I don't need the file,' I said, implying that was well briefed. If the general wanted to discuss the nuances, well and good; if he wanted to read the files, I would attach my comments and send them to him. The way I saw it, in that case, he didn't need me in his office.

'I want the files,' said the general, with an air of finality. I went back to my office, bundled them together, dictated a note for the Colonel GS to attach, and sent them to the corps commander. For the year that we worked together, this became our pattern of functioning.

I was to see yet another change in command in XI Corps; Nagraj was succeeded by Lieutenant General S Pattabhiraman, an engineer officer and an excellent person who went on to become the vice chief. We had served in the MO Directorate together where I had spent a month briefing him on various issues after he shifted from MO6 to MO3. Pattabhiraman was moving to Jalandhar from Secunderabad where he was commanding 54 Division. The general called me up and asked me to do what I had done with him in MO: take him over each and every inch of the terrain and the associated problems. Under his command, the Corps HQ once again became tension-free.

I was to complete more than two-and-a-half years in Jalandhar. Towards the end of 2001, Mrinalini had given birth to a baby boy, who was promptly named Vikramaditya. The baby was born in Jalandhar, and Bharti and myself were in close attendance, the proud grandparents. Yogja was continuing in the hostel in Chandigarh and moving into her final year as I was finishing my tenure in Jalandhar. She subsequently moved to Punjab University to pursue her masters. Apart from having served with three GOCs in the corps, I had also seen various divisional commanders come and go. It was almost like a merry-go-round and sometimes it was hard to keep track; Samantray in 15 Division had replaced Tarzan Kapoor and was in turn replaced by Balraj Nagal, one of the first from my batch to don two stars; Nandrajog was replaced by NS Brar who in turn was replaced by Shivashanker; Arun Chopra was replaced by RK Singh from Sikh LI who in turn was replaced by Bobby Saiyyad.

In the board held for brigadier to major general, I had not made the grade. It looked like my career in the Indian Army was coming to an end.

'What happened?' The voice at the other end of the phone was that of Lieutenant General Ram Subramanyam, the last of my GOCs in 12 Division. At the time, he was commanding XII Corps and waiting to take over the Central Army.

I didn't have to look far to know that my brief tenure in Faizabad as CO 2 Rajput on the watch of Brigadier Mahabir Singh had put the skids under my career. I had been expecting the axe to fall earlier, but somehow it had not happened. My ambition in life had been to command my battalion and I had, in fact, gone past the rank my father had held. Both these achievements were behind me now. It was the luck of the draw that I had run into Mahabir Singh. Though I had protested the report at the time, others further up the chain of command had obviously not overruled my brigade commander.

Ram Subramanyam thought I was giving up too soon, and he sent me a draft with suggestions on what to put down in my letter to seek redress. Around the same time, my GOC in XI Corps, General Pattabhiraman, also called me in and advised that I must represent against the Promotion Board's decision. With two senior officers backing me, I decided to take their advice and formally complained against Mahabir Singh's report. My case, routed through command, went to the Complaint and Advisory Board to the chief, General NC Vij who had taken over from General Padmanabhan. The board decided that Mahabir Singh's report was completely out of sync with every other report that I had earned through my military career. Without any fuss, my case was reviewed four months later and I was cleared for the rank of major general.

Unknown to me, General Vij had asked Shantanu Chaudhary, who had taken over as the vice chief, that I be posted to Victor Force in the Kashmir Valley. He then called up my previous corps commander, General Nagraj, who gave me an immediate thumbs down. With one positive and one negative vote, the chief then called my immediate boss. 'He'll do a good job,' said Pattabhiraman. The matter was sealed. I was the next GOC of Victor Force and I was told to move immediately to the Kashmir Valley. I had been given my second star four months after Balraj Nagal. My chestnuts had once again been pulled out of the fire.

PART III

LIFE AT THE TOP

10

COMMAND AND CONTROL

Victor Force

Though I knew the Poonch and Naushera region like the back of my hand, my knowledge of the Kashmir Valley was somewhat limited. I also had no first-hand knowledge of the Rashtriya Rifles (RR) as I had not been exposed to any environment other than regular army units. There was still a war game to be conducted in XI Corps before I could move, and this time, I was extremely careful not to script anything half as dramatic as an 'attack on the Indian Parliament'. Even as the war game ended, I was already moving into the Kashmir Valley, hoping to spend most of February getting familiar with the new area.

Major General (later Lieutenant General and, subsequently, with the United Nations) Jasbir Singh Lidder was an infantry officer from the Grenadiers. He was one of the five GOCs who were commanding Counter Insurgency (CI) Force HQs in Jammu and Kashmir. While Victor Force was looking after Anantnag, Pulwana, Shopian and Badgam districts in south Kashmir, Kilo Force was tasked with fighting insurgency in Kupwara and Baramula districts in north Kashmir. Delta Force was looking after Doda district, which was outside the Kashmir Valley area, straddling the narrow valley of the Chenab River. Similarly, Romeo Force, too, was deployed south of the Pir Panjal, its AOR primarily being Poonch and Rajouri.

While Victor Force and Kilo Force were under the direct operational command of XV Corps, the other three CI Force HQs were under XVI Corps. Lieutenant General Nirbhay Sharma (now Governor of Arunachal), a paratrooper who had been a part of the famous Tangail drop during the Bangladesh War, would be my immediate boss while Lieutenant General Hari Prasad was the Northern Army Commander with his Command HQ in Udhampur.

I spent the entire month going over as much detail as I could with General Lidder, trying to understand the nuances of the Rashtriya Rifles. I also met all sector commanders and tried to get to know the various units that would be operating under my command. 1 Sector under OP Gurung of the Mahar Regiment was at Khanabal looking after Anantnag district; 2 Sector was under the stewardship of 'Tanker' Gill, a paratrooper, and was located at Wuzur, next to Qazikund, the first township on the National Highway after dropping down into the Valley from Banihal; 12 Sector was located at Badgam and was being commanded by Shukla, a Rajput Regiment officer; and 70 Brigade, under AK Singh of the Punjab Regiment, was looking after the southern side of our AOR, its headquarters at Balapur in Shopian.

Since 1990, when it had become clear that the insurgency in Kashmir was Pakistan's motivated attempt to destabilize the Valley, the need to segregate our army into two parts became a top priority. Initially, as Pakistan upped the ante, very few people in India realized the seriousness of the situation, with the government of the day merely indulging in vote-bank politics. We eventually woke up to the magnitude of the threat and it soon became obvious that we were in for the long haul. Accordingly, plans were drawn up for the creation of the Rashtriya Rifles, a force to be placed under the administrative control of the Ministry of Home Affairs, but consisting entirely of troops on deputation from the Indian Army.

The RR was raised under the watch of General BC Joshi. Initially, troops and equipment were skimmed out of regular formations, resulting in the regular divisions in the Valley facing severe shortages, especially as it was decided that RR units must be at full operational strength. After the creation of the RR, even though the regular army units continued to be deployed in a CI role as well, their main task was to be on call in the event of trouble along the border. Battalions manning the LOC were naturally not involved in CI operations.

In March, I formally took over from Lidder. Of all the places, we met on the road at Udhampur. He was driving down to meet an urgent commitment, while I was on my way up. We shook hands, and the double-triangular GOC flag now fluttered on my vehicle's bonnet as I was escorted across the Pir Panjal, through the Banihal Tunnel into the Kashmir Valley. I drove along the National Highway through Anantnag, also known as Islamabad, and arrived at the ancient city of Awantipur. The hill slopes to my right were marked on the maps as 'stony waste'. My convoy turned north and, a few minutes later, we came to a halt at the Victor Force HQ.

Major General (later Lieutenant General) Gurbaksh Singh Sihota had been the first GOC and he was credited with the selection of the location. An aviator, he had picked a spot which dominated the entire area. From where I stood, I could see nearly 70 per cent of my entire AOR and, on a clear day, easily identify most of the features. During major firefights, we could sometimes even hear the gunshots and explosions. General Sihota had been succeeded by a string of highly competent officers, each one of them contributing to making the place a virtual Eden. Major General RK Kaushal, in particular, had literally 'greened' the area in a manner that made the 'stony waste' quite unrecognizable. The picturesque 'Victorpura', as it is known today, became home for me for the next seventeen months, a location that I was to completely fall in love with.

My staff told me that flying the GOC's flag within the Valley was a complete no-no. That went completely against the grain of what I wanted to do, which was to assert ourselves. If you were going to be targeted, you were going to get hit, flag or no flag. Body counts, as far as I was concerned, had absolutely no meaning; what mattered was the complete domination of the area. If there was any movement in our AOR, we wanted to know of it even before it happened. As a matter of principle, I went everywhere with the flag fluttering on my bonnet. Taking their cue from me, it was a matter of time before all commanders in the formation were doing the same.

Interaction with local officials in the administration and with the paramilitary and the police was combined with networking at every level. Units were assured that the resources they needed to get information would be made available, no questions asked. The lessons I had learnt on the ground in Sri Lanka were always at the back of my mind, and the endeavour was to implement them after adapting them to the specifics of the area. There are no templates that can be applied, for the people are different, the terrain is different and the insurgent or terrorist's tactics are different. Yet, the basic principles remained the same. A humane approach towards the population, where they know they will not be targeted, combined with area domination always yields positive results.

As GOC Victor Force, I couldn't have asked for better officers and troops on the ground; it almost looked like they were a handpicked force. Shortly after I took over, a party (which included a lady doctor) that had gone into Shopian town came under fire. I suggested to AK Singh that we station troops in the dead centre of the town.

'I want to be able to drive in an open jeep through Shopian,' I told the commander and the men. By the end of the year, they had created the environment for me to be able to do just that.

The XV Corps commander was a hard taskmaster, constantly pushing all formations under his command. A wonderful human being, he had a few quirky habits. First, the Corps HQ would work till late at night, something that created a ripple effect in the chain of command with everyone down to field formations having to be perpetually on call. Second, every time I asked Nirbhay Sharma for leave, the response would be exactly the same.

'Certainly. You must go.'

The leave would be granted, but by nightfall the corps commander would assign you a task that made sure you simply could not go. It was enough to make you want to tear your hair out.

55 RR had laid a cordon in a village during the night. In the morning, a couple of people broke through, breaking into a run when challenged. The stops opened fire and the escaping men were killed. In the absence of any weapon, there was no hard evidence that they were terrorists. By the end of the day, all the necessary paperwork had been done and the requisite police reports had been filed. The next day, I was to go on leave, so I drove to Srinagar airport, checked in my baggage, and was awaiting the boarding call when my communications team informed me the corps commander wanted to speak to me. 'Where are you?' he wanted to know.

'I've checked in and am waiting to take off,' I told him. I knew what was coming, and despite my protestations that everything was under control, I had to take my bags off the plane.

▪

In any formation, people who have preceded you are as much a part of any subsequent success, for each man contributes to the organisational building blocks. With the strengthening of our intelligence network, we began to have spectacular successes. In a particular incident, ten terrorists were taken out in a single night. I promptly got a phone call from my immediate predecessor, Jasbir Singh Lidder, who had been posted to the MO Directorate at Army HQ. Once in Victor Force always in Victor Force—he told me to have two drinks on him that evening. Even today, almost a decade after I've left Victor Force, my thoughts often drift to the men who make up the Force. Though I probably know none of them, every success of theirs is also my success.

A lot of terrorists were knocked off during that period. Pakistan kept a regular stream of them coming, many of them Afghans who brought with them fearsome reputations. However, our biggest success was in taking out the kingpins, among them a prominent 'commander' based in Pahalgam. Ashiq Hussein was known to be close to one of the most powerful political families. After we brought him down, another 'divisional commander' replaced him but we got him too. Soon, we were getting radio intercepts that suggested none of the terrorists in our AOR wanted any leadership posts as it spelt certain death.

Our biggest success, however, was in killing Shakeel Bhaduri who had been operating in the region since insurgency began in 1989. For a while he had worked as an ikhwani (militant who has surrendered and works with the army as a spotter/scout), but had then crossed back over to the militants. Due to his stint as an ikhwani, he was familiar with our methods of operating. He had a good network, and it took a lot of work to break through his protective cordon. After eliminating him, we were honour-bound to pay the sources who had helped nail Shakeel Bhaduri, but XV Corps refused to sanction any money. It was an extremely embarrassing situation to be in, but we eventually scrounged around and got the money from various units. Even though it's not about body counts, an idea of the intensity and seriousness of the situation can be assessed from the fact that during a period of seventeen months, Victor Force took out over two hundred confirmed Pakistani mujahids and fidayeens.

During this period, we also conducted two incident-free Amarnath yatras, each one extending over sixty days, and registered the largest number of pilgrims at that time. However, in the highly volatile situation, we were sometimes at the receiving end. On 3 December 2004, a young captain, a Jat officer, along with ten men from 1 RR, had gone in mufti to Khanabal, all crammed into a civilian Sumo in the manner of the local population. While returning, the officer decided to take a different route, which was perfectly acceptable according to our existing SOPs. They were probably spotted, as an IED blew the vehicle to smithereens. Though the incident happened at around 1730 hours and just five hundred metres away from a CRPF checkpoint, strangely, it was not reported.

With no sign of the party, 1 RR immediately sent out patrols to look for the missing officer and men. Finally, some locals reported having heard a blast and at 2200 hours the mangled remains of the vehicle and its passengers were discovered. I got there shortly afterwards. The explosion had left a huge crater, and body parts were strewn all over the place. I immediately ordered that lights be installed and each and every piece of human remains be picked up before sunrise. I particularly did not want any civilians gawking at the carnage in the morning. It took the doctors over three days to identify the various parts and sew them up, so that the bodies could be sent to their respective homes for cremation.

We were determined to nail the people behind the blast. Every intelligence resource was brought into play, and all information, including radio intercepts, was sifted through and analysed. We identified the perpetrators of the attack as being a team of eight. By the time I relinquished command, we had chased down and taken out six of them. Two of them were still at large, but my big advantage was that I was being shifted laterally to HQ XV Corps as chief of staff. When the orders for my move came, my first thought was that I still had time to pursue the remaining two terrorists who had evaded us until then. In the next few months, while I was still in Srinagar, Victor Force got one of them, and eventually reports came in a year later that the last of the terrorists had also been killed.

XV Corps

My tenure with Victor Force lasted a year-and-a-half; after having seen the start of the second Amarnath Yatra, I moved into Badami Bagh. Nirbhay Sharma had handed over by then and his successor was Sarabh Dhillon from the Grenadiers. As chief of staff, my job was primarily to assist the corps commander. One of the first things I did was to get Sarabh Dhillon to put his weight behind the allocation of resources for intelligence purposes. We did not want a repeat of the Shakeel Bhaduri incident where we were in danger of losing face and faith with carefully cultivated sources.

From the insulated world of Victor Force, one was suddenly exposed to the outside world. Lieutenant General (retired) SK Sinha was the Governor of Jammu and Kashmir and the ruling government was a coalition of the People's Democratic Party (PDP) and the Congress (headed by Mufti Mohammad Sayeed). It was interesting to interact with a variety of people ranging from those in the political hierarchy to those in the security forces who were playing their role in keeping the situation under control.

I was the officiating corps commander when a massive earthquake, measuring 7.6 on the Richter scale, jolted Kashmir during the morning hours of 8 October 2005. The epicentre was twelve miles northeast of Muzaffarabad, the capital of Pakistan Occupied Kashmir (POK). It was estimated that around 80,000 people were killed while around four million were left homeless. While the destruction on the Indian side was severe, that on the Pakistani side was catastrophic. The western and southern regions of the Kashmir

Valley took the brunt of the quake. Other parts of north India were also affected: tremors were felt in Amritsar, Delhi and across Rajasthan, Uttar Pradesh, Uttaranchal, Himachal Pradesh and Madhya Pradesh.

Uri, one of our brigade locations, took a terrible hammering with a major part of the town being damaged, as did some of our positions and posts all along the LOC. In Uri alone, 1,360 people were killed, a figure that did not include army personnel. The army didn't wait for orders to put relief measures into place. The Uri Field Hospital did outstanding work in treating casualties, swinging into action to save civilian lives, even as the army was still taking stock of its own situation. To make matters worse, it started to snow heavily on our side a few days after the earthquake. In the Tithwal Sector, the Pakistani side had suffered the most. We did our best to provide relief by way of rations and medical relief. By then, humanitarian aid was pouring in from various parts of the country.

For the people of Kashmir who lived through that period, the bonds that developed with the army had a huge psychological impact. A lot of people realized that the army was not quite what the propagandists were projecting.

For me, the two combined tenures in the Valley were eye-openers. The biggest sufferers in the state were the people. Kashmir today begs governance that is not obstructed by narrow political gains. The state needs a policy where the people are taken care of. There are still areas where there are no roads, the most basic of infrastructure. This begs the question: where has all the money that has been pumped into the state disappeared?

The answer is evident. It has been siphoned off by the rich and the powerful since it suits the powers that be to maintain the status quo. In a state in the grips of insurgency for almost a quarter of a century, it is surprising to see the frenetic pace with which multistorey houses are mushrooming. It is almost as if the Srinagar Valley is experiencing an economic boom. If things are to improve in Kashmir, we need extremely good administration with a monitoring mechanism that ensures development takes place across the board.

Under Sadhbhavna, the army has undertaken civil works to build hospitals, schools, bridges etc. One of the reasons the army commands huge respect in the rural areas is because it has, time and again, delivered on every promise, no matter how big or small the project may be. So much so that state officials are loath to let the army take on projects under Sadhbhavna—for it shows them up for what they are. There is a desperate need to re-energize the system and make it accountable.

On 15 April 2006, the results for the board of officers who were found fit for promotion to the rank of lieutenant general were declassified, and we were all informed accordingly. As is always the case, telephone lines came alive, with friends and colleagues calling to congratulate me. The Rajput Regiment flag fluttered proudly, for quite a few of us were a part of the three-star club. Milan Naidu was the ARTRAC army commander, shortly slated to move to Army HQ as the vice chief; Tom Mathews was the adjutant general and a host of others from the regiment were doing extremely well professionally.

The Chief of Army Staff at the time was General Joginder Jaswant 'JJ' Singh from the Maratha LI Regiment who had replaced Vij a year earlier. I had accompanied the general to Oman and the UK as part of his entourage. Among other things, one of my responsibilities was to help prepare a presentation on the Indian Army that the chief would make to brigadier-level officers doing the Royal College of Defence Studies course in Britain. Other than the week-long trip where I was a part of his team, my interactions with JJ had been limited to the chief's visits to XV Corps where, frankly, as the chief of staff, I had no major role to play in the briefings or otherwise.

I was pleasantly surprised when I was told I was being considered to take over II Corps. Though there had been infantry officers who had commanded the formation earlier, it had been commanded by armoured corps officers ever since it was designated a 'strike corps' (with its resultant leaning on armour). While I was flattered at the professional trust being reposed in me, I was acutely aware of the fact that I had no previous armoured experience.

However, even as I awaited orders to move from Srinagar to Ambala, there were moves afoot at Army HQ that would be designed to affect the rest of my career. A list of names had to be put up to the Ministry of Defence for the postings to be approved. A covering letter prepared by the MS Branch accompanied the file in which my year of birth was shown as 1950. This made no sense, for my entire dossier showed the correct year of birth as 1951. Predictably, the Ministry of Defence pointed out this anomaly to Army HQ, asking them to correct the year. I received a letter from the MS, Lieutenant General Richard Khare, asking me to explain the disparity in the dates.

I wrote back and also met the MS, pointing out to him that there was no disparity whatsoever. In April, the promotion board had gone by the service records put up by his own branch and had cleared me for the next rank based on the correct date of birth. He then said the disparity existed, saying my original UPSC form reflected 1950. I told him the error had been sorted out even before I joined the Academy and that I had submitted my original school leaving certificate through 2 Rajput after being commissioned.

'We'll check your father's records,' Khare persisted.

'Check 14 Rajput's records as well. I was born when my father was serving in the battalion,' I responded, wondering why this matter was being raked up.

Khare seemed to relent, saying that he would check all my previous promotion boards, and if indeed my date of birth had uniformly and correctly been entered, he didn't foresee any problem.

I returned to Srinagar. Then, in quick succession, I received two letters: the first was from the MS Branch (signed by Khare) stating that it had been decided by the COAS that my year of birth would be 1950. The second communication said I was to proceed to Ambala to take over II Corps forthwith.

II Corps

On 19 July 2006, I took over from Lieutenant General 'Dolly' Shekhawat, an outstanding armoured corps officer. II Corps had just completed Exercise Sanghe Shakti and everything was all spit and polish. In comparison with XV Corps that was confined to the expanse of the Kashmir Valley, my new formation was spread over a large geographical area that extended from Pathankot to Faridkot, Patiala, Sangrur, Dehradun, Meerut and also Delhi. I had under my command an armoured division that was being commanded by Chetinder Singh (later QMG), an independent armoured brigade under JP Singh, a RAPID (Re-organised Army Plains Infantry Division) division and an infantry division under the charge of S Chatterjee (later DG Resettlement) and Digvijay Thakur (later DGMI). In addition, there were air defence formations and a host of other support formations that were the direct responsibility of II Corps.

My immediate concern was to familiarize myself with the armoured units and accordingly some tanks and BMPs were made available for me to handle, for I was keen to get a feel of the equipment myself. I learnt to drive both the T-72 and the T-90 tanks, as also the BMPs, while being put through the paces on various support mechanisms, especially the transporting systems that included the process of loading and unloading of armour. At the same time, I decided to take a fresh look at all the files that pertained to Operation Parakram and study the reasons for the formation's inability to stick to its stipulated time schedule. I felt that my infantry experience and perspective would help further streamline the measures that had been put into place by commanders before me.

I think the exercise proved to be educative, not just for me, but also for the armoured units and the formation as a whole. The Western Army Commander was Daljit Singh, who had been the BGS in II Corps. Given to keeping his subordinates on their toes and also blowing his fuse at the drop of a hat, he would initially try and catch me off guard. Fortunately for me, I had served as a Colonel GS in the desert, the BGS in Punjab, commanded 168 Infantry Brigade just north of Pathankot and served with MO3, all of which had given me reasonable knowledge of the Western Sector. I held my own, and gradually everyone along the chain of command began to understand that our aim was to put into place plans that were practical and attainable, in case we needed to mobilize.

Indian armoured regiments are universally superb units with an ethos that is quite different from that of the infantry. Most of the senior officers who have worked their way through the system have been outstanding individuals who have contributed greatly to the overall proficiency of the Indian Army.

The problem was that sometimes the swaggering flamboyance of armour would override key issues. A lot of terms sounded wonderful in exercises and war games, but the feeling that I got was that these terms were generally taken for granted without much thought to action on the ground. For example, a phrase regularly used was 'we'll bounce the obstacle'.

I asked a CO who had just used this term during a sand model exercise what he meant by 'bounce'.

'Err... sir, we'll bounce them,' he said a bit hesitantly.

To hammer home the message I asked one of his squadron commanders what the CO meant.

'Umm, bounce, sir, means we'll bounce them...'

A lot of basic terminology was being taken for granted. Bouncing basically meant an encounter crossing as fast as possible. This entailed various other tactical issues, but these were not being looked at. Just as the infantry needed to understand and learn from armour, the tank boys could also learn a lot from the infantry. Sometimes, those who are zipping past 'bouncing' objectives miss the required attention to detail and 'bounce' themselves out of the equation. The entire thrust was to get the armoured formations out of a theoretical construct and into practical mode. At the end of my twenty months as corps commander, I think we were in a position where, if told to mobilize, things would go according to plan.

Shammi Mehta, who had earlier commanded II Corps, was quite closely involved with the Confederation of Indian Industry (CII). Having retired as the Western Army Commander, he obtained the necessary permission for the visit of a delegation of Indian industrialists. As we brainstormed on how best to handle the visit, it was suggested that we break down the military infrastructure in pure monetary terms. The general consensus was that attached financial values would help the visitors understand the situation 'in their language' rather than ours.

Even if we gave ourselves a wide margin of error, I don't think any of us in uniform had even the slightest idea of the army's net worth. It was jaw-dropping stuff, the final number running into figures that we were finding hard to comprehend. Just II Corps itself, without including the cost of the 70,000 plus workforce, was worth an incredible ₹3,000 crore. We then laid out a demonstration that focused on the technical advances within the army, and I think the majority of the delegation went back extremely impressed. Their perception of brainless soldiers marching up and down in drill boots took quite the hammering that day.

The presentation impacted me as well, for I went over all the shortages once again—be it the state and type of ammunition, war stores and even basic maintenance of the equipment—for this was one area that continued to stymie our actual war fighting capabilities. The irony of the situation was inescapable: on the one hand, we had this highly-motivated and professional fighting force worth millions/billions/trillions and, on the other, petty mind-sets and rampant corruption at multiple levels reduced our fighting abilities considerably. So, as a corps commander, I continued to highlight the shortages to Western Command. The answer would always be the same, 'It has been taken note of and it has been projected.' Then, nothing would happen. I wondered if we had actually become a hollow army, crippled as it were by archaic procedures combined with political and bureaucratic indifference. If that wasn't a deadly enough combination, we had to deal with the all-pervasive corruption that seemed to eat into the very heart of our existence.

One did not have to look very far to see how rampant corruption was and how even the inbuilt checks and balances had been subverted. Ambala's cantonment is dotted with old grant bungalows, each property built on a few acres of prime defence land. These bungalows had been given on lease, mainly during British times. According to the conditions of the lease, these properties could not be sold to any third party. However, through the power of attorney system, powerful politicians or local businessmen today own almost all these bungalows.

In the Cantonment Board, there exists the office of the PDDE (Principal Director of Defence Estates). Earlier, there was some semblance of control over the PDDE and his subordinates as they reported to the local military authority and the station commander. Somewhere along the line, the Ministry of Defence quietly took the decision to remove the military authorities from the chain of reporting. Every time any of the old grant bungalows in Ambala would start altering the basic structures, the owner would put in an application to the army commander to levy a sanction. The PDDE was the procedural channel through which the complaints had to go to the army commander—only after this could legal action be contemplated. The beauty of the system is that in 2006 there were three hundred complaints pending with the PDDE which had not seen the light of day. These had been pending for—hold your breath—twenty years!

What do you tell your men when they go for a run in the morning and see these swanky bungalows all around them with the nameplates of not just the politicians of the day, but even people who exercised some minor power in the past? The same men who get blown up because they have to fit wrong size fuses into anti-personnel mines just because someone somewhere did not bother to check, or was willing to sign off on a certificate because he got his two blankets from the canteen. We may have impressed the delegates from the CII, but I was beginning to feel more and more that we senior officers were letting down our men. How long were we to settle for the standard 'it has been noted' reply? As middle-ranking officers, we had fretted and fumed, for at our pay grade, there was nothing we could do. As a corps commander, I was beginning to wonder: at what point do we stand up and confront the system.

Being stationed in Ambala, I was continuously on the lookout to expand my horizons. Apart from trying to look at life from the mechanized point of view, the opportunity to fly in a Jaguar presented itself when Air Marshal AK Singh from Western Air Command came on a farewell visit just prior to his retirement. Throughout my six terms at NDA, I had been an air force cadet until my father had pulled the plug and had rooted me to terra firma for the rest of my life. Hardly had the offer been made, than I was strapping myself into the cockpit of the twin-engine trainer version. I had earlier done a sortie in a MiG 29 from Adampur (when I was the BGS in Jalandhar), and now looked forward to seeing how the IAF's low-level interdictors operated. It was, to put it mildly, an exhilarating experience. After going through various manoeuvres, we returned to base.

'You do realize, sir,' said the squadron commander, 'most of this actually happens at night.'

Next thing, we were slotted for a night sortie. In the pitch darkness of the night, I found myself strapped into yet another Jaguar. In the trainer cockpit, I was on my own, for the pilot sits in front and is not visible from the rear. We were communicating through internal radio transmitters.

Probably concerned about my comfort, the pilot told me to feel for a button on the left side so I could adjust my seat. Low and behold, I pressed something and triggered the fire extinguishing system! Fortunately, we were still on the ground doing our checks.

We transferred to a standby aircraft. 'Never ask an army chap in a confined place to press things which are sensitive,' I told the pilot.

Once again we were airborne, flying by instruments, making our way through the inky black night. Other than some occasional lights, the ground was not visible, while the sky was lit with hundreds of twinkling stars. After a while, it was hard to tell what was up and what was down. It required nerves of steel to fly the way our boys did, endless hours of training making them into first-class aviators.

Later, I was to do a third sortie, accompanying the station commander, Rahul Dhar, on a bombing run. We then flew formation with an IL 78 and did an air-to-air refuelling. A youngster who had just returned from leave was piloting another Jaguar, flying as our wingman. Three times the aircraft tried to get into position for the tanker's trailing fuel nozzle to lock into his tank, but on all three occasions he failed to make contact. Eventually, it was our turn. Dhar slid the aircraft into position with the precision of a surgeon and we were locked with the mother ship way up in the sky. It underlined the complexities of flying and the high degree of training that was called for. It was extremely educative and added considerably to my knowledge of air support.

■

Punjab in British times was based on the boundaries of Maharaja Ranjit Singh's Sikh empire but it had been fragmented by Partition. The resultant exodus from either side of the border had seen a virtual carnage, a bitter event in history that was one of the fault-lines between India and the newly created Pakistan. Indian Punjab then saw further subdivision along linguistic lines.

My earlier tenure in Punjab had primarily been a staff appointment. As the BGS, though I got to tour the forward areas, I had little or no time to see the hinterland. However, as GOC II Corps, I didn't miss any opportunity to head out into the countryside, always preferring to travel by road. As I advanced in rank, I began to miss the gay abandon with which I could take my scooter and drive around everywhere. As a corps commander, I was compensated to a great extent by the large area that I could cover, meeting literally hundreds of people.

I was fairly well acquainted with Haryana and I now took the opportunity to meet and interact with as wide a segment of society through the large ex-servicemen presence in the region. Time and again, doors would be thrown open, with the matrons of the family lavishly urging my entourage—officers, drivers, security details, everyone—to drink more lassi and dip into endless rounds of choorma or parathas. No matter how much we ate, the inevitable lament would follow, 'Khanda nahi hai, puttar.' (Son, you don't eat.) I was pretty sure I'd be found overweight in my next medical. Haryana or Punjab, it was the same story. The Doaba region tucked away between the Sutlej and the Beas; the Malwa region, which was our main operational area centering around Patiala and Sangrur, extending up to Ludhiana and the Majha belt north of the Beas, which is the heartland of Sikhism. As one interacted with and listened to the people, it was hard to believe the region had been so volatile and disturbed just a few years ago.

'How could we have got it so wrong?' I often asked myself, my mind drifting back to the Khalistan movement and Operation Blue Star. The colourful turbans, the endless fields of wheat, miles and miles of yellow mustard with both grey and black partridges calling, the poplar and eucalyptus trees, the network of dancing canals with frothing green water; and, above all, the down-to-earth sense of humour which defines the Punjabi: 'Satluj de niche Dilli hai. Aage sare tambi haige.' (South of the Sutlej lies Delhi. Beyond that, everyone is a Tamilian.)

■

For the first few months after taking over II Corps, I was too busy to worry about the rather strange letter I had received from the MS Branch pertaining to the change in my year of birth. However, once I settled into the job, I wrote to the MS asking them to enlighten me on the rationale and the logic behind changing my year of birth. Also stated in the letter was the rule that the date of birth could not be changed after two years of being commissioned. I pointed out to the MS that I was not the one asking for a change in my records.

My interaction with General JJ Singh had been minimal, and we had the usual formal and cordial relationship that exists between a senior and a subordinate officer. He had, after all, selected me to command the elite II Corps so I had no reason to suspect that there was any ulterior motive behind the deliberate creation of a controversy over my age. On the face of it, at the time, it seemed like yet another case of bureaucratic bungling. Besides, in any army, while you may have professional differences and may be judged accordingly, the Chief of Army Staff is the one person with whom you expect the buck to stop. I expected Army HQ to sort out the issue, not complicate it.

If there was a 'look down policy' that was looking at the appointment of future chiefs and their tenures, at the time, I personally knew nothing of it. Subsequently, the Defence Secretary and the Ministry of Defence were to go on record saying that since my age had been fixed (after I had become a lieutenant general) a year older, it could not be 'changed' as it would impact 'the line of succession'. It would also emerge later that not only had my age issue been created deliberately to truncate my career in the army, first at the army commander level and then as the chief, but there had been others too who had been deliberately and systematically targeted. While in the case of certain officers, the tactics to 'fix' them were subtle and within the system, the case of Major General Ravi Arora was as bizarre as the creation of the age issue itself.

With the benefit of hindsight, some facts are clear:

General JJ Singh had taken over as COAS in 2004 and his own tenure was to run till the end of September 2007. It is now an established fact that he had, within months of taking charge, initiated the 'look down policy' that would give a clear idea as to what the line of succession would, or could, be. That General Deepak Kapoor would take over from JJ himself was well known at the time, but Kapoor's successor would depend on the board that would be held towards the end of 2005 to decide on which officers were to be cleared for the lieutenant general rank. Since I was the most senior officer on it, it placed me in a fairly good position to attain the four-star rank and be next in line to Deepak Kapoor. To arrive at these conclusions, nobody needed a look down policy. However, the intention seemed to be to influence events even beyond that.

The 'look down policy' allowed every officer above the rank of brigadier, and still climbing the command pyramid, to work out his own list where, based on various permutations and combinations, the next three or four chiefs could be predicted. But the only list that mattered was the chief's own list, for as COAS he could tweak events to clear the way for his choice immediately after me, provided I did become the chief.

At this stage, it was probably brought to JJ's notice (I believe by an officer in the MS Branch, my original nemesis) that if the COAS could truncate my tenure as the chief to a two-year period, then the path could be cleared for the officer of his choice, and perhaps the choice of others in the government, to take over in 2012. A bit of deft manoeuvring was needed to remove impediments from the path of the officer on whom the chief had his eye. Among those who would have to be 'fixed' were Brigadiers Padam Budhwar, MM Chaudhary, followed by Major Generals Shujan Chatterjee, AK Singh, Ravi Arora and, finally, me. While all the others had to be 'fixed' in their brigadier to major general boards, or by other delaying tactics that allowed the designated favourite to overtake them, in the overall scheme of things it was probably an imperative that I become the chief, but only for a limited period.

The timing was critical—to have created the age issue before my lieutenant general board would have meant that I would not be in the running, thereby also knocking out the desired officer, which would have been counterproductive. So, barely two weeks after the declassification of the board results, the MS fired the first missile. All I could do was write again to the MS asking them for the rationale behind their advice to the COAS to fix my age on an arbitrary basis. Forget about the fact that I was a lieutenant general in the Indian Army; even as a citizen of India I was entitled to ask this one basic question. There was no immediate reply.

In September 2007 the baton of the army chief passed on to General Deepak Kapoor who had been the Northern Army Commander when I was the COS in XV Corps. Though General JJ Singh had retired, he was appointed the Governor of Arunachal Pradesh within a couple of months, a position he continued to hold till mid-2013.

After a year-and-a-half of commanding II Corps, Army HQ put up my name for army commander. Lieutenant General PR Gangadharan, a Maratha LI officer, had taken over as the MS from Richard Khare. I met the new MS, but there was no activity despite assurances that the issue would be settled. Bimal Julka was the Joint Secretary in the Ministry of Defence. Julka had first raked up the issue pertaining to the discrepancy between the MS Branch's note and my dossier when it had been sent up for corps commander. He now got quite hot under the collar, berating Gangadharan in no uncertain terms, for though the MS Branch had given a vague reply earlier, all documents in my dossier continued to indicate that I was born in 1951 and not 1950.

On the way to Gurgaon for my mami's funeral, Milan Naidu (who was vice chief now) asked me to come immediately to Army HQ since General Deepak Kapoor wanted to see me urgently. Milan had taken over the mantle of the colonel of the regiment, and it was but natural for me to seek his advice on any matter. The ministry, the chief said, was holding up my army commander's clearance because they were not satisfied with the earlier explanation on the issue of my birth year. He had mulled over the matter and had come to the conclusion that I must accept whatever decision Army HQ took on the matter.

'How can I do that?' I asked the chief. 'All my records, everything says 1951. How can I just give a statement that is not true? What do I do with my matriculation certificate and other documents like my passport?' I also pointed out that there was a media campaign orchestrated by someone from within Army HQ.

'It's a system's fault. We have to get over the hurdle with the ministry so that the file is not held up. We will sort out the issue subsequently.'

I made my way across to Milan Naidu. 'Likh ke de do,' said Milan. 'Doing what the chief wants doesn't change when you were actually born. All your records are clear, so it will not make any difference.' He then added, 'The Defence Secretary has also gone on record saying that just because an officer writes that "he accepts it" (date of birth) does not mean that the criterion for fixing age can change.'

'Don't do it, sir,' warned others on Milan's staff, as I stepped sideways into their office to dictate a reply.

'You know,' I said, 'I'm sick of all this nonsense. I've got a funeral to attend and here we are sitting discussing some fictitious date of birth.' I dictated a note saying 'as desired by the chief' whatever decision Army

HQ wanted to take 'in the organizational interest' was acceptable to me. Disgusted and fed up, I signed the letter and proceeded to Gurgaon.

As I was returning to Ambala that evening, Milan called again. 'He (the chief) doesn't like your saying "as directed by him" and the word "acceptable".'

I told Milan, 'Fine, fine, just cut out whatever he does not like and write whatever you want. You have my full authority.'

A few minutes later, Milan was back on the line. 'Chief doesn't want any kata-pitti. Tum phir se likh ke bhej do.' (Chief doesn't want any cutting out. Write the letter again and send it.) 'In any case, the chief says he has assured you that we will settle the matter subsequently.'

That settled the matter for the time being and I redrafted the letter as Deepak Kapoor wanted it. I should have known better, that there never was going to be any inquiry, for there was actually nothing to inquire about. I didn't know it then and would only realize it a lot later. In the mysterious ways of the Ministry of Defence and the Indian 'system', I had just been sucker-punched.

▪

Ambala was not all work and no play. On a visit to Patiala, Chetinder Singh's division decided to ask the 'infantry' corps commander if he would like to play polo. I hadn't sat a horse since my school and NDA days, but I knew my refusal to mount up would lead to many a shake of the head. Besides, in the worst case, I could only fall off. Fortunately, I managed to hold my own, though I doubt I connected with the ball at all.

Mrinalini and her husband Sangram were posted in Pune while Yogja had finished her masters from Chandigarh. She had applied for and got admission into the Army Institute of Management and had moved to Kolkata. Army HQ had told me that I would also be moving to the same city as I had been earmarked to take over Eastern Command. However, until hours before the orders were actually issued, television channels were reporting that I was taking over Northern Command. Bharti told me what was being reported on the ticker. I told her that the MS Branch would do what it had always done and we might as well get used to their ways. However, for once, there was no last-minute drama, for they actually posted me to Eastern Command.

11

THE SUN ALSO RISES

Neglect and Strife

I took over Eastern Command from Lieutenant General KS Jamwal at the end of February 2008. The Command HQ is situated in the historic Fort William in Kolkata. The scale of the command was massive; extending from Bengal to Sikkim, and then extending across the entire Northeast. I had three army corps and two area headquarters spread across the region. The eastern sweep of the Himalayas dominates the landscape, defining the northern borders while the Brahmaputra River descends into India from the extreme northeastern tip and, as it flows in a southwesterly direction, it claims the plains as its own, its waters swelling and receding annually.

Starting from the eastern flank of Arunachal, the north-south chain of the Naga-Patkai extends south into Nagaland and Manipur before linking up with the Chaifil Tlang and the Uiphum Tlang ranges in Mizoram, tapering off into the Chin and Arakan Yoma. Like the Eastern Himalayas, this region too was considered to be a natural barrier, separating the Indian subcontinent from Southeast Asia. The Bangladesh border runs along the south of Meghalaya, south Assam, Tripura and Mizoram. Post-independence, the Chicken Neck area became the gateway to the entire region, underlining its remoteness.

Eastern Command shares international boundaries with Nepal, Bhutan, China, Myanmar and Bangladesh. This, naturally, has security implications. Further complicating the issue, the region was synonymous with insurgency and underdevelopment. In 2008, law and order problems in Assam and Manipur were adversely impacting peace and stability in the region. Insurgent Naga groups were flexing their muscles not just within their own state, but claiming parts of Manipur and Arunachal as well. In the hill district of Darjeeling, the Gorkha National Liberation Front's (GNLF) demand for Gorkhaland was also creating problems, while further south, ethnic strife between the Bodos and Muslim migrants in the flood plains of the Brahmaputra was threatening to explode in our face.

That the history of the Northeast had been tortured not just by political strife but had also seen regular violence was not surprising given the fact that the region has more or less been ignored by the central government ever since Independence. Add to this, natural disasters, uncontrolled migration and displacement of entire peoples which had a cumulative impact in adding to the constant ferment which the region perpetually found itself in. Since 1947, India's population has expanded manifold, and the Northeast is no exception. The most natural result of this has been the struggle for land, which over a period of time got more and more complicated as the geographical boundaries within the region were constantly redefined.

Ethnic diversity within my AOR was but one face of the complexity; geographically, the region is a maze of rivers, hill ranges and mountains that have played a part in thwarting 'development' in the past. After Independence the country adopted its own Tribal Policy with respect to the hill areas of the Northeast. This hoped to preserve the existing cultures while at the same time offering the people a collective identity, a participative democratic political system and essentially the platform of nationalism to set aside their differences and build towards the future.

Conservative estimates suggest that nearly one million people have been forced to flee their homes over some issue or the other in just the last two decades, the latest and perhaps far worst exodus being the recent Bodoland disturbances in 2012 that also saw nearly a hundred people killed. Bodos are battling Muslims, Adivasis and Nepalis; Karbis are up in arms against Dimasas; the Nagas are constantly feuding with the Meiteis and Kukis; the Mizos are chasing the Brus (also known as Reangs); and in Tripura the original tribes have all but disappeared as this constant shift in demographical patterns continues to complicate matters.

In the six decades that have elapsed since Independence, India as a whole is a changed country, as more and more people move across the subcontinent, breaking out of regional and clannish cliques in search of the larger national identity. At the same time, ethnicity, which had always been central to their existence, was now becoming even more critical for others who were trying to cling to their lifestyles that defined their very existence. Surveys, based on linguistic and anthropological data, estimate that the mass of 46 million people in the region are divided into 475 ethnic groups that speak some four hundred languages.

Though I had served and travelled in some of these areas soon after I was commissioned into the army, I was far from familiar with Eastern Command.

So I got down to the business of first visiting the various corps headquarters. XXXIII Corps, based in Sukhna near Siliguri, was being commanded by Deepak Raj from the mechanized infantry; BS Jaswal from JAK RIF was looking after most of Arunachal at the time, with the IV Corps Headquarters in Tezpur; and MS Dadwal from the Dogra Regiment was responsible for the entire eastern flank with his Dimapur based III Corps. The Assam Rifles was under the command of Paramjit Singh from Garhwal Rifles (later replaced by Karan Yadava from the Gorkhas).

In terms of external security, the most sensitive area (and of immediate concern to Eastern Command) was the Indo-Tibet border (Sikkim and Arunachal) that runs across some of the most inaccessible terrain. Just before I had taken over Eastern Command, the Chinese had intruded into Sikkim in the area bordering the Chumbi Valley, south of Nathu La, and dismantled one of the bunkers.

Chinese Checkers

To understand the complex border problem with China, I needed a refresher course in history. I spent almost all my spare time poring over maps and reading whatever material I could find on the region. At the time of Independence, Arunachal, then known as the North East Frontier Tract (subsequently Tract was replaced by Agency and the area was known as NEFA) was unexplored and, to a great extent, 'unadministered' territory. The British Indian government had been quite content to exercise loose control over the area south of the Great Himalayan wall, secure in the belief that there was no external threat to the Raj from this axis. A handful of people did make inroads into the area, leaving their imprint on the region, which only just allowed for a peep into the mist-shrouded valleys of dense jungles inhabited by fierce warlike tribes. Despite the difficulties, some British officers successfully surveyed and charted the entire Himalayan watershed. Their work greatly influenced the demarcation of the McMahon Line that was drawn up in 1914 between the British and the Tibetans. The Chinese representative, who was present in Shimla when the treaty was signed, refused to endorse the treaty, not because he did not agree with it, but because he had come to discuss the demarcation of outer and inner Tibet. This strange fact of history rests in the archives and is not known to many. Gradually, almost hesitantly, the region opened up to others and over the years we have come to know something of the area and the people. NEFA was an evolving entity as independent India grappled with huge problems, not the least of which were its newly defined borders.

Tibet was annexed by Communist China in 1950 and the Chinese established a military government in the form of the 'Tibet Military District'. This was in direct violation of Peking's earlier pledge that it would allow Tibetan people 'the right of exercising national regional sovereignty'. In 1955 the Kham tribes started organized armed resistance against the Chinese, which soon became a full-fledged insurgency spreading from Chamdo to the Indo-Tibet border. An unequal fight at the best of times, the Khams received little or no support from the outside world, allowing the Chinese to build up their forces in Tibet considerably. These developments, combined with the fact that Peking was not a signatory to the 1914 Simla Agreement, foretold a potential threat, especially with the Chinese also stepping up their cartographical aggression by claiming almost the whole of NEFA and parts of Bhutan.

In response to the Chinese moves in Tibet, the Assam Rifles had formed the military vanguard, taking the Indian administration up to the border. New posts had been set up all along the watershed. Tibetan refugees had been steadily crossing into India. The climax came when the Dalai Lama, along with members of his family, escaped from the Tibetan capital and made for the Assam Rifles post at Chuthangmu. His Holiness then proceeded to Tawang, Bomdila and Tezpur, from where he subsequently went to Mussoorie.

By October 1962, an Infantry Division had operational control of the NEFA border. The Government of India decided on a 'Forward Policy' where thirty-four new Assam Rifles posts were established all along the McMahon Line with extensive patrolling of the border areas. The Forward Policy was based on the Intelligence Bureau's assessment that the Chinese would not go to war with India on the issue of the McMahon Line, so the international border would ultimately stabilize along the Line of Actual Control established by the presence of troops. By this time, twenty-four platoons of Assam Rifles were deployed in NEFA all along the watershed.

The fighting started on 19 October with heavy shelling at Khenzemane. The Chinese crossed the McMahon Line in other sectors also, always in superior numbers. 2 Rajput took the first real onslaught, but the battalion never stood a chance. Despite all the hardships faced by the men of the Indian Army and the Assam Rifles (there was even a lack of basic defensive requirements such as barbed wire), at no stage did any of these units fail to resist the Chinese onslaught giving rise to the phrase 'last man, last round!'

The Chinese, having achieved their objective of overrunning NEFA, withdrew to the McMahon Line leaving the people of India psychologically scarred. Though the Nathu La barbed wire incident in 1967, where 18 Rajput and 2 Grenadiers supported by artillery dented the myth of Chinese superiority by giving as good as they got, the boundary issue remained unsolved.

The bunker the Chinese had dismantled in East Sikkim underlined the high-handed manner in which they had been dealing with us. The GOC of 17 Division, Major General Vijay Lalotra, briefed me on the incident. In all their border disputes, the Chinese constantly probed into areas that were not physically manned, and then claimed, with the aid of doctored photographs, that the area was theirs. In case there were any further attempts by Chinese patrols, I gave Vijay Lalotra clear-cut orders on what to do.

As luck would have it, a thirty-man Chinese patrol soon surfaced in the area just north of the Indo-Bhutan-China tri-junction. The patrol was clearly on our side of the LAC when a captain from 9 Grenadiers confronted it. The Chinese officer leading the patrol grabbed hold of an old barbed wire fence that marked the area and angrily started to shake it, demanding that it be removed at once, claiming that it had been put up recently. The young captain coolly caught hold of the Chinese officer's hand and removed it from the post.

'Touch it again and I'll shoot you.'

The Chinese officer stood there for almost a minute, staring at the Indian captain who had let go of his hand. Troops on both sides eyed each other warily, and then the Chinese officer turned around and walked off with his men. As far as I know, the Chinese have not reappeared in that area. I salute this young officer for the way he handled the situation.

The plateau in North Sikkim, where troops man defences at a height of over 18,000 feet, was also reporting similar problems. In most parts, the boundary—well-established though not physically marked—runs across a flat plain. One small area was known as the 'finger' for it protruded into Chinese territory. We had decided to make a small track along the finger that would allow us to get to its furthest point. The Chinese immediately objected, and drove a few vehicles across the 'finger', deliberately trying to provoke us. I told 17 Division to sort out the problem firmly.

From our posts, we could see the Chinese vehicles driving towards the 'finger', so our boys positioned themselves for their arrival. They had decided to do a 'China' on the Chinese. Though we could not match the other side in their ability to produce doctored photographs, we had an old photograph of a herd of yaks that were being handed over to them many years ago. That the photograph had been taken at the tip of the finger could not be doubted. Our boys showed the black-and-white print to the Chinese soldiers; they gathered around and studied the photograph, then got back into their vehicles and drove away.

▪

As the Eastern Army Commander, I subsequently visited China on an official goodwill army-to-army tour. The Chinese were extremely hospitable and went out of their way to look after us. I was then a three-star general, and they broke protocol to arrange a meeting with a four-star general. In Beijing, where they have a demo regiment to impress foreigners, they put on quite a show. Chinese marksmen fired at targets and came and showed us the results: 198 out of 200; 197 out of 200. We were suitably impressed at these near-Olympic scores.

We then went to Chengdu. In May 2008, the 8.0 magnitude Sichuan earthquake had killed an estimated 70,000 people and was considered to be the worst natural calamity to befall China since 1976. The epicentre was 80 kilometres from the provincial capital of Chengdu. Official Chinese figures had put the homeless at around 4.8 million, but some sources claimed the figure could have been much higher than that. Tremors had been felt in Beijing, 1,700 kilometres away and almost 40,000 aftershocks had been registered.

In Chengdu we visited an aviation brigade, the first time any foreigners were being allowed there, or so we were told. It was a great honour. I asked the Chinese base commander through the interpreter, 'When the earthquake struck this region, how many helicopters could you get airborne?'

The commander's gaze shifted from the interpreter and me to the political commissar, who gave the briefest of nods.

Every question of mine addressed to the commander was answered in exactly the same way. Their serviceability was extremely good, around 70 per cent; the number of helicopters on call, everything was answered, but only after the political commissar's slight nod of approval. It was pretty obvious who wore the pants around this house.

They then took us around and showed us the barracks. The difference between the living standards of the men and the officers was negligible. The bulk of the Chinese troops on the border are all conscripts. Each regiment has a commanding officer, who in turn has a watchdog political commissar attached to his tail. There is nothing ambiguous about anything the Chinese do. The commissars have homogenous orders which go right back to the top. If we think that any incursion on the border is a local transgression, then we are kidding ourselves.

We landed at Lhasa where the Tibetan Military Region Commander, General Shu Chi, met us. We hit it off almost instantly and were soon comparing personal notes. He had one daughter, as was the norm in China; I had two daughters. We were both three-star generals and roughly the same age. I said to him that he could consider me to be his brother and the general got extremely emotional. Unlike India, the limited size of the family has impacted the social structure there quite severely.

It was soon time to get down to business. 'We must tell people below us in the chain of command not to have incidents on the border,' I said to him. 'Over there the men are younger and there is a lot of hot blood. Things can easily go wrong and then it is left to you and me to sort things out.'

Shu Chi and I parted as friends. I extended an invitation to him to visit India. He promised he would come. Subsequently, there was a lot of restraint shown on the Sikkim border and there were no further incidents for a while. In fact, the Chinese were keen that we have a lot more sporting events between the two armies at the border. I smiled to myself, for I recalled a volleyball match between Indian and Chinese troops many years ago at Nathu La when similar sentiments had been expressed. The Indian team had got trounced, for the Chinese had fielded the equivalent of their services team. A few days later, we reciprocated; the Chinese, perhaps embarrassed by the earlier one-sided match, fielded a regular side and we went in with our services team. Life on the border can be a lot of fun!

Joint exercises with the Chinese more or less follow this same pattern. Reports from Belgaum after one such exercise indicated that the Chinese were fielding 'specialists' while we tended to go in with balanced units. As a result, they would have experts who could wow the audience as individuals, but as a unit, our boys tended to have a much better level of performance. This lesson also became clear to the Chinese side after a while.

India as a NATO Country

Flanking us on our extreme eastern flank was Myanmar, formerly known as Burma. Our main concern was the existence of safe havens and camps of insurgent groups on their side of the border. At that time, they had a military government and, like the Chinese, they too had a system where everything would trickle down from the top. We knew the camps existed and could pinpoint their locations with absolute accuracy, but the answer from the Myanmar side never deviated from the standard 'we will check' and they would never get back to us. In fact, our intelligence networks indicated that most local military commanders received protection money from the insurgent groups, which would otherwise easily merge with the local population, with most tribes in the area straddling areas on either side of the border.

The second big problem that we faced from Myanmar was the inflow of Chins into southern Mizoram. Living conditions on the Indian side, though quite dismal, were far better than the conditions within Myanmar. This exodus of people, extending south from Champhai towards Saiha and Lawngtlai will sooner or later take a serious turn.

In mid-2008, the Eastern Army delegation landed at Nay Pyi Taw, the new administrative capital city of Myanmar after a night halt at Yangon. At the time, the military was firmly in control and the army-drafted constitution, Myanmar's third since independence, had been approved by referendum with a staggering 92 per cent favourable vote in an election that had a 99 per cent turnout. Once again we were visiting a country on the heels of a natural calamity; the entire Irrawaddy belt had been ravaged by Cyclone Nargis that had left in its wake around 200,000 dead and close to a billion homeless. The isolationist policies of the Myanmar government had come in for severe criticism for it had hampered relief measures in a big way. To make matters worse, the Government of India, kowtowing to western opinion rather than taking a realistic and pragmatic view, had also been following a policy of suspending military aid to Myanmar over the issue of human rights.

Myanmar's Parliament, Pyidaungsu Hluttaw, is made up of two houses, with the 224-seat Upper House, Amyotha Hluttaw (House of Nationalities) carrying fifty-six members appointed by the military, while the Lower House, Pyithu Hluttaw (House of Representatives), had 440 members of which a quarter were nominated by the military.

From the very outset, it became quite clear that the Myanmarese were far more comfortable talking to a military delegation rather than interacting with the diplomatic staff, though this is in no way a comment on our diplomats. The stiff-backed formal sessions with the diplomats always had the Myanmar generals speaking in Burmese, even if they were fluent in English. There would be absolutely no deviation from their official line, come what may. After the formal talks, they would joke and laugh with us with no inhibitions.

The Myanmar general, U Shwe Mann, who is now the speaker of the Pyidaungsu Hluttaw, was at the time the Joint Chief of Staff of Myanmar's Armed Forces, third in the hierarchy to Generals Than Shwe and Maung Aye. After one of the official meetings, he looked at my military attaché, Brigadier KH Singh. 'He looks like us,' he said, his face wrinkling with delight.

KH was the senior-most Manipuri officer in the Indian Army, a trailblazer for many others who have followed in his wake and done themselves and the Indian Army proud with their professionalism.

'He is one of yours,' I said jokingly.

'Ah, yes,' sighed the general, 'we do have so much in common. We would so very much like to work with India closely on many issues but the trouble is you are a NATO country.'

Surely the Myanmar general couldn't have been that badly briefed to think India was a part of the US-dominated North Atlantic Treaty Organization. 'No, no...' I protested, telling him we were a non-aligned country, even at the height of the Cold War.

U Shwe Mann was looking at me most kindly by then, his genial expression not changing at all. He waited for me to finish, then delivered the punch line with a little laugh, 'General, NATO means "No Action Talk Only".' You could have knocked me down with a feather. What could I say?

Despite the vaunted 'Look East Policy' being propagated by the prime minister himself, for fifteen years Myanmar's offer to explore for oil and gas had been lying in someone's pending tray. Fed up with India's inaction, they had finally asked the Chinese to come in. We were left making indignant noises while think tank experts got another reason to talk of China's growing influence all around us.

Later, as chief, I visited Myanmar again and was confronted with a host of similar problems. In Army HQ we were aware of an aid package that had been offered by India to build a road—a few road rollers and earth moving vehicles, probably adding up to not more than ₹20 crore. As usual, nothing was happening on the ground as bureaucrats studied every minute detail. During Army Day in 2012, Dr Manmohan Singh asked me about my visit to Myanmar. I told him in no uncertain terms what was happening, or rather, not happening. The prime minister listened most carefully.

'General saab, ab yeh procedural problems hain,' he said in a resigned manner, 'we are trying.'

How many times had I heard this before, I lost count years ago. Here was the Prime Minister of India, expressing his helplessness in matters that should have been trivial. Had the task been given to the army, we would have handed over the road rollers in less than a week. No wonder then that none of our neighbours trust us. If we are so stymied by the 'system', then why bother to make the offer in the first place?

These are countries that at a very basic level are wary of China. No one wants to be overwhelmed and reduced to a surrogate status. We should be building bridges, but here we were constantly shooting ourselves in the foot. It sounds very good to talk of the 'Look East Policy' and be concerned about the Chinese game plan of surrounding India. The point is, what are we doing about it?

Today, it is a well-established fact that almost all insurgent groups in the Northeast get arms through the Yunnan province of China. Though Kunming is on no one's security map in India, the fact of the matter is that Yunnan almost extends up to Arunachal Pradesh, separated by the northern tip of Myanmar. If our people believe that in China there are renegade groups operating on their own, they are only bluffing themselves. The Chinese have been playing the game since the 1950s. They have actively engaged Pakistan on the other end of the spectrum and developed it into a cat's paw mainly to keep India off balance. If we look at the Four Modernizations as set forth by the Chinese leadership, it was designed to make China a great economic power by the early part of the twenty-first century. Military expansion was prioritized behind agriculture, industry and science and technology. We have never quite understood that. In our case bureaucratic and procedural systems create endless delays, whether it has to do with engaging a country, procurement, or any other field where the government has half a foot in the door.

The story was much the same when it came to dealing with Bangladesh. Despite the problems over various issues, the goodwill towards the Indian Army in that country was phenomenal. Not just me, but every 1971 veteran who has visited Bangladesh is treated like a war hero.

In Bangladesh, the political order under Sheikh Hasina, the daughter of Mujibur Rahman, was relatively well disposed towards India after relations with the earlier Awami League had floundered. I was treated as one of their own, the media hailing me as a freedom fighter. Other retired army officers who had fought in Bangladesh in 1971, were also met with open arms; JFR Jacob, Ashok Kalyan Verma, Ian Cardozo, HS Panag, Lakshman Lehl,

'Bobby' Kapoor, PN Kathpalia, JS Bakshi, Joginder Singh, RKS Panwar, PN Kackar are just a few of those who were honoured by the grateful country. Almost everyone I had known then came to meet me. Major Rafique who had fought along with 2 Rajput and was the home minister in the previous government had an incredibly frank discussion with me about Indo-Bangla relations.

We talk of China making inroads into Bangladesh and Sri Lanka and strategically surrounding India from all sides; yet we, who have such strong, natural ties with the people of our neighbouring countries, fail to build and cement that relationship. More often than not, our domestic political compulsions affect our decisions and India's detractors have a field day, saying 'we told you not to trust these guys'. The Teesta River issue, the sharing of waters, transit rights across Bangladesh that will once again link up Silchar in Assam, Agartala in Tripura and Demagiri in Mizoram need to be followed up with a little bit of give and take. The Bangladesh Army, for example, has military equipment that is mainly of Chinese origin, modelled entirely on the Soviet pattern. Surely, we can help, not just with repairing and maintaining their existing hardware, but also take things forward by identifying areas of mutual interest. The questions, as always, are: who will do it, and what is the way through the competing bureaucratic procedural maze?

Nepal is yet another case in point. With such a large population that is deeply integrated with India through the military itself, there really should never have been a problem. When I visited the country as COAS, I was hugely relieved to meet the new ambassador, who seemed to be doing a much better job than his predecessor.

The danger of the Maoists spilling across the border and exploiting the situation in North Bengal was fairly serious. Since 1986 the GNLF had been demanding a Gorkha homeland, and two years later, the Darjeeling Gorkha Hill Council under Subash Ghising had supposedly been administering the region. However, members of the council including Ghising, had only lined their own pockets and development in the area came to an absolute standstill. The Governments of India and West Bengal also let matters rest following the ultimate form of governance: 'Paise de do, apne aap sab theek ho jayega.'

The emergence of Bimal Gurung as an alternate to Ghising had sparked off a fresh round of demands. With narrow tunnel vision, the emotive issue of Gorkhaland once again came to the fore, this time with the additional demand that Siliguri be a part of the new state, despite the fact that the city itself had only a small Gorkha presence. This had already sparked off similar demands from other ethnic groups including the Adivasis who wanted their own territory carved out of Bihar, North Bengal and Assam.

Eastern Command was keeping a close watch on the situation, for the Darjeeling area had a large number of ex-servicemen who were involved in the agitation. GNLF, as a part of their protest, had organized a peaceful march. As should have been expected, the march had at the forefront ex-servicemen bedecked with medals and their Gorkha topis. The state government lost its nerve and ordered the police to lathi-charge the march, and within the hour, pictures of blood-splattered medals and wounded ex-soldiers were all over the media. The people were told that the government did not even respect those who had fought and given their all for their country. It was a major public relations disaster, something the local authorities and the political class should have foreseen.

The central government had brought in Lieutenant General Vijay Madan, a retired officer from the Gorkha Regiment, into the fray as its interlocutor. The general had been working tirelessly and was extremely close to resolving some of the key issues. At Command HQ in Fort William, we had a detailed discussion where we spent a fair bit of time going over the various options. That same evening he was to proceed from Kolkata to Darjeeling by train.

Hardly had Vijay Madan left my office, when television channels started broadcasting the Government of India announcement that it had agreed to the formation of Telangana state. A bewildered Vijay Madan, appointed the interlocutor by the very same ministry that made the announcement, was left high and dry. To make matters worse, twenty days later, the Telangana decision was put on hold. It was a sad reflection of how the political class functioned. It underlined the fact that most of the time governance in India was nothing but firefighting. Political expediency does not run governments; it only saves the politician and the party from slipping into oblivion. Forget about our immediate neighbours, even our own people do not trust our governments.

Sukhna: Too Clever by Half

Sukhna, which probably gets its name from the rare case of a female Asian elephant with tusks, is situated a short distance from Siliguri. The location is flanked by jungles to its north and east, while the rest of the area is occupied by sprawling tea gardens. Ever since a landslide blocked the main highway to Darjeeling, a fair number of civilian vehicles traversed the army area. With Siliguri fast expanding, the pressure on land was being felt in all directions, including Sukhna that until now was isolated.

Sometime in 2008, on one of my visits to XXXIII Corps, Deepak Raj showed me an area overlooking the Corps HQ. He said that a developer, backed by industrialists, was trying to come into the area with plans of implementing various schemes. It was fairly obvious that there would be serious security concerns, especially as the location overlooked not just the main helipad but also the Corps HQ itself. Nevertheless, I asked Deepak if it compromised his security. He said yes.

'Then put a stop to it,' I said. For the government of West Bengal to transfer the land to the trust, it was mandatory that a no objection certificate (NOC) be obtained from XXXIII Corps. Deepak had been the area commander in Kolkata prior to moving to Sukhna and he made sure there was no political pressure brought to bear. From command, we were backing the corps to the hilt and the matter was shelved, or so we thought. Deepak Raj handed over command to Lieutenant General PK Rath shortly after that.

Subsequently, an officer from command HQ who had been in the loop on the Sukhna case had gone to the Writer's Building, the seat of the Bengal Government, in connection with some other matter. He was shocked when the person he was meeting said to him, 'Ab to Sukhna mein NOC mil gaya hai. Ab to koi problem nahi hai.' (The NOC has been issued in Sukhna. So there should be no problem now.) Returning to Fort William, the officer reported the matter to his immediate superior, and this latest development was brought to my notice. The complete about-turn by the Corps HQ on an issue it had been fighting made absolutely no sense. There has to be a simple explanation to this, I said to myself, as I dialled Sukhna and waited for PKR to come on the line.

I asked Rath if he had signed the NOC. 'Yes, sir, they are building a school there.'

'School? What school?' I asked PKR if he had gone through all the previous papers pertaining to the case. I also told him that this was the first time I was hearing about a school.

A few days passed and I got some wishy-washy and vague replies from Rath. The impression being given by Corps HQ was that not only was the land to be developed into a school, it would have 20 per cent reservation for army children and jobs reserved for army wives. This was all an attempt to create a smokescreen, trying to make it look like there was a noble social cause behind the move; in any case, a school hardly diluted the security risk, which was at the core of the matter. With all the evidence staring us in the face that outside influence had been brought to bear in this deal where commercial interests were being served, I ordered the Corps HQ to cancel the NOC and also ordered that a court of inquiry be held to find out why an about-turn had been done on an issue of security.

At that point of time, Eastern Command HQ had little or no idea whatsoever that the MS in Army HQ would also be involved. However, all the skeletons in the cupboard now began to tumble out. It transpired that Avadesh Prakash had visited Sukhna and had been in touch with Dilip Agarwal, who, it turned out, had been awarded quite a few contracts in IMTRAT when Avadesh Prakash had been commandant IMTRAT in Bhutan.

For the first two months after taking over Eastern Command, I had been too busy to follow up on the age issue with the army chief who had promised to sort out the issue. I wrote to General Deepak Kapoor reminding him of his commitment. I got no response. Three months later I was in Delhi and together with Milan Naidu walked into the chief's office.

'I'm not going to do anything about it,' said Deepak Kapoor. 'The matter is closed as far as I'm concerned.'

What does one say, or do, when a superior officer, that too the Chief of Army Staff, pulls the rug from under your feet? I think the genial and soft-spoken Milan Naidu was as much in shock, for we both said nothing more about it. I returned to Kolkata, determined now to stand up to this blatant manipulation. By now, the game plan put into place was beginning to become clear. The last meeting with Deepak Kapoor had also made one thing very clear—the chief was not interested in a level playing field. If I took any further action seeking justice, I would be entirely on my own.

At this stage, I had decided to write to the MS yet again, asking them to explain the reason for fixing my year of birth as 1950. Avadesh Prakash had replaced Gangadharan as the MS by then and my letter triggered off yet another chain of letters. Interestingly, not once did the MS Branch answer the key question—on what basis was the decision being taken? Instead, the focus now shifted to the dots and commas in the subsequent correspondence. Then Sukhna happened. Neither the MS nor the chief were implicated in the scam at that stage.

That the chief tried to drag his feet on the Sukhna issue, only to be hauled up by Defence Minister AK Antony, is well documented by the media. Not only was Avadesh Prakash his MS, he had been GOC 17 Division when Deepak Kapoor had been the XXXIII Corps Commander. Whatever happened later had nothing to do with Eastern Command. The only thing that had become obvious to me by then was the fact that the 'higher ups' were upset with my ordering a probe. If I continued to buck the system, I could kiss any chance of taking over from Deepak Kapoor goodbye! In my mind, I was crystal clear; I had to fight it out, no matter what. If it would impact the next rank, frankly, at that point, like Rhett Butler in *Gone With the Wind*, I couldn't have given a damn.

Transformation Study

With a fair amount of time was being taken up by mundane issues, I looked forward to the Transformation Study that was given to me as Army Commander Eastern Command. First of all, I scouted around for some pragmatic and practical officers in the organization; officers who I knew would go into every detail of a problem and whose professional backgrounds would supplement and contribute immensely to the eventual output. JP Singh, who had taken over II Corps from me, was one of my first choices, as was VK Ahluwalia who was the Central Army Commander, and AK Singh, then in charge of Perspective Planning. There would eventually be a host of officers from various commands working under them, who would make invaluable contributions to the study.

Over the years, the Indian Army and the security forces across the board have seen many changes. The process of evolution has seen many individuals, past and present, who have influenced the thinking. There have been many Expert Committees over the years that have focused on the tooth-to-tail ratio, while almost every aspect of the armed forces has been studied and evaluated in great detail. The contribution of virtually every army officer towards this process, in some form or the other, can never be undervalued.

Sometimes mistakes are made, or circumstances change and it becomes necessary to fall back on previous existing systems. One man who greatly influenced the army was the enigmatic General Sundarji. His handling of Blue Star, Brasstacks and IPKF apart, he fast-tracked modernization in the Indian Army and the concept of strike corps and RAPIDS came to the fore, giving us a proactive capability which was built on the old adage 'offence is the best form of defence'. During the tenures of General Bipin Joshi and Shankar Roychowdhury, the RR had been raised and honed into a specialist CI force and so on. Most of these changes, however, had been specific to the Western Sector.

The first thing I did was go over every study that had been done in the past; in addition to the Kargil Review Committee headed by K Subramaniam, there were path-breaking studies done by Generals Shamsher Mehta, Chandra Shekar, KV Krishna Rao and a host of others. Each and every one of them had tackled key issues and made precise and workable suggestions. To our horror, we realized that not more than 20 per cent of the recommendations had seen the light of day.

'The non-implementation of suggestions needs to be tackled,' I advised the core group, 'otherwise we are wasting our time. For each category, we need to prepare an executive summary. DGPP will have to make sure that at least the Defence Secretary is appropriately briefed and a copy of the recommendations is provided to him on completion of the study.'

During the next few months, I began to visit most of the formations and schools of instruction across the country. This was in addition to the trips I had to make within Eastern Command; this resulted in my setting a frenetic pace, which the team soon got used to. We talked to various commanders in various theatres and set for ourselves the scope and grid for a comprehensive evaluation of the existing system. After a while we decided that as far as the Western Sector was concerned, we would not go in for accretive changes; the Eastern Theatre, on the other hand, required an overhaul that could require the restructuring and realigning of existing troops and, if necessary, the addition of new forces. In the east, a lot of practices went back to World War II days. We needed to review the system with an eye towards how things stood today. The basic framework having been defined, we got on with the job.

The Transformation Study also assessed the various strike corps. On paper, they were supposedly similar, but on the ground, the situation was quite different. Certain areas needed more punch in the form of mechanized forces, some lessons and shortcomings highlighted by Op Parakram still needed to be tackled, but most importantly, the army needed to transform the existing mindset by seeking and giving the forces on the ground a capability that was far more proactive in nature.

A lot of the earlier transformations had side-stepped Eastern Command altogether, this despite the fact that almost all our major battles have been fought in this theatre, be it 1962 when we were caught napping, or 1971 when for the first (and last) time post-WWII, a decisive result had been achieved with the force of arms. As part of the study, it was imperative that we look at the various existing segments, especially areas where disputes existed or were likely to crop up in the future. Most importantly, it was soon quite obvious that the force levels holding ground in the east were woefully inadequate. Not only was the region crying out for an accretive approach, it needed an overhaul that gave us some proactive capability in this critical theatre as well.

One major aspect of the Transformation Study was the need to synergize the army with other security forces. A classic case study was the 1979 Sino-Vietnamese War. A year earlier, the Socialist Republic of Vietnam (North Vietnam) had sent troops into Cambodia with the intention of neutralizing the Khmer Rouge. In March 1979, 400,000 Chinese troops supported by armour rolled across the border. The Vietnamese Army was not even on its own soil, but a force of approximately 70,000 border guards put up fierce resistance. Having suffered greatly, the Chinese decided to pull back on learning that regular Vietnamese forces were in the process of joining the battle.

In India, the creation and control of security forces seems to be the ultimate weapon in the hands of the political system and the bureaucrats. Various deliberate schisms have been created ever since the ITBP and the BSF were raised as border-guarding arms in 1962 and 1965 respectively. As a part of the unwritten 'divide and rule' policy, the functional control has been so complicated that today while the BSF and ITBP hold the two main borders, there is a highly fractured relationship existing on the ground.

After the Sumdorong Chu incident, a presentation was made to Prime Minister Rajiv Gandhi where MO3 was involved. It had been pointed out by General Sundarji that the existing arrangement with the ITBP was fraught with danger, mainly because there are problems in coordination. If the chemistry at the lower level was not good between the ITBP and the army units on the ground, the information comes to the army units deployed in the region via Delhi. Rajiv Gandhi seemed to be quite convinced that the systems needed to be looked at, but at that moment the Home Secretary whispered something in his ear.

The prime minister now applied the brakes, 'No, no, everyone will sit down. You show me that file. In the meantime, work out the arrangements for putting ITBP on the border under operational control of the army. We will take a decision soon.'

The DGMO, the Defence, Home and Foreign ministries all worked through the night, making specific suggestions to iron out the flaws. But there was no action taken at the end of this exercise. When a nation's leadership starts thinking that the army is going to take over the country one day, and so we must have forces which will support the political class, then we really are in trouble. The latest Chinese incursion in the DBO area had similar problems of coordination between the ITBP and the army.

On the disputed part of the border with Pakistan, the army and BSF work in close coordination, the latter being under the operational control of the army. This does not mean that the BSF battalion or the CO will not get his due. Yet, the mistrust is not only created, it is constantly being fanned. In the Annual Confidential Report forms, the chain of command, which is the army, is given a miniscule box where you can barely fit in three lines. There is a mistrust that is created because the politicians and the bureaucracy are determined to keep the two streams apart. This then permeates down the chain of command, where even basic issues are opposed. The BSF mans and operates its nakas in a particular way; if you tell them this is not the way to go about it, they turn around and say, 'Aisa hi hota hai.' (This is how it's done.) The fact that the life of a BSF jawan is miserable is of no consequence.

Similarly, in the Northeast, the Assam Rifles is not just a good force, it is one of the finest paramilitary forces anywhere in the world. In most areas, in the absence of any credible administration, it has been the glue that has held things together. It has also performed creditably wherever it has been tasked to do a job, be it in Tamil Nadu, Sri Lanka or J&K. Since Independence, the Assam Rifles has been exclusively officered by the army and functioned under its operational control even though it was a force under the Ministry of Home Affairs.

But somehow over a period of time we are losing the plot, because the people in the ministry who deal with Assam Rifles don't really understand what the force is all about. They think it is like any other police force. We need to clearly understand that this is not the case, it is by far our greatest asset in the Northeast. You just have to look at its record and see how well it has performed. After the Fourth Pay Commission, it was ordered to have a similar rank structure as the rest of the paramilitary forces. Until then the rank structure was the same as that of the army. Today, a constable who is doing the duties of a runner or serving tea in an office, under the assured career progression policy, is getting the same rank as others who are defending the integrity of the border. Where is the motivation? At some point, the bureaucracy said it is a paramilitary force, we need to get it out of the army's control. On issues like this, the political bosses move with alacrity—there are no delays when the boot is on the other foot. This is the biggest problem in the country.

So much irreversible damage has been done due to political shortsightedness. Take the instance of the Manorama Devi case that grabbed the headlines in 2004. When the whole thing erupted, the propaganda blitz put out by the Imphal Valley based groups was excellent. Human rights organizations, the media, everyone jumped into the fray and there was a massive uproar—'Manorama Devi: Raped and Killed by the Assam Rifles'. The facts of the case were totally different. However, by then the prime minister had personally rushed to Imphal and handed over the Kangla Fort to the civil administration and the Imphal area was declared AFSPA (Armed Forces Special Powers Act) free. The militants who orchestrated the drama probably enjoyed a good laugh—the Assam Rifles had been kicked out of the city and now they could sit in the heart of Imphal and call the shots. As far as the media was concerned, the actual facts that emerged from the inquiry did not interest them—neither Manorama Devi nor Kangla Fort were news anymore.

Knowing the fate of most studies (I think all of us working on the Transformation Study were familiar with the BBC masterpiece *Yes Minister*) we tried our best to tackle political and bureaucratic indifference. Transformation would require time, perhaps as much as twenty years, for it involved reorientation, training, new raisings, re-equipping and the merging of existing forces. Our objective was to place before the country through the government of the day, a blueprint that would, over a stipulated period of time, convert the armed forces of India into a 'capability based' force rather than leave it to stagnate as a 'threat based' force.

We were determined to try and make a difference, especially as the strategic interests of the country and the lives of our future soldiers were involved. The 'system' had to be stood up to and we had to put across, without fear or favour, what experts in each field felt was absolutely essential.

Two critical areas were potential minefields. The first involved logistics. A large part of the transformation would rely on restructuring the supply chain, which in many areas was archaic, the existing systems having been in place since World War II. This was an area that would be most resistant to change because no matter how trivial a commodity may seem, when it came to the army, the sheer numbers made it highly lucrative with the possibility of business interests going right up to the door of the MOD.

The Transformation Study not only suggested overhauling and modifying the various time honoured methods, we suggested that each formation up to the level of a division, should have a 'logistics' battalion which is the single point responsible for dealing with the ASC, EME and ordnance. Similarly the medical setup needed an overhaul to make it more responsive and effective. Like all concepts, we put this through a test bed in Southern Command before recommending it for implementation. It was a huge success, even though it raised the hackles of individual corps who felt the recommendations of the study were intruding on their turf. In the UK, I had visited a logistics unit where the CO was from the EME. The mantra was, *work together and merge together.* Sharpen the tooth-to-tail ratio.

Second was the carefully orchestrated web of checks and counter checks designed and surreptitiously implemented over the years to keep the armed forces at their heel. The standard answer justifying the non-implementation of the Kargil Review's recommendations has been that it is an already Integrated HQ. In my opinion, there cannot be a bigger smokescreen than that. The MOD is a replication of Service HQ saddled with its own internal bureaucracy.

Integration implies integration in decision-making, not a single-file system where after it has been cleared by a principal staff officer, five babus go over it. How the armed forces have been reduced to toothless tigers becomes obvious if we examine the functioning of the Department of Personnel and Training. As per the Rules of Business that guide the functioning of the Government of India, the recommendations of the departmental promotion boards are final. In the case of the army, air force and navy, this ruling has been stood on its head; the recommendations are 'recommendatory' in nature and can be altered by even a desk officer in the MOD. No wonder then that some officers reach certain levels on the basis of their networking skills rather than their professional acumen.

Surely in the interest of the country, this has to be stopped. Otherwise, the shortages will continue to haunt us and when the time comes, it'll be our boys who die while fitting wrong sized fuses in mines. No one is accountable; we only play with words. ('General saab, ab yeh procedural problems hain, we are trying'.) We tried to change all that in the Transformation Study.

Cracks in the Wall

Until I came to Kolkata as the army commander, I had very little to do with the city, other than occasionally transit through or make a quick trip to the Eastern Command HQ inside Fort William. Calcutta, or Kolkata as it is now called, meant stories of traffic, football and a city with the Hooghly running through it. The Command House, rechristened 'Senapati Bhawan' by KS Jamwal, shared a wall with the Alipur Zoo and it was not at all strange to wake up in the morning to the sound of a tiger calling loudly. So long as we were not downwind of the zoo, we could step out on to the first floor terrace and have a cup of tea while we watched a herd of cheetal in the adjoining enclosure. The other problem was the profusion of civet cats. Come sundown, they would start scratching at the windows and if they sneaked into the kitchen, that would be the end of all eggs and other goodies.

I knew a smattering of Bengali, having progressed a bit since my 'mota mati' days. As Bharti and I settled down into our routine in the city and got to know a large number of people, we got more and more enamoured with the city, and its people—their culture, their warm hospitality and above all, their incredible respect and love for the armed forces. I'm quite sure that nowhere else in the country is the man in uniform treated as well. Time and again, in the confusion of one way-streets outside Fort William, unsuspecting army vehicles would be coming against the traffic. Every time, the police would smartly stop the traffic and let the army vehicles get their orientation. I'm quite sure a lot of it has to do with the '71 War when the city had a ringside view of Bangladesh being liberated by the Indian Army.

Until I moved to Eastern Command, my entire CI experience was limited to Sri Lanka and the Kashmir Valley. In the case of Kashmir, the key reason for insurgency was the critical role played by Pakistan. Since Independence, with a lot of help from within our own country due to poor governance, they had managed to keep the fires burning. Quite frankly, there should never have been a problem in the Northeast had we had a policy that was inclusive, comprehensive and looking purely at our national interest.

If one looked at the root of almost every problem, complete apathy and political expediency emerged as the key culprit. On the face of it, the situation, in New Delhi's parlance, was 'under control', but the region was like a tinderbox where anything could happen at any time. In Assam, there were militant groups operating in North Cachar and Karbi Anglong. KT Parnaik, from the Rajputana Rifles had taken over from BS Jaswal and his IV Corps reacted superbly to the developing situation, understanding ground realities and mounting sustained pressure on the militant groups to bring them quickly to the negotiating table. In both these regions, under

Section 6 of the Constitution, the Government had long ago abrogated their responsibility by giving 'autonomy' to the region.

Another area of concern was the Muslim-dominated regions bordering the Dhubri-Kokrajhar belt, extending to the north bank districts of Assam that were being administered by the Bodos. Sometime in 2009 we started receiving intelligence reports that were suggestive of impending violence between various ethnic groups in the region. Among the Bodos we had information that two MLAs—Hagrama Mohilary, a former Bodo Liberation Tiger then aligned with the Congress, and Pradeep Brahma of the Bodoland People's Front—were playing their own games with an eye on the coming elections. As per our information, both were working on using Bodo militant groups with the intention of inciting violence in certain areas. The political grouping with which they were aligned was also willing to play its part by turning its back at a crucial time—all that was required was a certain amount of delayed activity or inaction that would allow the situation to snowball. The unchecked influx of Muslims in the area had set up the perfect target grouping. Additional intelligence coming in indicated that the Muslim leadership was also planning something 'big'.

Information technology works both ways. If our 'ears are to the ground', we can pick up the signs. For any group to go on a rampage, weapons have to be moved, and fuel stocked to burn down villages. In this case, the liaison between the security forces, the local army units and the intelligence agencies was good and we picked up a few telltale signs. 21 Division, which had a brigade in Kokrajhar moved fast, rounding up the ringleaders on either side. They were spoken to individually and told that if a single person was killed, any woman raped or any village burnt, they themselves would be held answerable. The proactive response defused the situation and we could once again breathe easy. But only just.

The very fact that army patrols started sweeping the area increased the confidence of the local population manifold. More intelligence started coming in. The criminal element, quick to realize that we were on to them, melted away but only to bide their time. At Eastern Command, we didn't need sanctions or permissions from Army HQ, we just moved at the first sign of trouble. The commanders on the ground did not need sanctions from us either. The troops were already there, the Armed Forces Special Powers Act was in place to give them the protection they needed. If even one commander had failed to move, or wasted time seeking permission,

I would have sacked him. If he was proactive and did his job, all of us in the chain of command would hold his hand.

In 2012, Kokrajhar exploded on the very same lines. Surely the same signs were there, the same quantum of force was available. Yet, over five lakh people got displaced, women got raped and more than a hundred people were massacred. Forget about proactive action, the army failed to respond for four days even when district commissioners from Kokrajhar, Udalguri, Chirang and Baksa were asking the army to step in. 'System delays', we were glibly told, when questions were asked. The media, after making a few noises, bought that explanation and moved on to the next bit of breaking news. The fact that army units were already present on the ground was ignored. The fact that in the build-up to the violence, security forces in the four affected districts were whittled down from 146 companies to 96 was left hanging in the air. Not one head rolled. No one was held accountable. No one asked the question 'why'.

It's much the same story everywhere, complete apathy and corruption at every corner. If the people entrusted with law and order are only interested in feathering their own nest, down the chain of command, no one is going to give a damn. If and when there is a national emergency, unless we are prepared, our forces razor sharp and ready, there will be mayhem. You move around the region and the stories are endless. Even animals are not spared. How can thousands of cattle on their way to Bangladesh's slaughterhouses get across a fenced border every night? It's very easy to claim that the herds, which are marshalled from regions as far away as Gujarat and Rajasthan, are swept along in the Brahmaputra. Nobody cares, the guards look the other way. How can there be pride in their uniforms? Do we seriously expect our border guards to dig in the way the Vietnamese dug in against the Chinese?

Human cruelty, tempered with greed, throws up scenarios that are completely bizarre. Recent reports suggest that there is rampant smuggling of camels across the Bangladesh border. For meat! I am told they are brought across in vehicles, made to lie down one on top of the other, and are smuggled across the border. Maneka Gandhi has reportedly red-flagged the issue recently and is said to be in contact with various chief ministers whose states are involved in the racket. I doubt any serious steps have been taken, and it makes me wonder if we really care.

▪

Land-locked and almost like a fortress, Manipur finds itself enclosed by the Naga Hills to the north, Myanmar to the east, the Lushai and Chin Hills to the south and the state of Assam on its southwestern flank. An independent kingdom with a 2,000-year-old history, it was the last princely state to come under British colonial rule. Its first recorded kingdom was established in the year 33 CE, with the coronation of Pakhangba. Formed by the unification of ten major tribes, the present day population of Manipur consists of three major ethnic groups—the Meiteis, who inhabit the valley; the Nagas and the Kukis, who are the people of the hills and who, as per chronicled history, were settled to provide protection to the valley.

In the complex web of politics that exist in the Northeast, insurgency in Manipur began as an ideological movement for the restoration of the pre-British supremacy for the Meiteis. However, owing to the emergence of multiple power centres with their own agendas, the movement turned into an ethnic conflict; the growth of Naga militancy combined with the fact that it was closely linked to the Nagas of Manipur made the insurgent movement more of a power struggle. A certain segment of Meitei youth followed Arambam Somorendra Singh, formed the United National Liberation Front (UNLF) and launched an underground movement.

It was only after Mizoram and Nagaland became states that Manipur began to make noises about getting statehood. That is one of the reasons the valley-based groups have tremendous support from the people. How would they survive otherwise, despite the extortion, despite the killings, despite all the criminal activity? Over the years, insurgency in Manipur has evolved into a hydra-headed monster, with the common citizen often being caught in the crossfire between the multiple underground organizations and the security forces.

The handling of Manipur, Nagaland, Mizoram and Tripura has been nothing short of ham-fisted and the army waits in standby mode for the next fire to erupt, and then goes rushing in to douse the flames. With a single road link that is at the mercy of Naga insurgent groups, the situation so easily slips from bad to worse in Manipur every now and then. When the balloon goes up, the standard procedure is to call the army in. When that happens, people are bound to get hurt, no matter what, so a cry goes up to do away with AFSPA and blame the security forces for all the ills that have taken place. There is no effort at better governance, no effort to make sure things which have happened in the past do not happen again.

In Nagaland, Angami Zapu Phizo, around whom the radical elements of the Nagas had gravitated, had voiced the claim that the Naga Hills and Tuensang District had never been part of British India and hence he was fighting for the sovereignty of Nagaland as a separate nation. In March 1956, the hostile Nagas established a 'Naga Federal Government' and hoisted their flag at Phensiyu village in the Rengma area and adopted a constitution, complete with their own parliament, governors and magistrates virtually duplicating the official administration. The Naga Home Guards went on to form their own army with proper designations, badges of rank and uniforms. The fighting force at that stage numbered around 3,000 men and they let loose a reign of terror in the countryside, forcing villagers to cooperate with them while extracting money and supplies from the people on pain of severe reprisals.

It took years of bitter fighting for the army and the Assam Rifles to bring the situation under control. Ever since, it had been a continuing struggle to get the Manipur and Arunachal Nagas to realize that the concept of a Greater Nagaland was not possible. Just when they had begun to get used to the new reality, the central government got itself completely outmanoeuvred by the NSCN (IM) General Secretary, Thuingleng Muivah, who was given permission to 'visit' his village which is in the Naga-inhabited Ukhrul district of Manipur. As was to be expected, the hundred-vehicle long cavalcade of Muivah was stopped at the Nagaland-Manipur border. The resultant blockade meant that the entire state of Manipur had to go without essential commodities. Economic blockades of Manipur have now become so common that sometimes they don't even make it to the news. On the ground, apart from the economic chaos, human suffering is of little or no concern to anybody.

Whatever the reason, the displacement of any large human population is tragic. Throughout history the Northeast has seen waves of refugees flee from neighbouring regions and from within. The escapees from Tibet in the 1950s, the Chakma from East Pakistan in 1964, the 1971 Bangladesh exodus, or more recently, the Reang, who were dislocated from Mizoram and continue to live in refugee camps in the Kanchanpur sub-division of North Tripura. Ethnic clashes and persecution by the Mizos forced the Reang to leave their homes in Mamit and Lunglei districts. Thirty-five thousand of them took refuge in the North District of Tripura in late 1997 and they continue to languish in camps that have since claimed several lives. They continue to await a solution, waiting to return home. We would bring all this to the attention of the concerned government agencies and we would get the standard answer, 'We're looking into it.'

The 3 Ts: Trilogy, TSD and Tatra

Even within the communities in the Northeast, they know very little about each other, most areas having evolved in geographical isolation. The area was so vast and so fragmented that very few people had a mental grip on it. Years of neglect and indifference had resulted in the Northeast becoming a black hole in the collective consciousness of the country. This seclusion, however, is relative—the Northeast is perhaps the hub through which connectivity with the rest of Southeast Asia can and will develop, and the security of the region, both emotional and tactical, is vital to India's long-term place in the sun. In the plains and in the hills, many ethnic and sub-ethnic identities exist. Together they share through language, culture, migration history and even religion and faith an anthropological connectivity. Yet this ethnic identity can be a double-edged weapon; it can bring people together or divide them from one another by building 'narrow domestic walls'.

One of the biggest problems that we faced in Eastern Command was the complete lack of knowledge about the peoples in the entire Northeastern region. Sometime in early 2009, Rakesh Loomba, who had replaced MS Dadwal as the III Corps Commander came to see me in Kolkata. He was extremely excited about a book he was working on along with Dipti Bhalla and Kunal Verma.

'The corps is doing the book. Rather than do a publication about ourselves, we are doing it on the region and the people.' Loomba said the book was being done free of cost and that he wanted me, as the army commander, to release it on 15 August.

I knew Kunal and his filmmaker wife. They had visited me in 2005 in Awantipur when I was GOC Victor Force and had presented the formation with copies of their films on the Kargil War, the National Defence Academy (*The Standard Bearers*) and also on the IAF. Kunal was the son of Ashok Kalyan Verma, my former colonel of the regiment. Loomba suggested I go through the book while it was still in a dummy shape and also talk to the authors who he said were looking at expanding the concept to include the entire Northeastern region.

The Northeast Palette was superbly done, documenting the entire sweep of the Naga Patkai. However, it was a large sized book that would severely limit its distribution. Karan Yadava, the DGAR had already asked the husband-wife team to do a pictorial documentation of the Assam Rifles as the force was due to celebrate its 175th year in 2010.

'What if we document the entire region, and put out a trilogy of books that is distributed throughout the country?' asked Kunal as we were poring over the pages of the dummy. 'We could help change the entire perception of the region.'

My mind was already racing. We discussed a smaller format and what would be the scope of each book. 'Go to Sukhna and Tezpur and discuss the framework with Sidhu and KT Parnaik, I'll see how we can progress this from our end.' A few days later I discussed the subject with Shankar Roychowdhury who was our elder in Kolkata and always rendered sound advice.

'You do this,' said the former chief, 'and you'll change the face of this country. You'll have the time of your life getting it past the bureaucracy though.'

I called in my chief of staff, Prem Goel and the BGS IW (Intelligence Warfare), Brigadier S Vishwanathan and asked them to slot the project under the head 'Perception Management'. I asked for a meeting to be convened at Fort William where BGS IWs and senior officers from all three corps would be present. 'Gentleman,' I said to the assembled officers, 'this is Psy Ops. And this time our target is our own country.'

With Sidhu, Parnaik, Loomba and Karan Yadava, the framework was worked out. It was imperative that not just Sikkim, but even North Bengal and the Cooch Behar region be included in the trilogy. However, General Roychowdhury was right about one thing, there was no way we were going to be able to push this through from Eastern Command, for we needed a certain quantum of helicopter support. By then Loomba had been posted to Army HQ as the DGMI. He advised Kunal and Dipti to first finish work on Assam Rifles. 'We'll work on the trilogy later,' he told me.

By then the government had announced that I would be taking over the reins from Deepak Kapoor who was due to retire in March 2010. Loomba was sitting in my office, his brow puckered. He had flown to Kolkata to discuss with me certain developments that had taken place since the 26/11 Mumbai terrorist attack in 2008. Having finished with all other matters, he now gave me a detailed brief on the real purpose of his visit.

In the immediate aftermath of the seaborne assault that had created mayhem in the city, the NSA (National Security Advisor) had asked the various intelligence agencies in the country if India had any covert capability to hit back at Pakistan. There had been a deafening silence and the NSA had turned to the army chief and asked him if Military Intelligence could create an organization. Deepak Kapoor had said he would look into it, and had then instructed the DGMI to work out the details and revert to him. A few weeks later Loomba had reported back to the chief, who by then was not receptive to the project any more. At that point of time, the chief barely looked up and told Loomba to shelve it.

As the chief-designate, it seemed only fair that the matter should be discussed with me. The DGMI then spelt out the blueprint, having increased the scope of the proposed Intelligence unit so it could also develop tentacles in other neighbouring and surrounding areas. The proposed budget for the new unit, especially when compared to the masses of money allocated to our existing covert agencies, was almost laughable.

'Are you serious? That's what it will actually cost?' I asked.

'Well, during the Military World Games the cost of the opening and closing ceremonies was a thousandth of what any other association would take to organize an event like that. This was amply proved later when you compared it to what was spent on the CWG. By the way, we need a name for this new unit. Something vague and obscure that doesn't draw any attention. I was thinking of calling it the Technical Services Division—TSD for short.'

'Go ahead,' I said. The DGMI nodded and closed his files.

The Transformation Study had more or less been completed. One area that would cause a lot of trouble for me subsequently was the existing procurement practices. We knew even looking into this issue would ruffle a lot of feathers, some of them extremely high up in government circles. Yet, we could hardly ignore the issues, especially since wherever we went, the officers and men would point out the existing flaws. One name kept regularly popping up—Tatra. These vehicles were being sold to the Indian Army at fantastic prices since the mid-1980s and even though they had been mated to various weapon systems over the years, most formations said they were generally off-road for want of spares. In one unit we were shown a 'brand new' Tatra vehicle that had met with a minor accident. The EME officer briefing us bluntly stated that the vehicle was an old vehicle that had been repainted and refurbished by BEML.

The Tatra trucks were Czech manufactured, and the company that supplied these was owned by Vectra, a London-based company which in turn dealt on all matters with BEML, a public sector undertaking. BEML then assembled the vehicles and sold them to the army which since 1986 had purchased over 7,000 of the all-terrain vehicles. The trucks that otherwise cost approximately ₹26 lakh in Czechoslovakia, were costing the army close to a crore each.

'It's like fitting square pegs into round holes,' we were repeatedly told. Apart from the chronic shortage of spares, the company had not even bothered to customize the vehicles for Indian conditions. They were all left-hand drives. As we studied the field reports and analyzed the data, we soon realized that if ever there was a sweetheart deal, this was it.

As we scratched around and looked under carpets and inside bonnets, it soon became more and more obvious that we were sitting on a wooden keg crammed with explosives. The entire procurement process seemed warped. We also looked at the gun factory in Jabalpur, which despite having one of the finest production lines in Asia, had simply stopped manufacturing because the army had not placed any orders for the 105 mm weapons.

Towards the end of 2009, there was a lot of speculation in the media about my 'deteriorating' relationship with General Deepak Kapoor. The general rule of thumb until then had been for the senior-most three star general who was considered to be the next in line, to move to Delhi as the vice chief should the post fall vacant. This was considered to be particularly important if the officer concerned had never served in Army HQ at a relatively senior appointment. The appointment of PC Bhardwaj, one of our most highly decorated officers from the Parachute Regiment, as the vice chief sent the rumour mills into a tizzy. The fallout of Sukhna was being touted as one of the reasons for my having been 'bypassed' and eventually Deepak Kapoor had to clearly spell out to the media that there was a clear hierarchy and there was no question of a fallout.

As far as I was concerned there was no substance to all this. I needed to stay on in Eastern Command, for the Transformation Study was still a few months away from completion. The chief had taken a decision with the all-important continuity factor in mind. Besides, for the media to link him to the Sukhna scandal owing to the fact that Avadesh Prakash was one of his key officers was uncalled for.

General Deepak Kapoor and I may not have been golf buddies or shared great chemistry, but in the armed forces there is little scope for 'deteriorating' relationships, and the sooner the media realizes that, the better it will be in the future. He had been my army commander when I was chief of staff in

XV Corps and even though he had gone back on his commitment to sort out the age issue, it did not affect our day to day dealings on other issues. In addition, as the Chief of Army Staff he had reposed his faith in me and given me a free hand in the all-important Transformation Study. That in itself was a great honour. Despite his denial that there was a rift, journalists continued to speculate on various issues. There were even irresponsible reports that the chief had gone to the government asking for me to be sacked, while others reported that a compact disk had been rushed to the prime minister and the chairperson of the UPA, Sonia Gandhi, in which I was purported to have threatened all politicians in the country.

Deepak Kapoor retired on 31 March 2010 and as is the norm, one of the units from Delhi Area gave the outgoing chief a Guard of Honour. One thing was very clear in my mind—as the next in line, I had to carry forward the good work done by all my predecessors. One of the greatest failings in the Indian Army has been the 'I, me and mine' culture which tended to undo everything positive done by anybody in the past. The *'every guy before me was an ass'* culture had to be thrown out. Our loyalty has to be to the country and to the army. Nothing else mattered.

12

CHIEF OF ARMY STAFF

The Baton

Bharti and I boarded an Indian Airlines flight on 30 March 2010, getting into Delhi from where we proceeded to Noida. My coursemate, Sandeep Gupta, who had commanded 5 Armoured Regiment and had been a sergeant in Cassino Company during our cadet days, hosted a dinner where a few close friends joined us at his home. Pratima, his wife, was the perfect hostess and it felt particularly good to be among people with whom I had shared so much. On the drive back to the Eastern Army Commander's hut in Delhi Cantonment, I watched the city with its perennial traffic whizz past the window. It was very different from the Delhi I had visited when I came from Pilani to Dhaula Kuan looking for my father's regimental officer. Then, the city would be deserted shortly after sundown, with virtually no traffic on the road. I remembered the air force officer and his wife who had taken me in, saving me from having to spend a night at the bus stand.

The next day, after my morning pooja, I asked Colonel Girish, my AMA and Major Rahul, the ADC, to explain the details of the taking over ceremony. I had been briefed earlier in Kolkata and had been told that the entire family should be present for the occasion. At 1155 hours on 31 March, I, along with my family, walked into the office of the Chief of Army Staff. General Deepak Kapoor and his wife received us and, after a few pleasantries, the outgoing chief asked me to move to the business end of the table. We shook hands, wished each other the best of luck, and then I saw the general off.

The next day was easily one of my most special. I had been commissioned into 2 Rajput and had joined the battalion in Delhi. Apart from the Red Fort, the other half of our duties revolved around Rashtrapati Bhavan. The change of guard at Vijay Chowk, the head-butting ram from Tangdhar, the sound of boots marching down the slope past South Block, were all alive in my head as I approached the makeshift saluting base. Lined up in front, resplendent in their rhododendron-red safas, were men from my battalion, lined up to present me with a Guard of Honour. Commands were shouted and the band began to play. The Regimental Colours (on which were emblazoned battle honours that went back two hundred years and more), were held aloft proudly as I went past. The back of my throat felt dry as my hand came up in a salute. From being a subaltern in the battalion a long time ago, I was now the twenty-fourth chief of the Indian Army.

To one side of the Guard of Honour, the media was waiting. Major General Sanjeev Madhok from the Brigade of the Guards was the ADGPI and he had managed to do the impossible. He had the media standing respectfully behind a flimsy line during the ceremony. As I approached, there was bedlam and, before I realized it, I had television and still cameras in a tight circle around me.

After Independence, there had been two British chiefs. Field Marshal 'Kipper' Cariappa, had been the first of a distinguished line of Indians. Each one of my predecessors had brought something to the Indian Army in his own unique way. During highs and lows, triumphs and disasters, each man did what he could for the service.

Sitting in the chief's office in South Block, I would rarely get a minute to myself. I sat and mulled over my priorities, something I had been going over in my head. Theoretical points were one thing, converting them into actionable points was where the challenge would lie. At the top of the list was implementing the Transformation Study, partly because of its all-encompassing nature. The second point on my agenda was to give the Eastern Theatre a lot more emphasis. After General AS Vaidya, in 1983, I was the next chief from Eastern Command, which in itself was an indicator of our western orientation. Third, shortages needed to be tackled and solutions found to problems, even if they seemed insurmountable. Fourth, the working of Army HQ needed to be improved, for it sometimes seemed to me that we had begun to mirror the mentality of the babus. Fifth, we needed to take better care of our men—improve their rations, the quality of their uniforms, their living conditions, schooling for their children, speed up work on their KLPs, many of which were languishing and so on. Naturally, I would not be dealing with these issues myself, but would have to keep up the pressure on those who were to handle these key areas. Lastly, we needed to do away with the sahayak system and come up with an alternative.

In the days prior to my taking over as chief, the Sukhna incident had assumed much larger proportions than had ever been envisaged when I ordered the court of inquiry. Once the balloon had gone up, other names had started to emerge. During my farewell round across Eastern Command, I had been talking to officers and men across the board. What was most alarming, and very evident, was the widening gap between the junior and senior officers, as the former were increasingly sceptical about their seniors who seemed to be misusing resources and getting involved in all sorts of scams. Sukhna had shaken us all to the core, for it was amazing just how deep the malaise actually was. In the aftermath of the Bangladesh War, as junior officers, we had seen the entire war effort get diluted because of the greed of some senior officers at the time.

We had watched in horror then, when bribes were something that some border guards took to look the other way. We were the Indian Army and the only thing that mattered to us was the izzat of our respective units. Now the men were appraising us, especially in the aftermath of the Sukhna scam, to see if we could actually stand up and cleanse the system.

'We have to look at our internal health,' I said, underlining my main priority, 'we have to put our own house in order. We cannot fight unless we address a few core issues.' I knew it was a tall order for, in a million-strong army, there will be the occasional fish which dirties the pond. I also knew in our existing system of 'justice', it was well-nigh impossible to nail a man on the grounds of 'corruption'. However, we had to try and I also knew it would be a long process. Things would not happen overnight. But more than the officers, it was the men I was concerned about; they were watching our every step. We were fooling ourselves if we thought that the rank and file was unaware of what was happening.

As chief, my first visit was to the Kashmir Valley. I would say much the same thing to the men, be it individual units or groups of young and senior officers: we had to stand up and be counted. Once we became a part of the army, our lives were not ours anymore. Everything we did, or didn't do, reflected on the institution. Situations of combat often depended on blind obedience; but at other times, I told the men, we must refuse to follow orders if we thought we were being manipulated or felt that something was wrong. We had to do what was right and that was something I expected each and every soldier in the army to be able to discern.

I had taken over as the colonel of the Rajput Regiment from Milan Naidu while I was still the Eastern Army Commander. Milan had handed over the baton while he still had two months to go. However, even though the regimental secretariat shifted and I took on the work, I did not call myself the colonel of the regiment or fly the flag until Milan retired. Brigadier JP Singh, who had commanded 16 Independent Armoured Brigade when I was in Ambala, was my choice for the critical job of the MA (normally chiefs picked someone from their own regiment but I was of the view that the chief was for the entire army and not just the regiment he was commissioned into), while Lieutenant Colonel N Romeo from 2 Rajput came on board to help me handle regimental matters.

Shankar Ghosh, from the Brigade of the Guards was the Western Army Commander, while VK Ahluwalia was looking after Central Command; BS Jaswal had moved from IV Corps to Northern Command; CKS Sahu from the artillery was looking after South Western Command; Pradeep Khanna of the armoured corps was in Southern Command while ARTRAC was being commanded by AS Lamba, also from the artillery. Bikram Singh from Sikh LI had taken over Eastern Command from me.

We had an excellent bunch of PSOs (principal staff officers) and lieutenant generals at Army HQ, all of whom were my friends—I had served with them or done courses with them. The vice chief continued to be Prabodh Bhardwaj, while JP Singh from the Transformation Study was one of the deputy chiefs (P&S), the other being Virender Tonk from the Rajputs. GM Nair (he had been the brigade major in 76 Brigade in Sri Lanka) had taken over the job of the MS from Avadesh Prakash; Mukesh Sabharwal, also from the Rajputs, was the AG. The DGMO was my coursemate, Amarjit Sekhon, from Sikh LI; the QMG was SS Kumar from the Brigade of the Guards; Rakesh Loomba was the chief spook and Balraj Nagal was in charge of Strategic Forces Command.

The first few days as chief saw an almost endless stream of visitors. It was also incumbent on me to visit various people in government. So hectic was the pace that the initial period is a blur. With invitations pouring in for various functions, I soon had to instruct my staff to limit social engagements. Time management for the chief is always a big problem.

To complicate matters, the army commander's conference was slated for April. This gave me no time to prepare. I asked Army HQ to sound out the army commanders and the Ministry of Defence, and postpone the conference to May. During the previous two conferences, I had felt that there had been too many presentations and hardly any discussions. I let it be known that the conference would concentrate on discussing issues while presentations should be reduced drastically.

We moved into Army House on Rajaji Marg after Deepak Kapoor moved to 20 Mandir Marg in Dhaula Kuan, a house reserved for ex-chiefs who remain, for some time, under 'Z' category security. As was the norm, the army continued to afford him all the privileges for well over a year, before he moved out to his personal residence. Army House was close to Army HQ, and I quickly settled into my new routine.

Yogja had finished her management studies in Kolkata and had started working in Gurgaon. Sangram, now a lieutenant colonel, was posted in Central Ordnance Depot, Delhi. Once we moved to Army House, in spite of running her own establishment in the cantonment area, Mrinalini took over a fair amount of the social duties, allowing Bharti to concentrate on her job as President of AWWA.

Snakes and Ladders

The highest priority for us at Army HQ was to immediately implement the Transformation Study. JP Singh, who had been an integral part of the study group, was entrusted with translating the study into actionable points that could be handled within the army and did not require the involvement of the Ministry of Defence. There were long discussions with Vinay Sharma, the MGO (master general ordnance) and Ajay Chandele, the DGEME (director general electrical & mechanical engineering) pitching in with their expertise. I wanted a system that would monitor the entire progress and identify the immediate bottlenecks. JP did an outstanding job.

The other aspect that caught my attention at the very outset was the sense of resignation, almost despondency, at Army HQ. For a soldier file-pushing is never an exhilarating job, but pushing files where it is a foregone conclusion that everything you try to do is going to be mired in red tape the moment it leaves your desk can numb the brain.

For years, especially after I had taken over as the Colonel GS of 12 Division, it had become obvious to me that things were far from ideal on the ground. Every one of us who served on the staff in operational formations was acutely aware of the shortages—war stores, ammunition or the state of the equipment. As I've said earlier, all we could do at our level was to highlight the issue. We had to improvise most of the time, somehow managing with what we had. Exercises and war games were one thing, where shortages could be incorporated into the setting, but in an actual warlike scenario, it could knock the bottom out of even the best-laid plans. The failure of the strike corps to move according to the required time schedule after the Parliament attack had been the biggest eye opener.

We started to look for answers. Until I took over as the chief, I actually had no idea about how the overall system worked. One of my first priorities was to study how the procurement system functioned. I was assisted in understanding this by some of the best brains in the army. As we examined the complicated system in detail we grew ever more astonished. And despondent. Even though we knew the drawbacks of dealing with the political, bureaucratic and financial institutions, when looked at as a whole, we realized we were dealing with an impossible situation.

The reasons soon became obvious. Unlike the navy and the air force which were platform (single weapon) centric, the army's requirements were far more widespread and diverse. As far as the world of the babu was concerned, each requirement was a 'file' and it didn't matter if the item the army needed was worth one-millionth of what a ship or an aircraft would cost. It would have to go through exactly the same process and would take the same amount of time. In our case, from the moment we said we wanted X or Y piece of equipment, the minimum time required to get it was thirty-six months, *if everything went well.* At every corner there was a babu, armed with a 'procedure' book, waiting to nix whatever had been asked for or put up. Incidentally, they have a rather cute word for it. They call it 'observations'. It's a finely-honed game of snakes and ladders, where, as far as the services are concerned, the ladders have been taken away and only snakes rule the roost.

Year after year, the defence budget has a sizeable chunk of money allocated for acquisitions and other projects. Army HQ has to function within that and proposals are drawn up accordingly at the beginning of each financial year. Yet, amazingly, not once had the army ever been able to fully utilize the money and it would regularly be re-appropriated by the government at the end of the year as 'unutilized' money. We decided to treat the financial year 2010-2011 as a test case; we would try and identify the bottlenecks and JP and his team would then put their heart and soul into making sure the files were not tucked away somewhere.

Quite frankly, I think we took the finance boys in South Block completely by surprise, and actually overshot our budget. At the end of the year, it was the RM (raksha mantri) who pointed out that for the first time in India's history, the army had actually done what it had never done before: fully utilized the budget allocated.

Along with the rations, we had been plugging for the men to be given cloth for their uniforms, allowing them to get them stitched according to fit. Perhaps inspired by the readymade garment market, the Ordnance Factory Board had been given the task. The buzzword here was 'readymade' sizes. In the case of China, it is interesting to note that when the PLA decided to change their baggy uniforms to something smarter, a time limit of twelve months was stipulated. Four months before schedule, every member of the Chinese Army had been delivered two uniforms on hangers, the size a perfect fit. In our case, the 'large' would fit the 'small', while the colour of the shirt would differ by a few grades from the trousers. Our complaints were met with terse 'PSUs have the most modern plant and better than any private concern'. Makes you wonder who is supporting whom.

Two areas of immediate concern were (a) to replace the aging Cheetahs with light helicopters and (b) to bridge the deficiency in artillery. The helicopter deal had almost been inked with Eurocopter during General JJ Singh's time, but discrepancies in the selection of the helicopter had soon come to light. The deal had been scrapped. The process of shortlisting and looking at modifications was on.

A similar stand-off had arisen with guns. The army wanted an Ultra-Light Howitzer (ULH) and the project had been going round in circles even before my time. To our horror, we found that the GSQR (general staff qualitative requirement) for guns had been tweaked to favour Singapore Technologies' Pegasus 155 mm, virtually ensuring that it would boil down to just one gun system. However, Singapore Technologies ran into trouble and had come under a cloud, so we had no option but to start looking at the US M777 which the Americans were willing to sell under Foreign Military Sales (FMS). Here too, we found ourselves stuck, for the Defence Secretary, in his wisdom, insisted on the same GSQR being applied as for the Singapore gun. DG Arty and the DCOAS categorically stated that 'the stipulated conditions for the gun had no operational meaning under Indian conditions as also that the FMS system did not require GSQR', but the Defence Secretary was adamant, saying 'we'll give you deviations at the appropriate time'.

By now, I realized that in our existing scenario, one could not presume anything. My meeting with the Ordnance Factory Board (OFB) while I was in Eastern Command had stayed at the back of my mind. The Minister of State for Defence, Pallam Raju, had been present on the occasion. Ever since then, I had been trying to coax the OFB to snap out of its lethargy. I sent officers to take a look at the Gun Coach Factory in Jabalpur. They returned saying it was a state-of-the-art factory, but it had been lying unused now for years. Everyone was being paid their salaries, but since the IFG 105 mm was no longer in production, they had been sitting around and waiting for orders. I asked Army HQ to dig up every conceivable document we could find about the last successful artillery deal that had been struck with Bofors two decades ago. We were in for a shock.

'As part of the Bofors deal, we were supposed to produce the gun under license in India. A major part of the money that was paid to Bofors was for the transfer of technology,' my officers reported back.

'So…who has this technology?' I asked, acutely aware that the gun had never ever been manufactured in India.

Sure enough, when we asked, our superbly efficient Ordnance Factory Board reported back saying they had the technology, but they had never manufactured the gun because nobody ever told them to.

'The army kept changing the specifications,' said the Ordnance Factory Board, trying to explain why it had never even mentioned that it was sitting on the blueprints for twenty-five years, 'They wanted to change the calibre from 155/39 to 155/52.'

This was unbelievable, though completely in keeping with the nonsensical approach we have adopted towards our defence needs. Perhaps to keep the mud from splattering across their faces, the Ministry of Defence did not try to stop Army HQ from telling the Gun Coach Factory in Jabalpur to get moving and produce a couple of prototypes. Once the cat was out of the bag, the two prototypes were produced within no time and during the recently completed trials through 2012, the gun has performed admirably.

DRDO, which hitherto had been concentrating on other aspects of design, and having produced superb buildings and infrastructure to house themselves, now told the army that they could also look at producing the 155/52, which is what we ultimately want.

Someone seriously needs to look at the functioning of DRDO and for the sake of the country, shake it long and hard. Take the case of the INSAS rifle: when it was designed, the GSQR was that it should be able to penetrate NATO-standard body armour. The muzzle velocity resulted in a flat trajectory with a reasonably good barrel. However, the weapon had problems but these were not addressed beyond a point. Ordnance factories are absolutely dead when it comes to R&D, relying entirely on DRDO to throw up designs and solutions. DRDO, in turn, would rather design something new than work on the old design, since new projects attract better funding.

But the bigger shock was yet to come. Having first looked at BEML and the Tatra truck while looking at procurements as part of the Transformation Study, I asked for more information, especially as an order for approximately seven hundred additional vehicles was awaiting Army HQ's nod.

Basically, they were good vehicles, with an independent suspension which allows for easier all-terrain use. Even then (early 1980s), the GSQR seemed to have been tweaked to allow the deal to go through. Apart from the suspension, the other factor that sealed the deal in Tatra's favour was the fact that the vehicles had air-cooled engines. The weightage given to this seemed a bit far-fetched. The QR had stated that because the required vehicles would also be used in the desert, air-cooled engines were preferred because 'there would be no water to put into radiators'. Air-cooled engines were huge, and somewhere along the line, after having got the deal, the Czechs had switched to the smaller Renault engine. However, the assembly line for vehicles being sent to BEML was not changed kind courtesy the middleman who supplied these to BEML.

This just wasn't making any sense. We were continuing to pay BEML almost four times what the vehicles were costing them. What was even more amazing was the fact that the chairman and managing director of BEML had been at the helm for twelve years, and his networking skills had plugged him into a lot of 'helpful' friends. There were murmurings that the relatives of a senior bureaucrat at the PMO had been given plots in the BEML housing society and the son of a top official at the Planning Commission had been living in the BEML guest rooms for more than a year.

'Don't ask too many questions, sir,' I was advised by those in the know of the procurement business. 'The trail goes right up to a very high official in the PMO.'

'Of the seven hundred vehicles, I want a list of those which are the absolute necessary buys,' I said to the MGO, Vinay Sharma. 'Until then, red-flag the file till we have a more realistic picture of what is happening. No decisions will be taken without the consent of the chief's office. This fraudulent nonsense simply has to stop.'

It's not just BEML and Tatra, almost all public sector undertakings function in a manner that defies logic. The government wants them to show profits, which is impossible if they follow normal trade practices. Hence, over the years, they've actually devised a methodology of fictitious 'pricing' to enable them to do so. Nobody else in their right mind would accept these rates, so the armed forces are their bunnies through the bureaucrats.

Though I had more or less kept my opinion entirely to myself, the grapevine was abuzz, simply because we were asking a few questions. A senior naval officer, a former commandant of the National Defence Academy, while talking of civil-military relations, claimed I was jeopardizing the existing system. He suggested I was being naïve and attributed this to the fact that I had not served in the upper echelons of Army HQ earlier. 'You cannot beat the system,' was the refrain one heard from various quarters. I wondered what he expected me to do. In fact, I wondered if the whole lot of such senior officers had lost their sense of pride.

The Apple Tree

The military assistant (MA) managed my daily appointments. Keeping to the schedule was a major challenge, for there would always be someone or the other from Army HQ who would be waiting. As a rule, I hated having to keep any officer waiting. Soon others too realized there was no point wasting time on social chitchat. Take a decision, I kept telling myself. If, for some reason, I make a mistake, so long as our objectives and goals are clear, it will rectify itself.

A recently retired officer, whom I shall refer to as 'the middleman', was up next at 1100 hours on 22 September 2010. He had retired a couple of months earlier as a general. I had had very little interaction with him previously. Once or twice, while still in uniform, 'the middleman' had called on me at the office on regular work issues. Post-retirement, he was hoping to get a job with one of the organizations linked to the services and I assumed he was coming to see me in that connection. After some general talk, 'the middleman' came to the point.

'There is a file with you on Tatra. If the file is passed, you will get ₹14 crores.'

I found myself staring at him. It was like someone punching you in the solar plexus. 'The middleman' was looking at me intently.

'You don't need to get angry, sir. Aap ke pehle bhi log bagh lete rahen hai, aap ke baad bhi log bagh lete rahenge.' (People before you have taken money, and people after you will continue to do the same.)

'Just get out of my office,' I managed to tell him, 'get out and never come again.'

In my entire career, I had never had to face such a situation. Here was a man who had just hung up his uniform, having been honoured by the country that had allowed him to wear stars on his collar. He was a product of NDA, IMA and like so many of us, had been a part of the Indian Army. I had never felt smaller in my life. Everything was a whirl inside my head. I reached for the line that connected me to JP. 'See if the RM is in his office. I need to see him, now.'

It was almost lunchtime when I walked into the RM's office. I told him what had happened with 'the middleman'. AK Antony buried his face in his palms, then looked up and slapped his forehead.

'Hon'ble Minister,' I said to him, choosing my words very carefully, 'if you feel, if the government feels, I am a misfit in the system, just tell me and I will go now. Otherwise this sort of nonsense has to stop. We cannot have things like this happening.'

'Yes, yes, yes...' the RM was at a complete loss for words. 'No, no, I like your way of working. Nothing to be done, we have to be careful.'

'These files will not be cleared by me,' I said.

'Yes, yes, you take action.'

Apart from informing my immediate superior, the RM, of the incident, the options available to me were to stop the desired recommendation and ban the officer's entry from my office. I then asked for the MGO and Rajinder Singh, who was the DGSD. I told them that I wanted to know how we had arrived at a requirement of seven hundred vehicles. Apart from the systems that were Tatra-specific, I wanted to know the exact, actual, on-ground requirement. Subsequently, about 150 vehicles that were essential were ordered. Even the figure of seven hundred turned out to be a tweaked figure.

We got on with our work. One year and six months later, 'the middleman' would surface again.

I was not aware of it at that point of time, but wheels had already been set in motion that would unearth one of the most shameful scams that would involve a host of senior naval and army officers (including 'the middleman'). The Commander-in-Chief, Western Naval Command, Vice Admiral Sanjeev Bhasin, had a week earlier written to the Chief of Navy Staff, Nirmal Verma, alleging that a prime defence plot had been grabbed by senior bureaucrats, politicians and senior service officers.

The Southern Army Commander, Pradeep Khanna, had been asked to look into the matter. For quite a few years, there had been talk within the army that the defence land opposite the infantry mess in Mumbai had been hijacked and earmarked for flats.

Pradeep Khanna presented the report to me. 'We have deliberately not named the two former chiefs,' said Pradeep, 'though the entire list of officers is appended as a separate document.'

The report was not only damning, it was scandalous and sickening. Here we had not only the involvement of the defence estates officer, but the entire lot of army officers who could have put a stop to the nefarious scheme. Like the Sukhna case, where the developers had claimed they were building a school, the Adarsh Housing Scheme had given itself a fig leaf by claiming it was being done for Kargil widows. I was familiar with the area. The 25 Rajput officer's mess, when the unit was in Mumbai, had been bang opposite the plot that had been appropriated. To make matters worse, the building was a high-rise and had a spectacular view into just about every naval and army unit. Anybody could tell you it was a major security threat.

I read the attached list. I knew it was just a matter of time before the press got wind of the names, after which the services would be running for cover. My biggest worry was what I would tell the men and the junior officers who would see the news splashed across television channels and newspaper headlines. These men, sitting in faraway places, day in and day out putting on camouflage paint on their faces and moving out at sunset to guard the border, securing the country, and willing to pay any price for what they all believed in, would all be inundated by this 'breaking news'. The 'Kargil widows' touch made it even more cynical. I had never felt lonelier sitting in my office. Like Antony, I found myself holding my head in my hands.

The report went to the ministry. The names of one naval chief and two army chiefs could not be kept under wraps for long. However, all three of them immediately issued a statement offering to return the flats that had been allotted to them. Within the country, the dictionary got expanded, as 'Adarsh' became one more word that was synonymous with corruption in high places. The alleged involvement of the Maharashtra chief minister's family and a host of senior bureaucrats in the housing scam took some of the heat off us. By December, the chief minister had tendered his resignation.

■

Sometime in November, I was told that there had been two RTI applications filed from Kolkata and Delhi, respectively, pertaining to my year of birth. Ever since Deepak Kapoor had gone back on his word and refused to sort out the issue, I had walked away from the entire episode in disgust. Subsequently, I had been much too busy with the Transformation Study and then as the chief to bother with anything else. A section under the Provost Marshal which deals with these matters received the RTI applications and, since all records pertaining to the age of an officer are maintained by the AG's Branch, the file was sent there asking for a suitable answer.

At this point of time, the entire match was being played in the opposition's half. Tatra had been red-flagged and I had told the RM that Army HQ would not clear the file until we reviewed our requirements afresh. Though the ministry was doggedly dragging its feet on the implementation of the Transformation Study, the army was already going ahead with the actionable points which didn't involve the ministry. Most importantly, Army HQ under Deputy Chief JP Singh, was being extremely proactive, identifying the bottlenecks and roadblocks, and all our acquisitions-related proposals were moving. And, finally, in spite of the embarrassing involvement of senior officers and former chiefs in the Adarsh Housing Society scam, the army was clearly not going to brush anything under the carpet.

AG's Branch checked with the MS Branch and found that both departments had the same year on all the records, though the MS Branch was now in an embarrassing position owing to the stance taken on the issue ever since I had been approved for lieutenant general. Since the matter referred to my own case, I could obviously not give a ruling on the matter, so it was decided to refer it to the legal branch of the Ministry of Defence, headed by an officer from the Ministry of Law who was attached to the Ministry of Defence.

The law officer wrote out his comments and marked the file to the Ministry of Law. Various people in the Law Ministry looked at it, and it eventually came back with a simple ruling. 'The School Leaving Certificate will determine the age of the officer in question.' This document was now beginning to resemble the tattered flag on the ramparts of Bharatpur, for its authenticity, validity, genuineness and carbon dating had been done with the Birla Public School, the Rajasthan Education Board and god alone knows what else.

AG's Branch now wrote to the Ministry of Defence stating the opinion of the Law Ministry: the year of birth of the officer would stay at 1951 as it was in their records from the time the officer was commissioned. I asked for an appointment with the RM, and briefed him on the Law Ministry's ruling. I requested the minister to ask the Ministry of Defence to follow the law, sort out the matter once and for all. I also said that if he so desired, I was willing to give a commitment that I would demit office in May 2012.

'No, no, we will look into it,' said Antony. After a few seconds he added, 'We will send it to the Attorney General.'

I departed, wondering what the Ministry of Defence would do next. The matter was referred to Pradeep Kumar, then the Defence Secretary. What transpired in the next few hours would be conjecture, so suffice it to say that two questions were framed to the Attorney General. The questions were so simple that actually it was an insult to send it to the highest law officer in the country, for any two-year old could have answered them.

Question 1: Can an officer change his date of birth?

Question 2: Will it disturb the 'pre-set line of succession'?

The answer was no and yes, respectively. The Attorney General, however, added that 'under no circumstances should the line of succession be altered'. Just what that meant, nobody except Ghoolam E Vahanvati, the Attorney General of India could answer.

The RM called me to his office and told me what the Attorney General had said. I laughed and asked him what else could be expected if the questions were put in this manner. Besides, since when did the army or the navy or the air force have a 'line of succession'?

This nonsensical farce was now assuming yet another dimension. As laid down by the Government of India, an army chief's tenure is either three years from the day he takes over, or till the end of the month when he turns 62. Here I was, repeatedly telling the RM that I would give it in writing that I would quit at the end of May 2012 if the government wanted me to go, just don't go on and on making a tamasha out of nothing.

'Why don't you get the view of an independent body?'

'No, no,' said the RM, 'Attorney General only.'

It was beginning to feel like I was back in Poonch, making those endless hikes up and down from the post every day as every attempt was made to create a case against me. The people who had filed the RTI applications knew that all they had to do was throw a pebble, the ripples would take care of everything else. When I had decided to order a court of inquiry into the Sukhna episode, a senior regimental officer had said to me then: 'Soch lo, yeh cheez kabhi bhi prove nahin ho sakti. Idhar udhar se nikal jate hain, ulta tumhare peeche bhairiyon ke jaise ayenge.' (Think about it. These things are hard to prove. They'll escape, and then come after you like wolves.)

The knives were coming out. The main difference between Poonch and now was that I was no longer a junior officer, an anonymous face in a multitude of olive green. I was now the chief of the Indian Army and in this strength lay my vulnerability.

By now I had been in the hot seat long enough to know exactly what was going on. I knew I wasn't suffering from any paranoia, that there actually was an incestuous link between everything that was happening. Sukhna, Adarsh, Tatra, arms deals: the same people were involved, different circles with overlapping areas of interest, yet with a common core supporting them. For me this was the moment of truth. I had stood for what I believed to be right; I could run away, bury my head in the sand and forget about everything we had tried to do or were trying to do. Or, I could stand up and fight it out, knowing that the chances of succeeding were very small. I also knew that if I dug in, it would have to be a lonely battle. My own organization would stand behind me for a while, but gradually each man would have to safeguard his own future. The 'line of succession' in any case had already polarized the system.

On all my visits to various formations, I had been addressing the officers and the men. On all occasions, I had spoken to them frankly about procurements and the problems we faced. I wanted them to understand the system and how we were trying to fight it by simply standing up to it. I would ask them to do their bit by ensuring that they upheld the ethos of the army and concentrated on the job at hand. 'Nobody has seen tomorrow, so just concentrate on your today. Do your work with sincerity, you will be recognized. You don't have to do anything silly to jump over the heads of your colleagues and your peers.'

The system was being manipulated and that the strings were in the hands of some of the most powerful people in the country was obvious. I knew I was running out of options. I did not see myself as a hero trying to take on the system, nor did I look at it as some modern day David versus Goliath scenario. For me, it was a simple decision. I could roll over and get 'fixed' and never be able to look the organization, the officers and the men in the eye. Or, I could stand for what I believed in, even if it meant being isolated and fighting a private war for my honour. I don't think there ever was a choice in the matter.

The opinion of four retired Chief Justices of India was sought by well-wishers. They were unanimous in their opinion that the school leaving certificate was the final authority to establish an individual's age and since there was no ambiguity about its authenticity, the matter should end there. I made out a petition, attached the opinion of the four former Chief Justices and sent it to the RM. Copies were also sent to the President of India and the Prime Minister's Office. There was perhaps a slim hope that someone would see the logic, reason and the law of the land.

The End of the First Year

In March 2011, despite all the other problems with the kingdom of babus, Army HQ could take a lot of satisfaction from having used up the allocated budget. Emboldened by our success, we decided to leave nothing to chance for the 2011-2012 budget, and two months before the start of the new financial year, we had all our fresh proposals in place. The Defence Secretary was given a list of 106 proposals for the coming financial year. We now presumed that the bureaucrats and Defence Finance were also happy that we had finally broken through the glass ceiling. Finally, at least on this front, we thought we were making some progress.

We should have known better. During my first year, we had caught the bureaucrats unawares, as a result of which the ultimate miracle had taken place. In the month of April, the Joint Secretary (Acquisitions) was quietly posted out. For the next seven months, no one was posted in his place. It was as blatant as that. For nine months, all proposals sat in files that were not even opened, for no one else in the ministry could or would initiate the process. At the time, we had no clue of how things were going to pan out, but as days went by and weeks became months, the full realization of what we were up against began to emerge.

In the defence budget, the money earmarked for acquisitions is, in my jargon, an 'unplanned' budget. Using hypothetical figures, consider this: at the beginning of the year, the government allocates ₹10,000 crore towards 'acquisitions' for which Services HQ is expected to put up its proposals. In the past few decades, there could not have been a single year when Army HQ failed to put up proposals for 100 per cent utilization of this money. Yet amazingly not once had the army been able to utilize all the money that would regularly be re-appropriated by the Finance Ministry as 'unutilized' funds. Towards the end of each financial year, the government takes stock of how many proposals are through and how much money is likely to be 'unspent'. It is, quite simply, the biggest con that is played on the people of this country. The question that needs to be asked at this stage is: where does this money go?

Every year, government after government announces various populist schemes. How are these schemes run? Where does the money come from? The budget does not cater for it. Theoretically, other departments within the government also give up their unspent funds, but in most of their cases, the quantum of 'unplanned' funds is much lower. Hence, the first casualty is the defence budget which is treated as a cushion available for re-appropriation.

Defence accounts personnel are supposed to be 'advisors' and are not expected to behave as if they are the de facto commanders. Depending on the quantum of money required by the government to meet the unplanned expenditure, a regular unofficial 'advisory' is issued from time to time. Accordingly, the entire lot will flood the world with observations, many of them being so silly that it makes the entire process look like a gigantic spoof!

Having bushwhacked the system once, while the bureaucrats recovered and took stock, there would be absolutely no chances taken. With the Joint Secretary (Acquisitions) safely transferred, and with no replacement on the horizon, all that we could do was wait and watch. With two-thirds of the year gone, the media faithfully started carrying the sanctimonious sentiments of the babus who said the entire army budget was unspent. Some reports even suggested the chief, obsessed as he was with getting his age changed, was responsible for the proposals not having gone through. Having made a course correction, the Government of India finally appointed a Joint Secretary (Acquisitions). By the end of the year, only eight of the 106 proposals got past the finish line and 70 per cent of the original funds were unused. I am quite sure there must have been lot of clinking of glasses and high fives amidst the powers that be.

No wonder then, during the Kargil War, babus were running around the globe with suitcases of cash looking for ammunition. In most cases, we paid three or more times the amount we would have otherwise paid as 'emergency buys'.

Compared to officers dealing with procurement in the air force and the navy, we have a few other inherent problems as well. Mainly due to officer shortage and the basic requirement of balancing 'field' and 'peace' tenures, army officers have two-and-a-half to three-year tenures at best in Delhi. It easily takes a year to get to know the ropes, so productivity is limited. Years of dealing with the Ministry of Defence has ensured that the army's own internal thinking is beginning to mirror the mentality of the bureaucrats. Today, with Defence Finance sitting on each commander's shoulder, our own internal functioning is also getting warped.

The army has watched helplessly as the net around it has slowly and steadily been put into place. The Integrated Financial Advisor (IFA) is supposed to assist each formation understand the likely problem areas and roadblocks. Instead, at the formation level itself, there are multiple 'roadblocks' created by these advisors. These have to be tackled, after which the proposal moves out of the respective formation HQ with the noting, 'This proposal has the concurrence of the IFA'. Brilliant! You've just elevated the status of your own advisor to that of a decision-maker.

However, if the boot was on the other foot, then things moved like lightning. Let me quote one example. IFA took it into their heads that the warrant system in the army, 'dating back to pre-historic times', needed a makeover. Soldiers, both officers and men, travelling on duty or on leave, are issued railway warrants that are exchanged at the railway station for a ticket. On this occasion, instead of the army putting up a proposal, the IFA was putting up a presentation for Army HQ. The buzzword was 'e-ticketing' and the IFA wanted the entire army to convert to the system as soon as possible.

The presentation was very glitzy and full of fancy-sounding terms. However, there was one huge flaw that seemed to have escaped the normally observant babus from Integrated Defence Finance. Ninety per cent of our boys were from rural areas and the e-tickets that were being proposed were based on the existing computer ticketing grid of the Indian Railways that did not cover most of these rural areas.

Unfazed by the 'observation', Integrated Finance suggested e-tickets could be done up to the nearest station on the railway grid. This was ridiculous and self-defeating. A soldier going from any location to his village, let's say Kala Bakra, now had to get an e-ticket to the nearest station on the grid, which was Jalandhar. At Jalandhar, he had to leap off the train and purchase a ticket in cash to Kala Bakra. This money would then have to be refunded to him, for which he would have to make a claim. Other minor hitches like connectivity, the lack of credit cards needed to purchase the initial e-ticket, were all considered irrelevant. At stake were additional posts that the proposal would throw up for the finance people and a chance to further expand the 'Empire'.

Let me highlight the case of the National War memorial. We must be *the only country* in the world that has not considered it fit to honour the martyrs who have laid down their lives for the nation. (The Amar Jawan Jyoti which burns under India Gate was constructed by the British for the fallen soldiers of World War I.) I suggested to the RM that we could break the logjam on the issue of the memorial by siting it in line with the 'samadhis' along the Yamuna waterfront rather than seeking a place for it in the Lutyen Zone where it was facing opposition. He perked up, looked very pleased, picked up the phone and spoke to someone in Malayalam. Then he looked at me and smiled, 'Good idea. Go and meet TKA Nair at the PMO. This is a good suggestion.'

I dutifully went and explained the proposal to Nair. He was also very receptive and said that he would put people to work. Many reconnaissance trips were carried out but nothing emerged. As usual, there was a labyrinth of pressure groups, various turf battles and, of course, a sad mind set that this issue concerned only the armed forces. Where are we as a nation? I strongly believe that a nation that forgets its martyrs and soldiers will never attain greatness.

The Officer Corps

One of the biggest problems faced by the Indian Army since Independence has been the chronic shortage of officers. Of the army's sanctioned strength of officers, there was a shortage of around 12 per cent even during the 1950s. In the aftermath of the Indo-China and India-Pakistan wars, the gap was sought to be filled through Emergency and Short Service Commissions. However, the gap kept increasing and, today, the Indian Army is short by nearly 25 per cent. The criticality lies at the lower end of the pyramid, mainly at the level of captains and majors. While most staff appointments are not affected, the shortage is borne by most battalions and regiments who are actually deployed on the ground. A regular infantry battalion, for example, is authorized twenty plus officers. Today, the reality on the ground is that most units are functioning with less than half-a-dozen officers.

Apart from severely impacting the fighting capability of the units, this also adversely impacts unit tartib. A carefully evolved network of officers bridges the gap between the CO and the rest of the battalion, but this had long become a casualty of the acute shortage. A youngster reports to a battalion and he's more or less pushed into commanding a company. There is no time to learn, no time to understand the nuances that make every unit tick in its own special way.

It seemed incredible that no solution had been found over the years. On the contrary, the shortage kept increasing. Sometimes, some problems that have been lingering for years seem to become so big that no one wants to look at them anymore. We tend to presume that the obvious solutions have been tried, but have failed to resolve the problem.

'Let's look at the officer shortage with absolutely no baggage,' I told a small team of officers. 'We have a problem; let us find methods to resolve it.'

A few months later, the team made a presentation at the army commander's conference and the matter was further discussed and the proposed solutions further fine-tuned. At last, though there were still many variables that would need ironing out, the framework of a proposal was ready.

Every six months, NDA takes in approximately three hundred cadets after the written exam. Around six to seven hundred boys clear the SSB, where they are required to pass a minimum physical and psychological standard. NDA is limited by its inability to take more cadets, so we are left with three to four hundred boys who are keen to join the armed forces, meeting the standards, but being sent home.

The proposal was simple: take this lot of boys and put them through specific colleges chosen by the army, getting them to specialize in areas where we feel we can use them best in the organization. At the end of each academic term, the individual is given a short course of military orientation. After graduation, these boys are then put through one year's training at an OTA (Officer Training Academy) from where he is given a short service commission and is expected to serve for six years.

It was further proposed that we could uniformly apply this contractual service methodology at all entry levels; it would not matter if one had gone the NDA-IMA route, or whether he was a direct entry, or from an OTA. Everybody, across the board, is given a short service commission of six years. At the end of the six years, give them a choice of a permanent commission. At this stage, put them through the most stringent of tests, both mental and physical, and choose the very best to stay on in the army as career officers. Not only does the shortage get addressed, but you are also tackling the problems associated with the pyramid system. The possibilities are endless; if further synergized with the paramilitary, the police and administrative services, it can create a quantum increase in the overall quality of leadership.

What we were proposing was not that unique. In fact, most countries across the globe follow the contractual system in their armies. Take the US Army and West Point. Graduates are free to leave after five years, though most West Pointers will invariably carry on as professional soldiers. The need to keep educating our officers, even using this education as an incentive to stay on and serve in the army were all part of the final proposal.

The Defence Secretary flipped through the pages of the proposal after Army HQ put it up to him.

'What type of education will they get? We know what kind of colleges there are,' said Pradeep Kumar, seemingly bored at having to even look at the file. 'We'll look in to it,' he added, putting it aside on his table.

The proposal died there and then. It had no meaning that the file had the collective weightage of a group of officers who had gone into the problem in great detail and identified a possible route that would not only help solve the problem of the shortage, but would also tackle other equally serious issues of subsequent advancement. The collective wisdom of the army commanders also got nixed at the very first hurdle on the premise that the Defence Secretary, being a bureaucrat, knew better. After the mandatory polite gap, as chief of the Indian Army, I could only nudge the RM to light a fire under the Defence Secretary in the hope that the proposal would get smoked out of his office.

Around the same time, I asked the AG's Branch to prepare a detailed proposal that aimed at abolishing the sahayak system. Not only is it demeaning for a soldier to be 'working' in an officer's house, it was a huge drain on manpower. It was also costing the exchequer two to three times the amount, when compared to the alternative that we were proposing.

Various systems across countries, including Pakistan, were looked at. Once again, the proposal was pragmatic and simple. It was also based on the premise that the overall good of the country was more important than petty self-interest.

First, the proposal recognized that each officer in the Indian Army must have a buddy to help him perform his professional duties, as defined. In peace areas, recognizing that officers above a certain rank need help, civilian staff (hired as tradesmen and given salaries based on the NERRICK system), are assigned to each family. Even today, in established stations like Mhow, one civilian bearer looks after three to four officers.

Once again, the proposal that was handed over by Army HQ to the bureaucrats was met with indifferent 'we'll look at it' yawns. As usual, there had been little or no movement on the file. At Army HQ, we could only shake our heads and wonder why such sensitive issues should be stonewalled.

AK Antony is a good human being. In 2011, he was in his seventh year as the RM. It is difficult not to be charmed by his obvious sincerity, for as an individual, he is extremely receptive to all good ideas. Some schemes are very close to his heart and he makes every effort to get them through, especially where the welfare and morale of troops is concerned. For years, we had been talking of bringing the rations for the men on a par with that of the officers. 'There should be no difference. They lead the same life, do the same work—perhaps, physically even more,' I said to him, sensing that perhaps in this one field we might be able to sneak past the rock-like indifference of the babus.

'Yes, yes. We must have the same,' the RM turned to the Defence Secretary, who sensing the mood of the house decided to let this slip through. There would be many more lines of defence we would have to break down before we actually got down to the details of eggs, meat and fresh vegetables.

The RM would usually give clear, lucid instructions. Shamefully, I would catch myself trying to think like a babu, trying to anticipate their next move. It was a useless exercise, for they defied logic, rationale and common sense. However, on the front of better rations and uniforms for men, I sensed we had a chance.

The babus knew AK Antony better than anybody else. They knew the minister was absolutely against corruption, and they were adept at playing him, capitalizing on his abhorrence for crooked deals. In any scenario, the RM's style of functioning was absolutely clear—there must be complete unanimity if a project was to be passed. Our officer intake proposal went through this process. The Defence Secretary, after a million prods, decided to brief the RM.

'The proposal is okay,' he says, 'but the selection of colleges, the sanctioning of the money to universities, it's all very difficult. It can become a scandal.'

'Scandal?' No, no, we must have a consensus,' said the earnest RM. (Sir Humphrey, step aside, here was the real thing.)

AK Antony was a highly accomplished person who had also been the chief minister of Kerala. But he couldn't always get around the mafia of babus. Despite all the good intentions on his part, he too was a victim, unable to break free of the shackles of babudom. If the shackles of red tape were removed from around the minister's office for just two years and he was given a free hand to implement the Transformation Study with no 'observations' holding him back, half our issues would have been addressed. Instead, we had the former Defence Secretary Vijay Singh, going on record to say, 'Just because it is VK Singh's study, why should it go through?'

Finding the right people whose integrity could not be compromised to deal with key issues is half the challenge. Take cadre reviews, for instance, that were ostensibly held for the 'betterment' of the armed forces but in reality have damaged it to a great degree. Interestingly, these proposals, which in the long run have further damaged the basic fabric and structure of the armed forces, have sailed through the complex web spun by babus while every other committee or study group's recommendations start resembling a porcupine, embedded as they are with poisonous quills masquerading as 'observations'.

During British times a senior superintendent of police was known as a 'police kaptan', the three stars on his shoulders equating him with an army 'kaptan saab'. In addition, quite a few captains went on deputation as police officers. The district commissioner, with roughly similar years of service, was at best equivalent to a major saab. The cadre reviews thoughtlessly did away with basing seniority on service, shifting the emphasis on to pay grades. 'I get more money than you, hence I'm higher up in everything, including protocol.' By this logic, the Ambanis should move around in the presidential buggy!

Let me put it on record that the last few cadre reviews have only helped those who were part of the 'think tank' attain higher ranks for themselves. Everything else is a mitigated disaster. AV Singh II (Phase-II of the Ajay Vikram Singh Committee Report) upgraded everything outside the main 'fighting' system. A sub-area commander became a major general and the GOC of an area today drives around with three stars on his vehicle and collar. All 'funny' posts were upgraded and the army stampeded itself into not only accepting, but also implementing, the proposals within four years. What was General Vij, the chief at that time, thinking? He not only accepted it, he actually pushed for it. Look at what has happened—the sub-area commander is still dealing with the same people in the civil world, only it is a major general now tackling the same level of issues. We have not upgraded the appointment; we have succeeded in downgrading an entire rank!

The Indian Army took a decision sometime back on the continuity issue, laying down the guidelines which took into account 'residual service' when appointing both corps and army commanders. Thanks to the AV Singh II Committee's recommendations, the tenure of corps commanders has gone completely haywire, a large number barely completing a year before they are moved. Thankfully, the army commanders are in the saddle for two years, bringing some stability to a mad merry-go-round. Recent events show that even this is taking a hit but who will explain the continuity factor to our Ministry of Defence?

I was lucky, but my case was an exception—I got three years as the CO with 2 Rajput; as commander 168 Brigade, my tenure in Samba was two years and nine months (mainly due to the increase in the retirement age); as GOC, Victor Force, I was in the saddle for almost eighteen months but was lucky to stay on in XV Corps for another year, allowing me to contribute meaningfully to a greater extent; I held the reins of II Corps for twenty months and, as army commander, I had a twenty-five-month tenure. Now consider this: in II Corps, I saw three sets of GOCs at the divisional level and, as army commander, three sets of corps commanders. On staff too, I had two years and nine months as Colonel GS and BGS where again I worked with three sets of GOCs.

The situation, as it has come about, is completely unacceptable, and was one of the issues we looked at in great detail, suggesting certain measures to address the immediate problem. The problem was explained to the powers that be at the ministry. 'Very interesting,' says the Defence Secretary, 'do put it up as proposal.' Nothing happened, it's lying in the deep freeze. Army HQ makes a few noises, they start coming up with lame excuses like, 'so many people have to be promoted' and so on. We make more noises, taking the matter to the RM, telling him continuity is critical, this is not the police where people get shunted out at the drop of a hat.

'Very serious matter,' says the RM, almost as if he's hearing of the problem for the first time. 'You put up a proposal…' Harry Belafonte most probably got his inspiration for the famous song 'There's a Hole in my Bucket' from South Block. The system has been completely hijacked by the bureaucrats!

Nevertheless, hijacked or not, it was my job as the Chief of Army Staff to point out to the government the problems that should have been obvious even at the time of implementation of the cadre review. The navy had dug in, refusing to tamper with the rank structure and eventually a compromise was reached wherein the navy would implement the AV Singh II Committee recommendations over ten years as against the much shorter time span accepted by the air force and army.

Almost immediately, we ran into a wall of protest. 'The cabinet had approved the Ministry of Defence's proposal to upgrade the 1,800-odd posts. There was no way we could go back to them,' we were told. The latest round of shuffling army commanders around with little or no thought to continuity actually baffles the mind. If anything, the history of India has repeatedly taught us one lesson and the babus would do well to keep it in mind as they go on and on with their power games: the gates to the country have always been opened from within.

Statutory Complaint

Visiting other countries is part and parcel of an army chief's job. Right at the outset, I told Army HQ that we should concentrate on our immediate neighbours, and a few countries in the region. In addition, I was keen on visiting Vietnam, Laos and Cambodia in Southeast Asia, while, in Central Asia, we narrowed the list to Tajikistan and Mongolia. I was told that these countries were not classified as 'Category A' by the Ministry of External Affairs (MEA); besides reciprocal trips to the USA and UK were due. Regardless of what MEA thought, we had pencilled in visits to Bhutan, Bangladesh, Myanmar, Nepal and Sri Lanka. I had visited some of these countries as the Eastern Army Commander, and I wanted to follow up.

By mid-2011, the Government of India had had plenty of time to examine the petition I had sent to the RM and to the president. I had briefed the president, Pratibha Patil, earlier in the year, and I had reiterated that I was willing to give the government a written undertaking that I would seek premature retirement if they wanted me out of the way. By deliberately creating a tamasha, the message being given to the army in particular was horrendously wrong. How could every citizen in the country be judged on one yardstick and the army chief on another? People in the highest position had told me then, 'General, you will have no option but to go to court.'

Legal recourse was still a long way off. With the petition completely ignored by the RM, finally, in August 2011, a statutory complaint was put up to the minister. No service chief before me had ever taken this step. The accepted practice in the case of a statutory complaint was that the Government of India had to answer me within three months.

However, the Attorney General's remark about the established 'line of succession' had triggered off another chain of events. Having received a green signal, the CO of an Intelligence unit under III Corps in Dimapur surfaced in Delhi and began to masquerade as a part of Army HQ. A few journalists, both from television and the print media, were coming back to me wanting to 'authenticate' the 'information' being doled out. I was also being told that the 'Chandigarh think tank', with a very senior bureaucrat in the PMO as its ex-officio head, was also working overtime to 'go for the jugular'.

I called up Dalbir Suhag, GOC III Corps, and asked him what was going on. As far as I knew, this particular CO had been under a cloud when I left Eastern Command, for his own 2IC had made written allegations against him accusing the officer of having shot three Naga boys in cold blood. The three youth, it had been alleged, were initially buried in the army area, but a couple of days later they had been exhumed and dumped in the river where the Assam Police had subsequently found them. Suhag, who now knew that he himself was in the running for the top job, made some vague noises on the other end of the line.

Not only was the media being used to drum up a 'controversy' (with a number of articles in national newspapers and magazines), talk shows began talking of 'three acceptances' where it was alleged I had agreed that my date of birth was 1950.

On 30 December 2011, the Government of India finally responded to the statutory complaint. I was told that my year of birth had been fixed at 1950 and it could not be changed.

I did not want to go to court. Time and again, there had been plenty of opportunities to put an end to the entire charade, but whoever was calling the shots was determined to keep the pot boiling. At every stage I had told the RM that I would give it in writing that I'd take premature retirement and go home.

By the middle of January, I had exhausted every legal step within the army available to me to stop this blatantly illegal act. Reams and reams of newsprint had been devoted to a complete non-issue.

Going to the High Court may have meant a prolonged battle. I had already made up my mind that even if the courts ruled in my favour, I would not stay on. The RM knew it, as did the finance minister and, through them, I assumed the PM and the cabinet knew it too.

On the other hand, knocking on the doors of the Supreme Court required big money. Though I had a few fixed assets by way of agricultural land invested in over the last forty-two years of service, I still had to figure out where we would live after retirement. The last thing I could afford to do was squander my savings on legal fees. Justice in India is an expensive business. How does anybody with modest means ever knock on its doors, I wonder.

Over 90 per cent of the lawyers I consulted during this period offered to fight the case pro bono. However, should I decide to go to court, I was determined not to pick an attorney who was associated with any political party.

In the beginning of January, a PIL had been filed in the Supreme Court about my age in which I was also a respondent. A senior parliamentarian who was quite the legal eagle came to see me about it, offering to add his name to the PIL. He asked to see the writ. I told him frankly I hadn't seen it.

'General,' he said, his eyes widening, 'are you serious? How can you not know its contents?'

On the morning of 14 January there was a scramble to get hold of the filed writ. No one seemed to have a copy. Finally, Brijraj Dahiya, my senior from Birla Public School, who had commanded 20 Grenadiers, managed to obtain it. The PIL had been filed by the Grenadier's Association and was to be argued by Bhim Singh of the Jammu-based Panthers Party.

The legal eagle parliamentarian was even more incensed after he had seen the petition. 'It's insidious,' he declared. 'The writ, on the face of it, seems to support your stand on the age issue. However, some fairly wild allegations linking the PM to your successor in the line of succession will ensure the Supreme Court throws this petition out. The spin doctors and the media will do the rest. You would have lost your case without even having fought it.' This insight was discussed with a couple of other lawyers. They all agreed it was a carefully engineered trap.

15 January was Army Day and, as usual, the parade was superb. The special forces, in combat fatigue for the first time, jogged past, followed by the marching infantry and mechanized columns. For the army, it was also a dress rehearsal for Republic Day where the same contingents would dazzle the people of India. After addressing the men, there was the usual ceremony where fallen comrades were honoured and battalions that had performed exceedingly well were presented Unit Citations.

A year earlier, Dr Manmohan Singh had been briefed on the *Northeast Trilogy*, a project we in the army believed would be a small step in helping integrate the region with the rest of the country. This had been followed up with a detailed proposal from Army HQ suggesting that the books be translated into the vernacular and be distributed to schools and colleges in each and every state. However, since August 2011, the prime minister's office had refused to respond to repeated requests to even release the *Northeast Trilogy*. With no response coming forth, it was decided that along with the navy and the air force chiefs, Nirmal Verma and NAK Browne, I would jointly launch the book at the end of the parade. Later in the evening, at the Army House, the president, prime minister and all the bigwigs were ceremonially presented a set each.

The Grenadier's PIL was to be listed in front of a bench comprising Sarosh Homi Kapadia, the Chief Justice of India, in the next few days. After the departure of the 'black label' VVIPs and the other guests, I sat down with Udai Lalit and his small team. Lalit had a good record in the Supreme Court and had no political leanings. We again went over the Grenadier's PIL while Brijraj Dahia on his regimental net was hoping to get the PIL withdrawn. By midnight I received a call from Brij saying no one had been able to find the real people behind the PIL. 'Irony is,' said Brij on the phone, 'everybody is convinced you've filed the PIL by proxy.'

During the previous twenty-four hours, Lalit's team had hurriedly put together the writ petition, which with all the attachments was looking like a typical Ministry of Defence file. I leafed through it again. At every step, ever since this bogey had been raised, I had tried to fight the case within the system. Lalit and virtually every other legal expert had said there was no judge in the country who could look me in the eye and tell me that my school leaving certificate did not determine my year of birth. 'Go ahead,' I told Lalit, 'file the case.'

The writ, a virtual copy of the statutory complaint, was filed on the morning of 16 January and the matter was listed for 3 February. As expected, the filing of the case itself made headlines.

In between, the Grenadier's PIL came and went. On 23 January, Justice Kapadia ruled that since I had already sought to redress the matter in the Supreme Court, the PIL had no role to play in the matter.

The Government of India sent in their biggest guns, the Attorney General and the Solicitor General. The bench, comprising Justices RM Lodha and HL Gokhale, after going through the writ, took strong objection to the 'vitiated' manner in which the Defence Ministry had gone about deciding my year of birth. The bench questioned the government about its 30 December order that rejected the statutory complaint. The fact that the Attorney General was asked to arbitrate on his own earlier judgment that led to the rejection of the statutory complaint was 'against the principles of natural justice'. The apex court sought to know why the government had taken the opinion of the Attorney General when he had already voiced, a year earlier, that the army chief's birth year should be fixed as 1950. The court pointedly asked why the government did not seek a fresh opinion. Finally, the bench asked the Attorney General to seek the government's opinion on what the Defence Ministry intended to do with the 30 December order—should it be withdrawn to pave the way for me to approach the government again? The court made it clear that if the 30 December order was not withdrawn, it would quash it for a fresh process to begin. The next hearing was fixed for 10 February, giving the Government of India exactly seven days.

What happened during the next seven days is anybody's guess. However, the Attorney General started by withdrawing the communiqué of 30 December that had rejected the statutory complaint. I was in my office in Army HQ and only got an update from Lalit when the court took a lunch break. He was sounding quite despondent. 'Things are not going well, it looks like you will lose the case and my arguments and logic are not cutting any ice.'

'How can we lose?'

'Well, that's how it looks.' The Government of India had already withdrawn the rejection of the statutory complaint, so that meant the RM still had to answer in a manner that was in accordance with the law. We had gone to the Supreme Court with the premise that we would get justice from the apex legal body of India. Udai Lalit was experienced enough to know how things were going and if he wasn't feeling very hopeful, there was nothing much either of us could have done about it.

'What are the options?'

'Withdraw—or wait and see what happens.'

We discussed it for a couple of minutes more. The government was determined that what was wrong had to be seen as right. There wasn't a whole lot that I could do about it, so after giving the matter considered thought I took the only decision I could in the circumstances that presented themselves. 'Withdraw,' I told Lalit.

There was a long pause on the phone. Udai Lalit then said, 'Sir, I think you are right—we'll withdraw.'

That afternoon I was scheduled to visit South Western Command. On the short flight to Jaipur, I thought of putting in my papers, but I quickly brushed that thought aside. Right from the outset, I had known I was up against a system that either expected me to conform to their accepted age-old practices or just look the other way. The age issue had been brought into play with certain objectives, but as I moved up the chain of command towards the very top, it had become the one and only weapon my adversaries had to neutralize me. My loyalty had always been to the army and the establishment; in my book, resigning would mean I was putting myself ahead of everything else. Even some close friends and analysts like Maroof Raza who had known and understood what I was fighting for, were advocating resigning a la General Thimayya. I just felt that they were wrong; it would have simply played into the hands of those who were calling the shots.

Have You Read the Order, I Say?

The events in the Supreme Court had created a buzz that had almost every newspaper and television channel in the country in a frenzy, with bold headlines saying 'The General has Lost'. Television channels had quickly rounded up all the regulars who had been spewing venom on the issue, speaking endlessly with no regard to the facts on the ground. They were now drawing comparisons between General Thimayya's case in 1961 and it seemed they would only rest if I went out in a blaze of glory having handed in my resignation to the Government of India. The media fortunately was not aware of my having met the president, Her Excellency Pratibha Patil, after I returned from Jaipur. I was scheduled to leave on an official tour of the UK the next morning.

'I hope you are not thinking of resigning,' said the president, pointing out the importance of the official visit starting the next day. 'If you do that, history will say you were only interested in your age extension. You must carry on the work you are doing.'

The second hearing had certainly come as a big blow. The fact of the matter was that I had gone to the Supreme Court, the apex court in the country, expecting justice as per the law of land. *My petition to the court also categorically mentioned that I was not seeking additional time as chief.* I had told the Government of India through the RM and quite a few senior cabinet ministers that I had no intention of staying on beyond 31 May and all I wanted was this charade of my year of birth to be dropped.

The media frenzy was beginning to abate a bit, but I still had NDTV crews dogging me outside the hotel in London where we were staying.

I had just been jumped by them and had told the correspondent for the millionth time that my going to the Supreme Court was a personal issue. As I entered my room, an aide handed me a phone saying a Mr Devasahayam from Chennai wanted to speak to me urgently. 'Do you remember me?' he asked.

The voice on the other end of the telephone was typically south Indian. Major MG Devasahayam had served with the Madras Regiment and fought in the 1965 Indo-Pak War and participated in counter-insurgency operations in Nagaland before joining the Indian Administrative Service. He had been the District Commissioner in Bhiwani when I had just got commissioned and, since retirement, he had been writing profusely. Apart from writing a book on Jayaprakash Narayan, his movement and the Emergency, MGD had been following the age issue fairly closely and had been vociferous in calling a spade a spade. Being familiar with the inner workings of the government, he had categorically said what was happening was nothing short of 'kleptocracy' in articles that had appeared in *g-files*.

'I most certainly do, sir. My father took me to meet you in Bhiwani when you were the DC a few days after I was commissioned into the army.'

That seemed to please the voice at the other end of the phone, for he chuckled happily. Then he was all business. 'I have been following this age issue nonsense, I say. I have been writing about it.'

'I am aware of that, sir...'

'Tell me,' he asked, 'have you read the order of the Supreme Court? It has just been posted online.'

'I instructed my lawyers to withdraw my case...'

'No, no. You are not listening to me. Have you read the order, I say?'

I said I hadn't. 'Then you better read it because it puts the ball back in the court of the Government of India to "recognize a particular date of birth of General VK Singh in the official service record". Unless this is done you cannot be given retirement orders,' snapped the no-nonsense MGD. 'Nice talking to you, General.' The line went dead.

What order? I had no clue about how the legal system worked. I called up Mrinalini in Delhi and told her to find out about this order from Lalit.

The two-man bench had said nothing at all in the order. They had simply stated that the Government of India letter rejecting the statutory complaint was withdrawn. Though I knew this had happened, its actual import did not sink in for some time. The statutory complaint was alive. The Government of India had to answer it. They still had to fix my date of birth as per set legal practices. In an interview with *Outlook* magazine, I made this point, saying I would demit office at the end of May but neither the AG nor the MS Branch can actually hand me a retirement order.

As the copies of the magazine hit the stands, their correspondent left a message saying the interview had stirred a hornet's nest in the PMO. She said we could expect an announcement the next day that the Appointments Committee of the Cabinet had cleared the name of my successor, designated to take over on 30 May 2012. It seemed a bit odd, for a new chief was always announced two months earlier. I still had three months to go and the Ministry of Defence had to settle the little matter of answering my statutory complaint. Lo and behold, the next morning the PMO issued the statement, proving once and for all that this was a government that could work at lightning speed!

I placed a call to Eastern Command and congratulated Lieutenant General Bikram Singh on his being designated the twenty-fifth chief of the Indian Army.

By now, there was little doubt that a very senior bureaucrat in the PMO was orchestrating the entire age issue. Ever since I had blocked the Tatra files, the name of this person had been cropping up regularly. Not only was he directly involved with PSUs where there was direct evidence linking him to plots given to his family in the BEML complex, almost every move of the government seemed to originate from the same shadowy quarters. In what was obviously a smokescreen, around that time, I was approached with a bribe to clear the Tatra files. This bureaucrat had also been dropping hints that the age issue had been raked up by one of the former chiefs at the behest of the wife of a very important political personality.

Despite the prime minister and the PMO's non-response to the *Northeast Trilogy*, the RRM, Dr Pallam Raju was one of the first ministers to realize the tremendous potential of the project. Everyone who had seen the books had been impressed by what we had managed to put together. For the first time in independent India, all the peoples of the Northeast, its geography and its history had been put together in a spectacular manner to offer our own people a glimpse into one of the most important regions of our country.

'We need to take this across to the people. Why don't we start with a special release in Hyderabad where we have people of Northeast working in many fields or studying in various colleges,' he had suggested.

The suggestion was in keeping with what had been earlier proposed to the PMO. Instructions were sent to the EME Centre in Secunderabad to make the necessary arrangements and invite a large body of civilians, including citizens in the city who hailed from the Northeast. The media was also to be cranked up and Dipti Bhalla and Kunal Verma, the two authors, were told to be in Hyderabad on 5 March.

On the morning of 5 March, as I headed for the airport to get to Hyderabad, news headlines were saying that the army chief had deployed off-the-air interceptors at key points to eavesdrop on the powers that be. I have to admit that even though I was getting used to some real warped reporting, this one was the product of a really creative imagination. There was something familiar about these vehicles, but I could not immediately place my finger on it. 'Find out who is behind this report,' I told Army HQ and got airborne for Hyderabad.

On the aircraft, while thinking over this issue, I remembered seeing a note pertaining to off-the-air interceptors that had been put up to the service chiefs. The equipment had been purchased by the DG DIA for ₹37 crore without proper sanction. NTRO, who had been asked to make an inventory of all 'snoop' platforms that included UAVs and other James Bond toys, had also pointed out that the DIA was not one of the government agencies authorized to deploy these high tech gizmos without clearance. The CNS, Nirmal Verma (later Ambassador to Canada) had suggested we don't waste time on such trivial matters and had closed the matter, much to the relief of the CISC, Vice Admiral Sinha (later C-in-C Western Naval Command). As soon as I landed, I told the ADGPI to see if DIA or anyone linked with the organization had a role to play in this drama.

The media was in a frenzy about the 'army chief spying on the government'. I categorically told the media the report was pure fiction.

Back in Delhi later in the evening, I was told that my hunch had been correct and the former DG DIA, retired Lieutenant General Tejinder Singh was the 'anonymous' source. A statement by Army HQ was being drafted naming Tejinder Singh.

The Leaky PMO

Ever since I 'lost the case' in February, there had been a lot of jubilation in the babu circles. The general belief was that I would completely lose interest in the job and adopt a defeatist outlook to everything. One thing was very clear in my mind; my style of functioning was not going to change. We continued to push for the ULH case to go through and at the same time made a detailed presentation on the aviation issue that had become a real menace for the army.

The role of helicopters has assumed a completely different dimension ever since the Siachen conflict started in 1984. Two years later, the Army Aviation Corps was established and, ever since, the feats of our flyboys has been the stuff legends are made of. While trying to stay within prescribed safety limits, the pilots, drawn from various regiments, would constantly push the envelope, especially when lives of injured or critically ill soldiers was at stake.

The bulk of army aviation's tasks pertain to flying in some of the most demanding terrain in the world. The bulk of the machines operating at these daunting heights are the single-engine Cheetahs that have now been in service for more than four decades.

During General JJ Singh's tenure, the proposal to replace the Cheetah and the Chetak helicopters had finally come through. Eurocopter had bagged the deal for 194 helicopters, but almost immediately there had been reports suggesting the trials had been tweaked in favour of the European company. Ravi Rishi, a middleman in the Tatra deal was once again one of the key people involved in the Eurocopter deal. Once the allegations started to fly thick and fast, the RM had cancelled the contract without hesitation. The grapevine had been abuzz as people in high places had to scramble to return luxuriously appointed villas in France. However, that amusing spectacle hardly provided solace to the pilots who had to continue to make do with the old machines.

Around this time Eurocopter was doing some extremely aggressive marketing. Technical specifications ruled out Augusta, Bell and others, narrowing the field once again to the Eurocopter and the Russian Kamov. If the contract was to be awarded on the basis of the lowest price, then, once again, Eurocopter would take it. The Kamov, however, was twin-engined, and gave the pilots a semblance of a chance if an engine flamed out. It also came to our notice that some of the modifications being spoken of were only cosmetic. For example, the 'bulge doors' being fitted to accommodate casualties hardly added four inches on each side. Also, these trials had been done in 'vendor premises'. There is no way conditions in France could be compared to wind velocities and the dynamics of flying in Siachen. The final call had to be made by experts. By any standard, all of the armed forces requirements are huge. If we were to concentrate our energies and the money we were spending into getting these companies to enter into joint ventures with our own industry, the country would benefit enormously.

The carefully orchestrated attempt to pin the off-the-air interceptors on to the Technical Services Division had backfired. Even though the newspapers had quoted 'anonymous sources', it hadn't taken long for the person to be exposed. An Army HQ statement the next day had not only identified him by name, the release had also stated that the officer had been involved in nefarious activities and, after a bribe attempt, had been banned from entering Army HQ.

Though the army press release had mentioned the bribe attempt, the media chose not to give it more than a cursory glance. Vidya Subrahmaniam, a correspondent from *The Hindu* asked me about the spying allegations and I told her it was pure rubbish and that we had identified the person as being the same individual who had offered me a bribe. The main focus of the interview was on the steps we were trying to take to improve the lot of our men and retired personnel.

A few weeks later, around mid-March, *The Hindu* story broke. Even though quite a few journalists were in the know of the bribe offer, it is perhaps a sign of the times that it didn't seem to warrant attention. Besides, at the time of the incident in September 2010, he had not attained the heights of notoriety that he was on his way to achieving. In the Adarsh Housing scam, his was one of the key names. *He had had extremely strong objections on security grounds, but had not pursued these after being allotted a flat.* Suddenly, the Tatra story—until then restricted to the *DNA* newspaper—and he were big news. The mainstream media, which had until now tried to ignore the Tatra scandal, had no choice but to report it.

The 'bribe' issue also got highlighted, with the matter being discussed in Parliament. The RM corroborated the facts and a CBI enquiry was finally ordered into the matter. Tatra now went into damage control. The facts were there before the nation and there was very little they could do to stuff the genie back into the bottle. However, the 'shouting brigade' was now let loose on television, trying to make an issue out of the fact that no action had been taken. They even made grandiose statements saying I should have called in the Military Police. The comments, coming as they did from senior officers, now retired, were ridiculous in the extreme and smacked of the tutoring they had received. According to the law of the land, I was supposed to inform my superior authority, which in this case was the RM. At Army HQ, we had already red-flagged Tatra.

BEML threatened television channels with lawsuits and issued front-page advertisements in three or four national newspapers. The story virtually disappeared off the front pages in a matter of days. A senior opposition leader told me off record, 'General saab, lapetna tha to aapne Tatra kyon pakra?

Isme hum halla machayenge to hum bhi phaste hain.' (General, if you had to catch them, why Tatra? If we back you, we'll also get exposed).

'Bribegate' and Tatra had the sutradhars on the back foot. Within days, they played their next card.

I had sent a letter to the prime minister that focused entirely on the shortages that continued to plague the army, especially ammunition that affected the infantry and the mechanized forces. As the Ministry of Defence, till that time, hadn't cleared a single project in 2011-2012, I pointed out the 'hollowness' of our defence system—in some cases, we were down to our war reserves. My writing to the prime minister was nothing extraordinary. A similar communiqué, even more detailed, had been prepared and sent to the Ministry of Defence a few days earlier. The Military Operations Directorate (MO) prepares letters with such sensitive information. After discussing the broad framework with the DGMO, the draft comes back to the chief directly, bypassing even the COAS's secretariat. Once I had made my corrections by hand, the letter was finalized and I signed it. Subsequently, the letter was sealed in the MO Directorate and delivered to the PMO. This confidential document was somehow leaked to the media.

Subsequent media speculation placed the leak of the letter at the doorstep of a junior lady functionary in the PMO. I personally doubt that very much as only a very senior bureaucrat in the PMO would handle such letters. What motivated the leak can at best be an educated guess, but the next thing I knew, television channels were going viral, and with Parliament in session, there was an uproar in both the Houses.

I was visiting formations in J&K and was getting sporadic reports on the developments in Delhi. The entire country's media was suggesting the letter had been 'leaked by VK Singh', and the RJD President, Laloo Prasad Yadav, a key member of the government known for his acerbic wit, rose to say, 'Makkhi ke jaise hata do!'(Shoo him away like a fly), or words to that effect.

By then, I was absolutely furious. There had to be some limit to the 'dirty tricks' department's nonsense. How could a letter written by an army chief to the PM pointing out critical shortages in the country's defence structure be used as a political weapon? The timing of the leak was also perfect. Not only was Parliament in session, in J&K, I was generally out of communication as I was constantly moving from one location to the other. After Laloo Yadav's statement, I drafted a terse message and had it released to the media:

'This is an outrage! Official communication with the PM, RM, or anybody for that matter, with the COAS is privileged information. The leaking of the letter should be treated as high treason. This cynical approach to tar my reputation has to stop. The source of the leak has to be found and dealt with ruthlessly.'

The statement helped douse the populist fires that were being deliberately stoked. The RM assured Parliament that the Intelligence Bureau would get to the bottom of who leaked the letter while also assuring the members that the contents of my letter would be taken note of. The editor of the newspaper which had originally run the leaked letter published a tongue-in-cheek article suggesting 'someone very close to the PM' was responsible for the leak, while a few months later PTI also carried a story saying a 'relatively junior' officer from the Indian Economic Service in the Cabinet Secretariat was behind the leak. Whatever it was, the sick mind of the 'dirty tricks department' was fairly evident, and it was quite obvious even the most sensitive matters had no sanctity in the endeavour to get at me.

Since Independence, the top political leadership in the country has been haunted by the possibility of a military takeover. It is no secret that people around Nehru exploited his paranoia of a military coup and started chipping away at the army in an evolving civil-military relationship. The appointment of Baldev Singh as India's first Defence Minister—a man known for his political 'fix it' ability rather than any military acumen—set the tone for the future. Had Nehru had his way, Field Marshal Cariappa would never have been the chief. Subsequently, Thimayya's popularity as an individual would give Prime Minister Nehru more nightmares than the Chinese on the border. When the attack did come in October 1962, the Indian Army was engaged in 'Op Amar' where they were building houses while our ordnance factories were making coffee percolators.

Thorat, Prem Bhagat, SK Sinha—they were all dumped by the wayside. Indira Gandhi not only inherited the leadership of the country from her father, she too never stopped looking over her shoulder. The examples are endless, the lesson the same. If you want to spook the system, raise the spectre of a military takeover. It always works.

Every move of the think tank to stymie me had floundered simply because there was no truth to any of the so-called issues. Yet, each move was hacking away further at the one institution that has somehow stood firm and remained efficient despite every attempt to reduce it to the basic common denominator where it is considered to be just like everybody else. So what was one more lie?

A national daily broke the story of a coup which had all the masala of a C-grade movie script. Fiction or not, a banner headline greeted readers on 6 April claiming that I had moved a mechanized unit (on transporters) from Hissar and a parachute battalion from Agra towards Delhi on the night of 15 January. The Defence Secretary, Shashi Kant Sharma, had to abort his trip to Malaysia and rush back to New Delhi. I'm not sure which of the two attempts to throw mud at me was more ludicrous—the 5 March anonymous story where the off-the-air interceptors were brought into play, or the 6 April coup story.

Fortunately, the coup story was such a farce that it smashed itself and the principal author lost credibility completely. In subsequent months, he would continue to publish a few blatant untruths, but in a scenario where the waters were being churned round-the-clock to hide the truth, those were minor issues. I thought this particular journalist not only let himself down, but also let down his entire newspaper that had been nurtured by one of the great stalwarts of the country who had been one of the few people to stand up and be counted during the Emergency.

By this time, my tenure was coming to an end and I got busy with my farewell visits. I spoke to the officers and men of each command one last time as their chief. I could squarely meet their gaze and look each one of them in the eye. I had the conviction to tell them to stand firm against wrongdoings.

Throughout my tenure as the chief, I had decided to stand up to the system. I knew where I stood and I also knew my efforts to take on the babus was a bit like trying to straighten a dog's tail. At the base of it all, the main issue was always procurement and acquisitions, something which has made the armed forces the cash cow for successive governments in India. The author Philip Mason called bureaucrats 'the heaven born', but today very few in the top echelons are willing to rock the boat. They did not need me to tell them the system was rotten. They knew it all along. My job was, and is, to tell my story as honestly and truthfully as I can, so that people, not just those within the army but outside of it as well, know what is happening to this wonderful country of ours.

Bikram Singh, my successor came to formally call on me after he had been designated chief. A wonderfully charming man, I had no problems with him at a personal level. Bikram felt the need to say a few nice things about my tenure, rounding it off with 'I will always be loyal to you.'

'Just be loyal to the army and the country,' I told him, wishing him well.

The Government of India still hadn't answered my statutory complaint and recognized my actual date of birth. In the absence of a final decision, neither the MS Branch nor the AG could issue me a retirement notice. All the government could do was make the announcement that my tenure ended on 31 May. As far as I was concerned, I would keep working till the last day, then hand over and move on.

With three weeks to go, I received a phone call and a letter from two different people, neither of which I could ignore. This would set into motion one last event that would require the collective skills of the cover up team to 'save one of their own'. The matter would get swept under the carpet, but one must remember that truth always has a way of resurfacing.

▪

In spite of Army HQ constantly prodding Eastern Command to investigate the Rangapahar killings, there had been no major movement against the concerned officer, Colonel Sreekumar, the CO of the Intelligence Unit in III Corps. Sometime in early 2012, the officer was again in the news, his people having stolen a variety of electronic items and a licenced pistol during a botched raid in Jorhat. When one of the cell phones was switched on, the team was traced and caught red-handed by the Assam Police. However, despite the blatant violation of the law, III Corps tried to duck behind AFSPA, hoping the higher ups would hold their hand.

Though we were aware of the matter, and urging Eastern Command to follow the laid down SOPs in a case like this, I received a call from the chief minister of Assam, Tarun Gogoi, who said that only perfunctory steps were being taken by Eastern Command and III Corps towards punishing the guilty. I promised Gogoi that I would do what I could, even though it was a matter where command usually called the shots.

Then came a signed letter from a senior serving service officer of the rank of an army commander; the letter stated that Sreekumar was related to him and had in the past molested his daughter. To protect the girl, the family had ostracized Sreekumar more than a decade ago. However, as the young girl was due to get married, Sreekumar had resurfaced and was trying to queer the pitch by spreading all sorts of untruths.

I spoke to GOC III Corps, Dalbir Suhag, and told him in no uncertain terms that, whatever his compulsions, covering up was not acceptable. I had once before spoken to Suhag when Sreekumar was masquerading as a part of the Intelligence Unit in Delhi and was the main source of information for the magazine that broke the coup story. Suhag once again hemmed and hawed, and eventually the BGS III Corps passed some mild strictures against Sreekumar that actually had no meaning.

Sections of the media would subsequently try and make it look like I was being vindictive towards Dalbir Suhag who was marking time to take over as the Eastern Army Commander. I wonder what they would have expected any army chief true to his salt to do. A show cause notice 'as to why no action was being taken against the CO of his intelligence unit' was issued by the AG's Branch. I told the Adjutant General, JP Nehra, to call up Suhag and, as was the usual practice, inform him that the show cause notice was on its way and that I expected him to explain his position or better still, come and clarify matters in person.

Dalbir Suhag's staff officer received the notice as the corps commander had left for Delhi on 'leave' after the AG had spoken to him. The sealed envelope was then placed in a safe, awaiting the general's return to active duty. Most miraculously, that night the contents of the letter were unsealed and Headlines Today, a subsidiary of *India Today*, started splashing the contents of the notice on television. The television anchor seemed intent on proving my 'vindictiveness' and Suhag's innocence.

The focus seemed to be on how many days I had left rather than what the actual notice was all about. In keeping with the 'stalling tactics', Suhag wrote to Army HQ asking for more time. 'Give him all the time he wants,' I told Nehra. The show cause notice also meant that there would be a DV (discipline and vigilance) ban in place. Unless the matter was satisfactorily resolved, Suhag could not become the Eastern Army Commander. I had done what I had to do, and after midnight on 31 May it was no longer any of my business.

That evening, as the reveille sounded and the flags came down for the day, I was no longer the chief of the Indian Army. I was an ordinary citizen of India. After forty-six years in uniform, I changed into civvies for good that day. As the final notes of the bugle wafted through the air, I felt like an uncaged bird.

EPILOGUE: RECLAIM INDIA

After a month's break post-retirement, I felt my job as a citizen of this country was only half-done. I had long discussions with colleagues and others, who over time, had become friends. More or less, all said the same thing: go out into the countryside and see what is happening. A former soldier/bureaucrat, whose relentless fight against corruption has thrown up a new word 'kleptocracy', said to me, 'You have seen the rot that has set in on defence matters. Grassroots, man, get down to the grassroots,' he emphasized, 'only then can you expose the rascals who are in power today and are relentlessly eating up this country.'

Over the last couple of years, one had seen how Anna Hazare's movement had led to a surge of anger and hope, as the multitudes took to the streets waving the national flag and chanting vande mataram. Others like Baba Ramdev were attacking black money and talking of issues that needed desperately to be addressed. There were serious problems that were affecting the farmers, many of whom were committing suicide. Other people were talking of electoral reforms, some were looking at the need for alternate energy as against nuclear energy, while still others were doing yeoman service in various other fields, be it the judiciary or police or even the armed forces. However, the most interesting thing was that all these groups and individuals, fiercely committed to building a better country, were almost universally seen as being anti-government by those in power. 'We were very happy with the system,' Foreign Affairs Minister Salman Khurshid told IAS achievers at a function, 'until Anna Hazare came along and created all this trouble.'

All my life I had been in the army and the only thing that I knew intimately was the armed forces. So I started discussing issues with ex-servicemen. Almost all the officers I spoke to said that there was a desperate need to unite or put under a common umbrella organization all the ex-servicemen organizations. Today there are more than 360 of them and babudom is having a field day dividing and ruling. As a result, even key issues—such as one-rank-one-pay and disability pensions—had dragged on and on until those fighting the case just gave up or passed away.

I started meeting people and listening to them. Far too often we have predetermined ideas and we shut our mind to other points of view even before we've heard what the other person has to say. I was invited to join the farmers in the sugarcane agitation, so I went, more in a listening and absorbing mode. I met with Baba Ramdev, trying to understand what he stood for and what his objectives were. We talked at length about key issues like black money and tried to understand each other's perspective on critical issues. Anna Hazare invited me to his village in Maharashtra, and along with others on his team we looked at the Mahatma Gandhi model where democracy was rooted to villages which would be the first unit of development. Lokpal, hunger, education, urban migration, the constitution, black money, FDI, neo-liberal economics, the desperate need to resuscitate institutions and a host of other subjects. I went to help break Anna's fast and was also invited to do the same for Baba Ramdev. I also came into contact with other social activists as well as political leaders of all colours, be it the right, left, Congress, as well as others. It has been an education, at the end of which I realized there are many more questions than answers.

The systems are all available. Our Constitution is a robust document but over the last sixty years it has been hijacked. It took a while for the political-bureaucratic nexus to get into the act. The irony is, over 95 per cent of the people, including the bureaucrats are deeply committed to their work and the country, but these people are systematically brushed aside. In the army, as lieutenants, captains, even through to colonels, everyone talked the same language where nothing but the nation, the army and the men mattered. We would always wonder how some senior officers could behave in a certain way for they too had been junior and mid-level officers once.

The December 2012 rape case that saw our children spill on to the streets, with the state responding with lathi charges and water cannons, underlines the abject state of affairs that exists in our society today. While on the face of it, the rape was the reason for the public outcry, it was also a collective cry for better governance. I wonder what would have happened if the president of the country had walked down the slopes of Raisina Hill and enveloped those protesting children in his arms. The trouble is, ours is no longer a government for the people.

When the nuclear debate raged in Parliament, the prime minister had risen to state that history would decide 'if I am a strong or a weak prime minister'. Despite all the warning signs, nothing seems to change, except that anyone showing the red flag is a marked man. How long can this sort of indifference be tolerated and, more importantly, who will pay the price when we are faced with a major crisis. Take the 'hollowness issue' for example. A year before I sent my letter to the prime minister, we had invited him to the Army HQ and made the same presentation to him. Nothing happened. When I wrote to the PM, the letter was used as a political weapon to try and discredit me rather than try and address the actual problem.

What are the solutions? We have the institutions, we just need to let them function without interference. Define the roadmap for every Indian, bring him into the loop of national security and then leave it to those who know the subject to deliver. Whether we are willing to admit it or not, today we face greater security challenges than ever before. The US is withdrawing from Afghanistan, creating a void that this time around is likely to be filled by the Chinese. History has taught us valuable lessons, but we can only see something if we are willing to look.

The Transformation Study recognized the threats and analysed various likely scenarios. Wherever possible, we pushed hard and got things done, especially in areas where the ministry's direct intervention was not required. The first of our new accretions had started coming in while I was still in Kolkata and a detailed roadmap to absorb subsequent additions was made. At Army HQ we had worked out details for the required accretions. The locations and the infrastructure needed were worked out in great detail. Yet, it is a shame that the proposed corps is still stuck in a bureaucratic maze. The former Defence Secretary wryly commented that since this was a VK Singh proposal, it will not get through. How much more myopic can we be? It is a pity that none of our bureaucrats are ever held responsible for any shortages or failures. There is an urgent need to bring about accountability if the nation wants to protect itself.

The Naxal or Maoist or, using politically correct terminology, 'left wing extremism' threat had been growing as a problem. The Dantewada massacre only highlighted the intensity and ruthlessness of the extremists which was further underlined by the ruthless attack on Congress Party functionaries. Every now and then, a case is made for deploying the army. It needs to be understood that army is already stretched and is having a problem managing the peace and field tenure of the units. At the same time, the central police forces and the paramilitary have been seeking accretions (and getting them) as also better weaponry. The earlier we realize that it is training, dedication and involvement of officers that gets results in such situations, the better it would be. Today, almost without exception, most of the deployment of security forces in the Maoist affected areas is defensive in nature.

In the army, we were concerned with this issue and I did suggest a model to the home minister. I believe it was shot down by the so-called security experts in Home Ministry under the excuse that 'General is looking at accretions for the army to get more ranks for his people'. There cannot be anything more absurd than this. I had tasked the Central Command to carry out a detailed analysis and monitor the situation. They did an excellent job and made worthwhile practical suggestions. All the army commanders were taken on board and I also ensured that the RM visited Central Command to get updated on this issue.

In one of the conferences I attended in Delhi as an army commander, the issue of dilution or removal of AFSPA had been brought up by General Deepak Kapoor. I pointed out the pitfalls and was supported in this by the majority of army commanders who believed that we should not tinker with this enabling act, for it ensured that our troops were not dragged into court by anti-national elements. I was very clear in my mind that the army had already laid down guidelines and instructions to avoid any misuse of the provisions of this act and the army should not succumb to some gimmickry by vested interests, as it would have a major negative fallout for the troops operating on the ground.

It was thus amusing to find the chief minister of J&K joining the issue on the AFSPA because, for him, this was a political issue as it was in the manifesto of his party. All kinds of statements emanated from Omar Abdullah who did not understand the actual ground position. I was surprised that his advisors did not tell him that the army was not operating in any major town and the so-called partial withdrawal would have serious consequences

We need to tackle issues that are being swept under the carpet. A country is best judged by how it treats its fighting men—be they soldiers, airmen or sailors. Today, the ex-servicemen are a hugely divided lot, each headed by a group that fiercely protects its own turf. In our political system, since this body is so fragmented, it is not seen as a vote bank and hence nobody cares. This large body needs to be harnessed and brought under a common umbrella. Let us just take one example—the army created an environmental battalion in the 1980s with the specific task of re-greening the Himalayan foothills in the Doon Valley, between Jammu and Pathankot, as also the area between Gurgaon and Faridabad. The results have been spectacular.

Why can we not amalgamate this large body of disciplined soldiers with the Ministry of Environment and Forests or for some social work for the benefit of the nation? Millions of rupees have been poured into the cleaning of our rivers. What has happened? Why can't we make specialist units to look after each and every district in the country?

Today, we endeavour to make sure that all our men, by the time they leave the army, are at least graduates. Across the country, we may have schools, but so many are empty shells with no teachers. If society wants, these men can be further trained to fan out as educators at the primary level. But for all this, we need a vibrant system that is alive and throbbing, not bogged down in endless red tape that is cynically used to divert funds.

The solutions are simple—the budget for acquisitions should not be appropriated as unspent money. Just because the financial year rolls over, it doesn't mean we stop requiring ammunition or fresh systems. The moment this is done, Defence Finance actually has no role to play in the matter. If we are looking at the ULH, DG Artillery should be the ultimate authority in that case. Secretary, Defence Production, should be sitting outside his office waiting to make a presentation, so that the ordnance factories are also in the running for the order, not the other way around. Similarly, the call on helicopters should rest with DG Aviation and so on and so forth. Have your checks and balances by all means, but for god's sake we need to stop the tamasha.

The sooner the political class realize that the army in India is not a threat to them but the single, largest institution that is a tool for nation building, the better it will be for all of us. This is the only institution that lives with the motto 'The Nation Comes First Always and Every Time'. The bureaucrats have played this game for much too long—divide and rule worked wonders for the British who were after all, an alien power. Today, we must realize this is our country and we are only axing our feet if we continue to accept the current state of affairs. How else do we explain the fact that successive defence secretaries have moved to that exalted position from Defence Production? They spend their two years or so as defence secretaries covering up and exonerating themselves for all the scandals and scams that get unearthed. The system now has been fine-tuned even further, for defence secretaries become chief vigilance commissioners and comptrollers and auditor generals!

The current system has made a joke out of the institutions that hold our country together. Political expediency has already made a mockery of our defence budget. Today, virtually everything that we believed in, the very *honour code* that drove generations of army officers, is under attack. Taking a cue from the 'system', in fact with the active encouragement of the system, senior officers who are expected to set examples are playing right into the hands of those who are playing kingmakers. How else do we justify officers at the level of corps and army commanders using AFSPA as a protective shield from behind which their chosen few can operate at liberty?

Where does one draw the Lakshman Rekha? One of the highest seats of office in the country, blatantly tampered with the Appointments Committee of the Cabinet file when it announced my successor at the beginning of March. This file was summoned in the Supreme Court itself, where Justices Gokhale and Lodha themselves read out and quoted from documents that were dated April 2012, a full month-and-a-half after the file was supposed to have been closed. Much is made of the RTI Act, but till today, the government dare not show the original ACC file to the petitioners of the PIL who had gone to court to uphold the institutional integrity of the armed forces. They were not fighting for me or on my behalf, they were simply trying to stand up for what was considered by most to be right.

▪

More than a year has passed since I hung up my boots. The last twelve months have been a period of discovery and of introspection. The day I retired, we moved out of Army House and shifted into 20 Mandir Marg. I wanted a clean break, but that was not to be, for at 0700 hours I received a legal notice from the CMD of BEML, VRS Natarajan, demanding an apology for my 'false and motivated' allegations against BEML on the Tatra truck issue. The BEML CMD called a press conference and said, 'Legal notice has been issued today. If he does not apologize, we may file a defamation suit against General VK Singh.'

I had no idea what Natarajan wanted an apology about. The CBI had registered a Preliminary Enquiry in the bribery case and once Army HQ had raised the issue of the trucks being overpriced, every newspaper and television channel had done their own research and reported that BEML was billing the army thrice the actual amount. Seven thousand vehicles with an approximate mark-up of ₹75 lakh; any calculator with the appropriate amount of digits will tell you adds up to ₹5,250,00,00,000 (five thousand two hundred and fifty crore rupees). Obviously, the mandarins in the PMO who were calling the shots were not going to be satisfied with my retirement.

There was an immediate uproar in the press. Suddenly, after twelve years in the saddle, Natarajan had to go. Some others, however, continued to be protected, even though it would mean sacrificing an agency that had been created to guard our national interest. After the matter had exploded in March, the CBI had been given the task of conducting an enquiry into the bribe issue. Even though we continue to await the findings, a defamation suit was filed against me and four other officers, including the DGMI.

Even as I relinquished command of the Indian Army, two events took place in quick succession. The DV ban on GOC III Corps was revoked without any preamble and the way cleared for him to pick up his army commander's rank. The post had been kept vacant illegally for him, but that is another story. The second was the Defence Secretary, Shashikant Sharma, refusing to countersign the accounts pertaining to the TSD, thereby insinuating that all was not right with the Intelligence set up. Even though the TSD exclusively dealt with 'human Int' and had nothing to do with electronic surveillance, hints were being dropped all over that the off-the-air interceptors were actually deployed and operated by TSD. The fledgling organization had performed outstandingly well (we knew of the attempted coup in the Maldives before any other agency had even started looking in that direction) but it seemed to me that it would now be sacrificed in a final bid to throw mud at me.

After six-and-a-half decades of independence, I think our democracy stands at a critical crossroads. Why are we in a state where things seem to be going wrong, where corruption is becoming a way of life, where the electoral system is only breeding money and muscle power despite the fact that our Constitution is reasonably solid? The Constitution proclaims India a welfare state where the government is supposed to look after its people. But today the situation is different. You take a look at how neo-liberalism, which came in the 1990s, has impacted the economy where the gap between the rich and poor, the haves and have-nots, has only widened. All these have been constant issues for discussion with a wide variety of people from all shades of the political and social spectrum. It is amazing how at the core of most people, there seems to be a fire burning on how to rectify the situation, yet everyone seems to be helpless in the face of the hydra-headed system that has evolved over this period and sits like a sticky spider's net over our lives.

As things progressed, the idea to form the Jantantra Morcha was born. The idea was to try and create a socio-political reformist movement that would spread awareness amongst the people and motivate them to reach out for their rights. Why jantantra? The idea was that today democracy is not in the spirit of the Constitution, and the Preamble that says 'We, the people' has been relegated to the background and hence the movement must by its name espouse the cause of democracy. It was to create a movement to bring in democracy as envisaged by patriots like Mahatma Gandhi and Jayaprakash Narayan. Like Gandhi and JP, we needed to have a core of people who were incorruptible, whose only desire was to do their duty towards the country and the people, who would not seek something in return at each and every step. Only then could the movement hope to make a beginning, starting at the grassroots level. To achieve something on that scale, we have to reach out to the villages, for the common man to have a role to play. Today he doesn't have a voice, he gives his vote and then for the next five years he gets kicked around.

The rally in Patna on 30 January 2013 affirmed my belief that there was a desire amongst the masses for a positive change. So how do we get the system back on the rails and what kind of changes are needed, has been the theme of the Jantantra Morcha. In Hindi we called it 'moolbhoot parivartan' or 'sampoorna parivartan', which means fundamental and complete change. This would take into account the entire political and bureaucratic system. It implies that you are going to address electoral reforms so that you can clean up the system. You are going to address the way people are elected so that the whole process has the imprint of the common man taking part and the role of money goes away. We are looking at the education system that is nowhere close to delivering the desired results. We are looking at the health system that is not delivering. We are looking at greater development and autonomy for villages as a unit, we are looking at the plight of farmers and how to make their lot better, we are looking at the power sector and how to ensure that we can make it much more efficient, how to tackle corruption which is a major impediment to development.

We are also looking at better utilization of water resources of the country; the protection of natural resources so that they can be used for the good of the nation; land reforms and acquisition which should benefit the common man and not the land mafia as it is happening today; the entire economic spectrum so that it can be realigned for national growth and the welfare of its citizens; the menace of black money; the exploitation of tribal and other indigenous people; ensuring equal treatment on all matters for all minority groups and those who have been exploited; we were also addressing the shortfalls in the judicial system so that it becomes more responsive, people-friendly and easy for the common man; the overhauling of colonial era laws and regulations; police reforms; and ensuring that the veterans from the armed forces get their due recognition. All in all it is a vast palette and *it can be done* if there is a will, good intentions, no selfish motives and the support of the people.

Reclaim India is a very large project. There are certain things that can be done in a fixed time frame and certain things that will take a little longer as mindsets have also to be changed. But I am convinced that a lot of things that will make a difference to a common man's life can be done provided we want to put our hands to it. And after having spoken to a lot of people in the country, I find there are enough experts available who have solutions to these problems. Whether it is the judicial system, the education system, or the power sector, people have ideas that they have converted into workable solutions. What holds back India today is the personal greed of the political and the bureaucratic class that has merged into one common system that does not let anything happen in this country unless there is something in it for them. Until this changes, nothing will happen and that is why this parivartan/transformation/reclamation is required across the board.

Having interacted with the young officers and men of the Indian Army all my life and now as I speak to university students, farmers, people from all walks of life, I have no doubt that we as a nation can achieve whatever we want for our land and our people. We can only achieve that if we are willing to walk the selfless, moral path that puts the country ahead of everything else. Every soldier in the Indian Army has always done just that. We now need to borrow again from the British who influenced all our institutions and even our Constitution to a great degree. The famous words of Lord Nelson at Trafalgar have to be adapted and be our guiding light forever: India expects every man and woman to do their duty.

When I sat down to write my autobiography I was acutely conscious of the fact that my story could probably match that of any other officer in the Indian Army. I had been lucky, for I could well have gone home as a brigadier. Had it not been for the prodding of a former GOC, I wouldn't have bothered to seek redress. At the end of the day, I didn't want anything more from the state. I have got much more from the country and the army than anyone can hope to get in a lifetime. As I rose through the ranks, I tried very hard not to forget how every decision would impact the men in the trenches. To stand up for what you consider to be your duty towards your country is our ultimate dharma. Towards that end, I hope my story and the words I have written serve a purpose.

But are mere words enough to serve any purpose? Here I seek assurance from the famous clarion call of the Russian rebel writer Aleksandr Solzhenitsyn: 'It is infinitely difficult to begin when mere words must move a great block of matter. But there is no other way if none of the material strength is on your side. And a shout in the mountains has been known to cause an avalanche.'

ACKNOWLEDGMENTS

In acknowledging all those without whose inspiration, encouragement and persistence this book would not have been written, first and foremost is my publisher, David Davidar, who broached the subject shortly after I retired from the Indian Army in May 2012. An autobiography is always an extremely tricky subject—there is so much to tell, there is so much trivia that has given joy that one feels needs to be included and there is the conflict as to how much of 'I' there should be rather than something that will provide the reader the correct perspective of happenings of the time, that one needs someone who can provide good feedback on what it should contain. For this I thank Kunal Verma, not only for discussing what transpired but also for probing the why of it before the narration was penned. Kunal also deserves thanks for ensuring that no laptops or desktops were written off in the process of writing the book and for ensuring that timelines were constantly flagged.

I have been blessed to interact with many great people ranging from the soldiers, to officers of all ranks, to the highest in the political hierarchy and all those who were my teachers in life. Let me acknowledge the contribution of Late Shri Radha Raman Pathak (Ramanji as we all called him) for instilling in me values that allowed me to stand up for what is right. He was my headmaster in school for the entire duration that I spent in Pilani. Along with him are a galaxy of teachers—Tara Dutt Joshi, Pareekhji, Gopalji Rathore, OS Mehrotra, Kailashji, TN Goswami, Jyotsinghaniji, Gaurangji, Prajapatiji, Vibha Parthasarthy, Mrs Gabriel, Mr Wheeler, Mr Sealey, Mr Axt, Mr Brooks, Mr Craukers, Mr Mukherjee, Shakuntalaji, Miss Pandit, Miss Malkani, Markandey Upadhyay, BS Bhatnagar and all the staff who contributed to bringing me up in the hostel. I would like to thank all my classmates, seniors and all other Vinians who have stood by me and have been a source of encouragement. This list is really vast, but to name just a few: Brijraj Dahiya, Vinod Rai, Satendra Dahiya, Mahendra Joon, Mahavir Shoora, Charanjit Singh, Baljit Singh, Pravesh Kohli, Devraj Kohli, Kiran Kapoor, Ashok Yadav, Mahendra Sharma, Anil 'windy' Chaturvedi, Suresh Joshi, Vijay Punia, Joginder Mann, Satendra Sandhu, Jit Mann, Dinesh Sharma, Surendra Sharma, Bajrang Lal, Prithvi and the entire lot from Abohar–Fazilka,

Jasjit, Richhpal Mann, Ishwar Singh, Narendra 'munna' Bhati, Narvir; all Vinians from the Kolkata Chapter and countless others whose Vinian tag has boosted my morale.

My instructors at NDA and IMA, HS Dalal, Sukhwinder Singh, Dhupar, Abhijit Mamik, Chandra Khanduri, D. C. Saraswat, AS Adhikari and so many more who gave their best to teach and shape me. The contribution of the men, JCOs and officers of Kali Chindi and 25 Rajput—the Silver Paltan—in giving me a sound grounding, in taking care of me, in ensuring I did well and in protecting me when the chips were down is immense and I acknowledge this with thanks and my respect for all my seniors and juniors. Sohrab Vakil, Dev Raj Dutt, Bhup Singh, Vijay Druv Verma, Shailu Verma, Avinash Kapila, RN Malik, K. Mohinder Singh, KN Mishra, Nandu Gupta, Tom Mathews, Melwyn, Ashok, Satish Vashist, Nanaya, Prem, Kumud, Vijay Lal, Nandu Verma, Vijay Pillay, Ranbir, Surendra Yadav, Pradeep (T2), AK Singh, Virendra Gulia, Amulya, Anil Rathore, KH Singh, Yogesh, Bhupi Sahi, Nandu Verma, Ajay, Jimmy Abraham, Velayudhan, Nanjappa, Venkat, Pradhan, Manohar, Vijay Reddy, Hermon, Dasho Atri, Harinarain, Shanti Khalkon, Gurinder, Vikas, Kutty Sharma, Anil Bali, Suresh, Alankar are some of the names that immediately come to mind when I think of those from whom I benefitted. The role of father-figure-like colonels and seniors of the regiment has been immense and WAG Pinto, RS Dayal, Ashok Kalyan Verma, Rajeshwar Taragi, Nikki Kapur, HS Bagga, Bhupinder Singh, Milan Naidu, Ravi Eipe and PC Puri need special mention for what they passed on. I would also like to acknowledge the role of all those under whom I served for accepting me as I was and for what I gained from them in turn. Some names that come to mind are Eric Vas, Rustom Nanavaty, Surjit Sangra, Shammi Mehta, Jameel Mahmood, HB Kala, Lalit Bhatia, AS Bahiya, VK Vaid, Nabhjyoti Deka, Sushil Gupta, Arun Roye, Sudhir Sharma, N B Singh, VK Kapoor, Dilip Deore, IJ Khanna, RS Katoch, K Balaram, Bob Mahendra, MR Sharma, Trigunesh Mukherjee, CN Somanna, Ginger Bal, VR Raghvan, Dheeru Saklani, VK 'Tubby' Nayar, Hanut Singh, TP Singh, R Loganathan, Dheer, Jerry Gonsalves, Jitendra Singh, Bhopinder Singh, KS Sethi, Shankar Roychowdhury, Dinesh Chauhan, VP Malhotra, MB Singh, RC Chadda, HS Narang, Keshav Singh, HM Khanna, Pankaj Joshi, R Subramaniam, Pawan Chhibber, Shantonu Chaudhry, K Nagaraj, Pattabhiraman, Nirbhey Sharma, Sarabh Dhillon, Dolly Shekhawat and Daljeet Singh. There are countless others whose personality and wisdom rubbed off on me whether they were senior or junior and it would require another chapter to name them. And all my coursemates to whom all I can say is that you collectively provided me the courage to stand up for what is right with the full knowledge that your support and unseen hands were always there to shore me up.

I would also like to acknowledge the support of friends in the media especially during my tenure as chief. That some of you remained steadfast while some succumbed to commercial interests or egos is beside the point; however, I gained from your insights for which I thank all of you. I would be failing if I did not acknowledge the support and inspiration I had from Pradeep Naik and Nirmal Verma who were chiefs of air force and navy through most of my tenure, as also NAK Browne. Pradeep and Nirmal were also from the same squadron in NDA—the Hunter and that spirit was a great help. My special thanks to Dipti who not only helped Kunal and me go through each and every paragraph, but for also helping in transcribing sections of the book.

Lastly, all my family members, especially my wife Bharti and daughters Mrinalini and Yogja—all I can say is that you all have been my strength through all the trials and tribulations. This book would not have been possible without you. Faith, Family and Friends have been the anchors and beacons in life. Let me quote Winston Churchill as this quote means a lot to me:

> The only guide to a man is his conscience; the only shield to his conscience is the rectitude and sincerity of his actions. It is imprudent to walk through life without this shield, because we are so often mocked by the failure of our hopes and upsetting of our calculations; but with this shield, however the Fates may play, we march always in the ranks of Honour.

INDEX